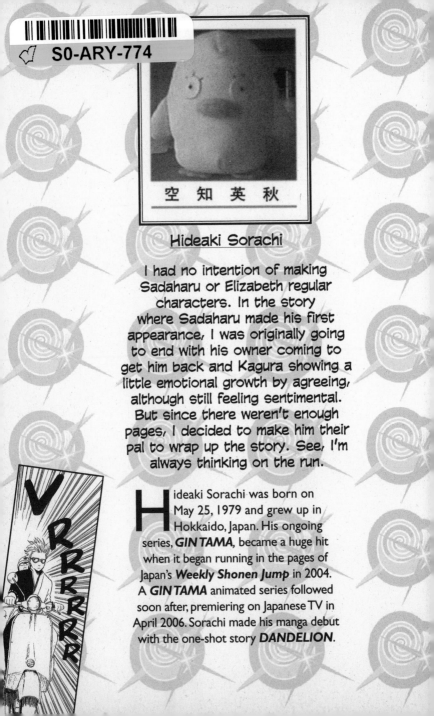

空 知 英 秋

Hideaki Sorachi

I had no intention of making Sadaharu or Elizabeth regular characters. In the story where Sadaharu made his first appearance, I was originally going to end with his owner coming to get him back and Kagura showing a little emotional growth by agreeing, although still feeling sentimental. But since there weren't enough pages, I decided to make him their pal to wrap up the story. See, I'm always thinking on the run.

Hideaki Sorachi was born on May 25, 1979 and grew up in Hokkaido, Japan. His ongoing series, *GIN TAMA*, became a huge hit when it began running in the pages of Japan's *Weekly Shonen Jump* in 2004. A *GIN TAMA* animated series followed soon after, premiering on Japanese TV in April 2006. Sorachi made his manga debut with the one-shot story *DANDELION*.

GIN TAMA VOL. 9
The SHONEN JUMP ADVANCED Manga Edition

STORY & ART BY HIDEAKI SORACHI

Translation/Matthew Rosin, Honyaku Center Inc.
English Adaptation/Gerard Jones
Touch-up Art & Lettering/Avril Averill
Cover Design/Sean Lee
Interior Design/Izumi Evers
Editor/Mike Montesa

Editor in Chief, Books/Alvin Lu
Editor in Chief, Magazines/Marc Weidenbaum
VP, Publishing Licensing/Rika Inouye
VP, Sales and Product Marketing/Gonzalo Ferreyra
VP, Creative/Linda Espinosa
Publisher/Hyoe Narita

Published by VIZ Media, LLC
P.O. Box 77010
San Francisco, CA 94107

SHONEN JUMP ADVANCED Manga edition
10 9 8 7 6 5 4 3 2 1
First printing, November 2008

THE WORLD'S MOST
CUTTING-EDGE MANGA

www.viz.com

www.shonenjump.com

GIN TAMA

STORY & ART BY
HIDEAKI SORACHI

Vol. 9
Whatever You Play, Play to Win!

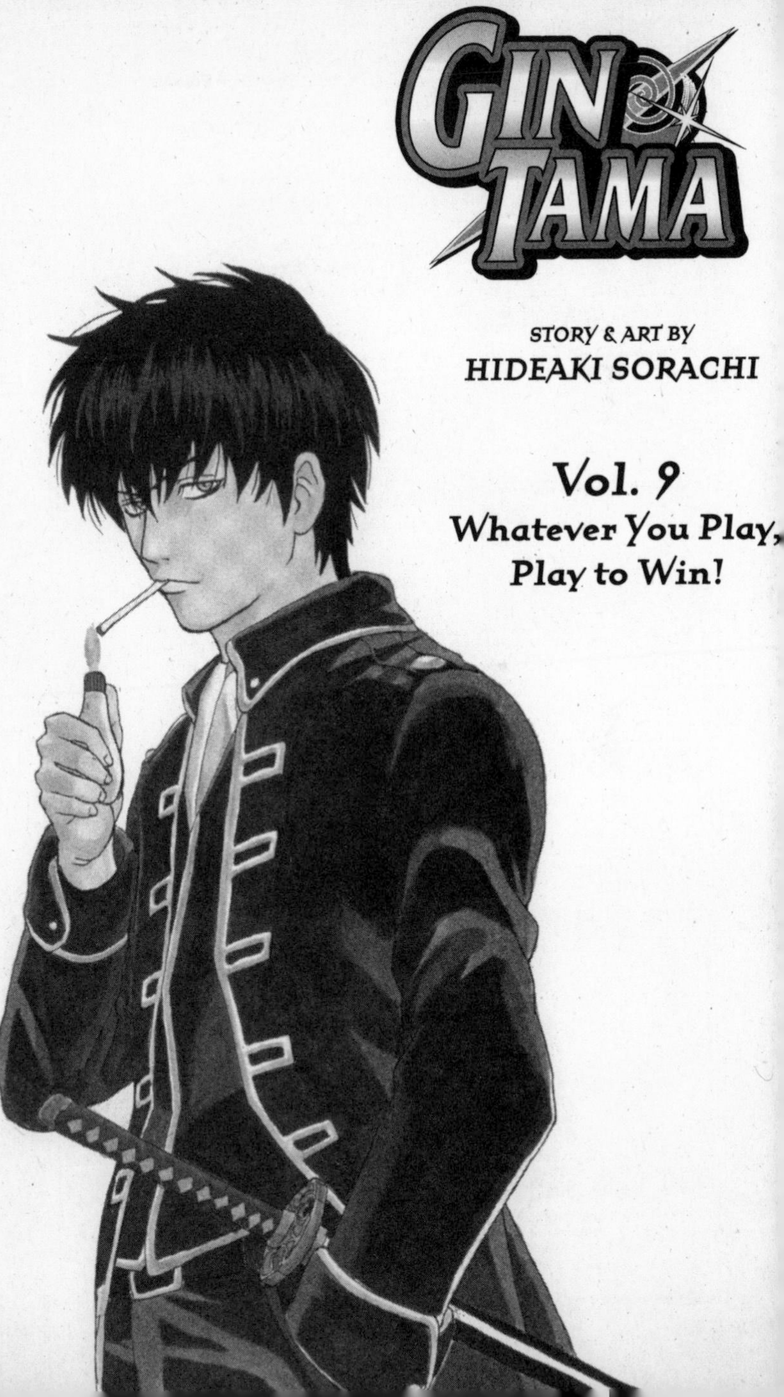

Cast of Characters

Yorozuya Members

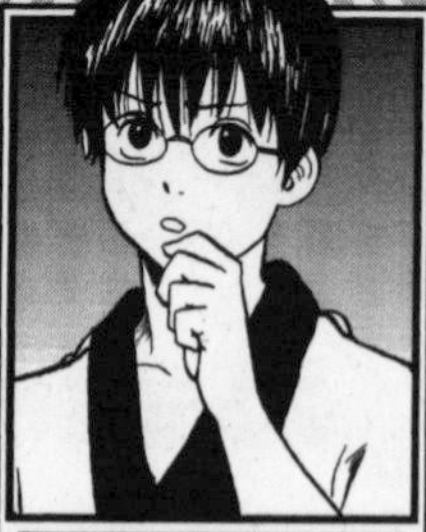

Shinpachi Shimura

Works under Gintoki in an attempt to learn about the samurai spirit, but has been regretting his decision recently. Also president of idol singer Tsu Terakado's fan club.

Gintoki Sakata

The hero of our story. He needs to eat something sweet periodically or he gets cranky. He commands a powerful sword arm but is one step away from diabetes. A former member of the exclusionist faction that seeks to eliminate the space aliens and protect the nation.

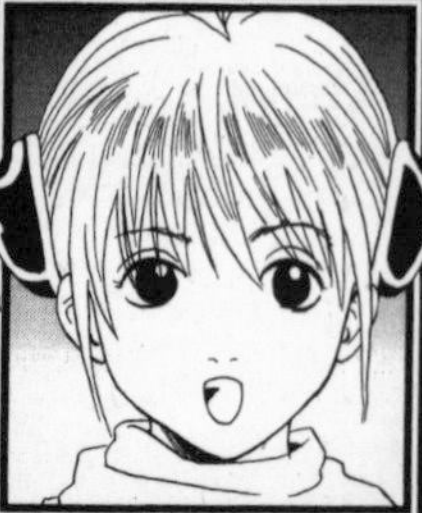

Kagura

A member of the "Yato Clan," the most powerful warrior race in the universe. Her voracious appetite and often inadvertent comic timing are unrivalled.

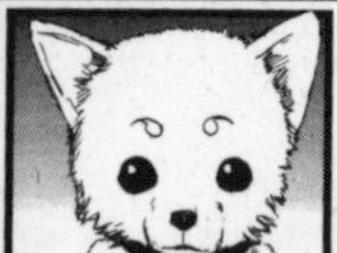

Sadaharu/animal

A giant space creature kept as a pet in the Yorozuya office. Likes to bites people (especially Gintoki).

Shinsengumi Soldiers

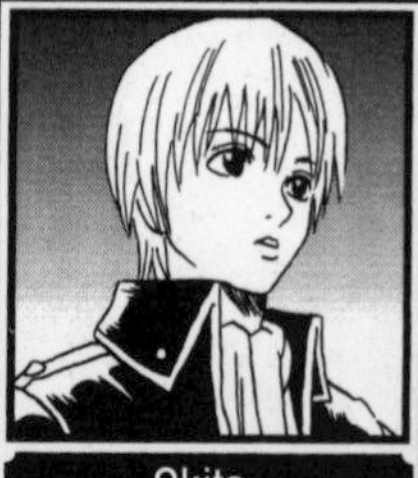

Okita

The most formidable swordsman in the Shinsengumi. His jovial attitude hides an utterly black heart. He wants to take over as the Vice-Chief.

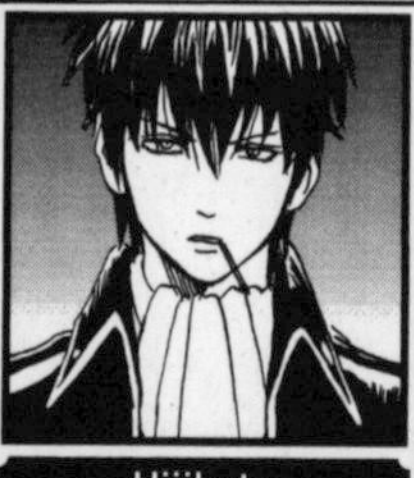

Hijikata

Vice-Chief of the Shinsengumi, Edo's elite Delta Force police unit. His cool demeanor turns to rage the moment he draws his sword. The pupils of his eyes always seem a bit dilated.

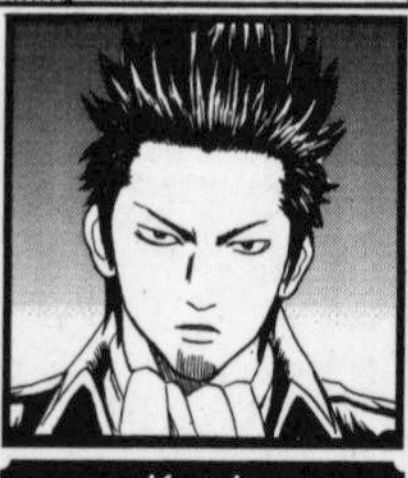

Kondo

Chief of the Shinsengumi, and trusted by all its soldiers. Also stalking Shinpachi's elder sister Otae.

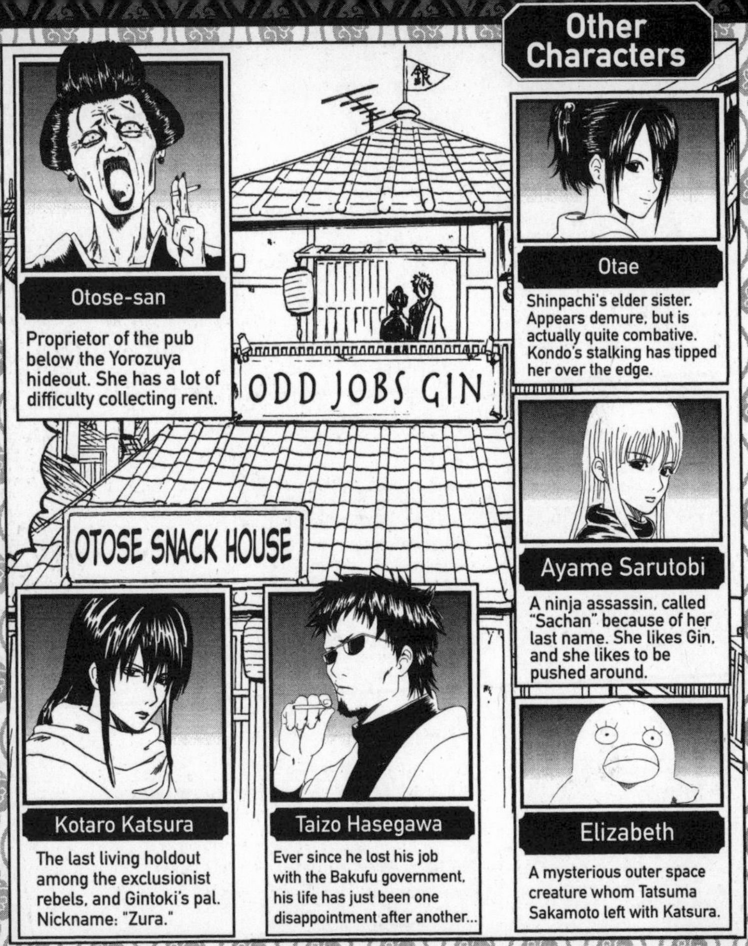
Other Characters
Otae
Shinpachi's elder sister. Appears demure, but is actually quite combative. Kondo's stalking has tipped her over the edge.
ODD JOBS GIN
Otose-san
Proprietor of the pub below the Yorozuya hideout. She has a lot of difficulty collecting rent.
Ayame Sarutobi
A ninja assassin, called "Sachan" because of her last name. She likes Gin, and she likes to be pushed around.
OTOSE SNACK HOUSE
Elizabeth
A mysterious outer space creature whom Tatsuma Sakamoto left with Katsura.
Taizo Hasegawa
Ever since he lost his job with the Bakufu government, his life has just been one disappointment after another...
Kotaro Katsura
The last living holdout among the exclusionist rebels, and Gintoki's pal. Nickname: "Zura."

The story thus far

In an alternate-universe Edo (Tokyo), extraterrestrials land in Japan and the new government issues an order outlawing swords. The samurai, who have reached the pinnacle of power and prosperity, fall into rapid decline.

Twenty years hence, only one samurai has managed to hold onto his fighting spirit: a somewhat eccentric fellow named Gintoki "Odd Jobs Gin" Sakata. A lover of sweets and near diabetic, our hero sets up shop as a *yorozuya*—an expert at managing trouble and handling the oddest jobs.

Joining "Gin" in his business is Shinpachi Shimura, whose sister Gin saved from the clutches of nefarious debt collectors. After a series of unexpected circumstances, the trio meet a powerful alien named Kagura, who becomes—after some arm-twisting—a part-time team member.

Kagura's father comes to Earth to take her back home…but at the same time they are attacked by an alien monster, Gintoki develops an inflammation in the worst possible area. Then they are terrified by a next-door neighbor...and now the whole gang is invading the magistrate's office to rescue a captured Elizabeth! What's next?!

WHAT THIS MANGA'S FULL OF
vol. 9

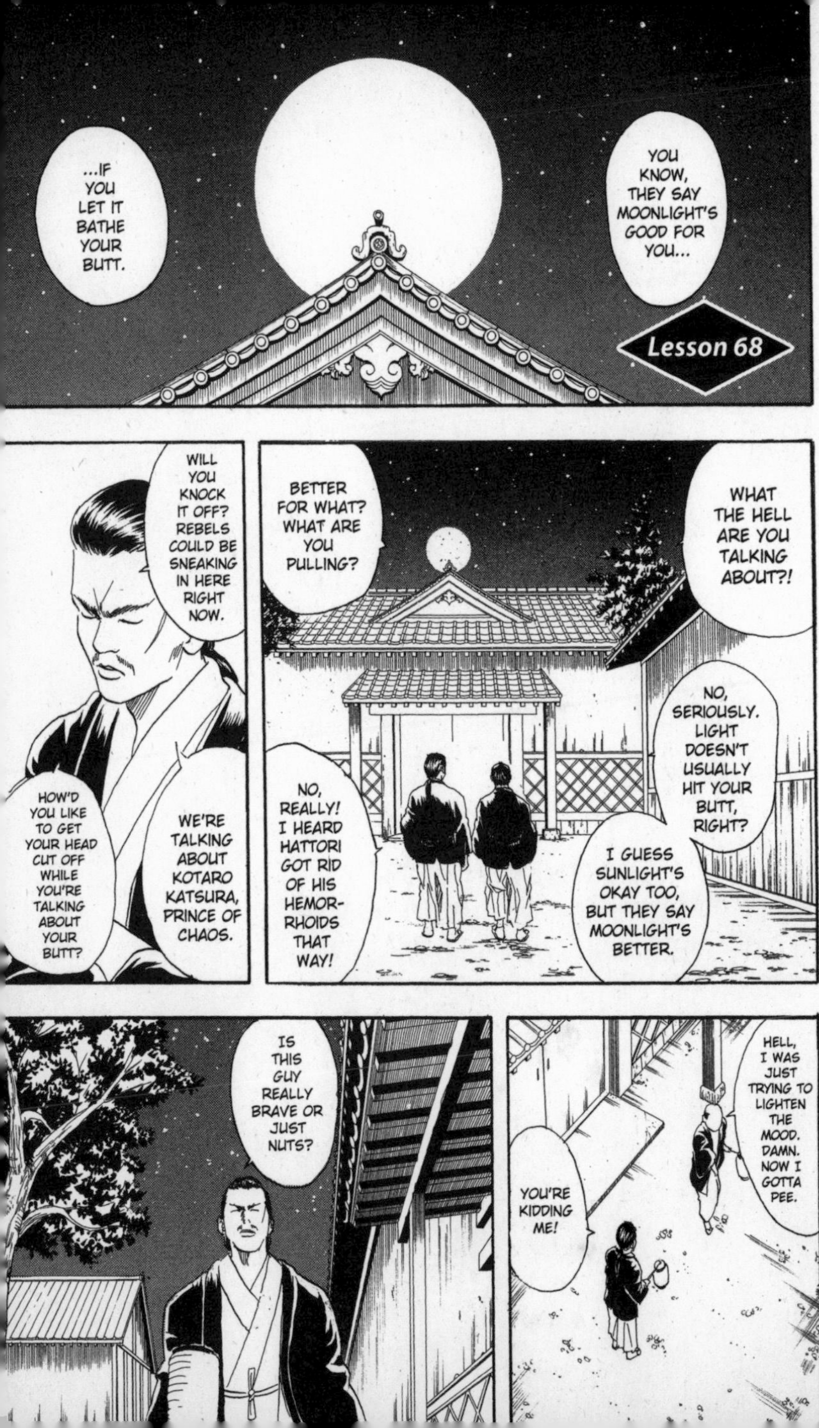

YOU KNOW, THEY SAY MOONLIGHT'S GOOD FOR YOU...
...IF YOU LET IT BATHE YOUR BUTT.
Lesson 68
WHAT THE HELL ARE YOU TALKING ABOUT?!
BETTER FOR WHAT? WHAT ARE YOU PULLING?
NO, SERIOUSLY. LIGHT DOESN'T USUALLY HIT YOUR BUTT, RIGHT?
I GUESS SUNLIGHT'S OKAY TOO, BUT THEY SAY MOONLIGHT'S BETTER.
NO, REALLY! I HEARD HATTORI GOT RID OF HIS HEMOR-RHOIDS THAT WAY!
WILL YOU KNOCK IT OFF? REBELS COULD BE SNEAKING IN HERE RIGHT NOW.
WE'RE TALKING ABOUT KOTARO KATSURA, PRINCE OF CHAOS.
HOW'D YOU LIKE TO GET YOUR HEAD CUT OFF WHILE YOU'RE TALKING ABOUT YOUR BUTT?
HELL, I WAS JUST TRYING TO LIGHTEN THE MOOD. DAMN. NOW I GOTTA PEE.
YOU'RE KIDDING ME!
IS THIS GUY REALLY BRAVE OR JUST NUTS?

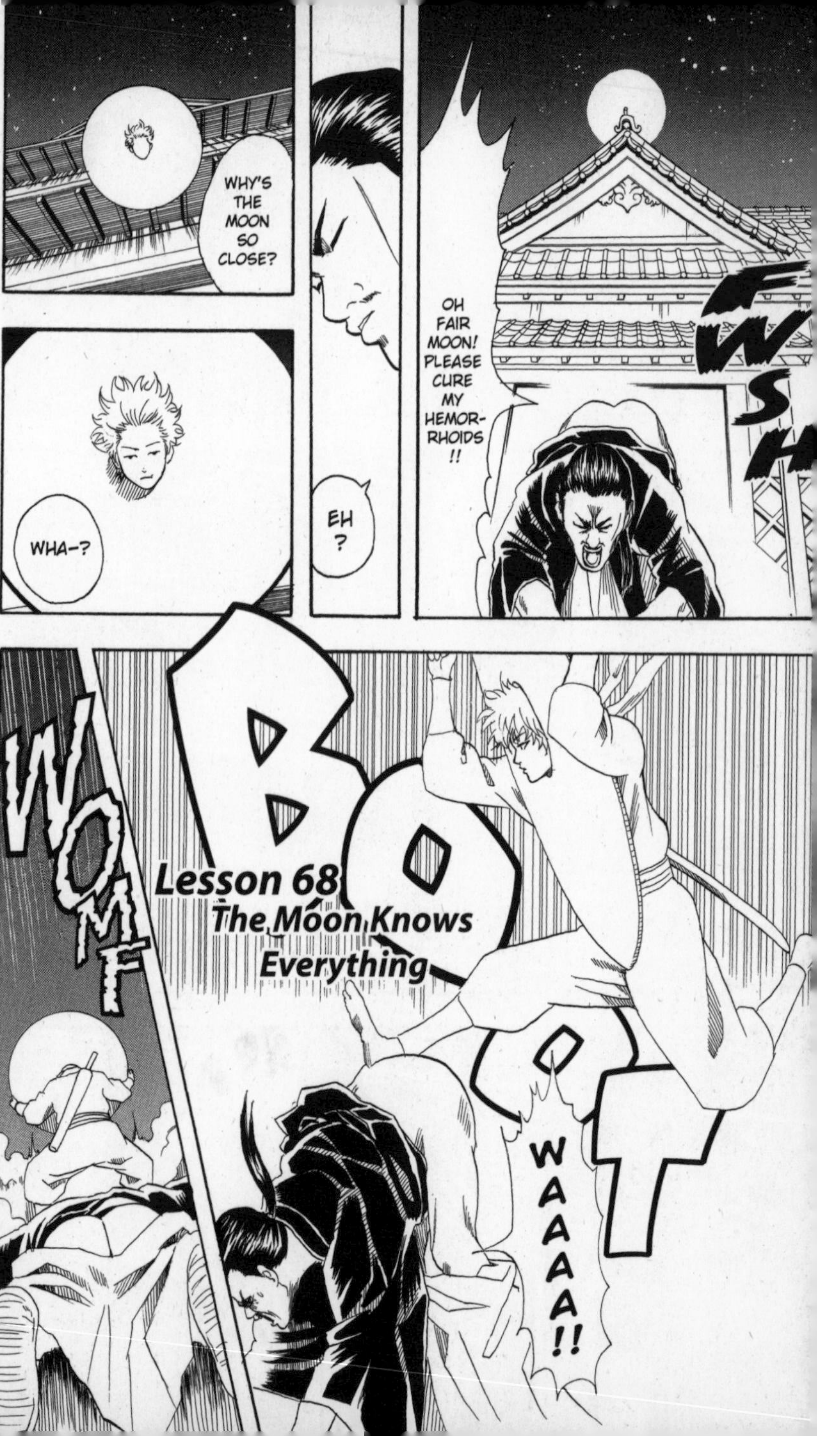
FWSH
OH FAIR MOON! PLEASE CURE MY HEMOR-RHOIDS !!
EH ?
WHY'S THE MOON SO CLOSE?
WHA-?
BOOT
WAAAA!!
Lesson 68 The Moon Knows Everything
WOMF

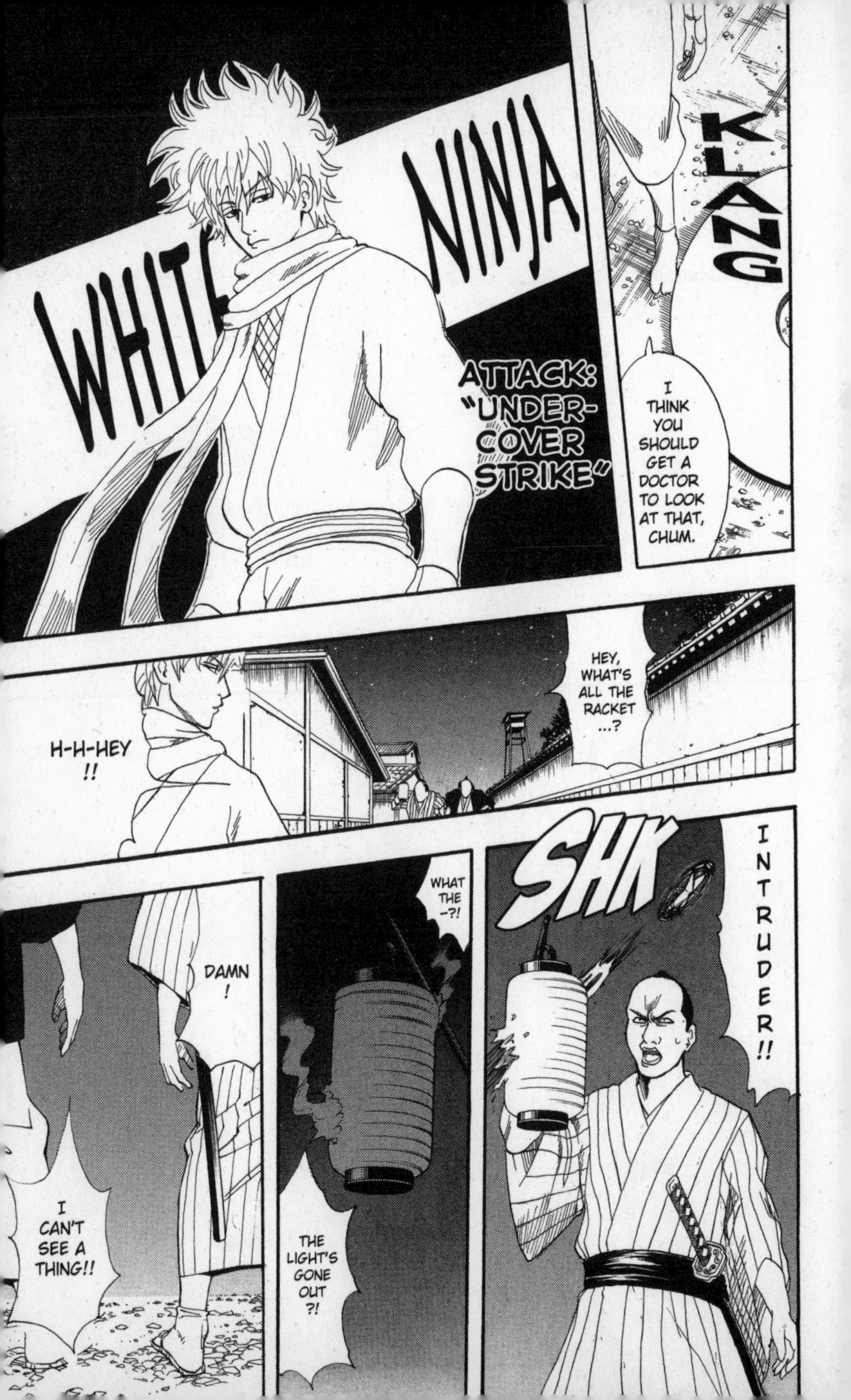
KLANG
I THINK YOU SHOULD GET A DOCTOR TO LOOK AT THAT, CHUM.
WHITE NINJA
ATTACK: "UNDER-COVER STRIKE"
HEY, WHAT'S ALL THE RACKET ...?
H-H-HEY !!
SHK
INTRUDER!!
WHAT THE -?!
THE LIGHT'S GONE OUT ?!
DAMN !
I CAN'T SEE A THING!!

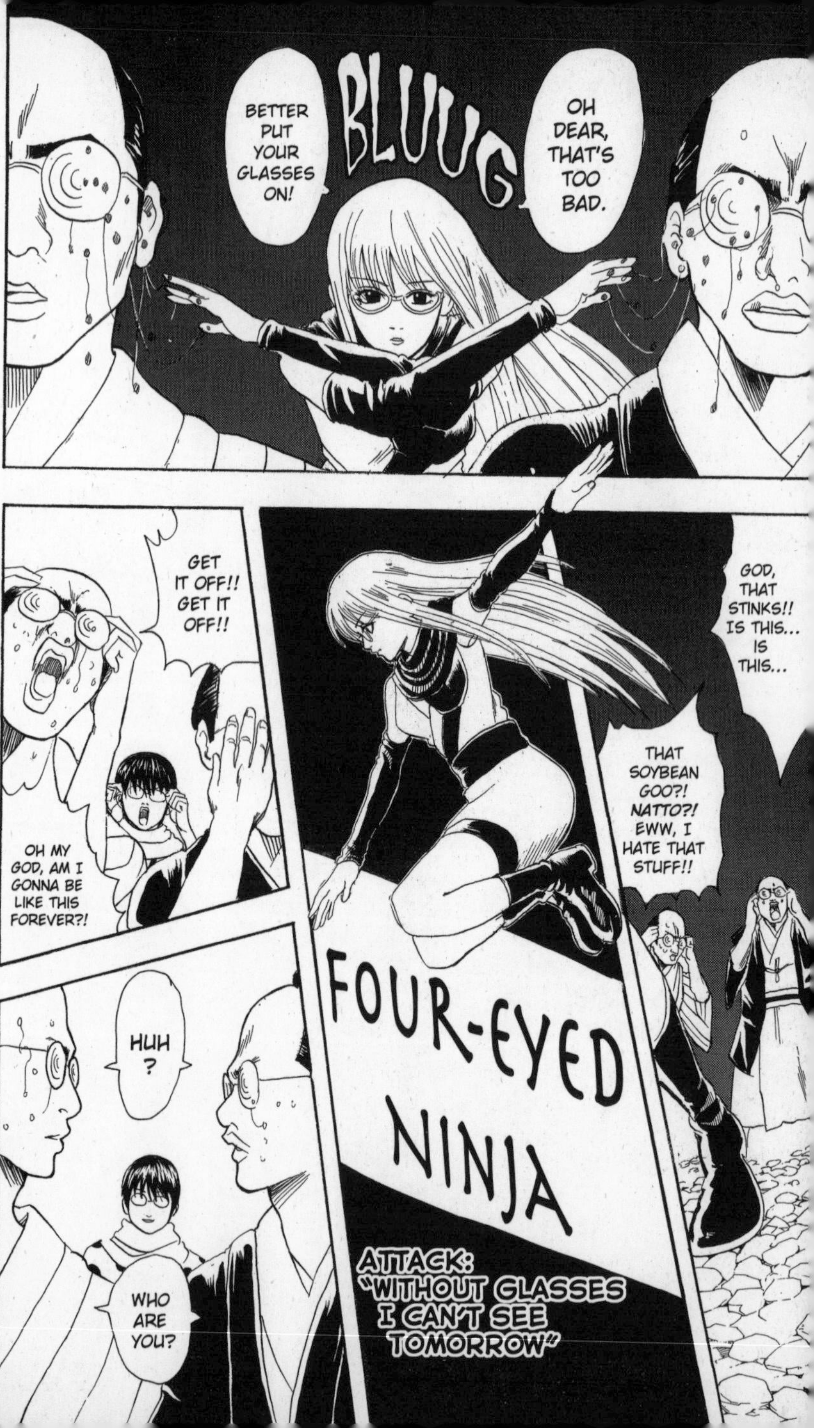
OH DEAR, THAT'S TOO BAD.
BLUUG
BETTER PUT YOUR GLASSES ON!
GOD, THAT STINKS!! IS THIS... IS THIS...
THAT SOYBEAN GOO?! NATTO?! EWW, I HATE THAT STUFF!!
FOUR-EYED NINJA
ATTACK: "WITHOUT GLASSES I CAN'T SEE TOMORROW"
GET IT OFF!! GET IT OFF!!
OH MY GOD, AM I GONNA BE LIKE THIS FOREVER?!
HUH?
WHO ARE YOU?

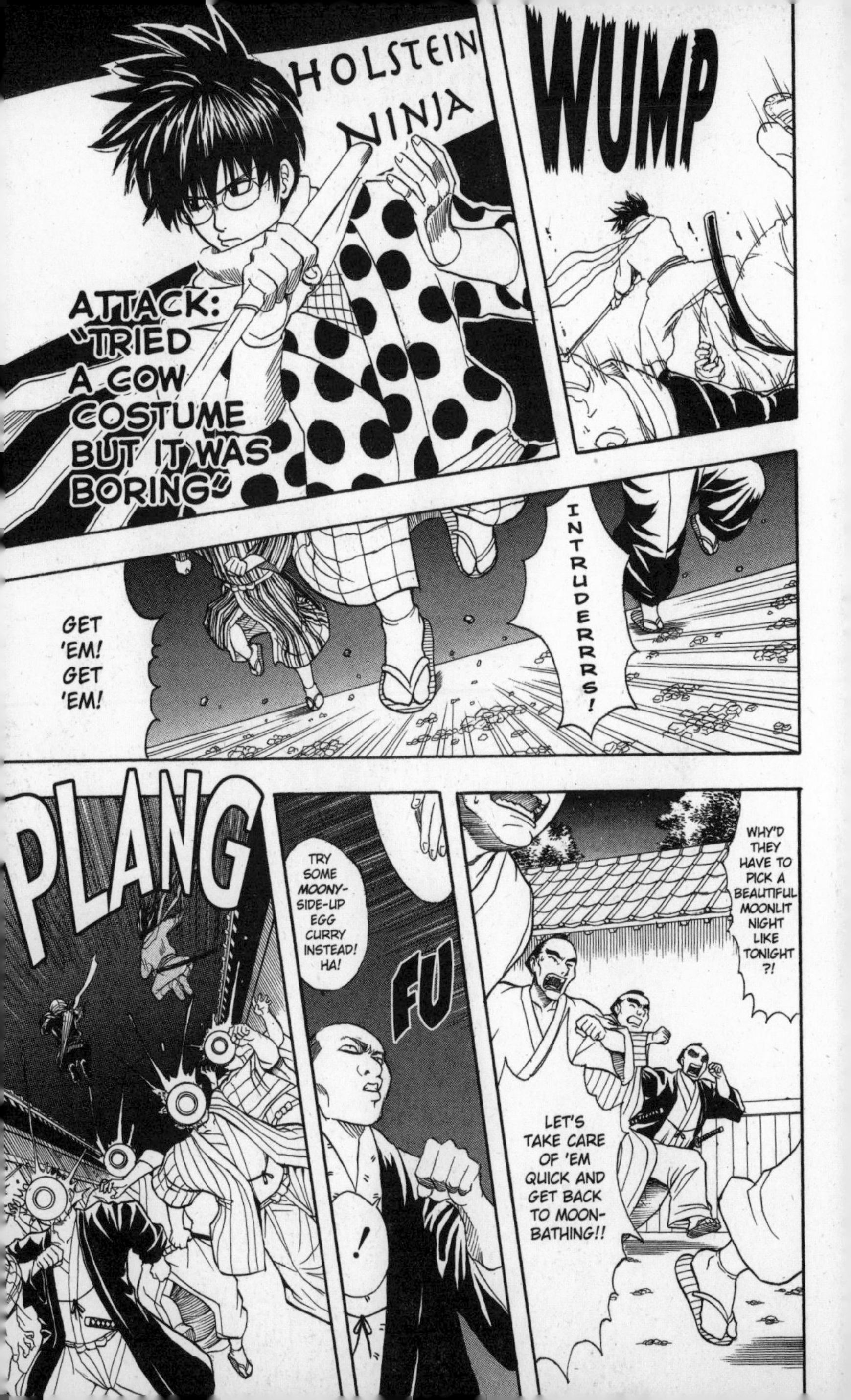
WUMP
HOLSTEIN NINJA
ATTACK: "TRIED A COW COSTUME BUT IT WAS BORING"
INTRUDERRRS!
GET 'EM! GET 'EM!
WHY'D THEY HAVE TO PICK A BEAUTIFUL MOONLIT NIGHT LIKE TONIGHT?!
LET'S TAKE CARE OF 'EM QUICK AND GET BACK TO MOON-BATHING!!
TRY SOME MOONY-SIDE-UP EGG CURRY INSTEAD! HA!
FU
!
PLANG

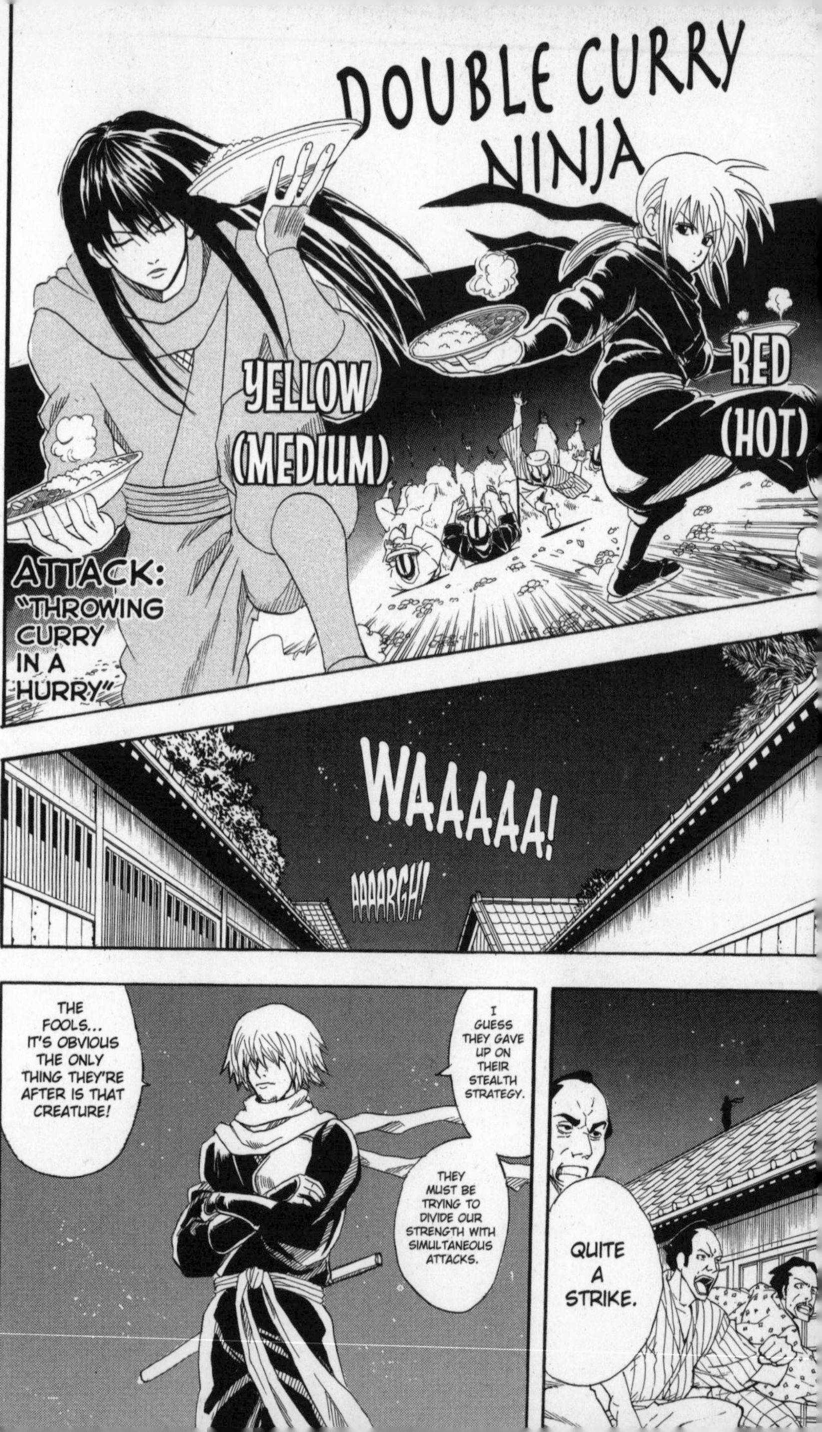
DOUBLE CURRY NINJA
RED (HOT)
YELLOW (MEDIUM)
ATTACK: "THROWING CURRY IN A HURRY"
WAAAAA!
AAAARGH!
QUITE A STRIKE.
I GUESS THEY GAVE UP ON THEIR STEALTH STRATEGY.
THE FOOLS... IT'S OBVIOUS THE ONLY THING THEY'RE AFTER IS THAT CREATURE!
THEY MUST BE TRYING TO DIVIDE OUR STRENGTH WITH SIMULTANEOUS ATTACKS.

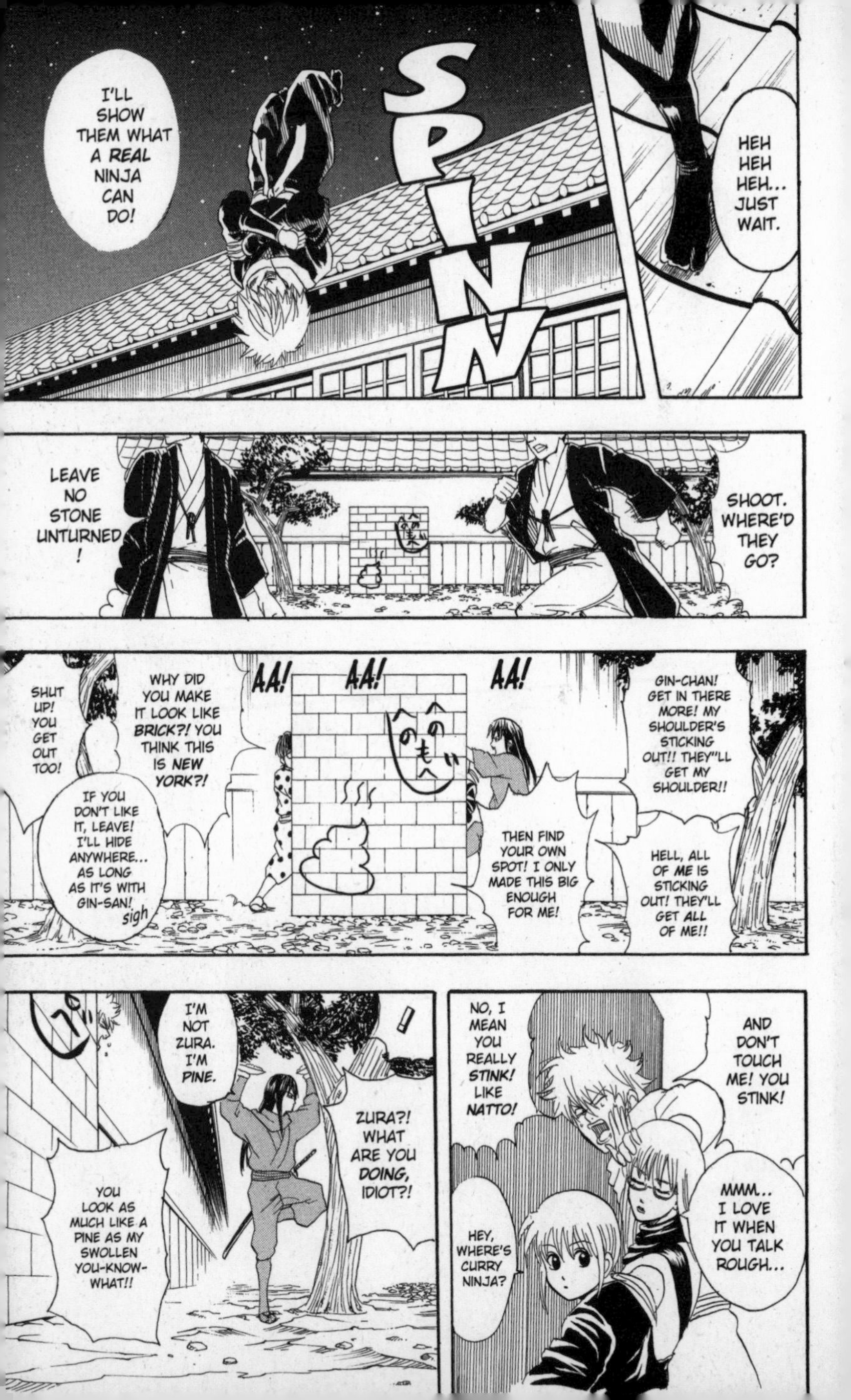
HEH HEH HEH... JUST WAIT.
SPINN
I'LL SHOW THEM WHAT A REAL NINJA CAN DO!
SHOOT. WHERE'D THEY GO?
LEAVE NO STONE UNTURNED!
GIN-CHAN! GET IN THERE MORE! MY SHOULDER'S STICKING OUT!! THEY"LL GET MY SHOULDER!!
AA!
AA!
AA!
HELL, ALL OF ME IS STICKING OUT! THEY'LL GET ALL OF ME!!
THEN FIND YOUR OWN SPOT! I ONLY MADE THIS BIG ENOUGH FOR ME!
WHY DID YOU MAKE IT LOOK LIKE BRICK?! YOU THINK THIS IS NEW YORK?!
SHUT UP! YOU GET OUT TOO!
IF YOU DON'T LIKE IT, LEAVE! I'LL HIDE ANYWHERE... AS LONG AS IT'S WITH GIN-SAN!
sigh
AND DON'T TOUCH ME! YOU STINK!
NO, I MEAN YOU REALLY STINK! LIKE NATTO!
MMM.. I LOVE IT WHEN YOU TALK ROUGH...
HEY, WHERE'S CURRY NINJA?
!
ZURA?! WHAT ARE YOU DOING, IDIOT?!
I'M NOT ZURA. I'M PINE.
YOU LOOK AS MUCH LIKE A PINE AS MY SWOLLEN YOU-KNOW-WHAT!!

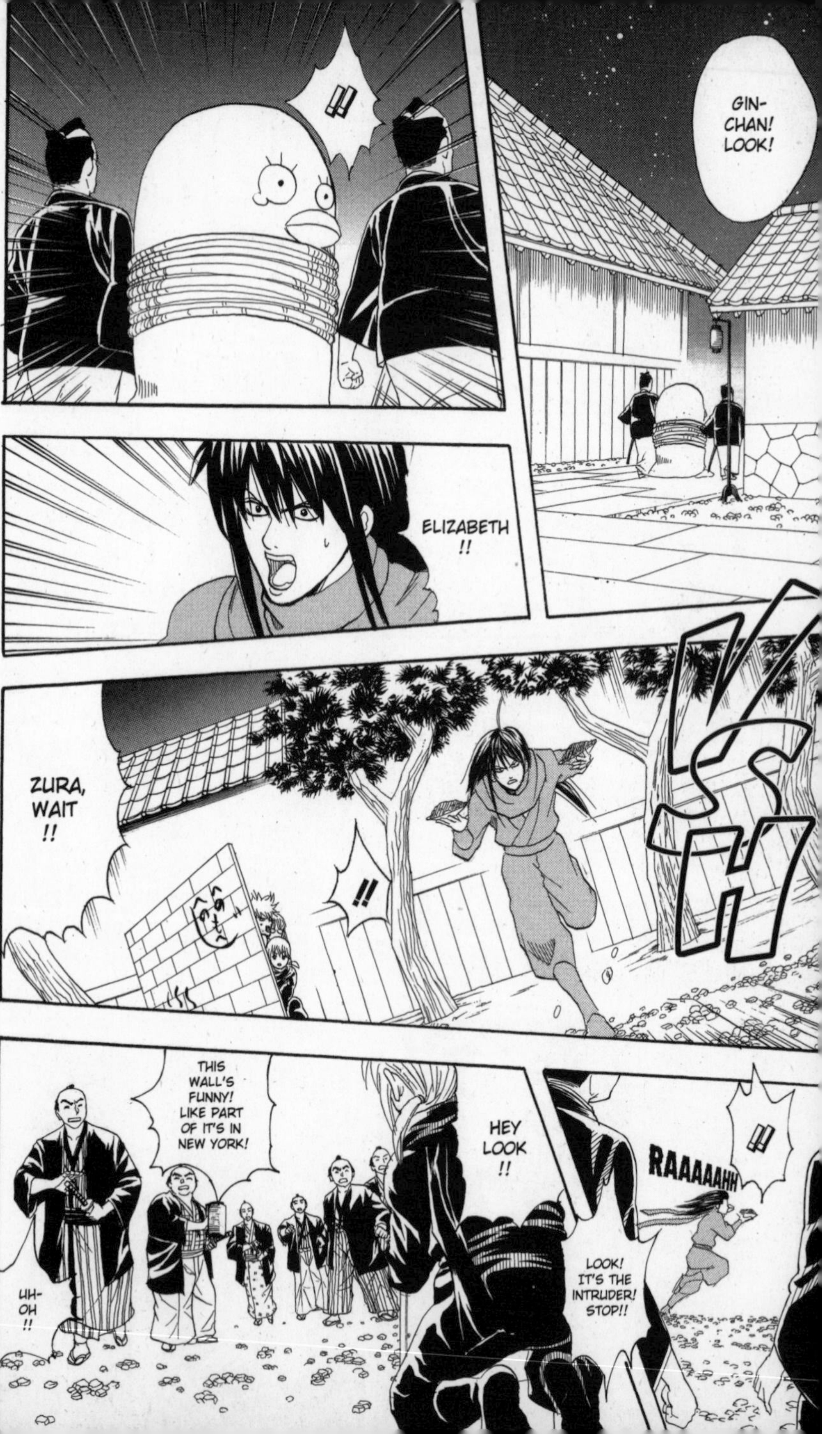
GIN-CHAN! LOOK!
!!
ELIZABETH!!
VSH
!!
ZURA, WAIT!!
!!
RAAAAAHH
LOOK! IT'S THE INTRUDER! STOP!!
HEY LOOK!!
THIS WALL'S FUNNY! LIKE PART OF IT'S IN NEW YORK!
UH-OH!!

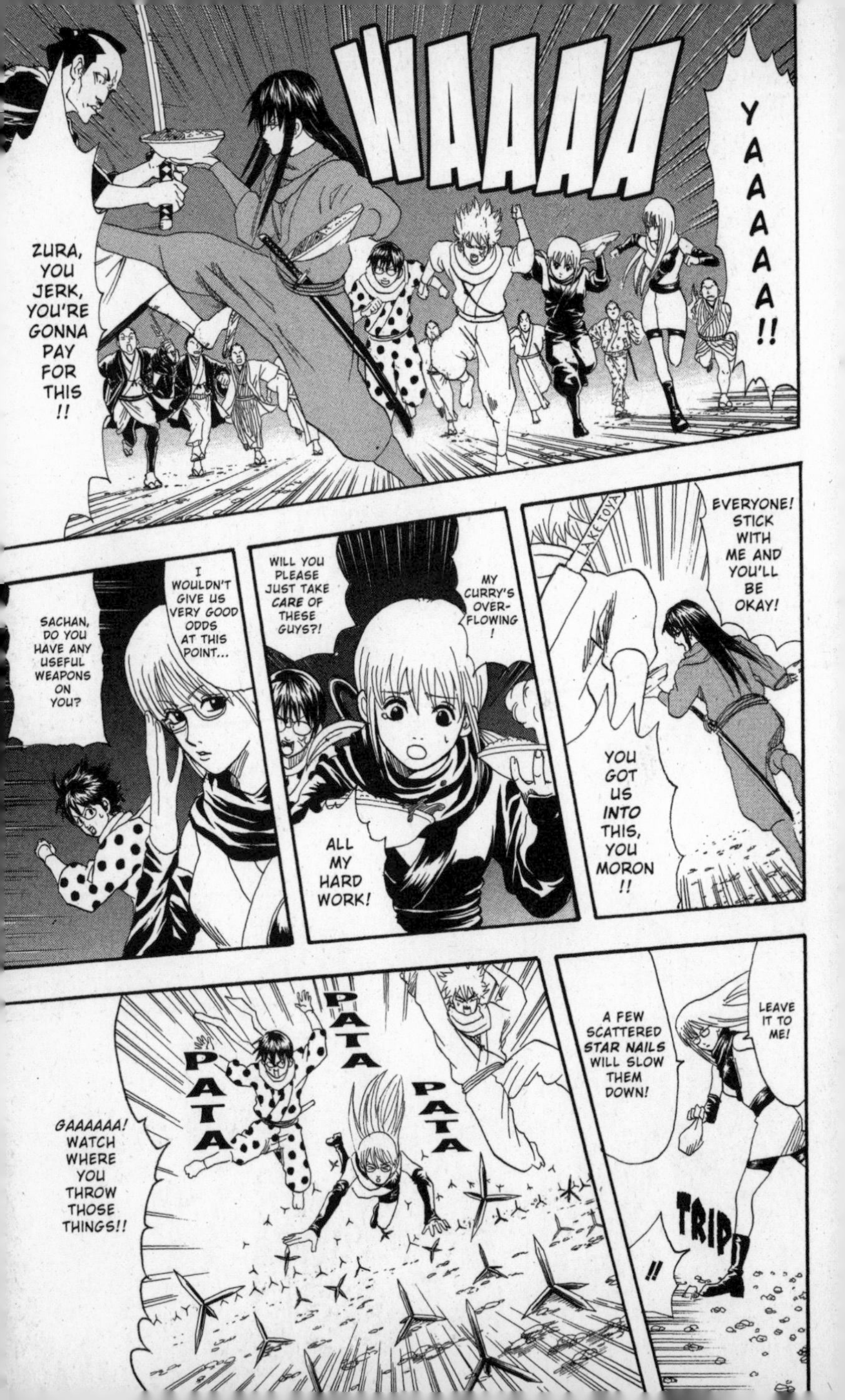
YAAAAAA!!
WAAAAA
ZURA, YOU JERK, YOU'RE GONNA PAY FOR THIS!!
EVERYONE! STICK WITH ME AND YOU'LL BE OKAY!
LAKETOYA
YOU GOT US INTO THIS, YOU MORON!!
MY CURRY'S OVER-FLOWING!
WILL YOU PLEASE JUST TAKE CARE OF THESE GUYS?!
ALL MY HARD WORK!
I WOULDN'T GIVE US VERY GOOD ODDS AT THIS POINT...
SACHAN, DO YOU HAVE ANY USEFUL WEAPONS ON YOU?
LEAVE IT TO ME!
A FEW SCATTERED STAR NAILS WILL SLOW THEM DOWN!
TRIP
!!
PATA
PATA
PATA
PATA
GAAAAAA! WATCH WHERE YOU THROW THOSE THINGS!!

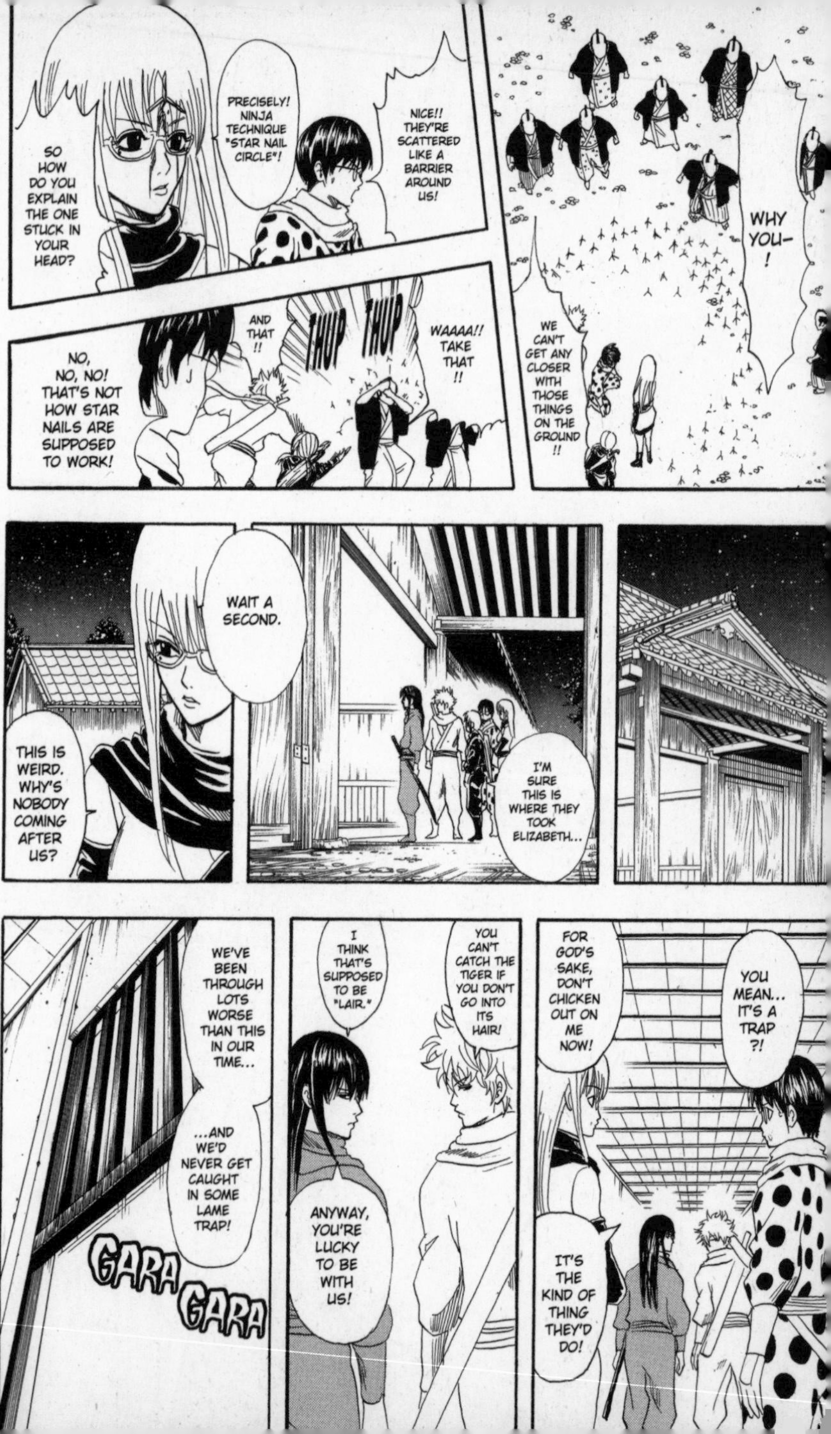
WHY YOU-!
WE CAN'T GET ANY CLOSER WITH THOSE THINGS ON THE GROUND!!
NICE!! THEY'RE SCATTERED LIKE A BARRIER AROUND US!
PRECISELY! NINJA TECHNIQUE "STAR NAIL CIRCLE"!
SO HOW DO YOU EXPLAIN THE ONE STUCK IN YOUR HEAD?
WAAAA!! TAKE THAT!!
THUP THUP
AND THAT!!
NO, NO, NO! THAT'S NOT HOW STAR NAILS ARE SUPPOSED TO WORK!
I'M SURE THIS IS WHERE THEY TOOK ELIZABETH...
WAIT A SECOND.
THIS IS WEIRD. WHY'S NOBODY COMING AFTER US?
YOU MEAN... IT'S A TRAP?!
FOR GOD'S SAKE, DON'T CHICKEN OUT ON ME NOW!
IT'S THE KIND OF THING THEY'D DO!
YOU CAN'T CATCH THE TIGER IF YOU DON'T GO INTO ITS HAIR!
I THINK THAT'S SUPPOSED TO BE "LAIR."
ANYWAY, YOU'RE LUCKY TO BE WITH US!
WE'VE BEEN THROUGH LOTS WORSE THAN THIS IN OUR TIME...
...AND WE'D NEVER GET CAUGHT IN SOME LAME TRAP!
GARA GARA

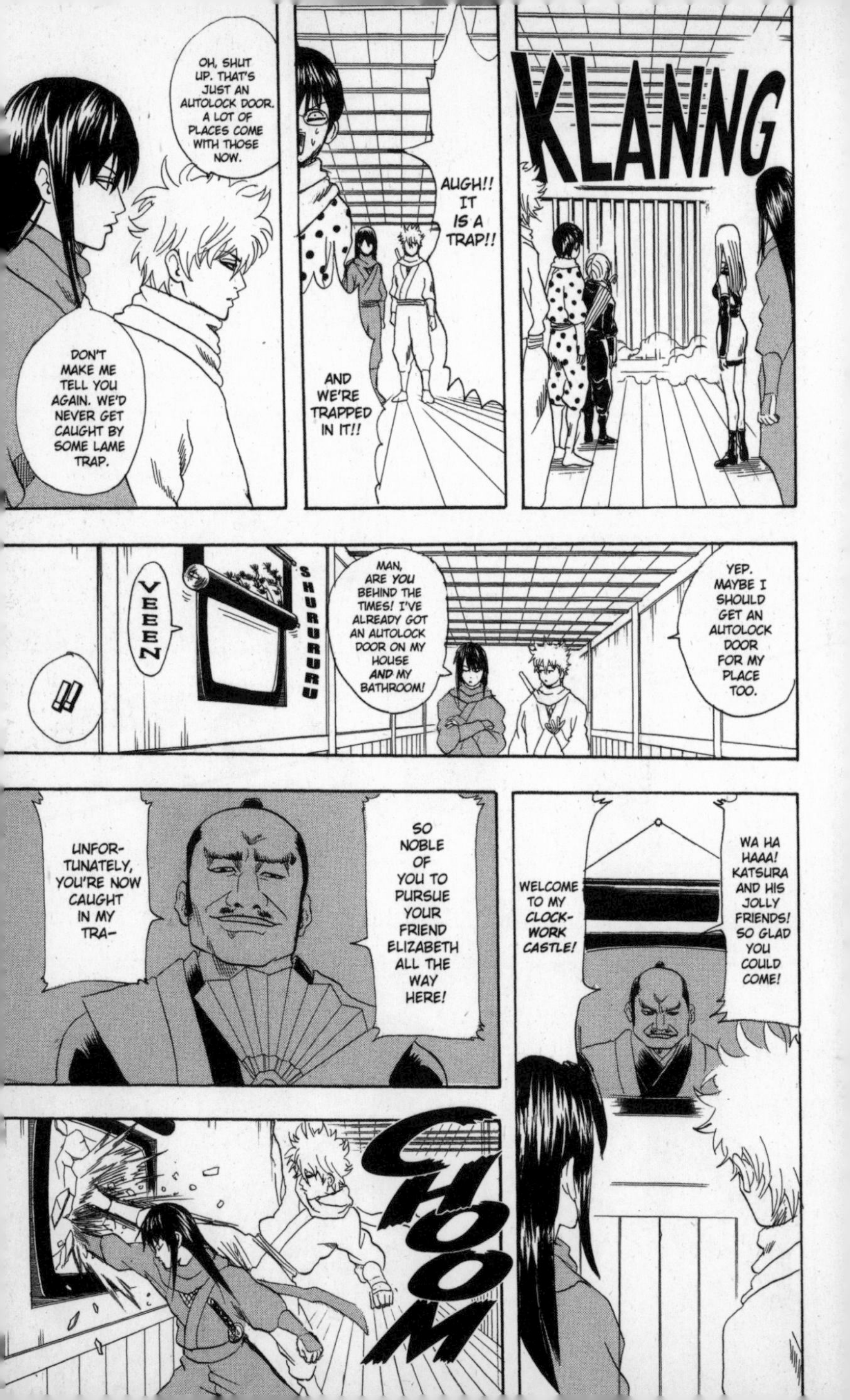
KLANNG
AUGH!! IT IS A TRAP!!
AND WE'RE TRAPPED IN IT!!
OH, SHUT UP. THAT'S JUST AN AUTOLOCK DOOR. A LOT OF PLACES COME WITH THOSE NOW.
DON'T MAKE ME TELL YOU AGAIN. WE'D NEVER GET CAUGHT BY SOME LAME TRAP.
YEP. MAYBE I SHOULD GET AN AUTOLOCK DOOR FOR MY PLACE TOO.
MAN, ARE YOU BEHIND THE TIMES! I'VE ALREADY GOT AN AUTOLOCK DOOR ON MY HOUSE AND MY BATHROOM!
SHURURURURU
VEEEN
!!
WA HA HAAA! KATSURA AND HIS JOLLY FRIENDS! SO GLAD YOU COULD COME!
WELCOME TO MY CLOCKWORK CASTLE!
SO NOBLE OF YOU TO PURSUE YOUR FRIEND ELIZABETH ALL THE WAY HERE!
UNFORTUNATELY, YOU'RE NOW CAUGHT IN MY TRA-
CHOOM

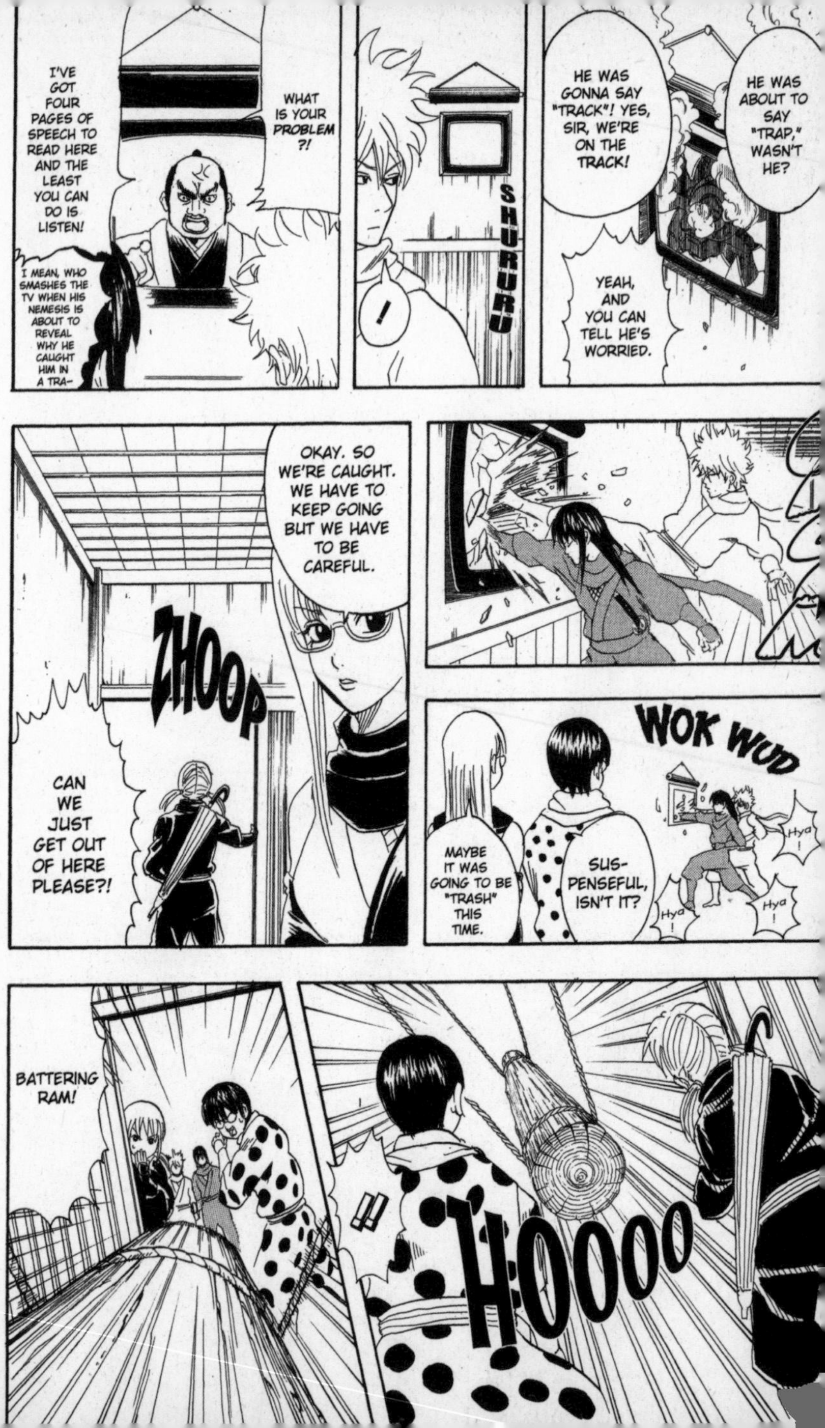
HE WAS ABOUT TO SAY "TRAP," WASN'T HE?
HE WAS GONNA SAY "TRACK"! YES, SIR, WE'RE ON THE TRACK!
YEAH, AND YOU CAN TELL HE'S WORRIED.
!
SHURURU
WHAT IS YOUR PROBLEM ?!
I'VE GOT FOUR PAGES OF SPEECH TO READ HERE AND THE LEAST YOU CAN DO IS LISTEN!
I MEAN, WHO SMASHES THE TV WHEN HIS NEMESIS IS ABOUT TO REVEAL WHY HE CAUGHT HIM IN A TRA-
WOK WUD
Hya!
Hya!
Hya!
SUS-PENSEFUL, ISN'T IT?
MAYBE IT WAS GOING TO BE "TRASH" THIS TIME.
OKAY. SO WE'RE CAUGHT. WE HAVE TO KEEP GOING BUT WE HAVE TO BE CAREFUL.
ZHOOP
CAN WE JUST GET OUT OF HERE PLEASE?!
!!
HOOOO
BATTERING RAM!

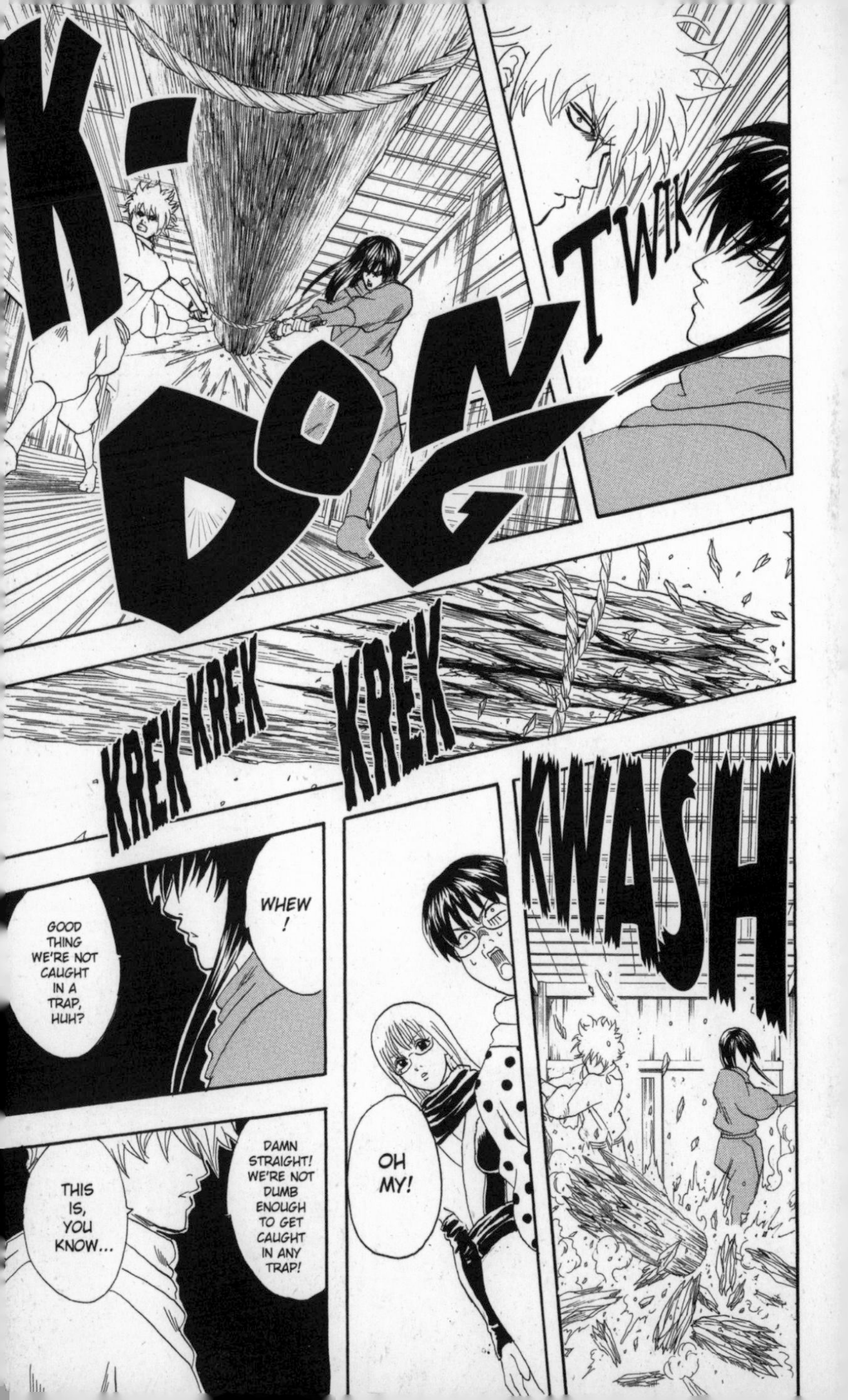
TWIK
K-DONG
KREK KREK KREK
KWASH
OH MY!
WHEW!
GOOD THING WE'RE NOT CAUGHT IN A TRAP, HUH?
DAMN STRAIGHT! WE'RE NOT DUMB ENOUGH TO GET CAUGHT IN ANY TRAP!
THIS IS, YOU KNOW...

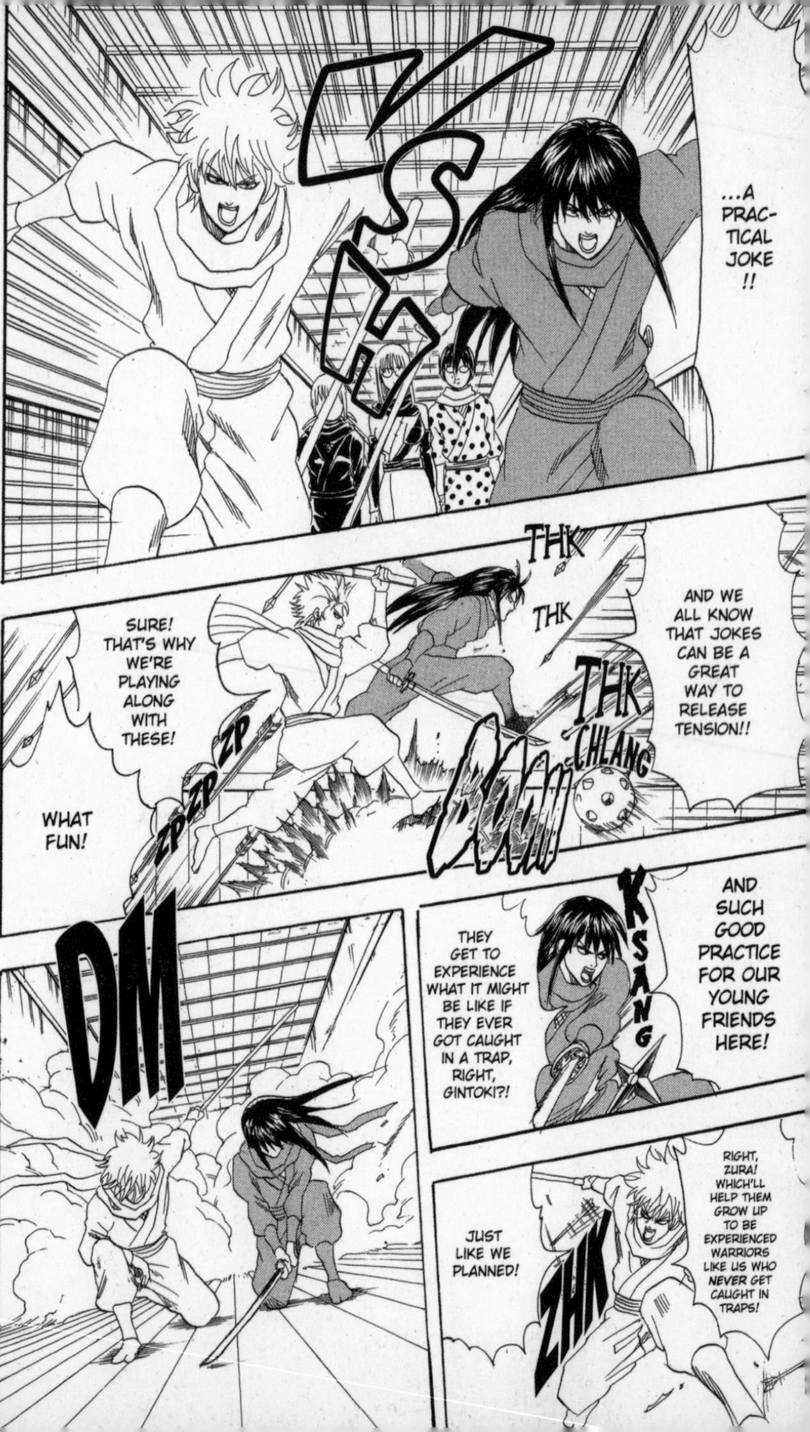

...A PRAC-TICAL JOKE !!
AND WE ALL KNOW THAT JOKES CAN BE A GREAT WAY TO RELEASE TENSION!!
THK
THK
THK
CHLANG
SURE! THAT'S WHY WE'RE PLAYING ALONG WITH THESE!
ZP ZP ZP ZP
WHAT FUN!
AND SUCH GOOD PRACTICE FOR OUR YOUNG FRIENDS HERE!
KSANG
THEY GET TO EXPERIENCE WHAT IT MIGHT BE LIKE IF THEY EVER GOT CAUGHT IN A TRAP, RIGHT, GINTOKI?!
RIGHT, ZURA! WHICH'LL HELP THEM GROW UP TO BE EXPERIENCED WARRIORS LIKE US WHO NEVER GET CAUGHT IN TRAPS!
ZHK
JUST LIKE WE PLANNED!
DM

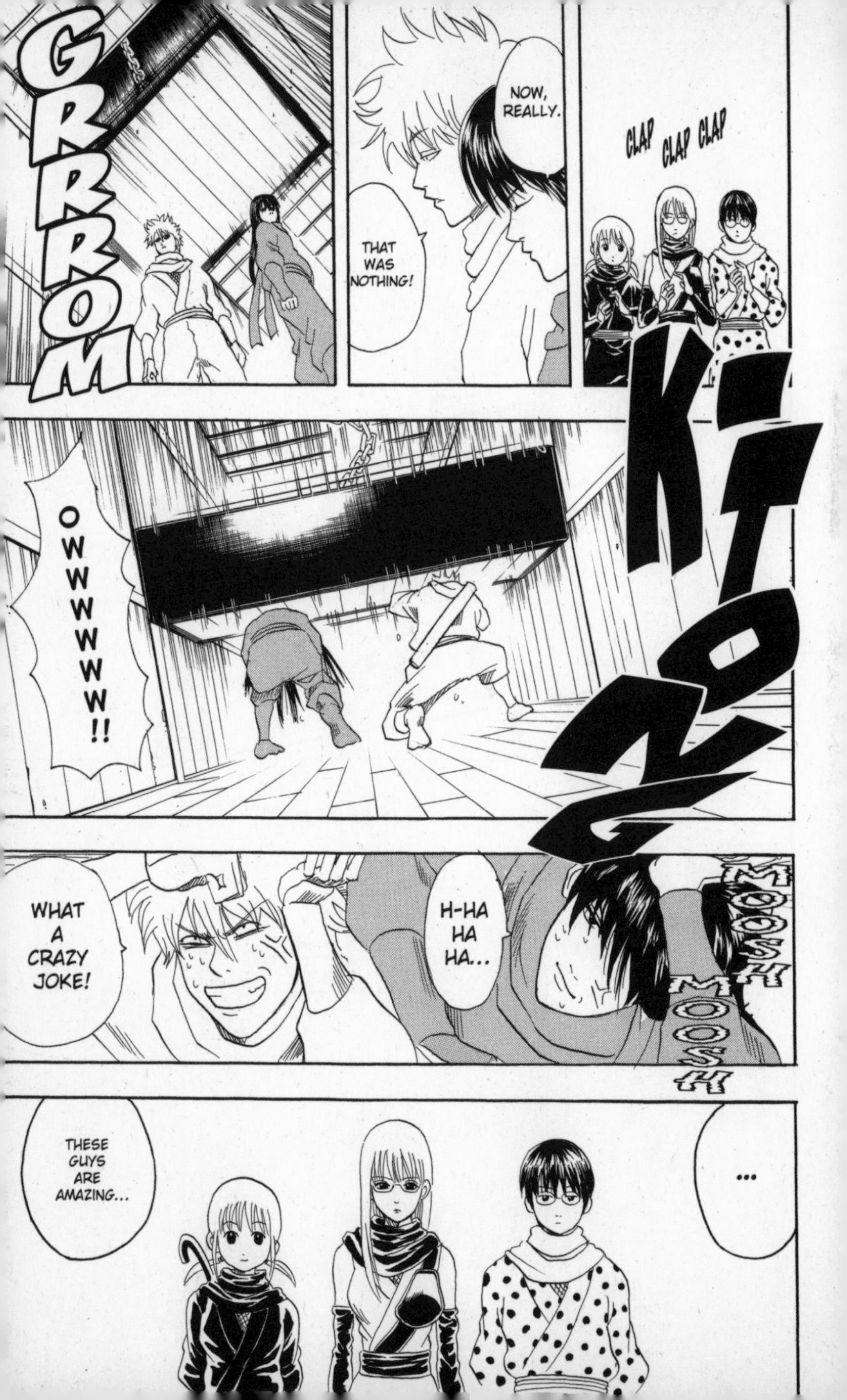

CLAP CLAP CLAP
NOW, REALLY.
THAT WAS NOTHING!
GRRROM
KIDONG
OWWWWWW!!
MOOSH MOOSH
H-HA HA HA...
WHAT A CRAZY JOKE!
...
THESE GUYS ARE AMAZING...

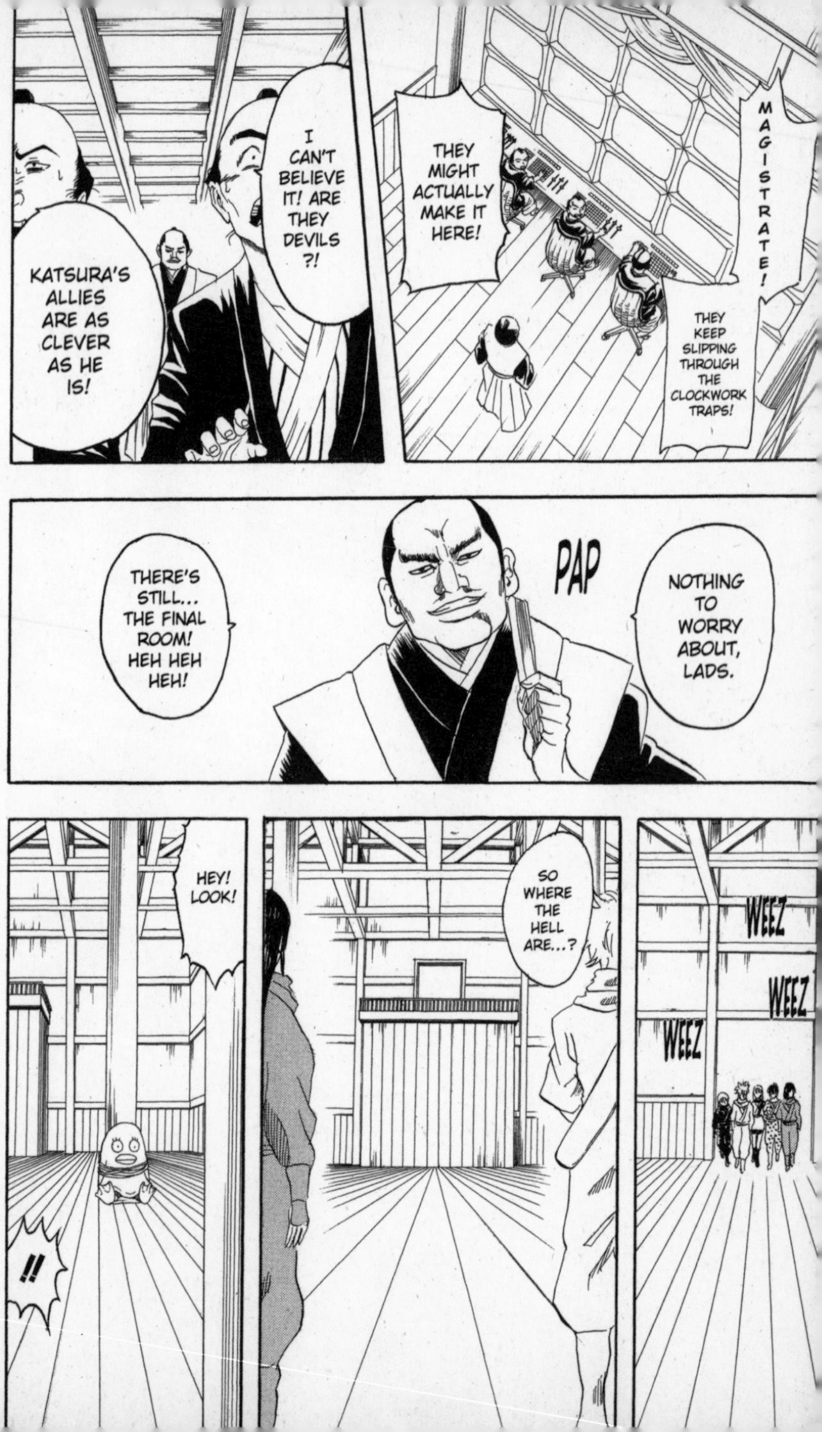
MAGISTRATE!
THEY KEEP SLIPPING THROUGH THE CLOCKWORK TRAPS!
THEY MIGHT ACTUALLY MAKE IT HERE!
I CAN'T BELIEVE IT! ARE THEY DEVILS?!
KATSURA'S ALLIES ARE AS CLEVER AS HE IS!
NOTHING TO WORRY ABOUT, LADS.
PAP
THERE'S STILL... THE FINAL ROOM! HEH HEH HEH!
WEEZ
WEEZ
WEEZ
SO WHERE THE HELL ARE...?
HEY! LOOK!
!!

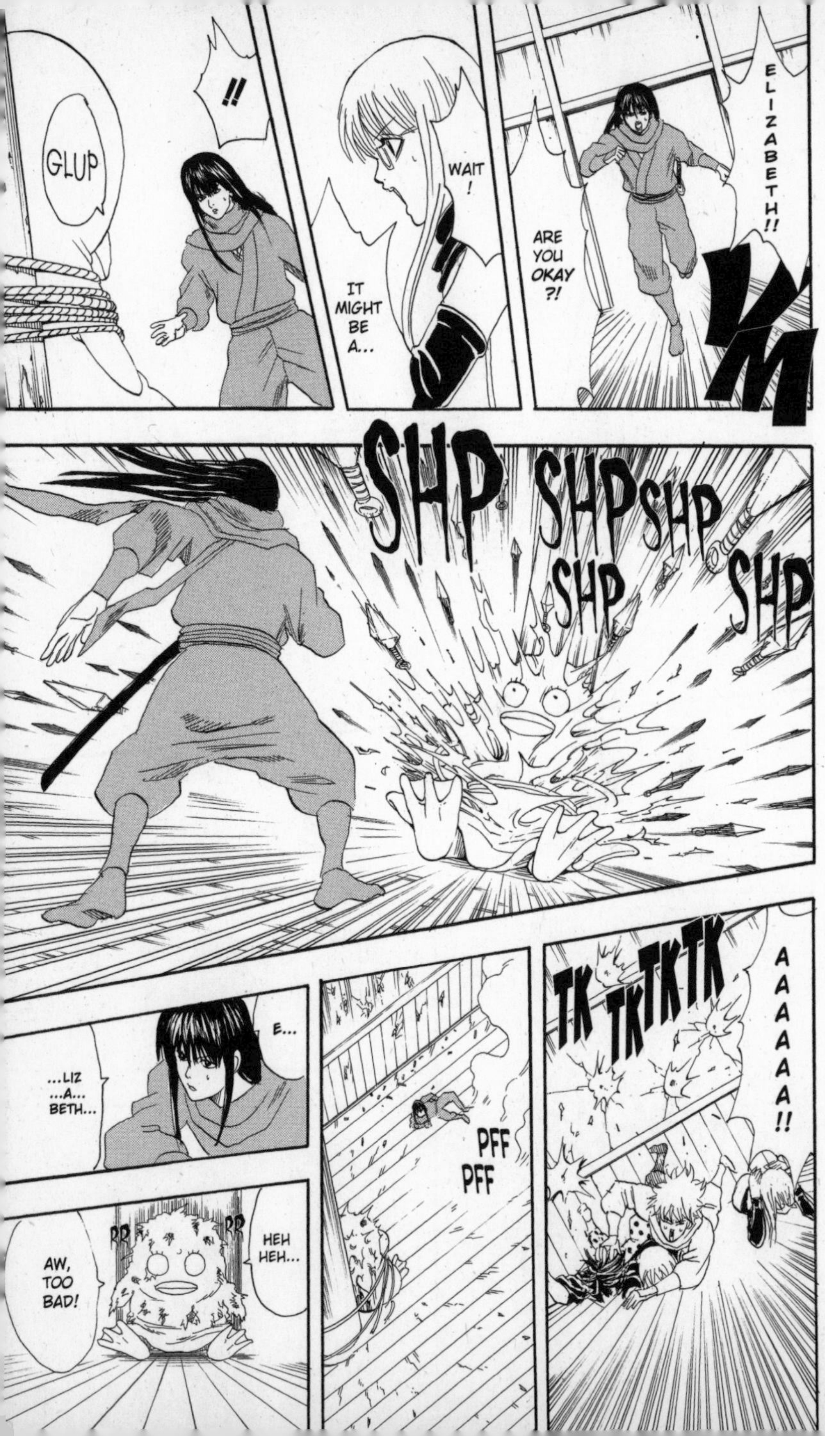
ELIZABETH!!
ARE YOU OKAY?!
WM
WAIT!
IT MIGHT BE A...
!!
GLUP
SHP
SHP SHP
SHP
SHP
TK TK TK TK
AAAAAAA!!
PFF PFF
E...
...LIZ ...A... BETH...
HEH HEH...
RR RR
AW, TOO BAD!

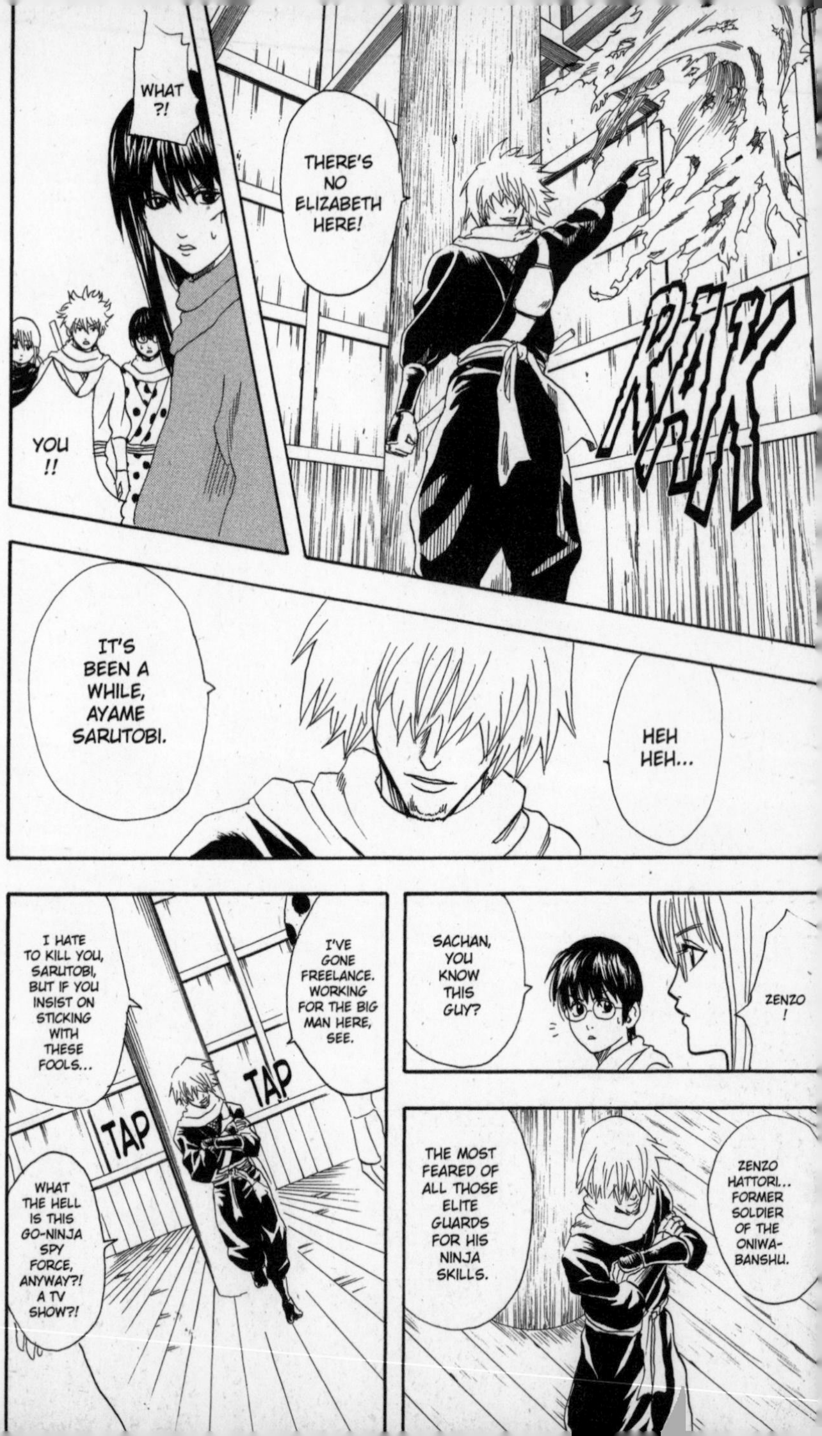
THERE'S NO ELIZABETH HERE!
RAK
WHAT ?!
YOU !!
HEH HEH...
IT'S BEEN A WHILE, AYAME SARUTOBI.
ZENZO !
SACHAN, YOU KNOW THIS GUY?
ZENZO HATTORI... FORMER SOLDIER OF THE ONIWA-BANSHU.
THE MOST FEARED OF ALL THOSE ELITE GUARDS FOR HIS NINJA SKILLS.
I'VE GONE FREELANCE. WORKING FOR THE BIG MAN HERE, SEE.
I HATE TO KILL YOU, SARUTOBI, BUT IF YOU INSIST ON STICKING WITH THESE FOOLS...
TAP
TAP
WHAT THE HELL IS THIS GO-NINJA SPY FORCE, ANYWAY?! A TV SHOW?!

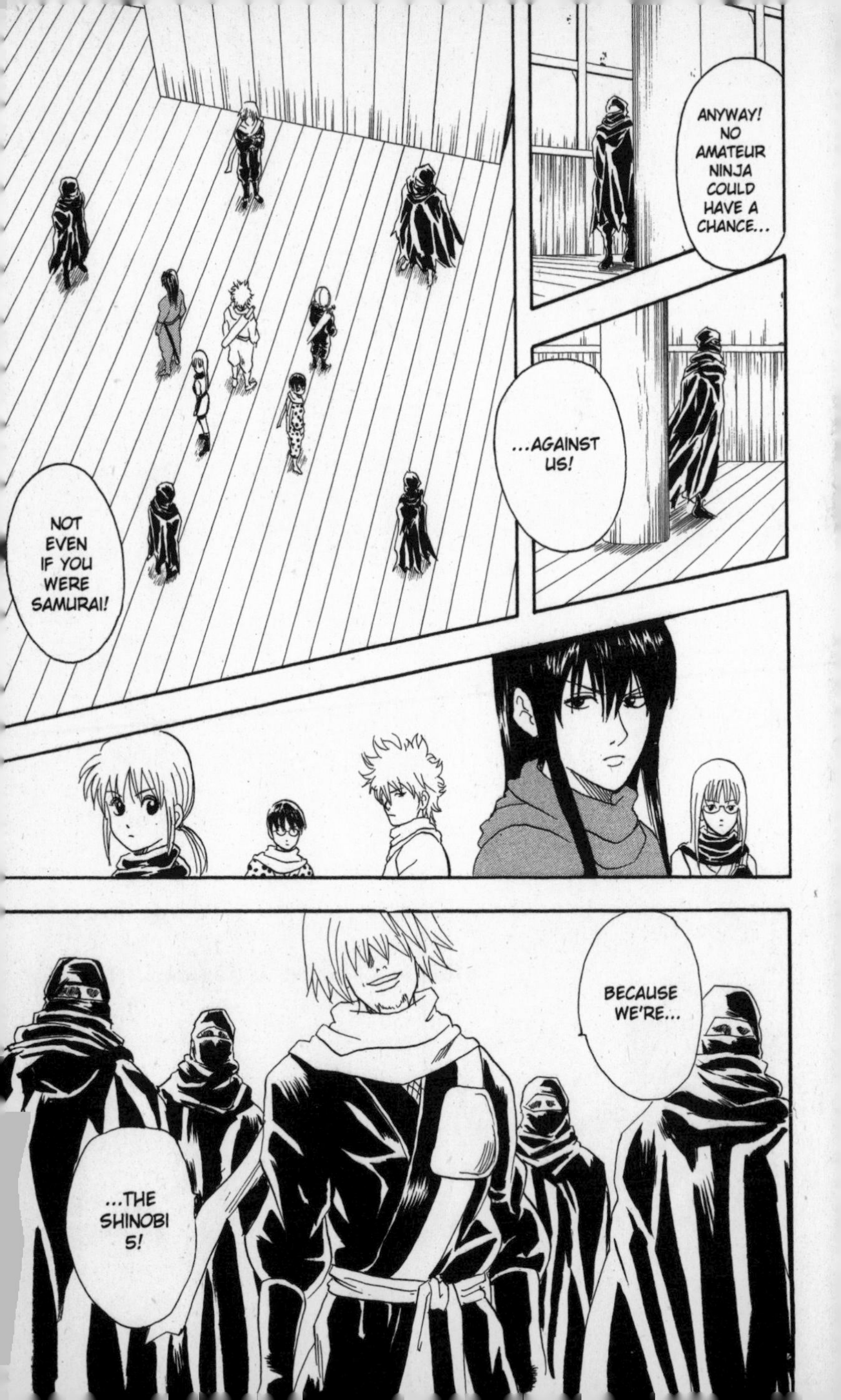
ANYWAY! NO AMATEUR NINJA COULD HAVE A CHANCE...
...AGAINST US!
NOT EVEN IF YOU WERE SAMURAI!
BECAUSE WE'RE...
...THE SHINOBI 5!

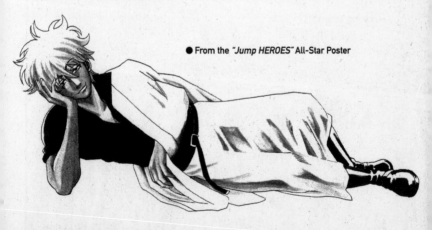

● From the *"Jump HEROES"* All-Star Poster

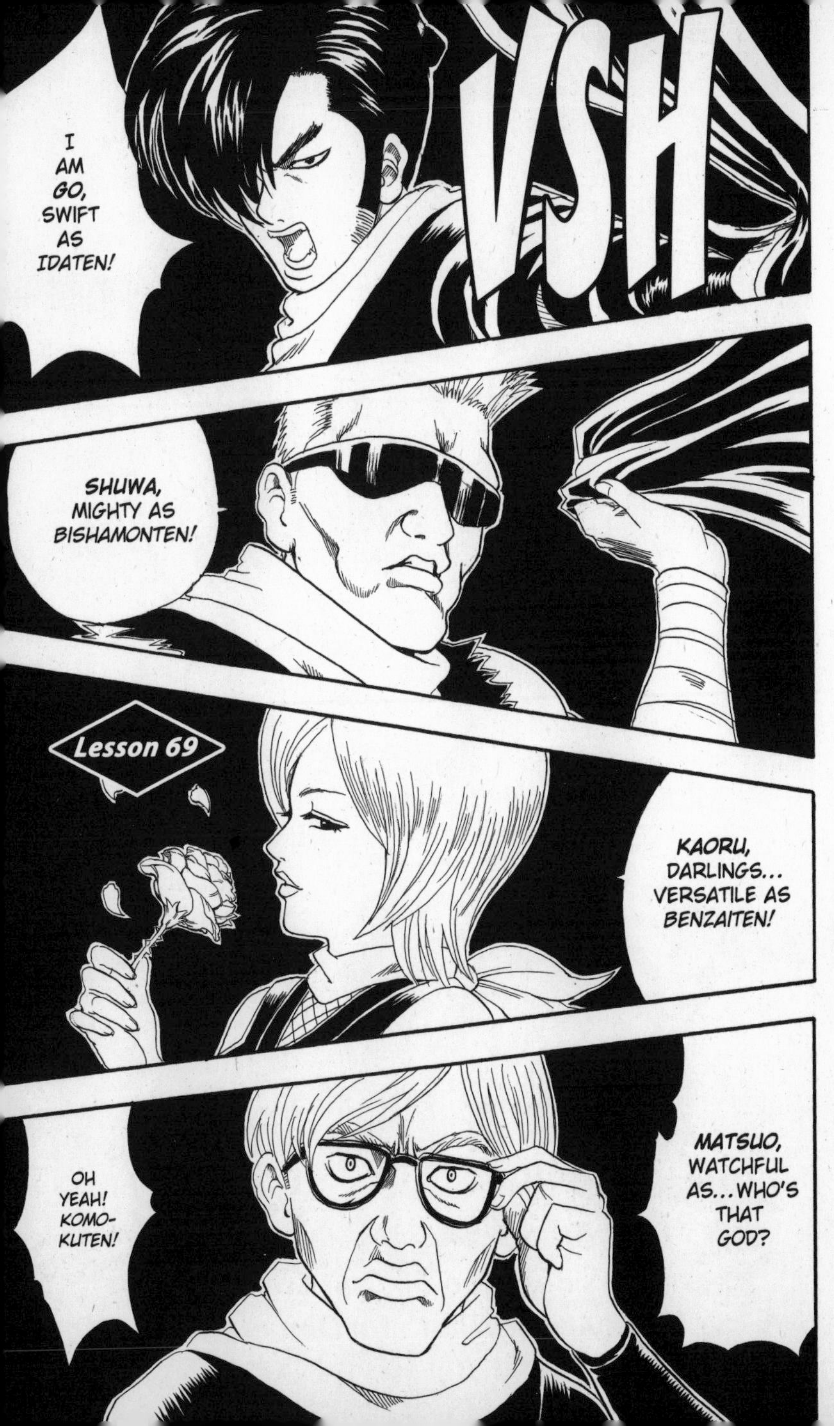

VSH
I AM GO, SWIFT AS IDATEN!
SHUWA, MIGHTY AS BISHAMONTEN!
KAORU, DARLINGS... VERSATILE AS BENZAITEN!
Lesson 69
MATSUO, WATCHFUL AS...WHO'S THAT GOD?
OH YEAH! KOMO-KUTEN!

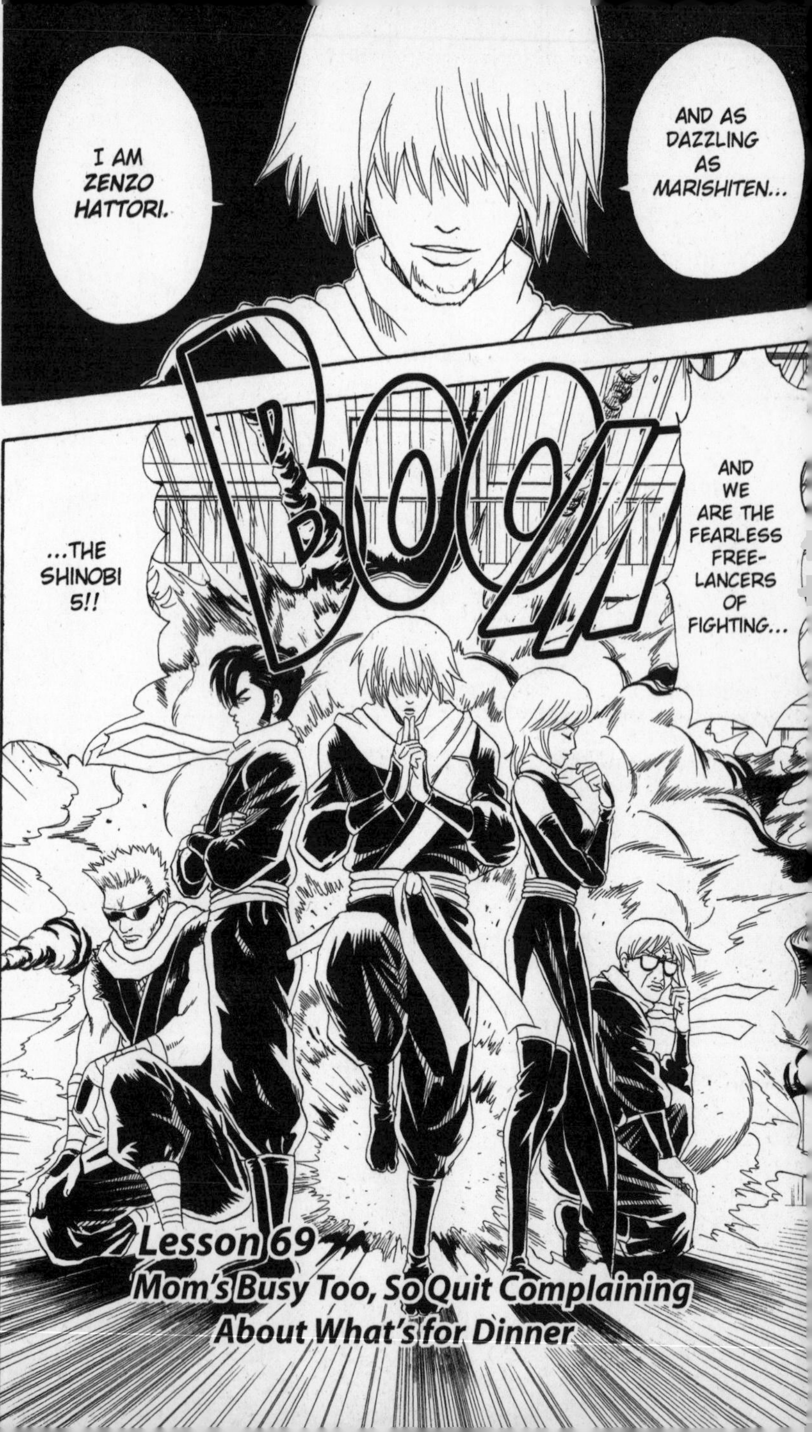
AND AS DAZZLING AS MARISHITEN...
I AM ZENZO HATTORI.
AND WE ARE THE FEARLESS FREE-LANCERS OF FIGHTING...
BOOM
...THE SHINOBI 5!!
Lesson 69
Mom's Busy Too, So Quit Complaining About What's for Dinner

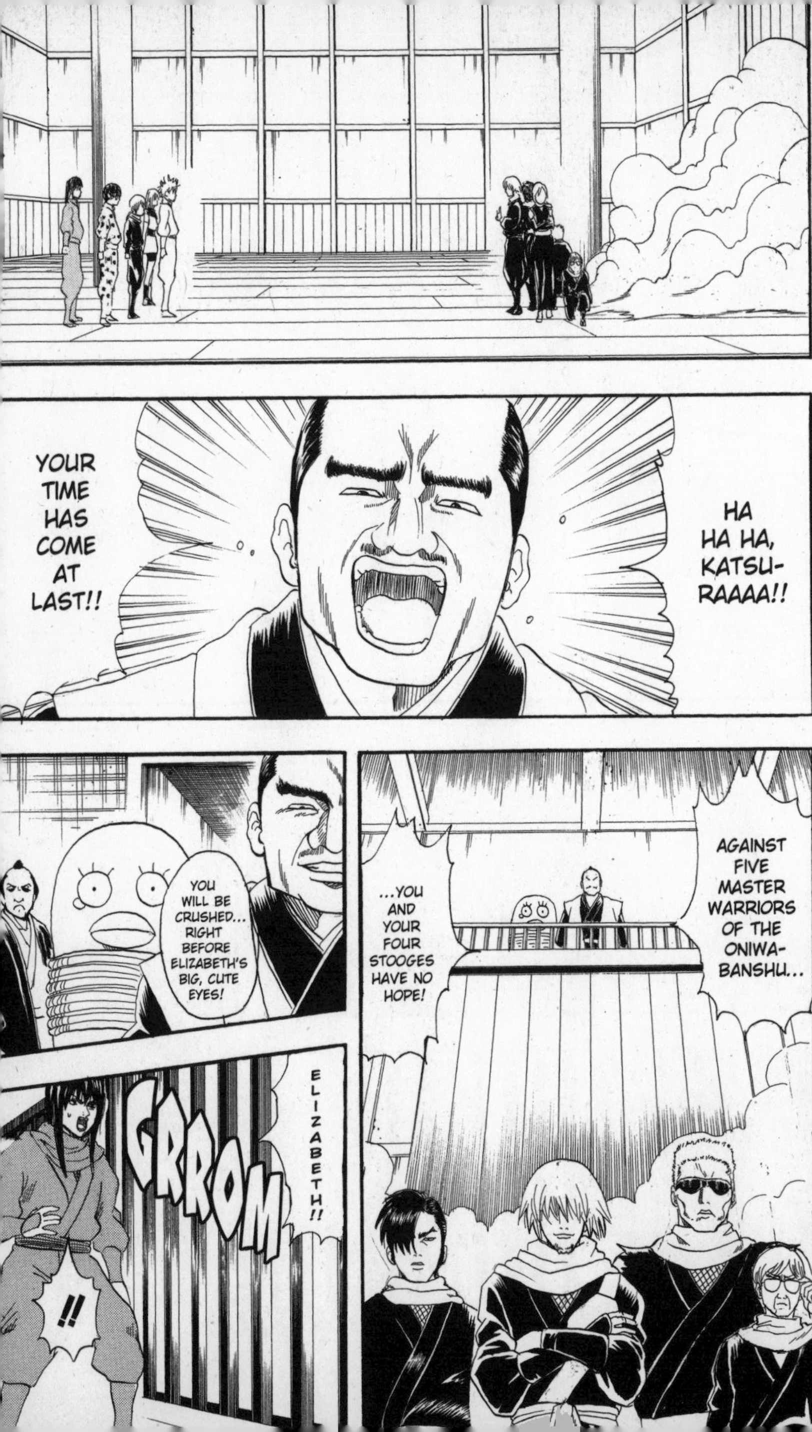
HA HA HA, KATSU-RAAAA!!
YOUR TIME HAS COME AT LAST!!
AGAINST FIVE MASTER WARRIORS OF THE ONIWA-BANSHU...
...YOU AND YOUR FOUR STOOGES HAVE NO HOPE!
YOU WILL BE CRUSHED... RIGHT BEFORE ELIZABETH'S BIG, CUTE EYES!
ELIZABETH!!
GRROM
!!

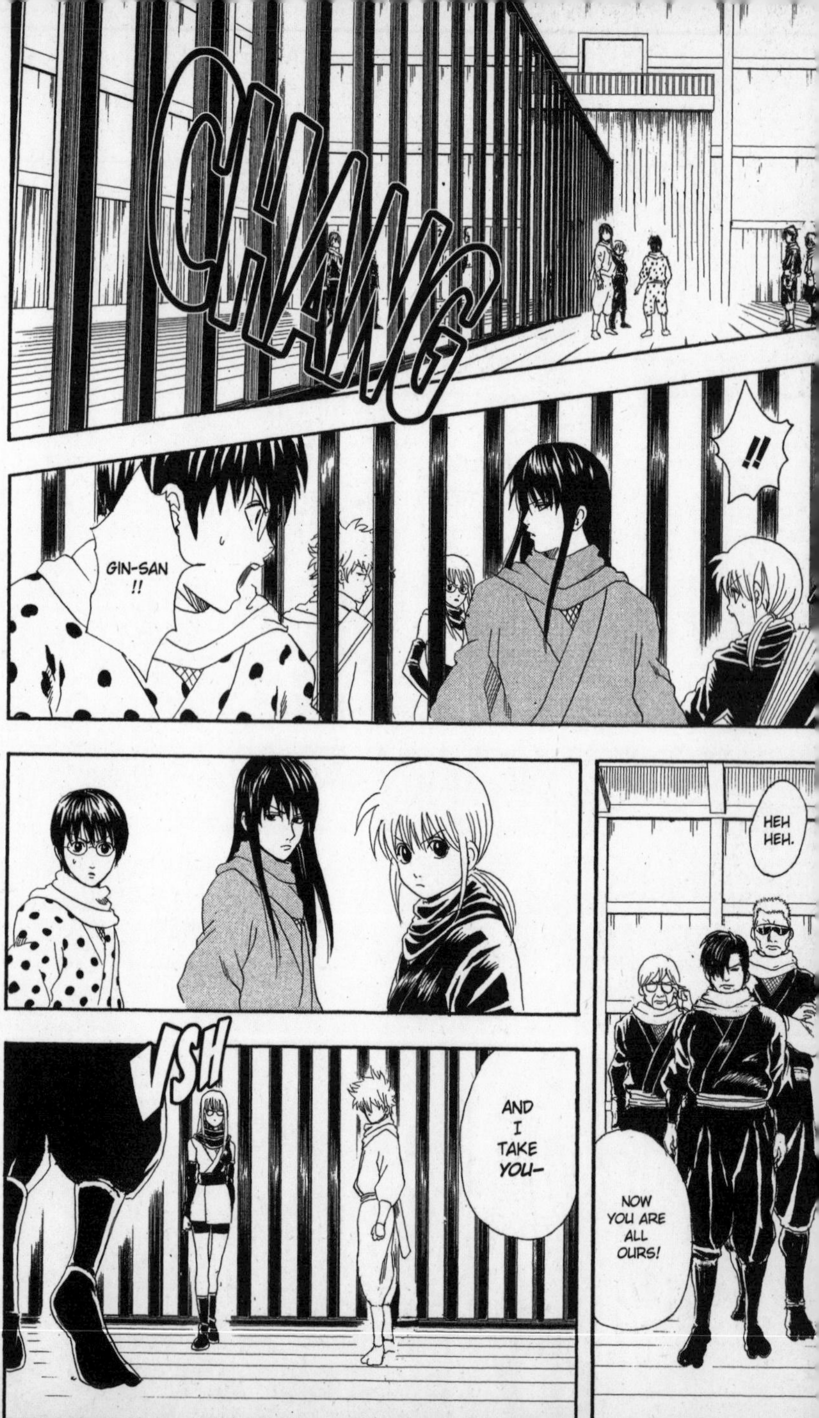
CHANG
!!
GIN-SAN !!
HEH HEH.
NOW YOU ARE ALL OURS!
VSH
AND I TAKE YOU-

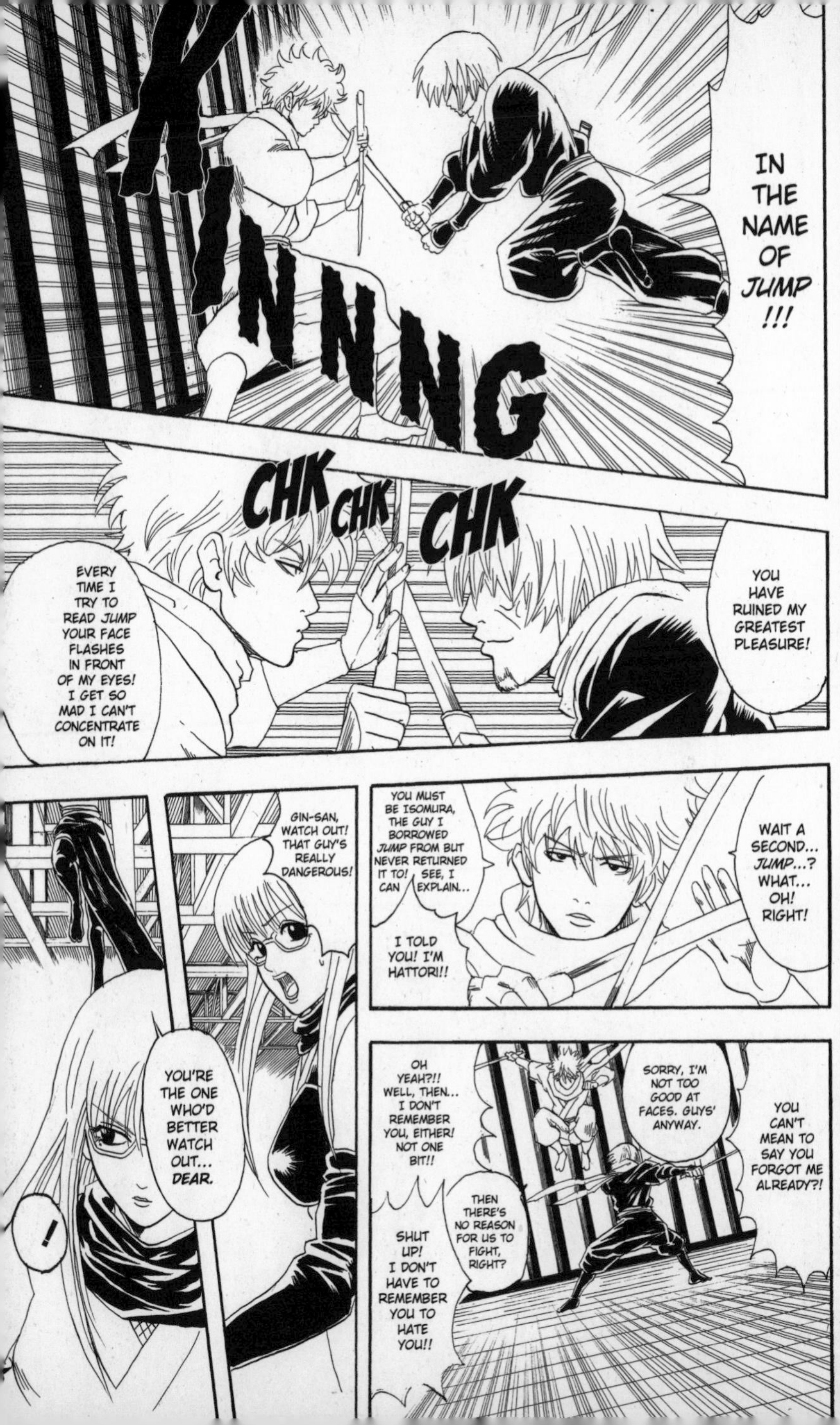
IN THE NAME OF JUMP!!!
KINNNG
CHK CHK CHK
YOU HAVE RUINED MY GREATEST PLEASURE!
EVERY TIME I TRY TO READ JUMP YOUR FACE FLASHES IN FRONT OF MY EYES! I GET SO MAD I CAN'T CONCENTRATE ON IT!
WAIT A SECOND... JUMP...? WHAT... OH! RIGHT!
YOU MUST BE ISOMURA, THE GUY I BORROWED JUMP FROM BUT NEVER RETURNED IT TO! SEE, I CAN EXPLAIN...
I TOLD YOU! I'M HATTORI!!
YOU CAN'T MEAN TO SAY YOU FORGOT ME ALREADY?!
SORRY, I'M NOT TOO GOOD AT FACES. GUYS' ANYWAY.
OH YEAH?!! WELL, THEN... I DON'T REMEMBER YOU, EITHER! NOT ONE BIT!!
THEN THERE'S NO REASON FOR US TO FIGHT, RIGHT?
SHUT UP! I DON'T HAVE TO REMEMBER YOU TO HATE YOU!!
GIN-SAN, WATCH OUT! THAT GUY'S REALLY DANGEROUS!
YOU'RE THE ONE WHO'D BETTER WATCH OUT... DEAR.
!

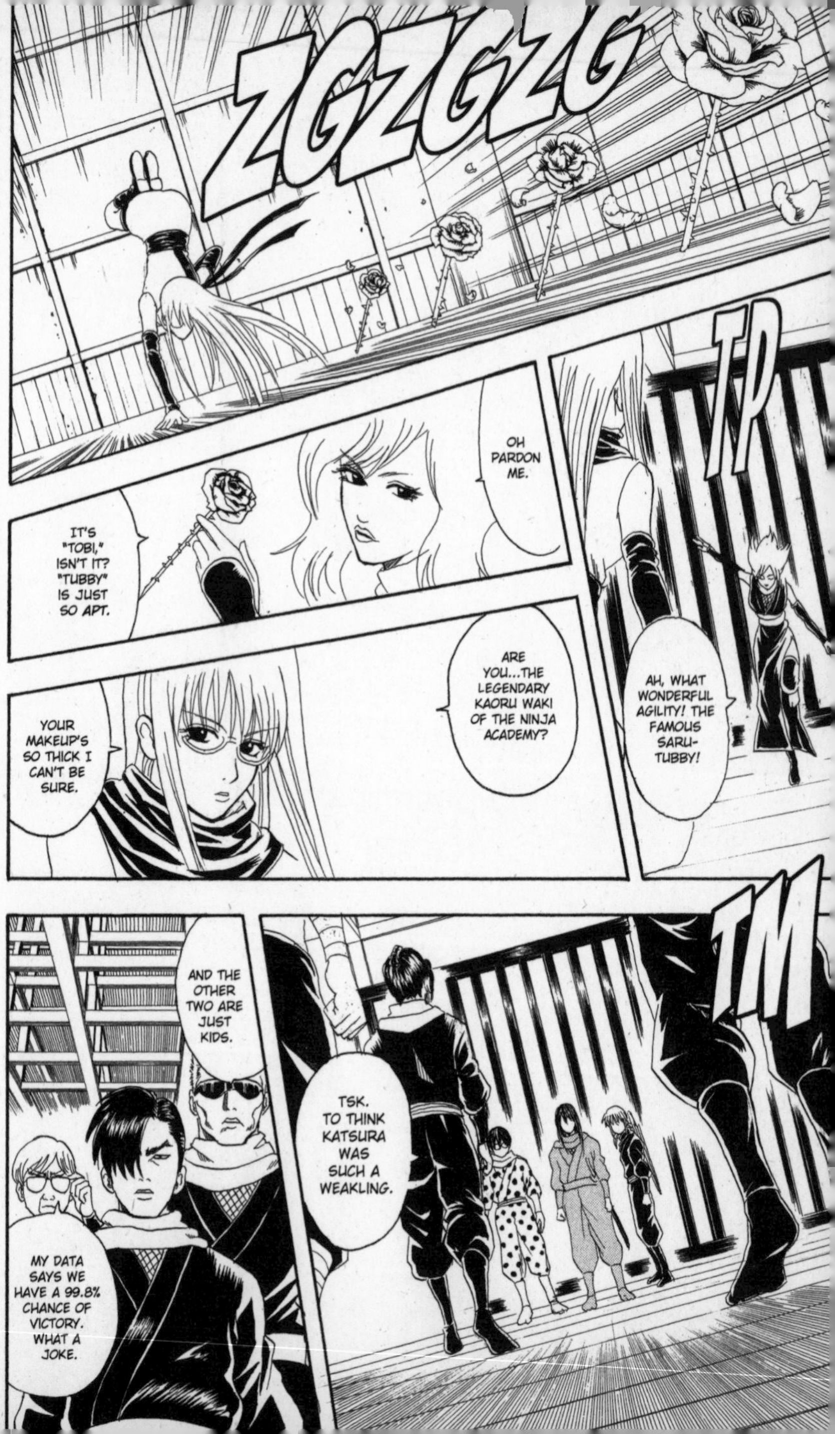
ZGZGZG
TP
AH, WHAT WONDERFUL AGILITY! THE FAMOUS SARU-TUBBY!
OH PARDON ME.
IT'S "TOBI," ISN'T IT? "TUBBY" IS JUST SO APT.
ARE YOU...THE LEGENDARY KAORU WAKI OF THE NINJA ACADEMY?
YOUR MAKEUP'S SO THICK I CAN'T BE SURE.
TM
TSK. TO THINK KATSURA WAS SUCH A WEAKLING.
AND THE OTHER TWO ARE JUST KIDS.
MY DATA SAYS WE HAVE A 99.8% CHANCE OF VICTORY. WHAT A JOKE.

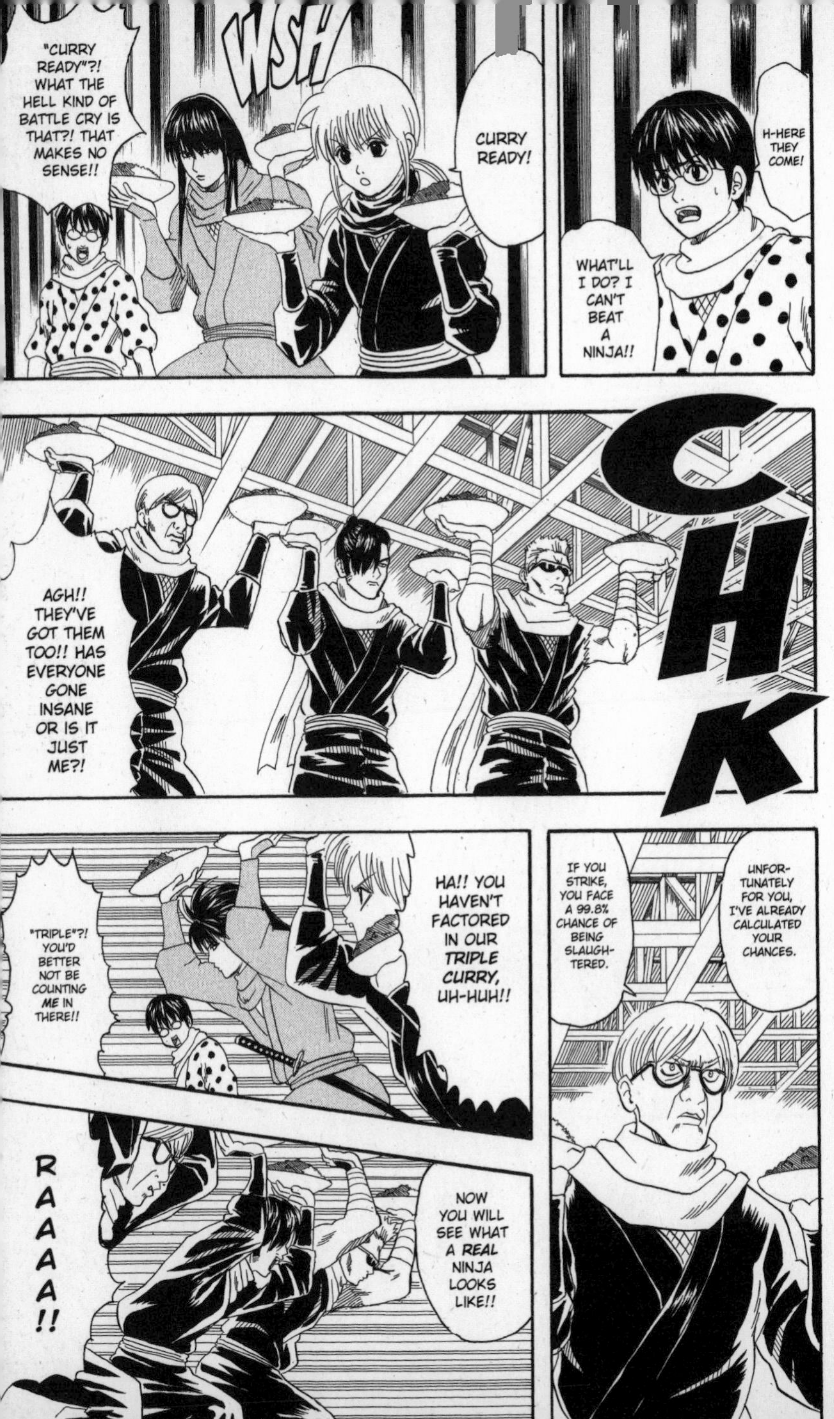
H-HERE THEY COME!
WHAT'LL I DO? I CAN'T BEAT A NINJA!!
CURRY READY!
WSH
"CURRY READY"?! WHAT THE HELL KIND OF BATTLE CRY IS THAT?! THAT MAKES NO SENSE!!
CHK
AGH!! THEY'VE GOT THEM TOO!! HAS EVERYONE GONE INSANE OR IS IT JUST ME?!
UNFOR-TUNATELY FOR YOU, I'VE ALREADY CALCULATED YOUR CHANCES.
IF YOU STRIKE, YOU FACE A 99.8% CHANCE OF BEING SLAUGH-TERED.
HA!! YOU HAVEN'T FACTORED IN OUR TRIPLE CURRY, UH-HUH!!
"TRIPLE"?! YOU'D BETTER NOT BE COUNTING ME IN THERE!!
NOW YOU WILL SEE WHAT A REAL NINJA LOOKS LIKE!!
RAAAAA!!

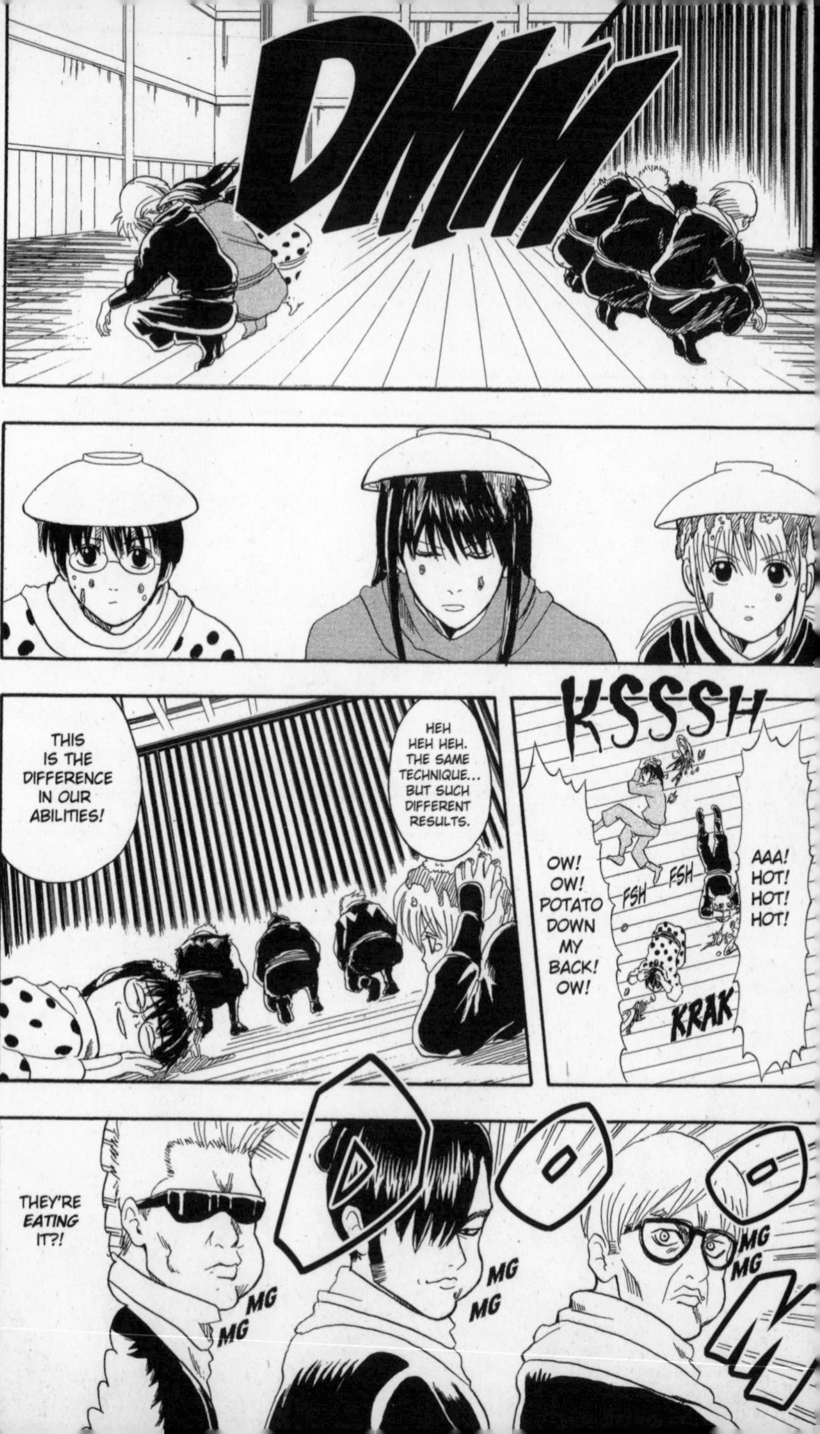
DMM
KSSSH
AAA! HOT! HOT! HOT!
FSH
FSH
OW! OW! POTATO DOWN MY BACK! OW!
KRAK
HEH HEH HEH. THE SAME TECHNIQUE... BUT SUCH DIFFERENT RESULTS.
THIS IS THE DIFFERENCE IN OUR ABILITIES!
DOOM
MG MG
MG MG
MG MG
THEY'RE EATING IT?!

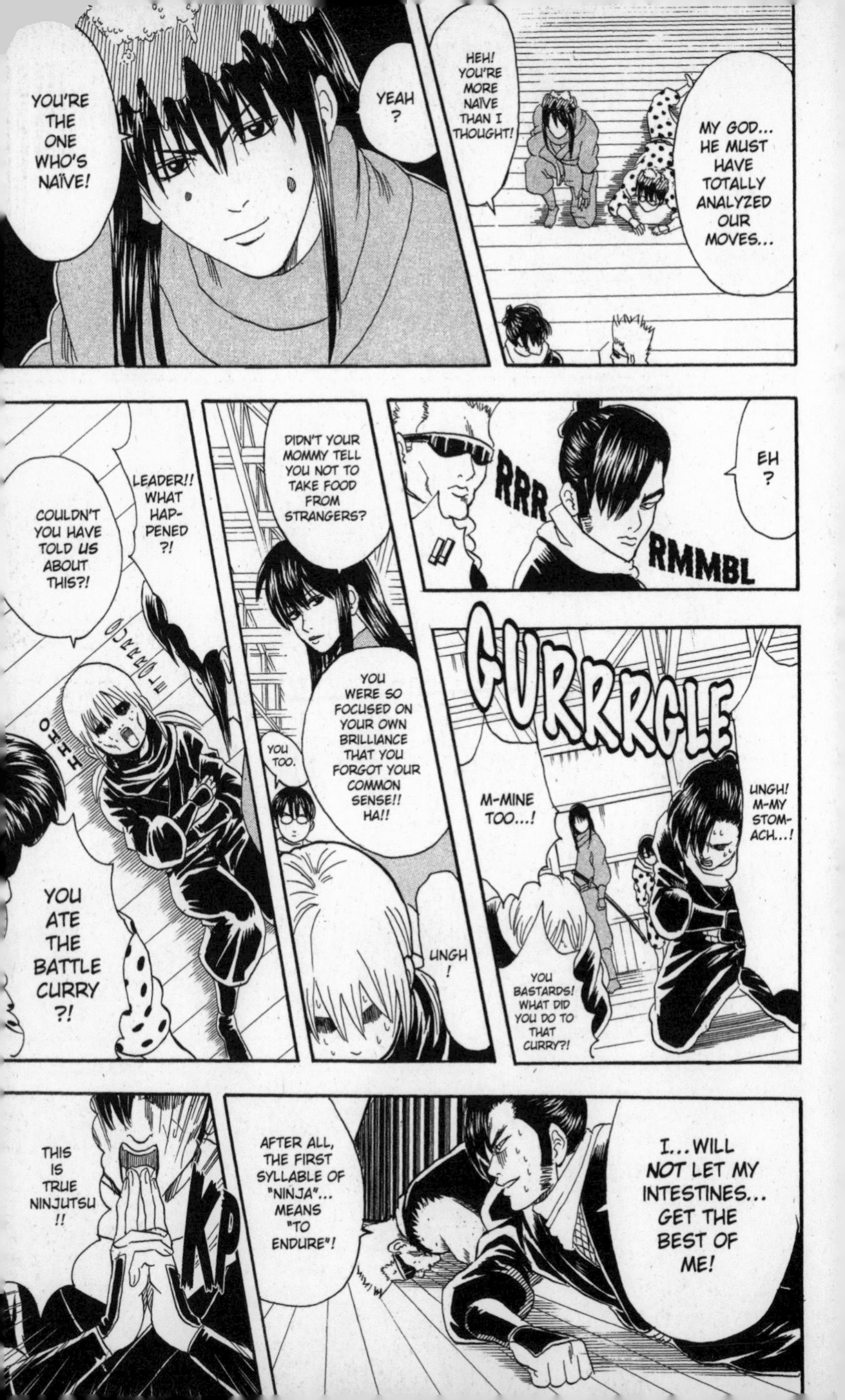
MY GOD... HE MUST HAVE TOTALLY ANALYZED OUR MOVES...
HEH! YOU'RE MORE NAÏVE THAN I THOUGHT!
YEAH?
YOU'RE THE ONE WHO'S NAÏVE!
EH?
RRR RMMBL
GURRRGLE
UNGH! M-MY STOMACH...!
M-MINE TOO...!
YOU BASTARDS! WHAT DID YOU DO TO THAT CURRY?!
DIDN'T YOUR MOMMY TELL YOU NOT TO TAKE FOOD FROM STRANGERS?
YOU WERE SO FOCUSED ON YOUR OWN BRILLIANCE THAT YOU FORGOT YOUR COMMON SENSE!! HA!!
YOU TOO.
UNGH!
LEADER!! WHAT HAPPENED?!
COULDN'T YOU HAVE TOLD US ABOUT THIS?!
OHHH
YOU ATE THE BATTLE CURRY?!
I...WILL NOT LET MY INTESTINES... GET THE BEST OF ME!
AFTER ALL, THE FIRST SYLLABLE OF "NINJA"... MEANS "TO ENDURE"!
KP
THIS IS TRUE NINJUTSU!!

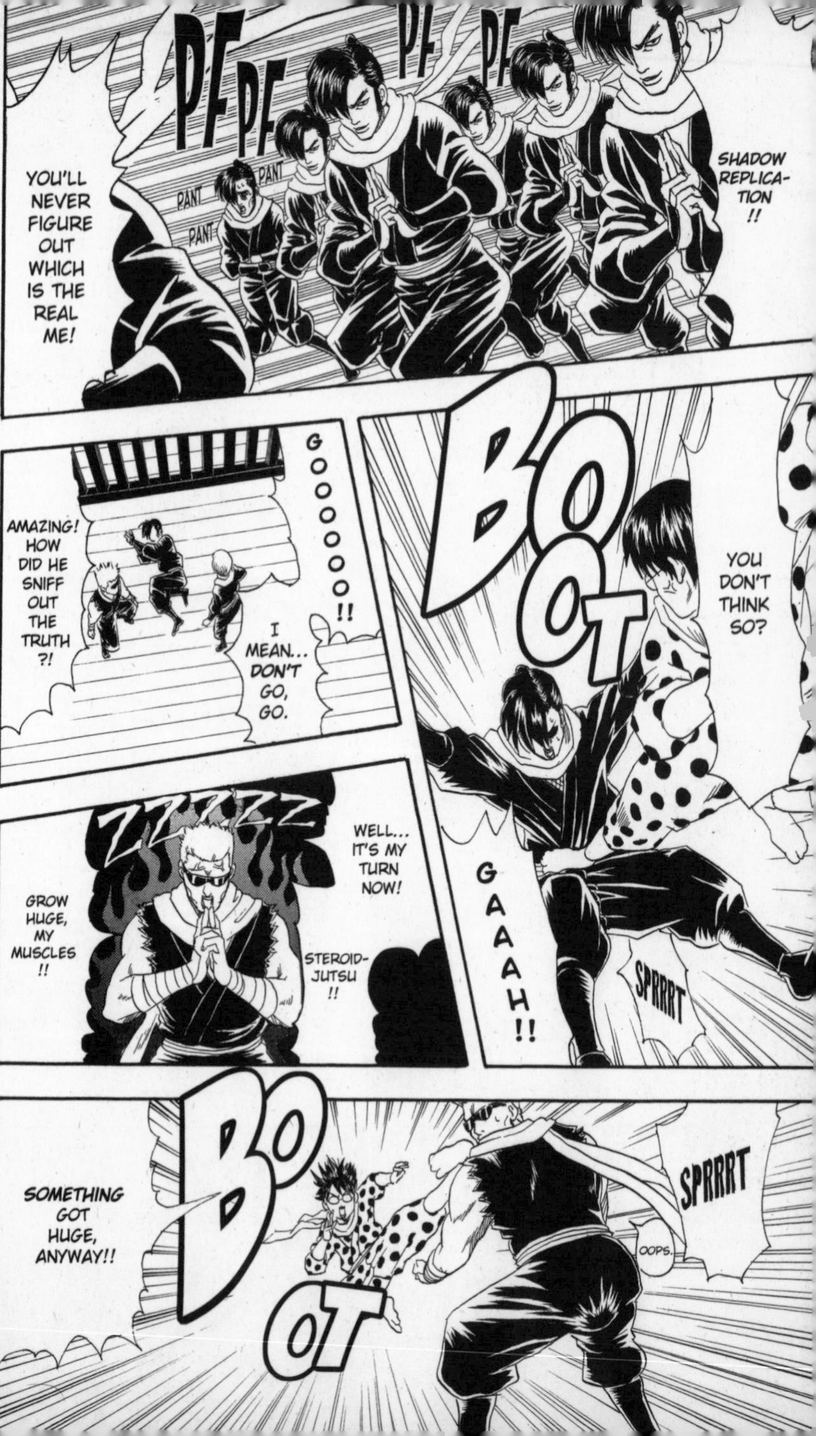
SHADOW REPLICATION!!
PF
PF
PF PF
PANT
PANT
PANT
YOU'LL NEVER FIGURE OUT WHICH IS THE REAL ME!
BOOT
YOU DON'T THINK SO?
GAAAH!!
SPRRRT
GOOOOOOO!!
I MEAN... DON'T GO, GO.
AMAZING! HOW DID HE SNIFF OUT THE TRUTH?!
WELL... IT'S MY TURN NOW!
STEROID-JUTSU!!
GROW HUGE, MY MUSCLES!!
SPRRRT
OOPS.
BOOT
SOMETHING GOT HUGE, ANYWAY!!

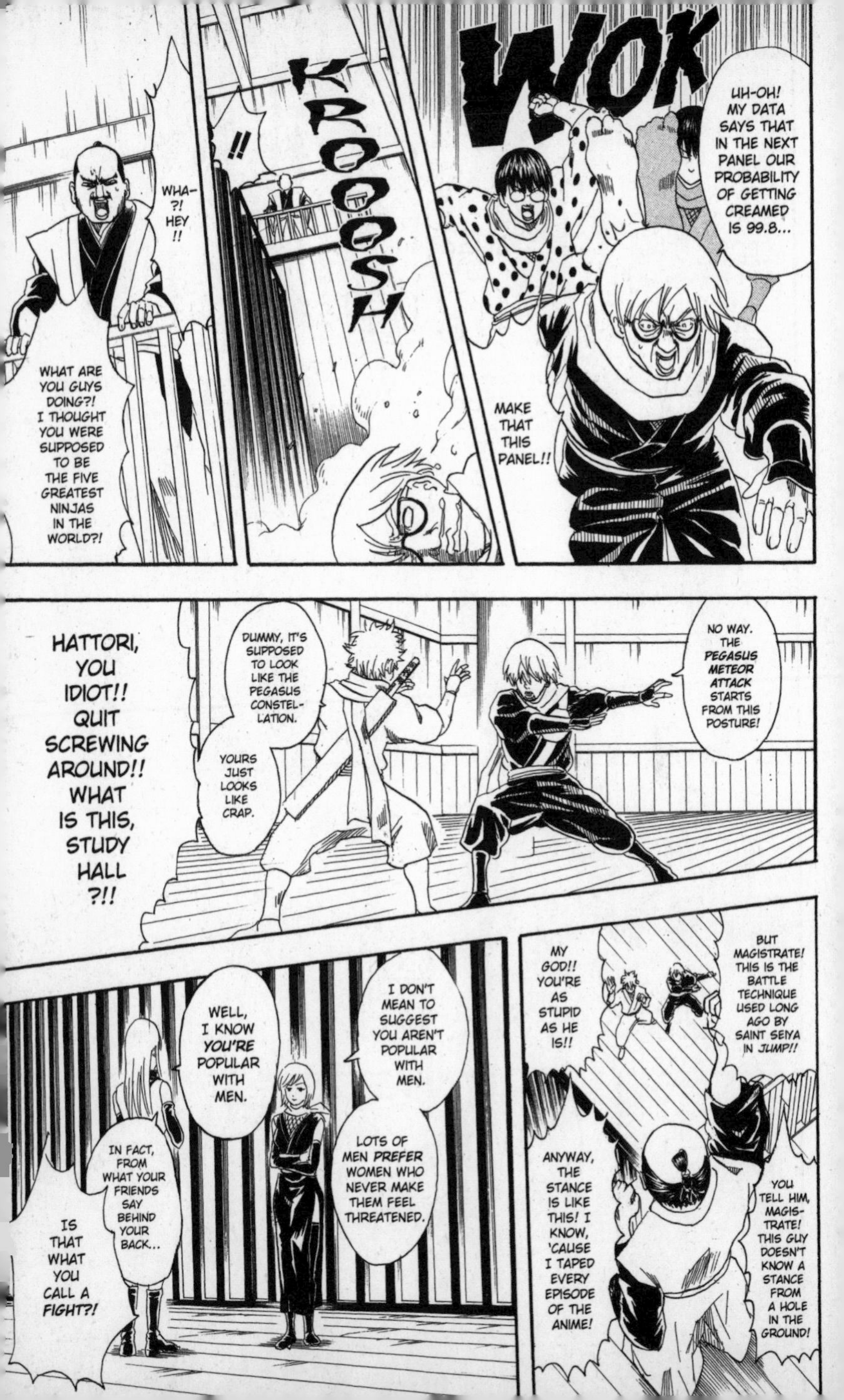
WOK
UH-OH! MY DATA SAYS THAT IN THE NEXT PANEL OUR PROBABILITY OF GETTING CREAMED IS 99.8...
MAKE THAT THIS PANEL!!
KROOOSH
!!
WHA-?! HEY!!
WHAT ARE YOU GUYS DOING?! I THOUGHT YOU WERE SUPPOSED TO BE THE FIVE GREATEST NINJAS IN THE WORLD?!
NO WAY. THE PEGASUS METEOR ATTACK STARTS FROM THIS POSTURE!
DUMMY, IT'S SUPPOSED TO LOOK LIKE THE PEGASUS CONSTEL-LATION.
YOURS JUST LOOKS LIKE CRAP.
HATTORI, YOU IDIOT!! QUIT SCREWING AROUND!! WHAT IS THIS, STUDY HALL?!!
BUT MAGISTRATE! THIS IS THE BATTLE TECHNIQUE USED LONG AGO BY SAINT SEIYA IN JUMP!!
MY GOD!! YOU'RE AS STUPID AS HE IS!!
YOU TELL HIM, MAGIS-TRATE! THIS GUY DOESN'T KNOW A STANCE FROM A HOLE IN THE GROUND!
ANYWAY, THE STANCE IS LIKE THIS! I KNOW, 'CAUSE I TAPED EVERY EPISODE OF THE ANIME!
I DON'T MEAN TO SUGGEST YOU AREN'T POPULAR WITH MEN.
WELL, I KNOW YOU'RE POPULAR WITH MEN.
LOTS OF MEN PREFER WOMEN WHO NEVER MAKE THEM FEEL THREATENED.
IN FACT, FROM WHAT YOUR FRIENDS SAY BEHIND YOUR BACK...
IS THAT WHAT YOU CALL A FIGHT?!

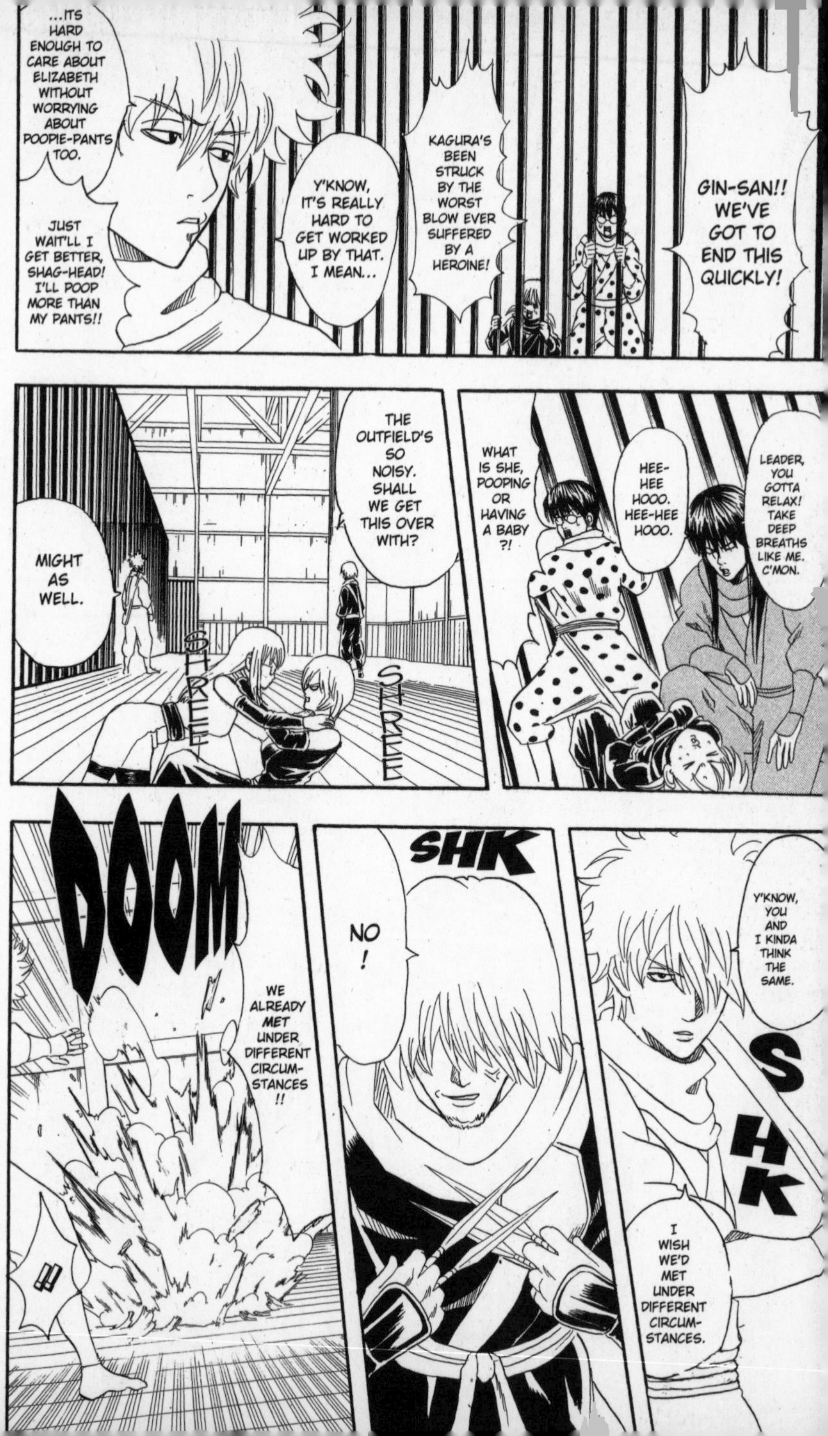
GIN-SAN!! WE'VE GOT TO END THIS QUICKLY!
KAGURA'S BEEN STRUCK BY THE WORST BLOW EVER SUFFERED BY A HEROINE!
Y'KNOW, IT'S REALLY HARD TO GET WORKED UP BY THAT. I MEAN...
...ITS HARD ENOUGH TO CARE ABOUT ELIZABETH WITHOUT WORRYING ABOUT POOPIE-PANTS TOO.
JUST WAIT'LL I GET BETTER, SHAG-HEAD! I'LL POOP MORE THAN MY PANTS!!
LEADER, YOU GOTTA RELAX! TAKE DEEP BREATHS LIKE ME. C'MON.
HEE-HEE HOOO. HEE-HEE HOOO.
WHAT IS SHE, POOPING OR HAVING A BABY?!
THE OUTFIELD'S SO NOISY. SHALL WE GET THIS OVER WITH?
SHREE
SHREE
MIGHT AS WELL.
Y'KNOW, YOU AND I KINDA THINK THE SAME.
SHK
I WISH WE'D MET UNDER DIFFERENT CIRCUM-STANCES.
SHK
NO!
DOOM
WE ALREADY MET UNDER DIFFERENT CIRCUM-STANCES!!
!!

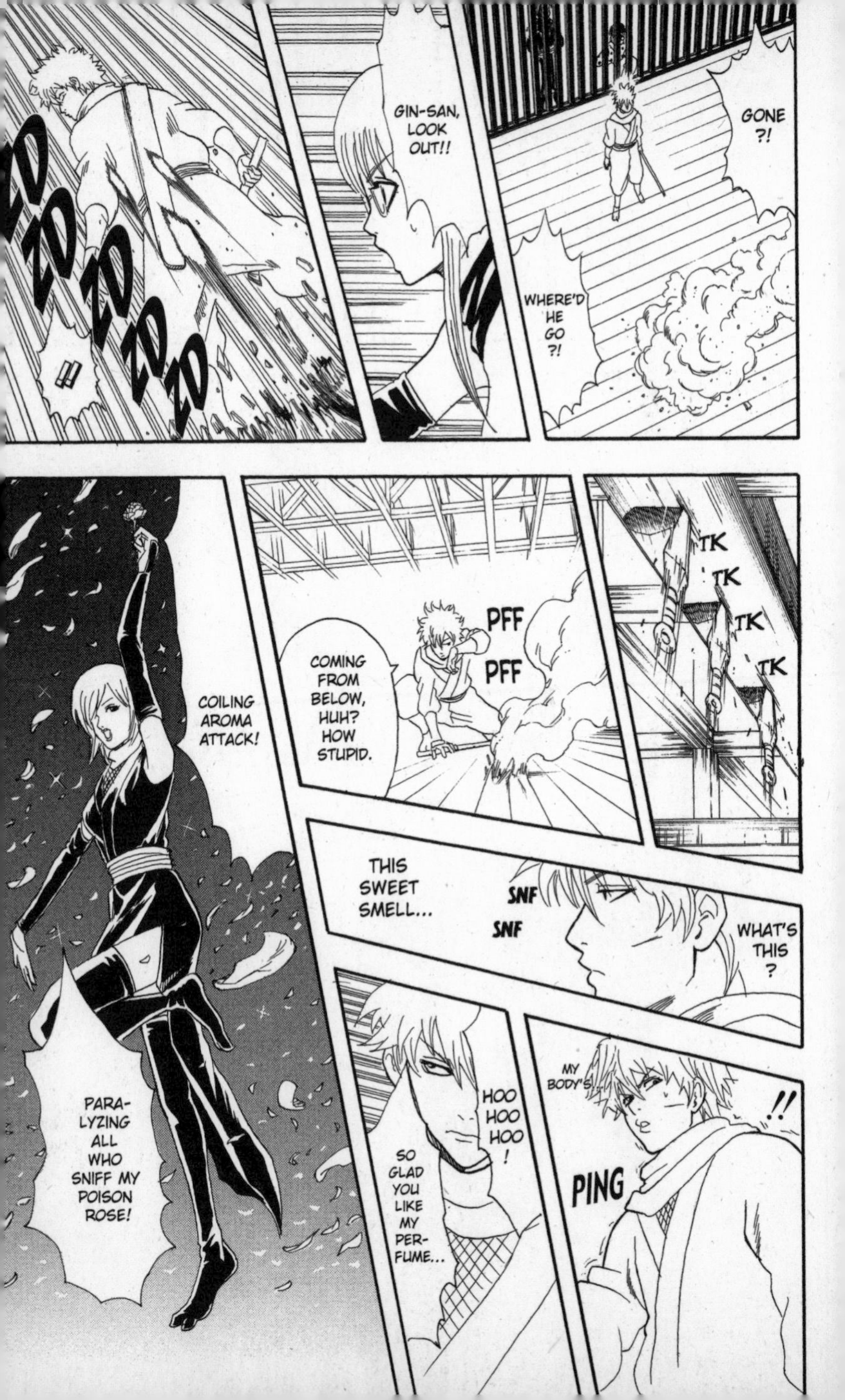
GONE ?!
WHERE'D HE GO ?!
GIN-SAN, LOOK OUT!!
ZD ZD ZD ZD ZD ZD ZD
!!
TK TK TK TK
PFF PFF
COMING FROM BELOW, HUH? HOW STUPID.
SNF SNF
THIS SWEET SMELL...
WHAT'S THIS ?
MY BODY'S
!!
PING
HOO HOO HOO !
SO GLAD YOU LIKE MY PERFUME...
COILING AROMA ATTACK!
PARALYZING ALL WHO SNIFF MY POISON ROSE!

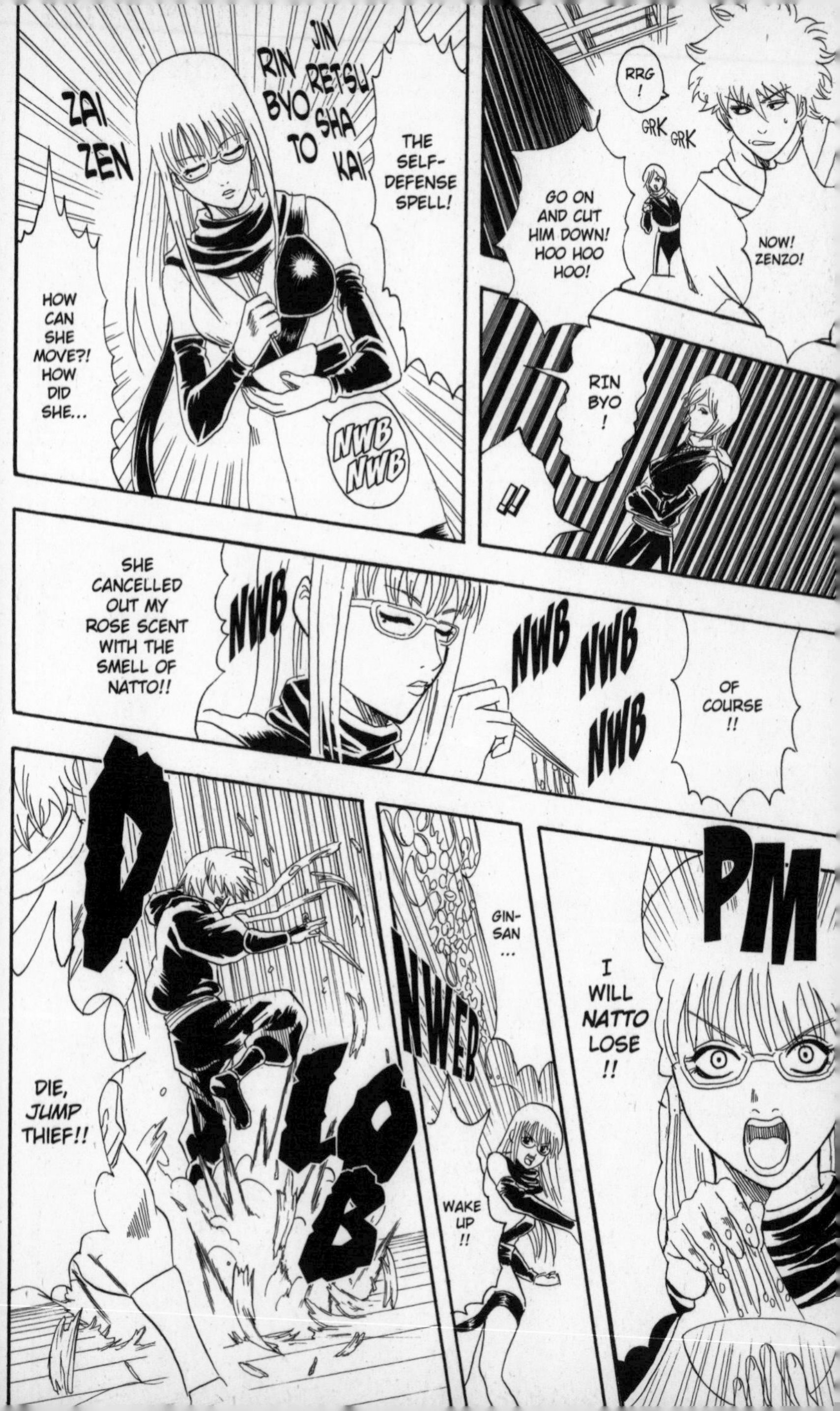
RRG!
GRK GRK
NOW! ZENZO!
GO ON AND CUT HIM DOWN! HOO HOO HOO!
RIN BYO!
!!
THE SELF-DEFENSE SPELL!
RIN BYO TO SHA KAI JIN RETSU
ZAI ZEN
HOW CAN SHE MOVE?! HOW DID SHE...
NWB NWB
OF COURSE!!
NWB NWB NWB
NWB
SHE CANCELLED OUT MY ROSE SCENT WITH THE SMELL OF NATTO!!
PM
I WILL NATTO LOSE!!
GIN-SAN...
NWEB
WAKE UP!!
DLOB
DIE, JUMP THIEF!!

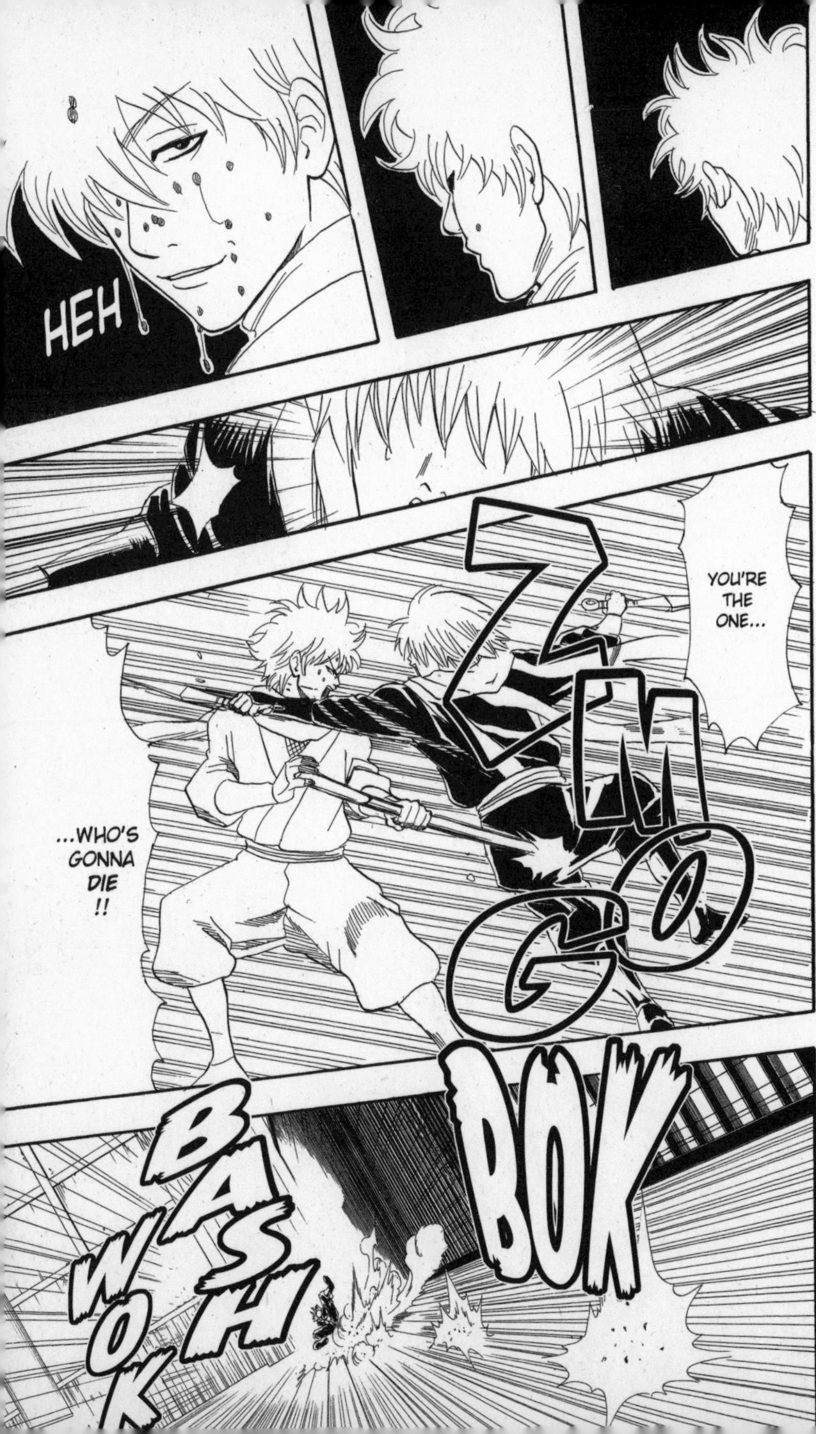
HEH
YOU'RE THE ONE...
ZMGO
...WHO'S GONNA DIE !!
BOK
BASH
WOK

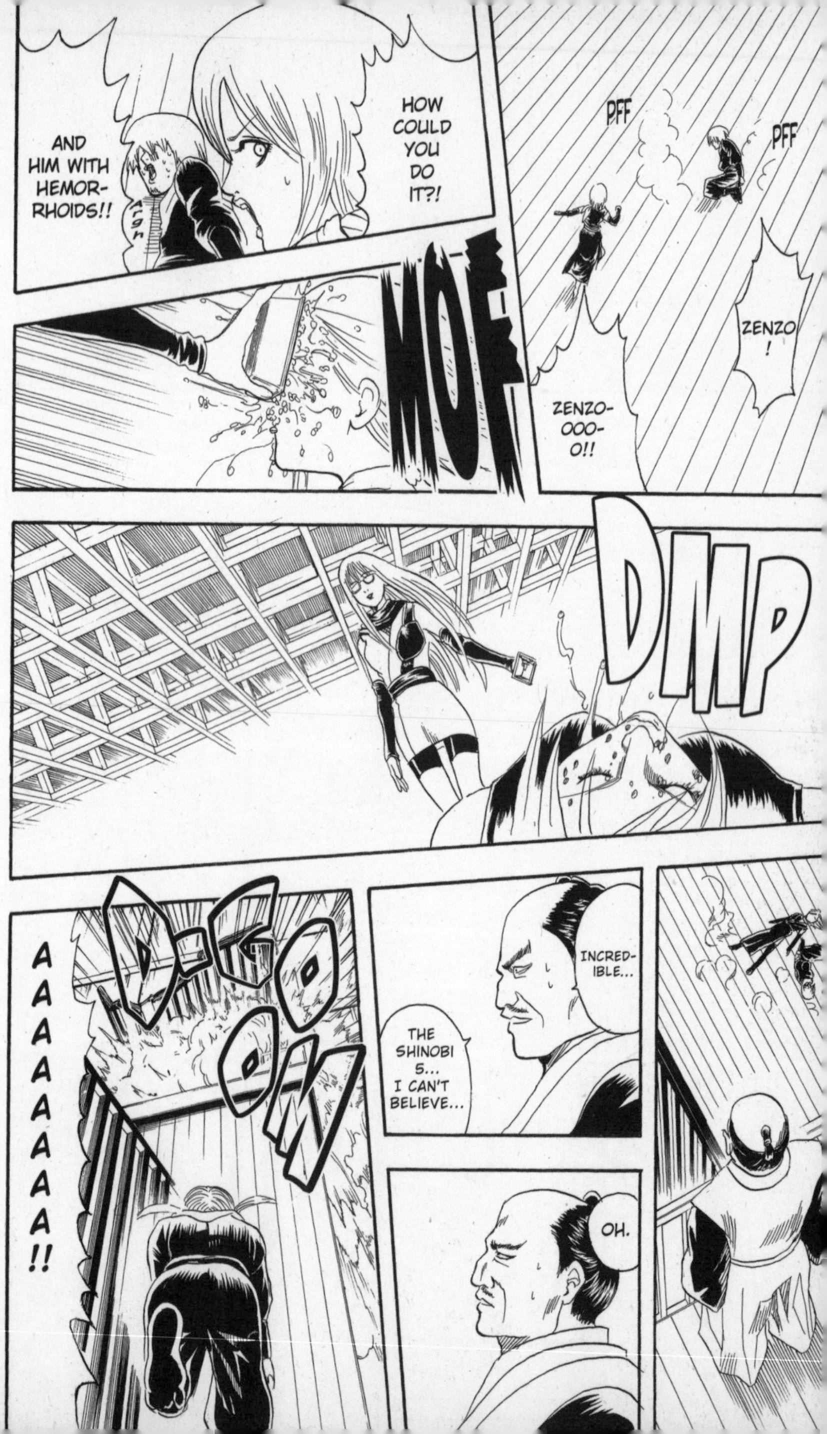
PFF
PFF
ZENZO!
ZENZO-OOO-O!!
HOW COULD YOU DO IT?!
AND HIM WITH HEMORRHOIDS!!
Argh
MOF
DMP
INCREDIBLE...
THE SHINOBI 5... I CAN'T BELIEVE...
OH.
DGOOOM
AAAAAAAAAAA!!

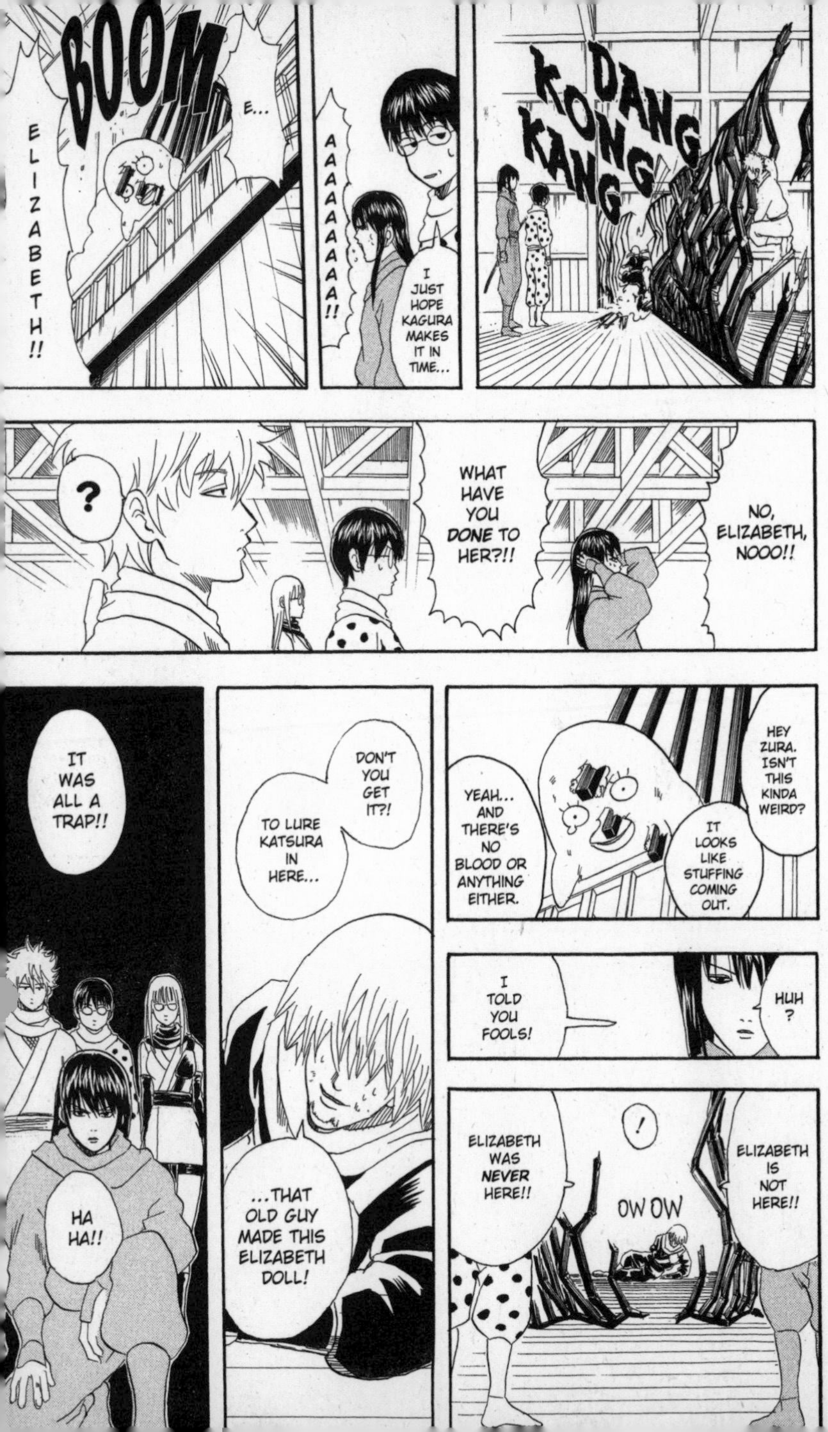
KONG DANG KANG
I JUST HOPE KAGURA MAKES IT IN TIME...
AAAAAAAAAAA!!
BOOM
E...
ELIZABETH!!
NO, ELIZABETH, NOOO!!
WHAT HAVE YOU *DONE* TO HER?!!
?
HEY ZURA. ISN'T THIS KINDA WEIRD?
IT LOOKS LIKE STUFFING COMING OUT.
YEAH... AND THERE'S NO BLOOD OR ANYTHING EITHER.
HUH?
I TOLD YOU FOOLS!
ELIZABETH IS NOT HERE!!
!
OW OW
ELIZABETH WAS *NEVER* HERE!!
DON'T YOU GET IT?!
TO LURE KATSURA IN HERE...
...THAT OLD GUY MADE THIS ELIZABETH DOLL!
IT WAS ALL A TRAP!!
HA HA!!

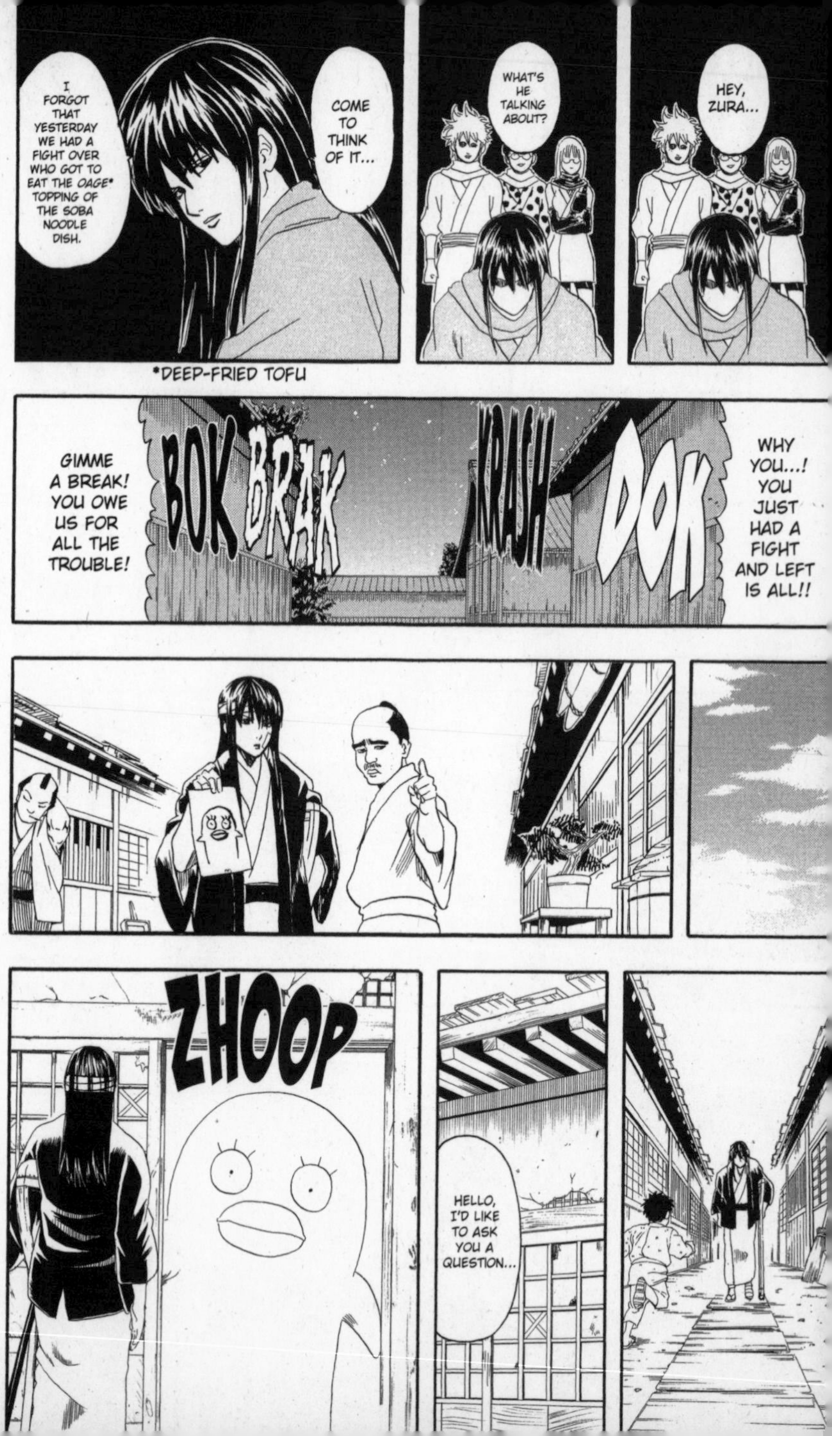
HEY, ZURA...
WHAT'S HE TALKING ABOUT?
COME TO THINK OF IT...
I FORGOT THAT YESTERDAY WE HAD A FIGHT OVER WHO GOT TO EAT THE *OAGE** TOPPING OF THE SOBA NOODLE DISH.
*DEEP-FRIED TOFU
WHY YOU...! YOU JUST HAD A FIGHT AND LEFT IS ALL!!
DOK
KRASH
BRAK
BOK
GIMME A BREAK! YOU OWE US FOR ALL THE TROUBLE!
HELLO, I'D LIKE TO ASK YOU A QUESTION...
ZHOOP

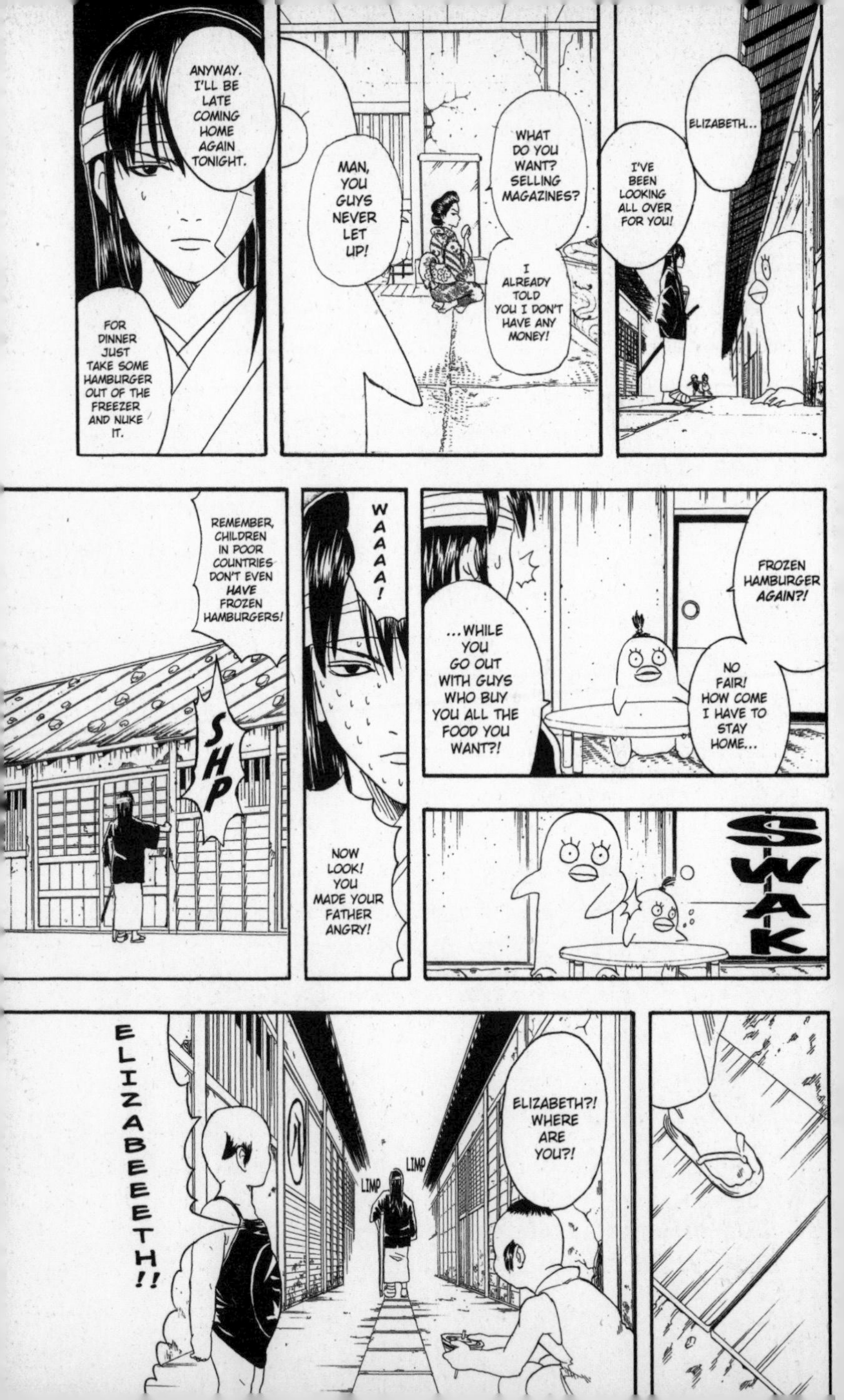
ELIZABETH...
I'VE BEEN LOOKING ALL OVER FOR YOU!
WHAT DO YOU WANT? SELLING MAGAZINES?
I ALREADY TOLD YOU I DON'T HAVE ANY MONEY!
MAN, YOU GUYS NEVER LET UP!
ANYWAY. I'LL BE LATE COMING HOME AGAIN TONIGHT.
FOR DINNER JUST TAKE SOME HAMBURGER OUT OF THE FREEZER AND NUKE IT.
FROZEN HAMBURGER AGAIN?!
NO FAIR! HOW COME I HAVE TO STAY HOME...
...WHILE YOU GO OUT WITH GUYS WHO BUY YOU ALL THE FOOD YOU WANT?!
SWAK
WAAAAA!
NOW LOOK! YOU MADE YOUR FATHER ANGRY!
REMEMBER, CHILDREN IN POOR COUNTRIES DON'T EVEN HAVE FROZEN HAMBURGERS!
SHP
ELIZABETH?! WHERE ARE YOU?!
LIMP
LIMP
ELIZABEEEETH!!

Thanks a lot for buying *Gin Tama 9*. Ummm...this time I was thinking of announcing the winning designs for new Amanto aliens from all the ones you submitted, but I kind of promised to announce it in the regular *JUMP* magazine, so I think I should stick to that. In other words, after the winners' Amantos appear in the magazine, they'll also be published in one of these tankobon. That way people who don't buy *JUMP* and just buy these volumes will find out who won too...and when the design appears in *JUMP*, we'll print the submitter's original postcard here. (Actually, one's already shown up *JUMP*, but there's a time lag before the book version comes out, so you won't see that postcard until around **Volume** 11. Sorry it takes so long.) Anyway, I promise the winners will be published, no matter what! Okay! Now that I've promised, I can't wiggle out. Now let's get back to **Volume** 9...

Sorachi Sensei is referring to a contest run in the Japanese version of *JUMP* magazine. –Editor

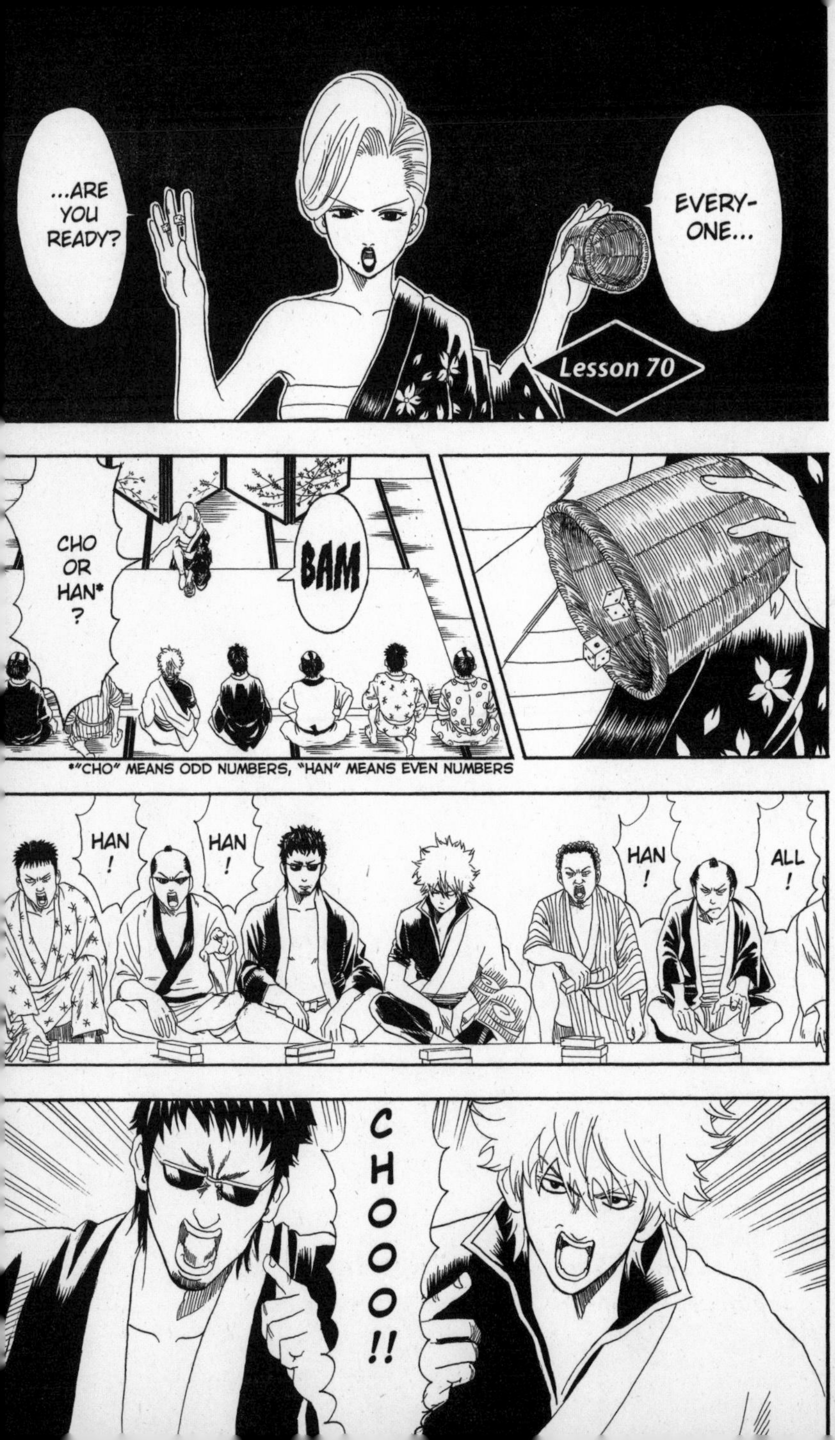
Lesson 70
EVERY-ONE...
...ARE YOU READY?
BAM
CHO OR HAN* ?
ALL !
HAN !
HAN !
HAN !
CHOOOO!!

*"CHO" MEANS ODD NUMBERS, "HAN" MEANS EVEN NUMBERS

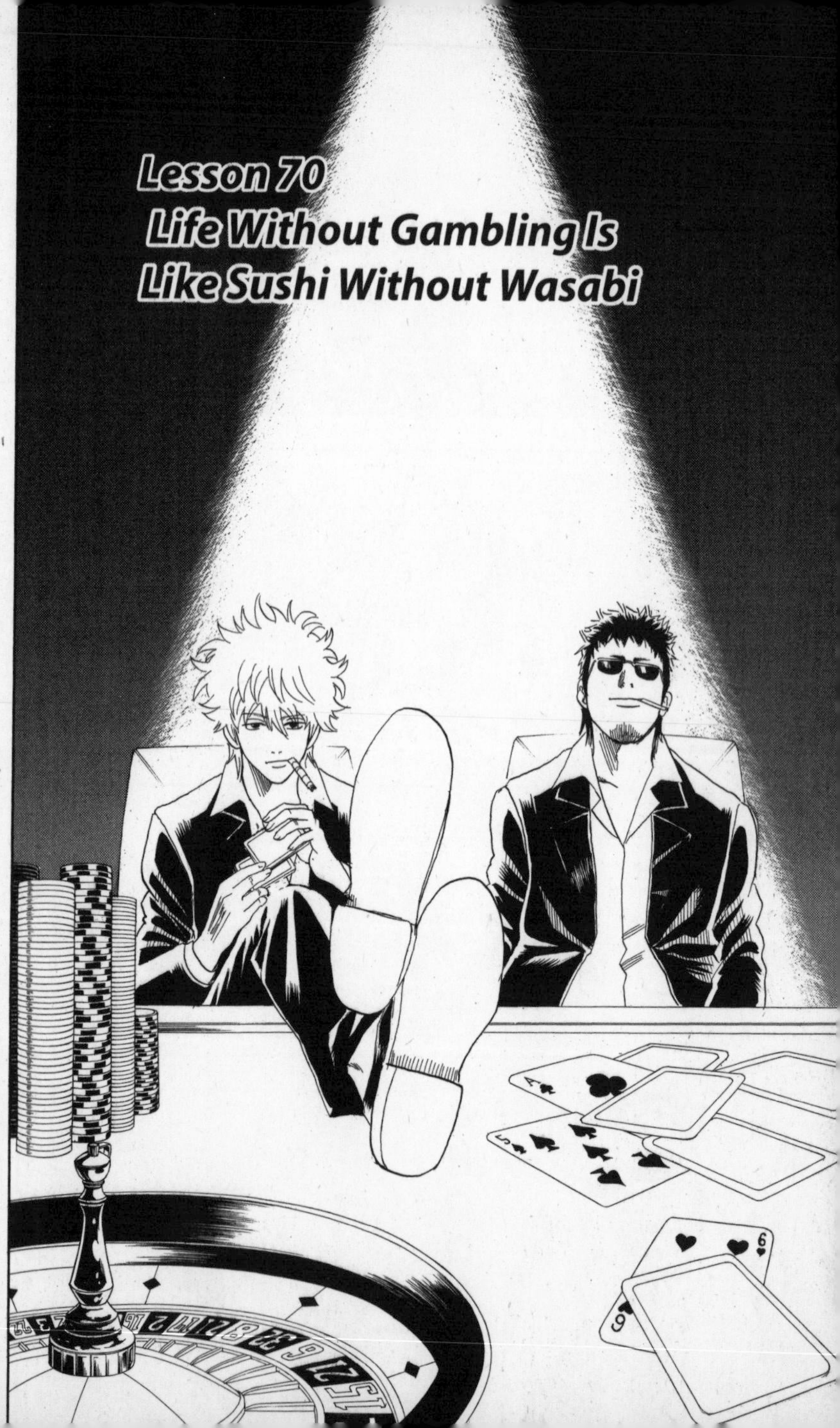
Lesson 70
Life Without Gambling Is
Like Sushi Without Wasabi

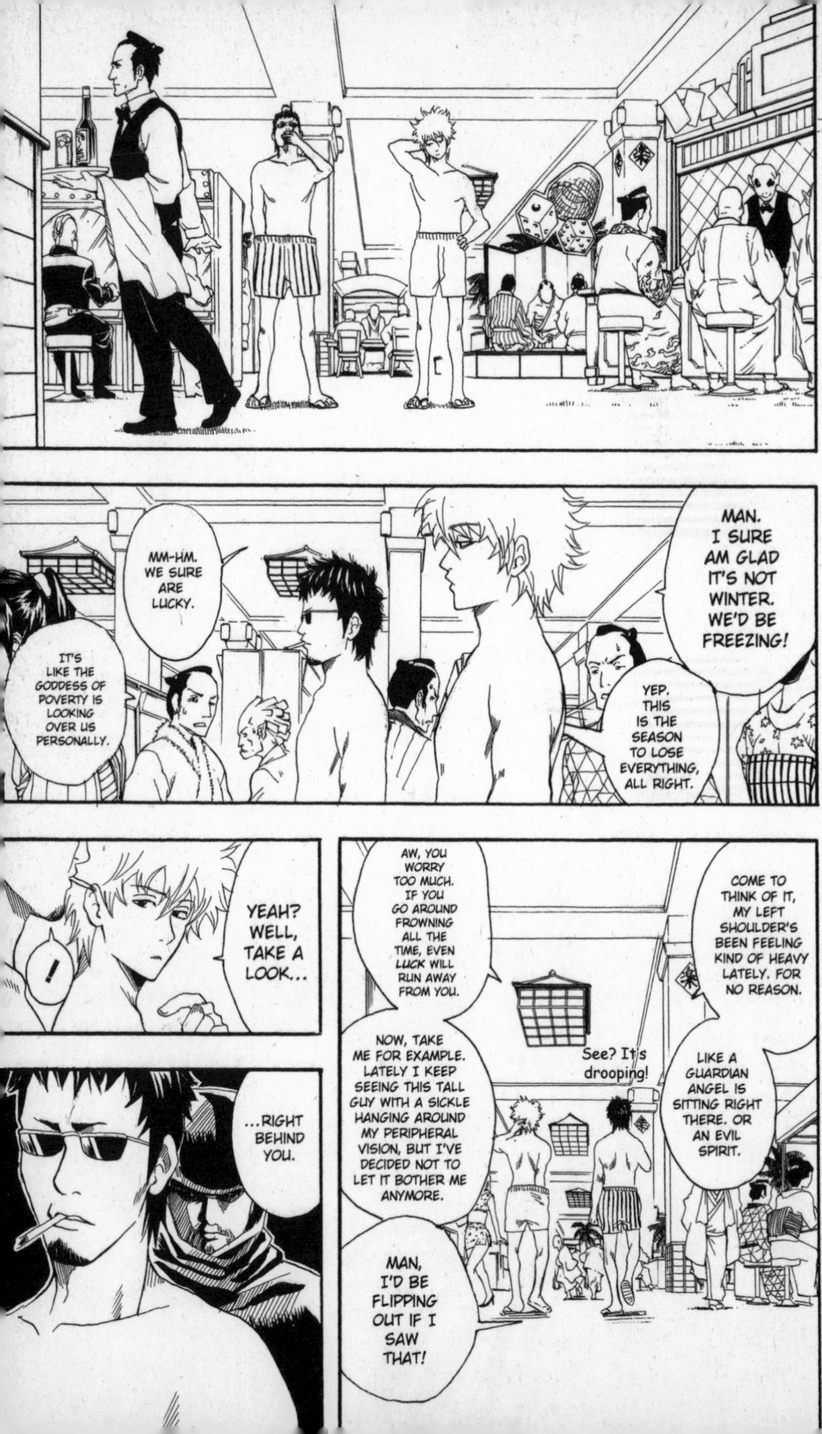
MAN. I SURE AM GLAD IT'S NOT WINTER. WE'D BE FREEZING!
YEP. THIS IS THE SEASON TO LOSE EVERYTHING, ALL RIGHT.
MM-HM. WE SURE ARE LUCKY.
IT'S LIKE THE GODDESS OF POVERTY IS LOOKING OVER US PERSONALLY.
COME TO THINK OF IT, MY LEFT SHOULDER'S BEEN FEELING KIND OF HEAVY LATELY. FOR NO REASON.
AW, YOU WORRY TOO MUCH. IF YOU GO AROUND FROWNING ALL THE TIME, EVEN LUCK WILL RUN AWAY FROM YOU.
LIKE A GUARDIAN ANGEL IS SITTING RIGHT THERE. OR AN EVIL SPIRIT.
See? It's drooping!
NOW, TAKE ME FOR EXAMPLE. LATELY I KEEP SEEING THIS TALL GUY WITH A SICKLE HANGING AROUND MY PERIPHERAL VISION, BUT I'VE DECIDED NOT TO LET IT BOTHER ME ANYMORE.
MAN, I'D BE FLIPPING OUT IF I SAW THAT!
YEAH? WELL, TAKE A LOOK...
!
...RIGHT BEHIND YOU.

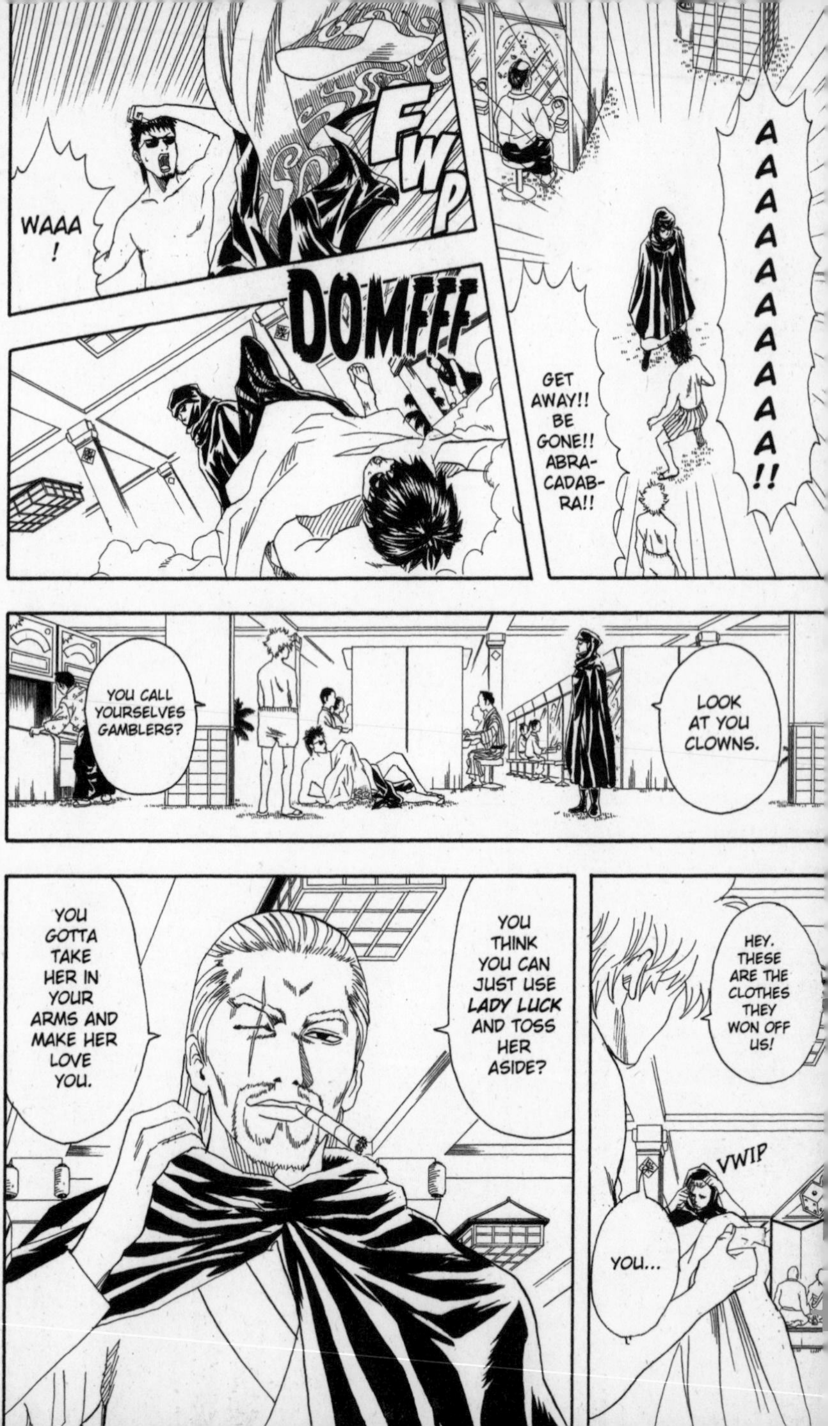
AAAAAAAAAAAAA!!
GET AWAY!! BE GONE!! ABRA-CADAB-RA!!
FWP
WAAA!
DOMFFF
LOOK AT YOU CLOWNS.
YOU CALL YOURSELVES GAMBLERS?
HEY. THESE ARE THE CLOTHES THEY WON OFF US!
VWIP
YOU...
YOU THINK YOU CAN JUST USE *LADY LUCK* AND TOSS HER ASIDE?
YOU GOTTA TAKE HER IN YOUR ARMS AND MAKE HER LOVE YOU.

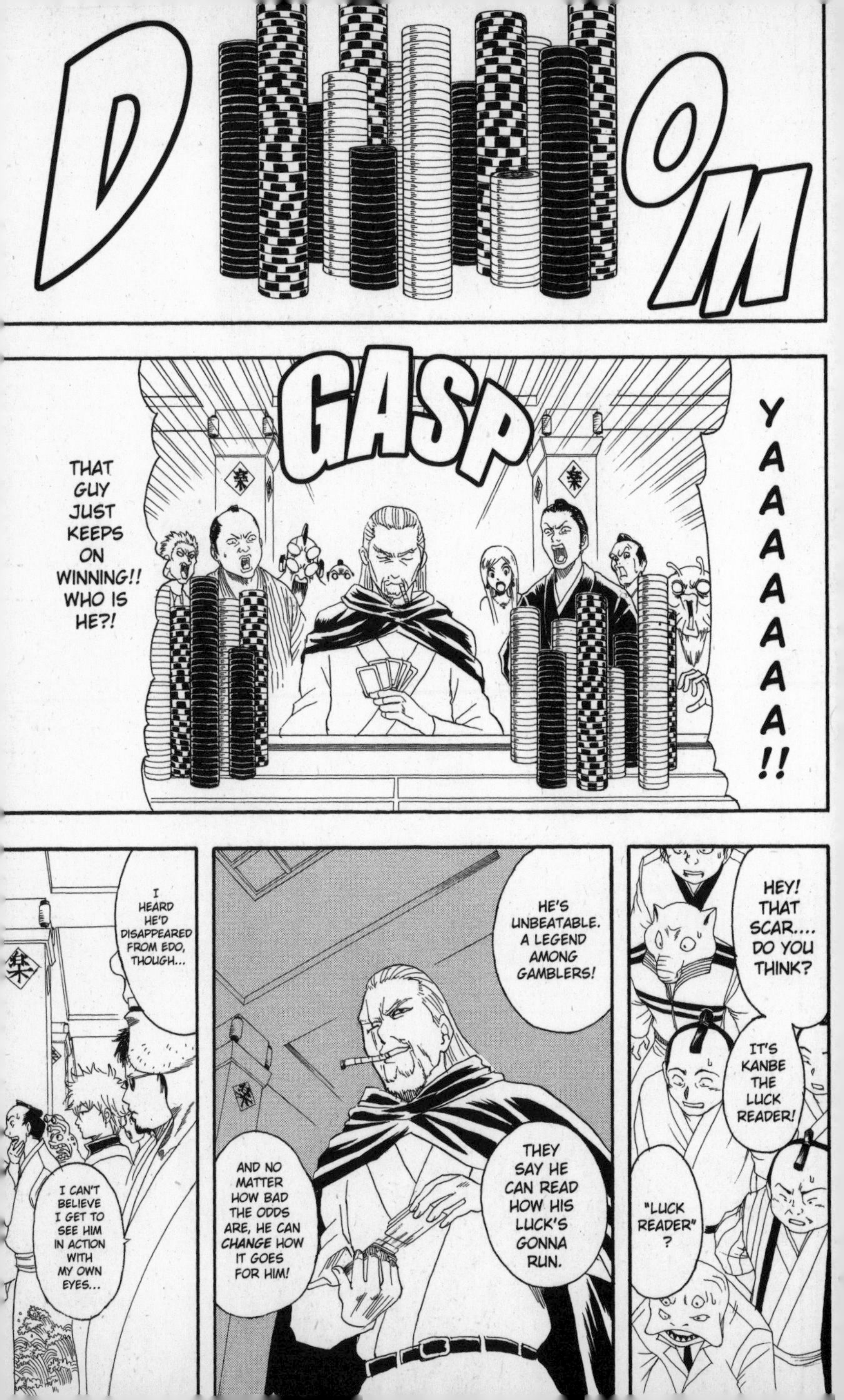
DOOM
GASP
YAAAAAAAAAA!!
THAT GUY JUST KEEPS ON WINNING!! WHO IS HE?!
HEY! THAT SCAR.... DO YOU THINK?
IT'S KANBE THE LUCK READER!
"LUCK READER"?
HE'S UNBEATABLE. A LEGEND AMONG GAMBLERS!
THEY SAY HE CAN READ HOW HIS LUCK'S GONNA RUN.
AND NO MATTER HOW BAD THE ODDS ARE, HE CAN CHANGE HOW IT GOES FOR HIM!
I HEARD HE'D DISAPPEARED FROM EDO, THOUGH...
I CAN'T BELIEVE I GET TO SEE HIM IN ACTION WITH MY OWN EYES...

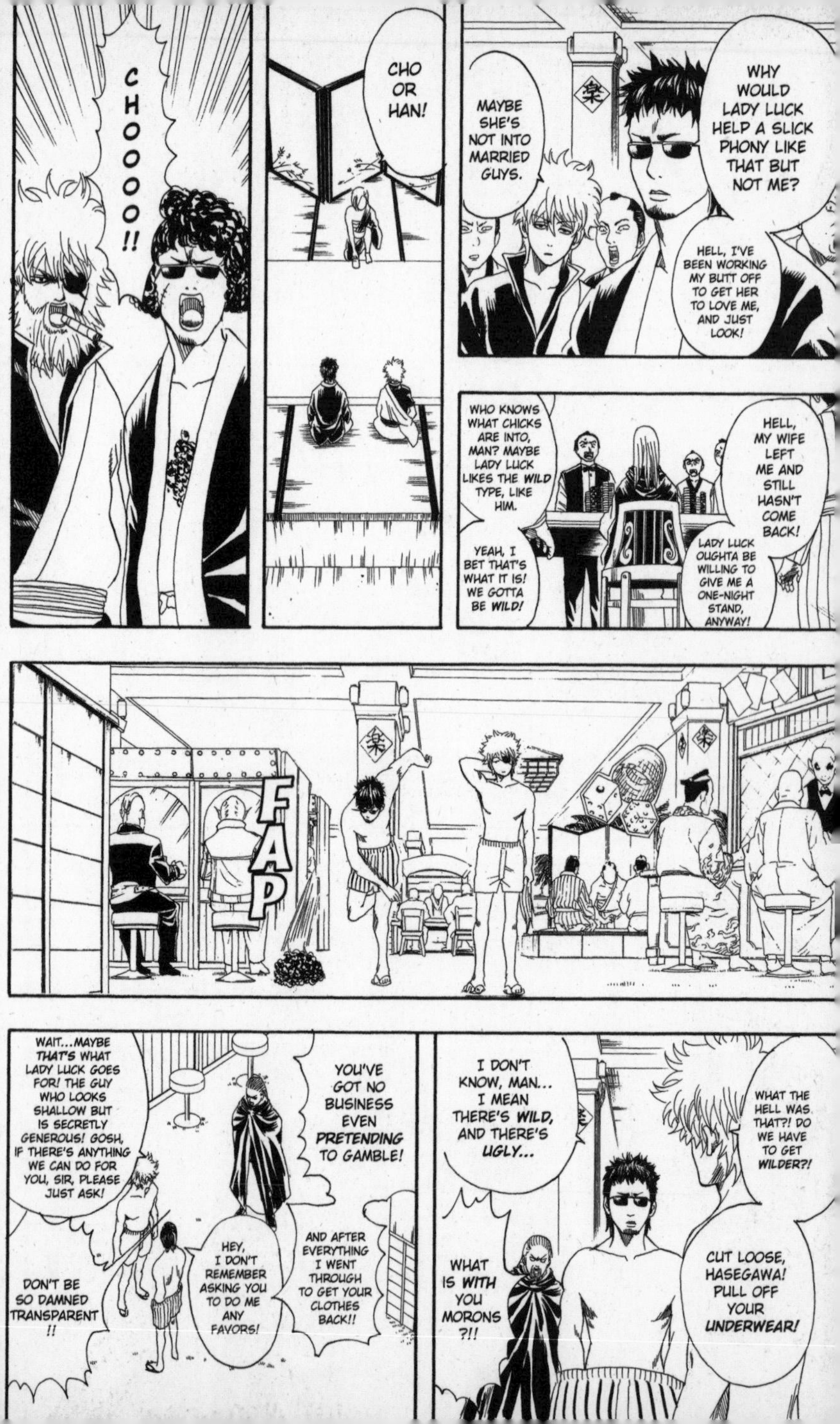
WHY WOULD LADY LUCK HELP A SLICK PHONY LIKE THAT BUT NOT ME?
HELL, I'VE BEEN WORKING MY BUTT OFF TO GET HER TO LOVE ME, AND JUST LOOK!
MAYBE SHE'S NOT INTO MARRIED GUYS.
HELL, MY WIFE LEFT ME AND STILL HASN'T COME BACK!
LADY LUCK OUGHTA BE WILLING TO GIVE ME A ONE-NIGHT STAND, ANYWAY!
WHO KNOWS WHAT CHICKS ARE INTO, MAN? MAYBE LADY LUCK LIKES THE WILD TYPE, LIKE HIM.
YEAH, I BET THAT'S WHAT IT IS! WE GOTTA BE WILD!
CHO OR HAN!
CHOOOOO!!
FAP
WHAT THE HELL WAS THAT?! DO WE HAVE TO GET WILDER?!
CUT LOOSE, HASEGAWA! PULL OFF YOUR UNDERWEAR!
I DON'T KNOW, MAN... I MEAN THERE'S WILD, AND THERE'S UGLY...
WHAT IS WITH YOU MORONS ?!!
YOU'VE GOT NO BUSINESS EVEN PRETENDING TO GAMBLE!
AND AFTER EVERYTHING I WENT THROUGH TO GET YOUR CLOTHES BACK!!
HEY, I DON'T REMEMBER ASKING YOU TO DO ME ANY FAVORS!
WAIT...MAYBE THAT'S WHAT LADY LUCK GOES FOR! THE GUY WHO LOOKS SHALLOW BUT IS SECRETLY GENEROUS! GOSH, IF THERE'S ANYTHING WE CAN DO FOR YOU, SIR, PLEASE JUST ASK!
DON'T BE SO DAMNED TRANSPARENT !!

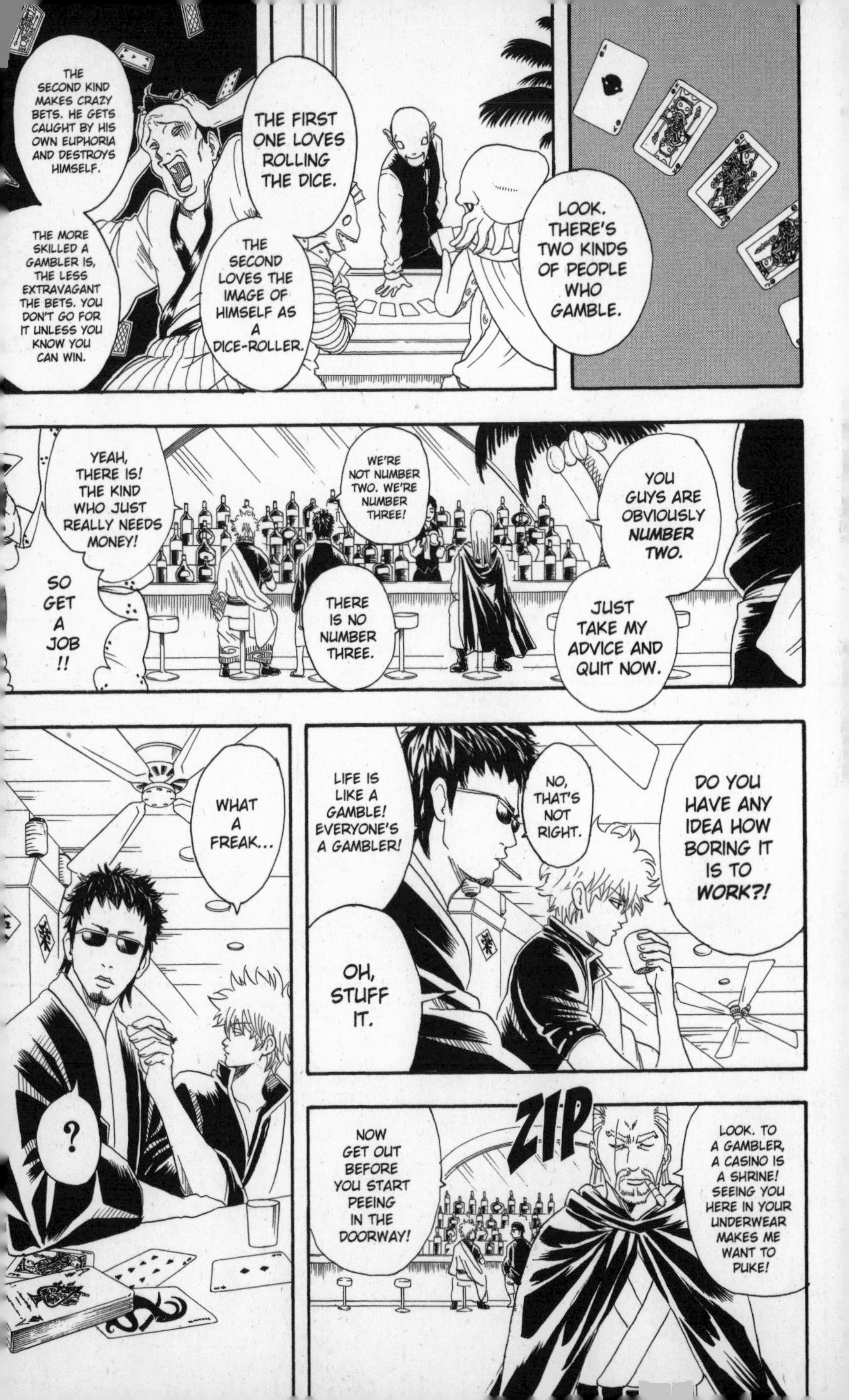
LOOK. THERE'S TWO KINDS OF PEOPLE WHO GAMBLE.
THE FIRST ONE LOVES ROLLING THE DICE.
THE SECOND LOVES THE IMAGE OF HIMSELF AS A DICE-ROLLER.
THE SECOND KIND MAKES CRAZY BETS. HE GETS CAUGHT BY HIS OWN EUPHORIA AND DESTROYS HIMSELF.
THE MORE SKILLED A GAMBLER IS, THE LESS EXTRAVAGANT THE BETS. YOU DON'T GO FOR IT UNLESS YOU KNOW YOU CAN WIN.
YOU GUYS ARE OBVIOUSLY NUMBER TWO.
JUST TAKE MY ADVICE AND QUIT NOW.
WE'RE NOT NUMBER TWO. WE'RE NUMBER THREE!
THERE IS NO NUMBER THREE.
YEAH, THERE IS! THE KIND WHO JUST REALLY NEEDS MONEY!
SO GET A JOB!!
DO YOU HAVE ANY IDEA HOW BORING IT IS TO WORK?!
NO, THAT'S NOT RIGHT.
LIFE IS LIKE A GAMBLE! EVERYONE'S A GAMBLER!
OH, STUFF IT.
LOOK. TO A GAMBLER, A CASINO IS A SHRINE! SEEING YOU HERE IN YOUR UNDERWEAR MAKES ME WANT TO PUKE!
ZIP
NOW GET OUT BEFORE YOU START PEEING IN THE DOORWAY!
WHAT A FREAK...
?

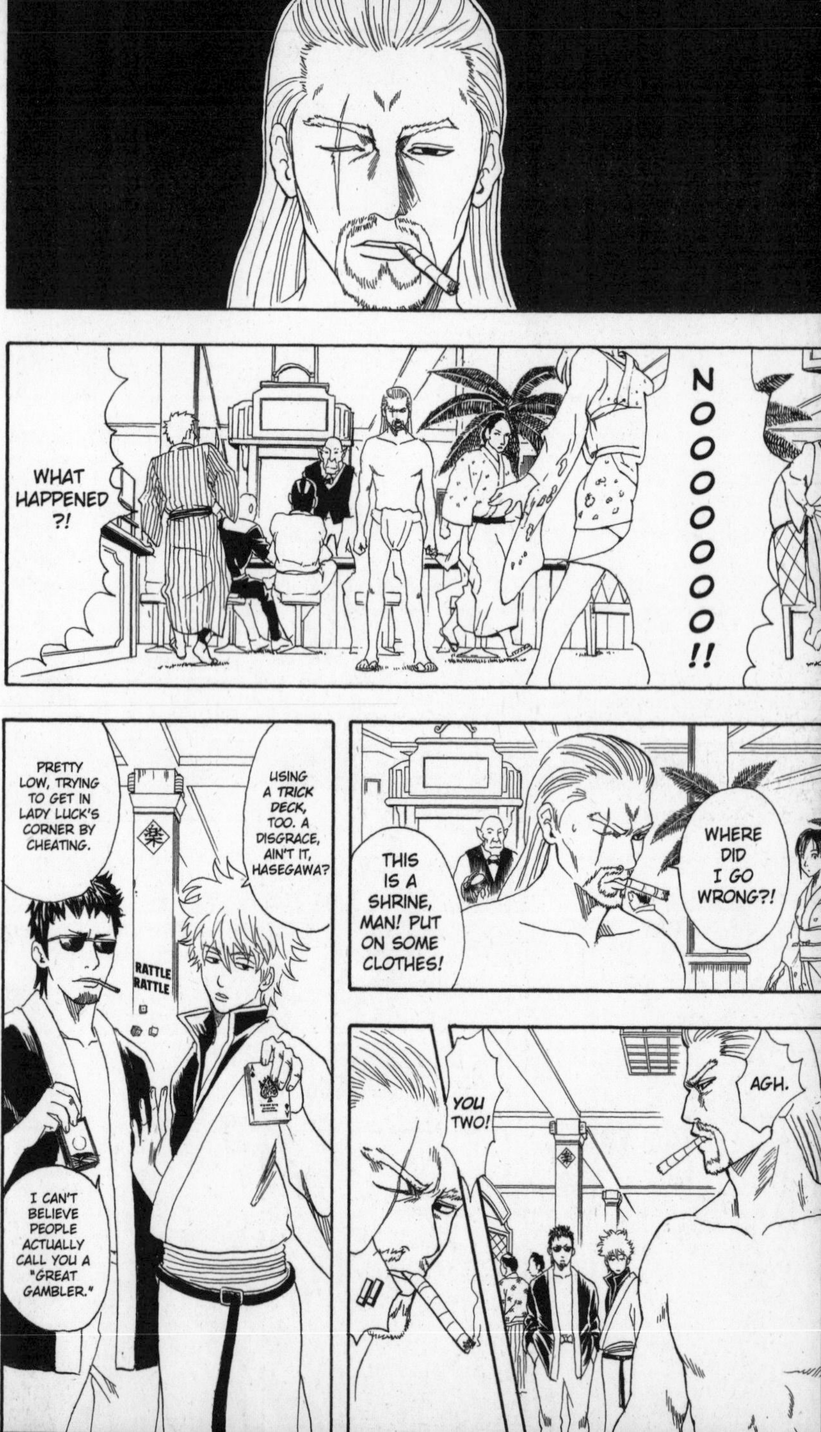
NOOOOOOOO!!
WHAT HAPPENED?!
WHERE DID I GO WRONG?!
THIS IS A SHRINE, MAN! PUT ON SOME CLOTHES!
AGH.
YOU TWO!
USING A TRICK DECK, TOO. A DISGRACE, AIN'T IT, HASEGAWA?
PRETTY LOW, TRYING TO GET IN LADY LUCK'S CORNER BY CHEATING.
RATTLE RATTLE
I CAN'T BELIEVE PEOPLE ACTUALLY CALL YOU A "GREAT GAMBLER."

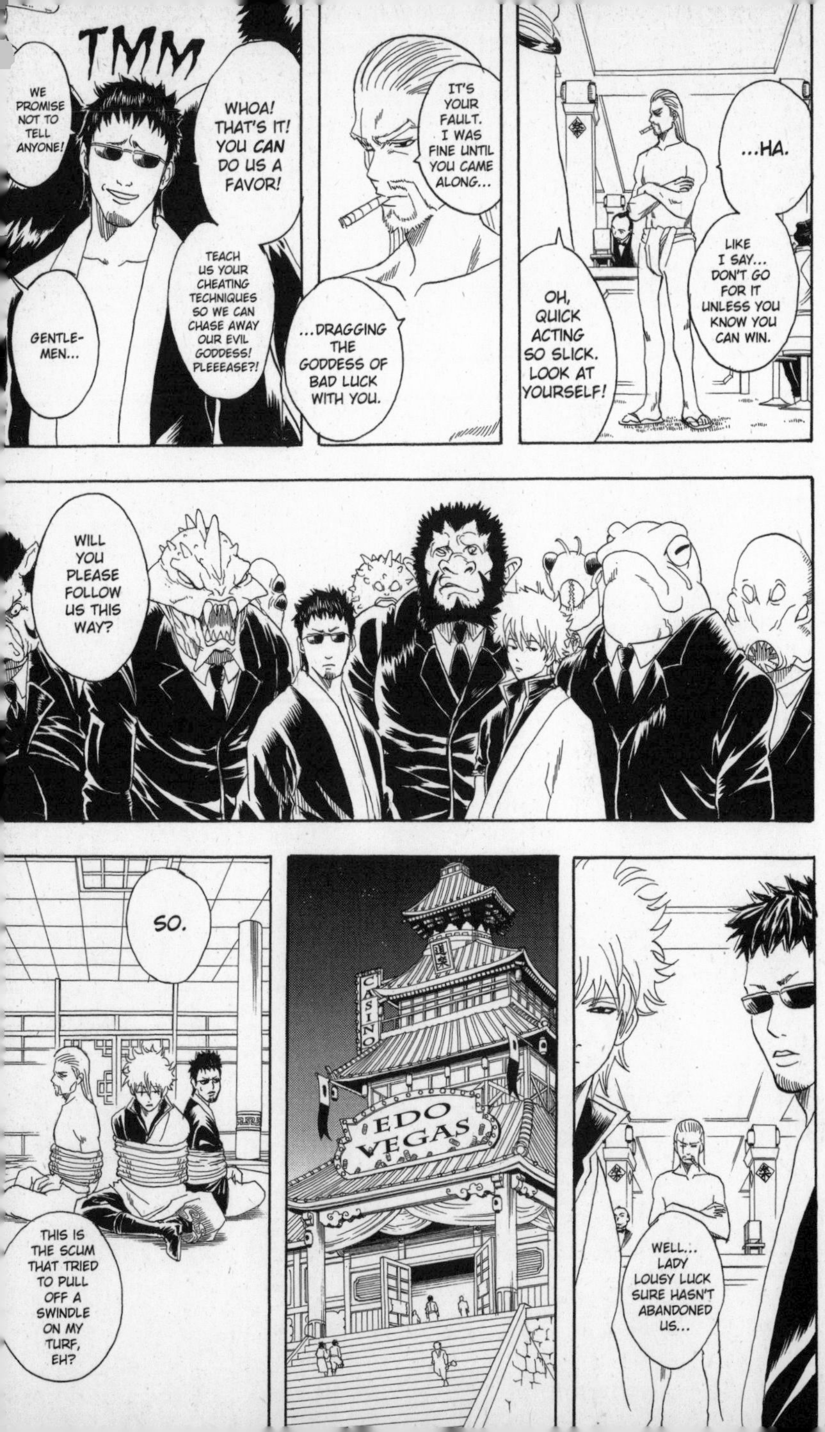
...HA.
LIKE I SAY... DON'T GO FOR IT UNLESS YOU KNOW YOU CAN WIN.
OH, QUICK ACTING SO SLICK. LOOK AT YOURSELF!
IT'S YOUR FAULT. I WAS FINE UNTIL YOU CAME ALONG...
...DRAGGING THE GODDESS OF BAD LUCK WITH YOU.
WHOA! THAT'S IT! YOU CAN DO US A FAVOR!
TMM
TEACH US YOUR CHEATING TECHNIQUES SO WE CAN CHASE AWAY OUR EVIL GODDESS! PLEEEASE?!
WE PROMISE NOT TO TELL ANYONE!
GENTLE-MEN...
WILL YOU PLEASE FOLLOW US THIS WAY?
WELL... LADY LOUSY LUCK SURE HASN'T ABANDONED US...
CASINO
EDO VEGAS
SO.
THIS IS THE SCUM THAT TRIED TO PULL OFF A SWINDLE ON MY TURF, EH?

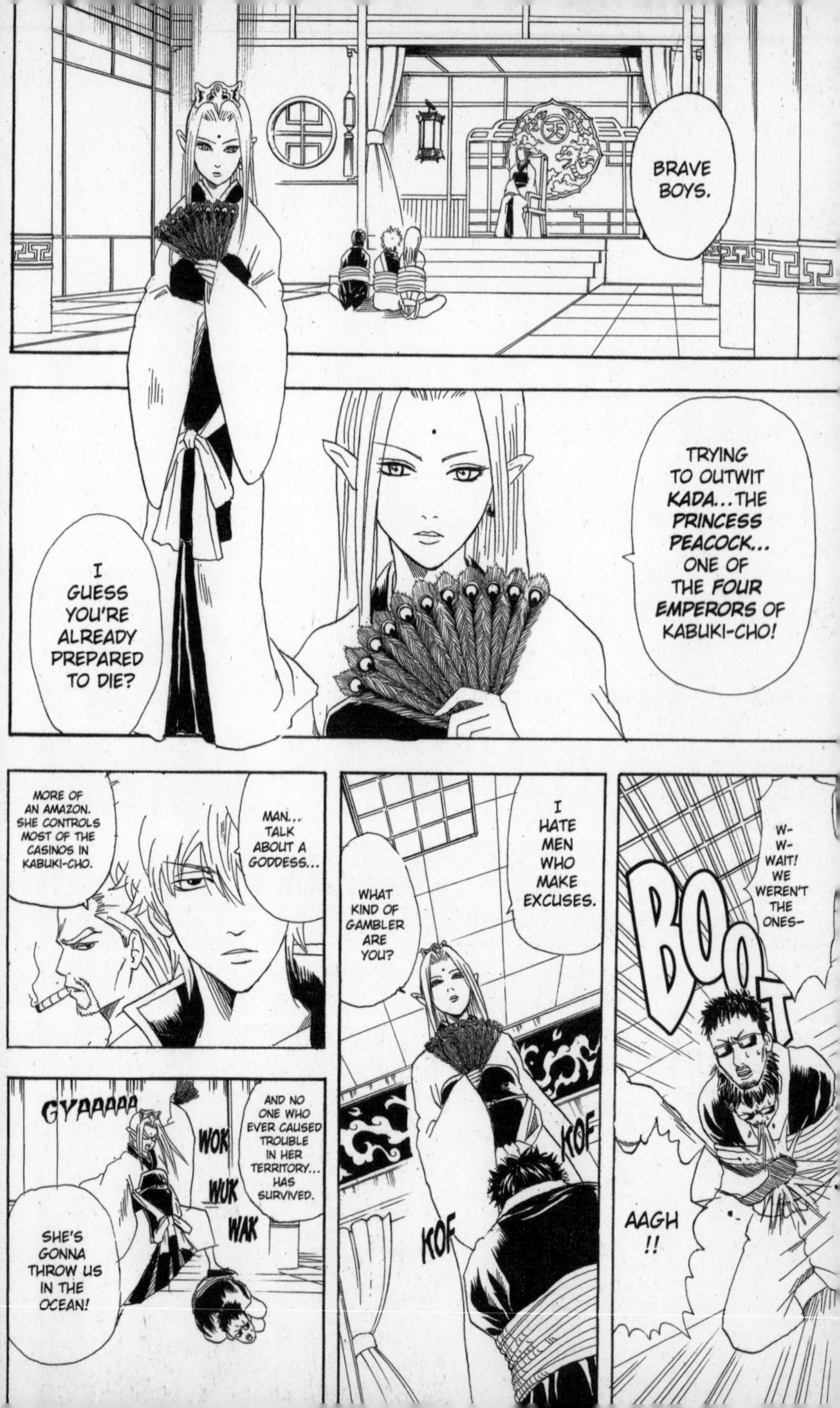
BRAVE BOYS.
TRYING TO OUTWIT KADA...THE PRINCESS PEACOCK... ONE OF THE FOUR EMPERORS OF KABUKI-CHO!
I GUESS YOU'RE ALREADY PREPARED TO DIE?
W-W-WAIT! WE WEREN'T THE ONES-
BOOOT
AAGH !!
I HATE MEN WHO MAKE EXCUSES.
WHAT KIND OF GAMBLER ARE YOU?
KOF
KOF
MAN... TALK ABOUT A GODDESS...
MORE OF AN AMAZON. SHE CONTROLS MOST OF THE CASINOS IN KABUKI-CHO.
AND NO ONE WHO EVER CAUSED TROUBLE IN HER TERRITORY... HAS SURVIVED.
GYAAAAA
WOK
WUK
WAK
SHE'S GONNA THROW US IN THE OCEAN!

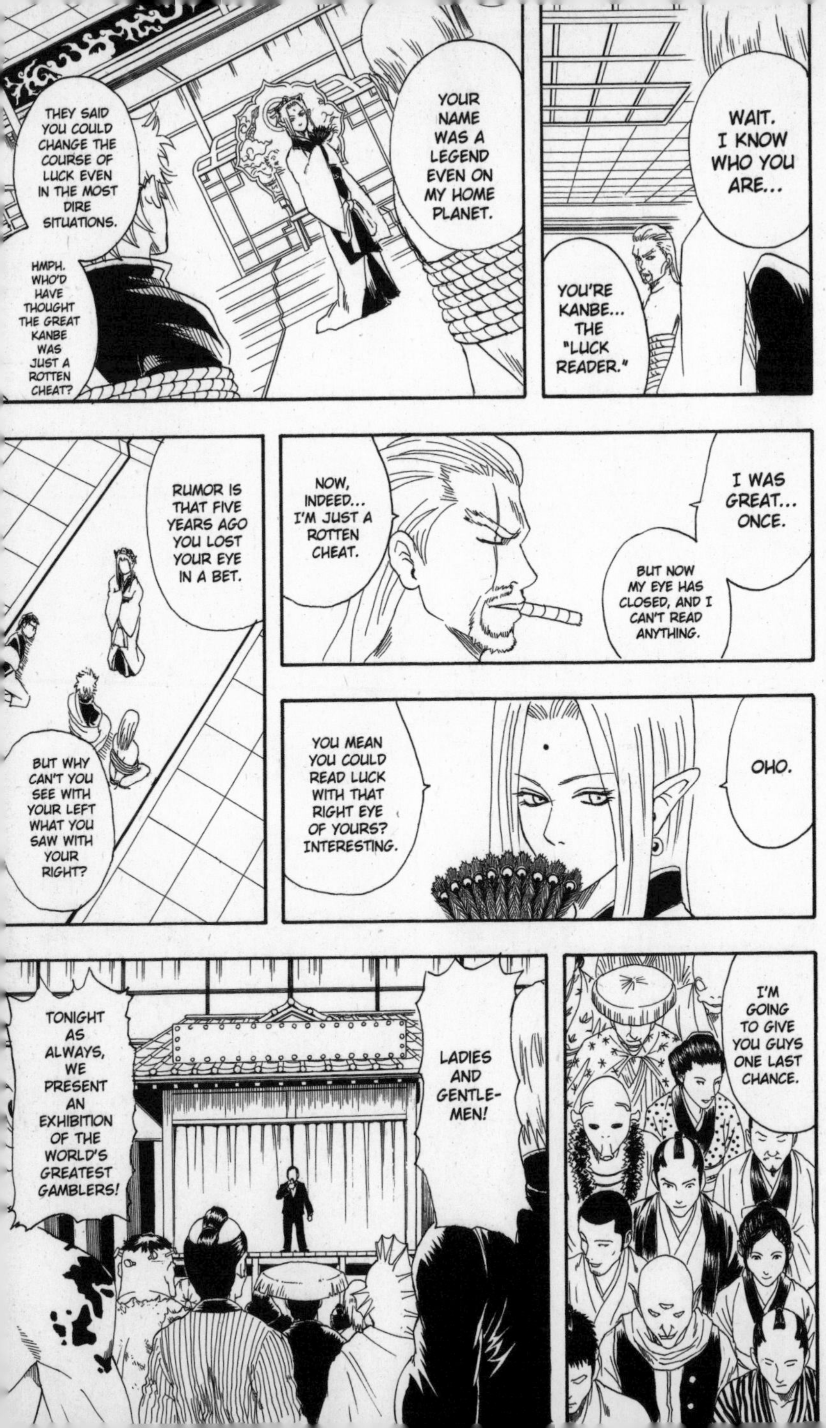
WAIT. I KNOW WHO YOU ARE...
YOU'RE KANBE... THE "LUCK READER."
YOUR NAME WAS A LEGEND EVEN ON MY HOME PLANET.
THEY SAID YOU COULD CHANGE THE COURSE OF LUCK EVEN IN THE MOST DIRE SITUATIONS.
HMPH. WHO'D HAVE THOUGHT THE GREAT KANBE WAS JUST A ROTTEN CHEAT?
I WAS GREAT... ONCE.
BUT NOW MY EYE HAS CLOSED, AND I CAN'T READ ANYTHING.
NOW, INDEED... I'M JUST A ROTTEN CHEAT.
OHO.
YOU MEAN YOU COULD READ LUCK WITH THAT RIGHT EYE OF YOURS? INTERESTING.
RUMOR IS THAT FIVE YEARS AGO YOU LOST YOUR EYE IN A BET.
BUT WHY CAN'T YOU SEE WITH YOUR LEFT WHAT YOU SAW WITH YOUR RIGHT?
I'M GOING TO GIVE YOU GUYS ONE LAST CHANCE.
LADIES AND GENTLE-MEN!
TONIGHT AS ALWAYS, WE PRESENT AN EXHIBITION OF THE WORLD'S GREATEST GAMBLERS!

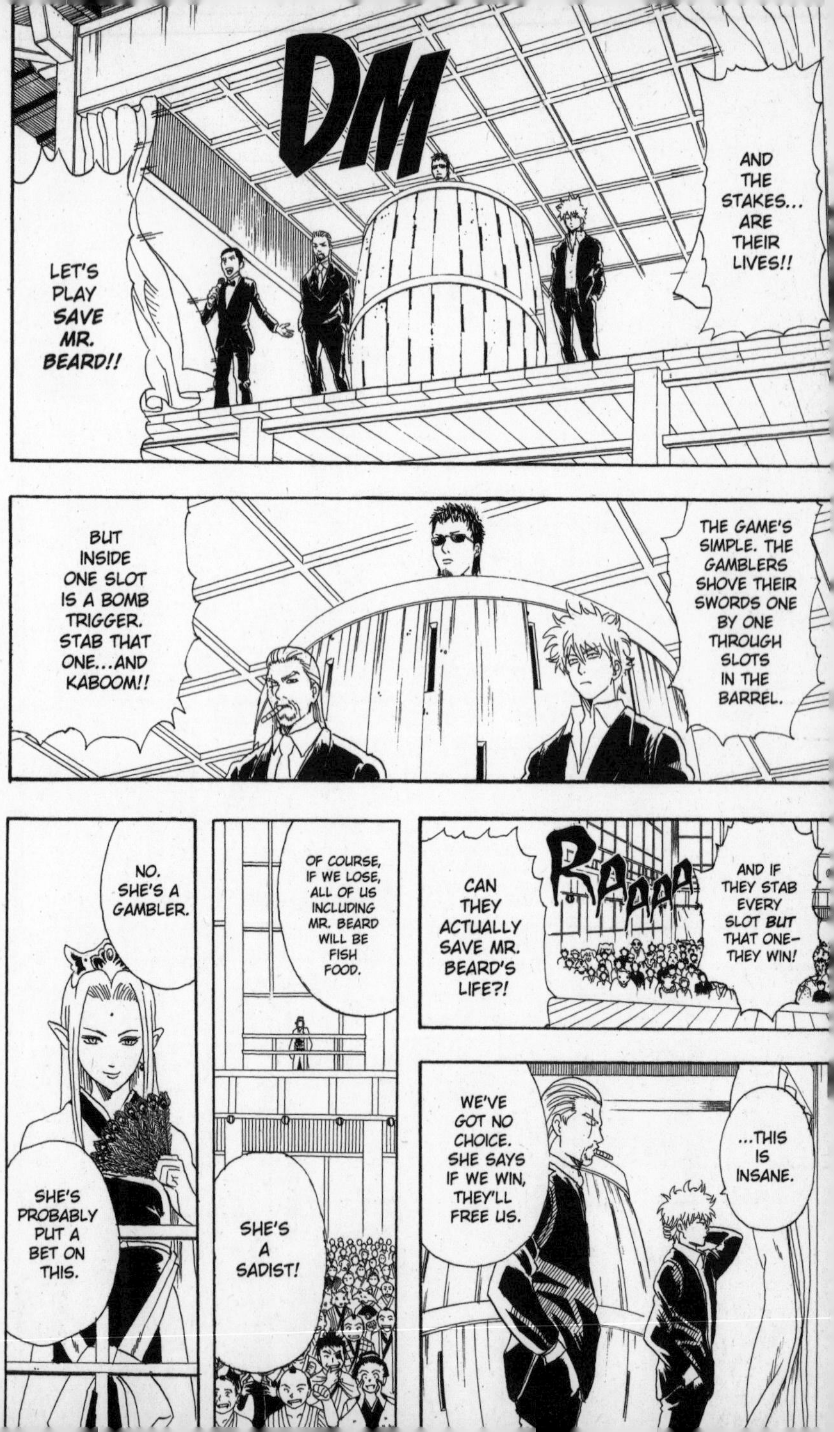
AND THE STAKES... ARE THEIR LIVES!!
DM
LET'S PLAY SAVE MR. BEARD!!
THE GAME'S SIMPLE. THE GAMBLERS SHOVE THEIR SWORDS ONE BY ONE THROUGH SLOTS IN THE BARREL.
BUT INSIDE ONE SLOT IS A BOMB TRIGGER. STAB THAT ONE...AND KABOOM!!
AND IF THEY STAB EVERY SLOT BUT THAT ONE— THEY WIN!
RAAAA
CAN THEY ACTUALLY SAVE MR. BEARD'S LIFE?!
...THIS IS INSANE.
WE'VE GOT NO CHOICE. SHE SAYS IF WE WIN, THEY'LL FREE US.
OF COURSE, IF WE LOSE, ALL OF US INCLUDING MR. BEARD WILL BE FISH FOOD.
SHE'S A SADIST!
NO. SHE'S A GAMBLER.
SHE'S PROBABLY PUT A BET ON THIS.

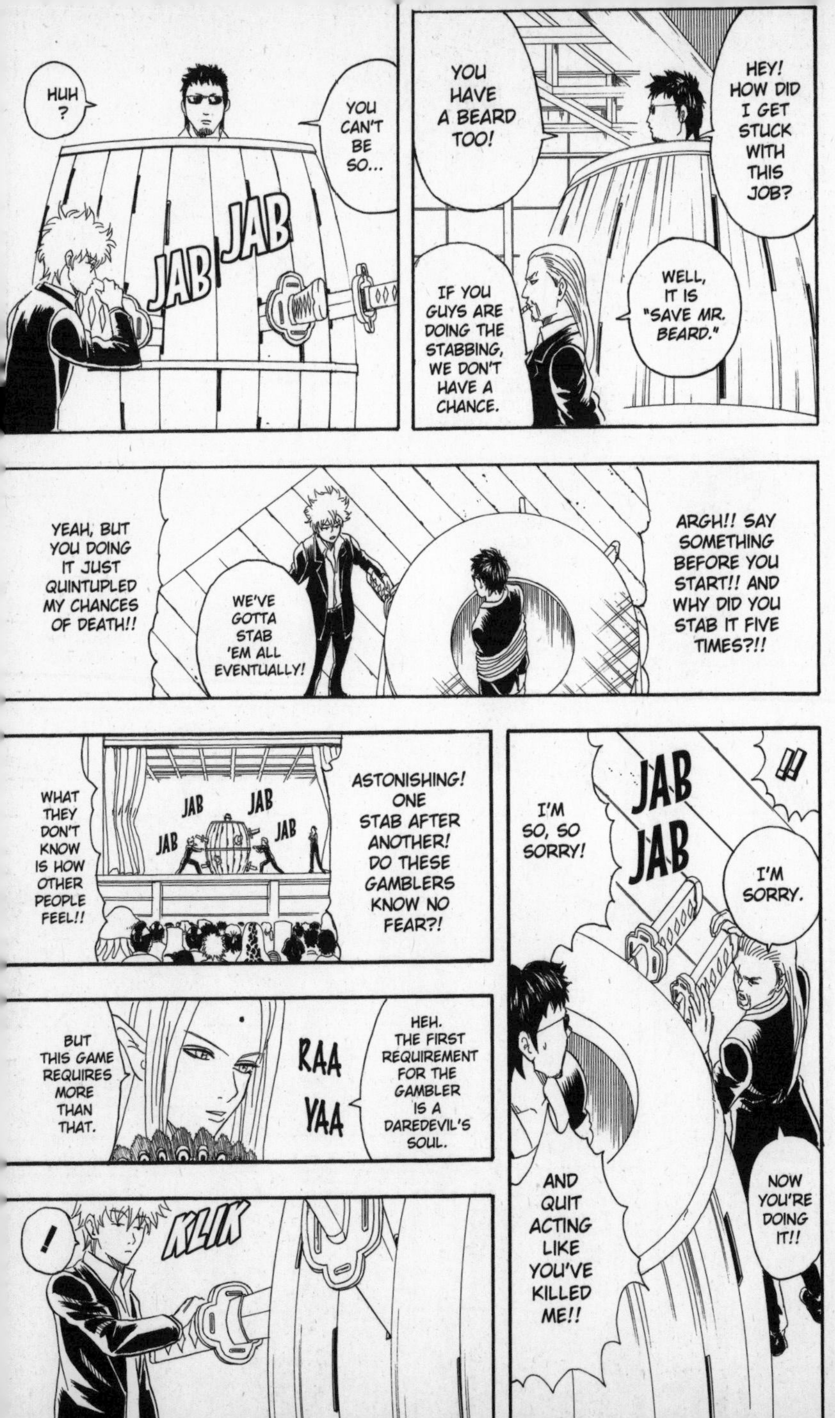
HEY! HOW DID I GET STUCK WITH THIS JOB?
YOU HAVE A BEARD TOO!
WELL, IT IS "SAVE MR. BEARD."
IF YOU GUYS ARE DOING THE STABBING, WE DON'T HAVE A CHANCE.
YOU CAN'T BE SO...
JAB JAB
HUH?
ARGH!! SAY SOMETHING BEFORE YOU START!! AND WHY DID YOU STAB IT FIVE TIMES?!!
WE'VE GOTTA STAB 'EM ALL EVENTUALLY!
YEAH, BUT YOU DOING IT JUST QUINTUPLED MY CHANCES OF DEATH!!
!!
JAB JAB
I'M SORRY.
I'M SO, SO SORRY!
NOW YOU'RE DOING IT!!
AND QUIT ACTING LIKE YOU'VE KILLED ME!!
ASTONISHING! ONE STAB AFTER ANOTHER! DO THESE GAMBLERS KNOW NO FEAR?!
JAB JAB JAB JAB
WHAT THEY DON'T KNOW IS HOW OTHER PEOPLE FEEL!!
HEH. THE FIRST REQUIREMENT FOR THE GAMBLER IS A DAREDEVIL'S SOUL.
RAA YAA
BUT THIS GAME REQUIRES MORE THAN THAT.
KLIK
!

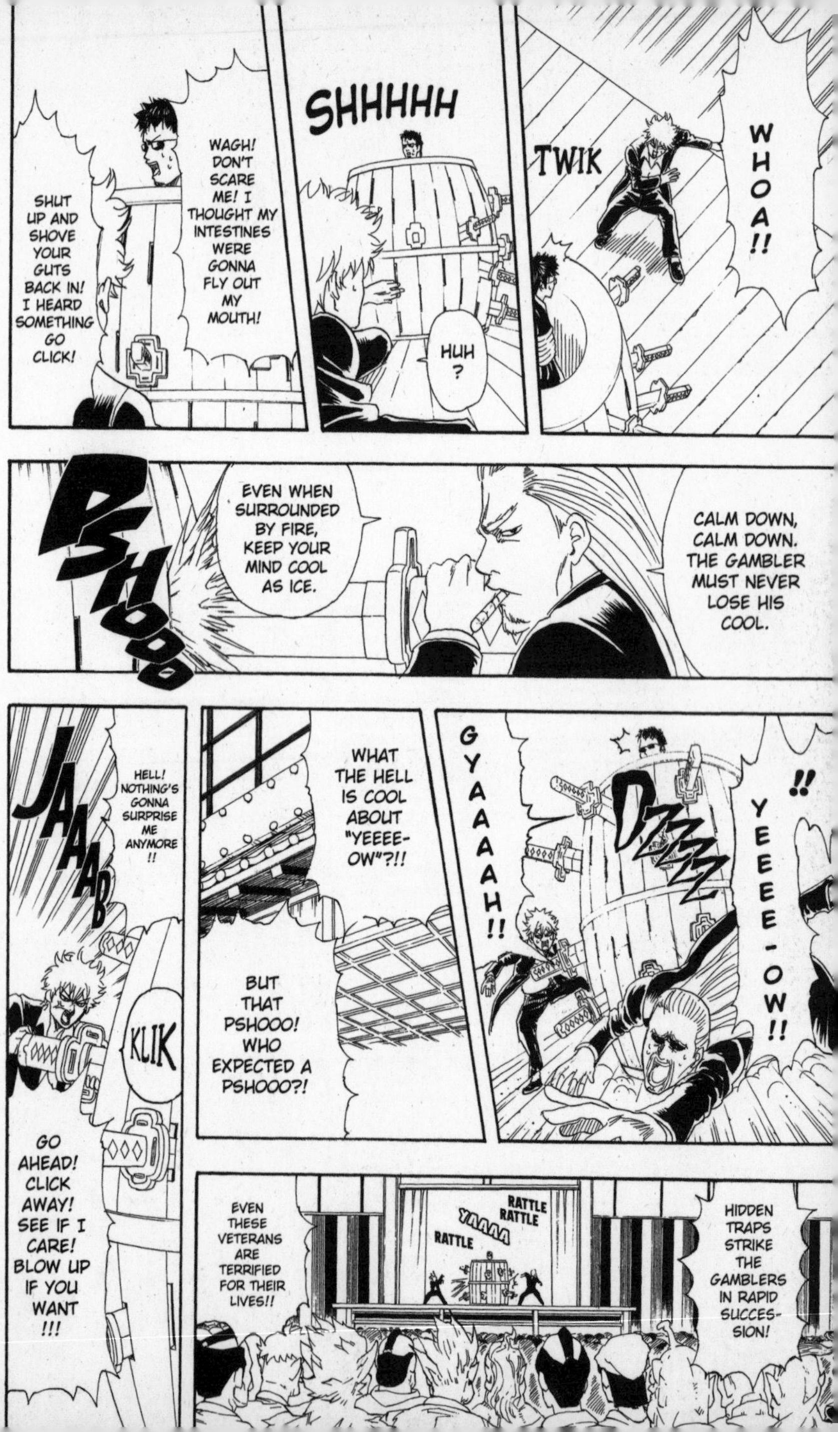
WHOA!!
TWIK
SHHHHH
HUH?
WAGH! DON'T SCARE ME! I THOUGHT MY INTESTINES WERE GONNA FLY OUT MY MOUTH!
SHUT UP AND SHOVE YOUR GUTS BACK IN! I HEARD SOMETHING GO CLICK!
CALM DOWN, CALM DOWN. THE GAMBLER MUST NEVER LOSE HIS COOL.
EVEN WHEN SURROUNDED BY FIRE, KEEP YOUR MIND COOL AS ICE.
PSHOOO
!!
YEEEE-OW!!
DZZZZ
GYAAAAH!!
WHAT THE HELL IS COOL ABOUT "YEEEE-OW"?!!
BUT THAT PSHOOO! WHO EXPECTED A PSHOOO?!
HIDDEN TRAPS STRIKE THE GAMBLERS IN RAPID SUCCES-SION!
RATTLE RATTLE
YAAAA
RATTLE
EVEN THESE VETERANS ARE TERRIFIED FOR THEIR LIVES!!
HELL! NOTHING'S GONNA SURPRISE ME ANYMORE!!
JAAAB
KLIK
GO AHEAD! CLICK AWAY! SEE IF I CARE! BLOW UP IF YOU WANT!!!

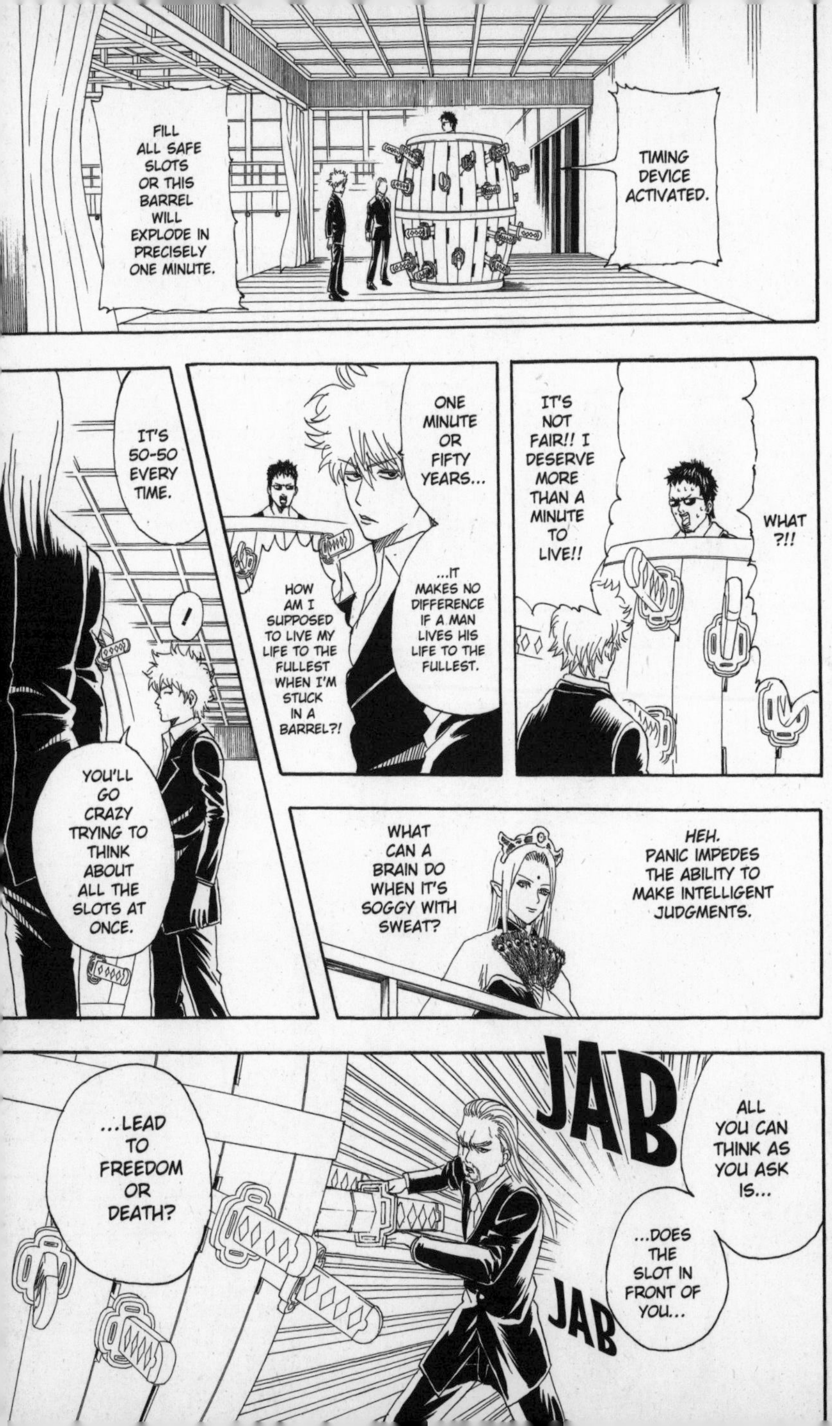
TIMING DEVICE ACTIVATED.
FILL ALL SAFE SLOTS OR THIS BARREL WILL EXPLODE IN PRECISELY ONE MINUTE.
WHAT ?!!
IT'S NOT FAIR!! I DESERVE MORE THAN A MINUTE TO LIVE!!
ONE MINUTE OR FIFTY YEARS...
...IT MAKES NO DIFFERENCE IF A MAN LIVES HIS LIFE TO THE FULLEST.
HOW AM I SUPPOSED TO LIVE MY LIFE TO THE FULLEST WHEN I'M STUCK IN A BARREL?!
HEH. PANIC IMPEDES THE ABILITY TO MAKE INTELLIGENT JUDGMENTS.
WHAT CAN A BRAIN DO WHEN IT'S SOGGY WITH SWEAT?
IT'S 50-50 EVERY TIME.
!
YOU'LL GO CRAZY TRYING TO THINK ABOUT ALL THE SLOTS AT ONCE.
JAB
ALL YOU CAN THINK AS YOU ASK IS...
...DOES THE SLOT IN FRONT OF YOU...
JAB
...LEAD TO FREEDOM OR DEATH?

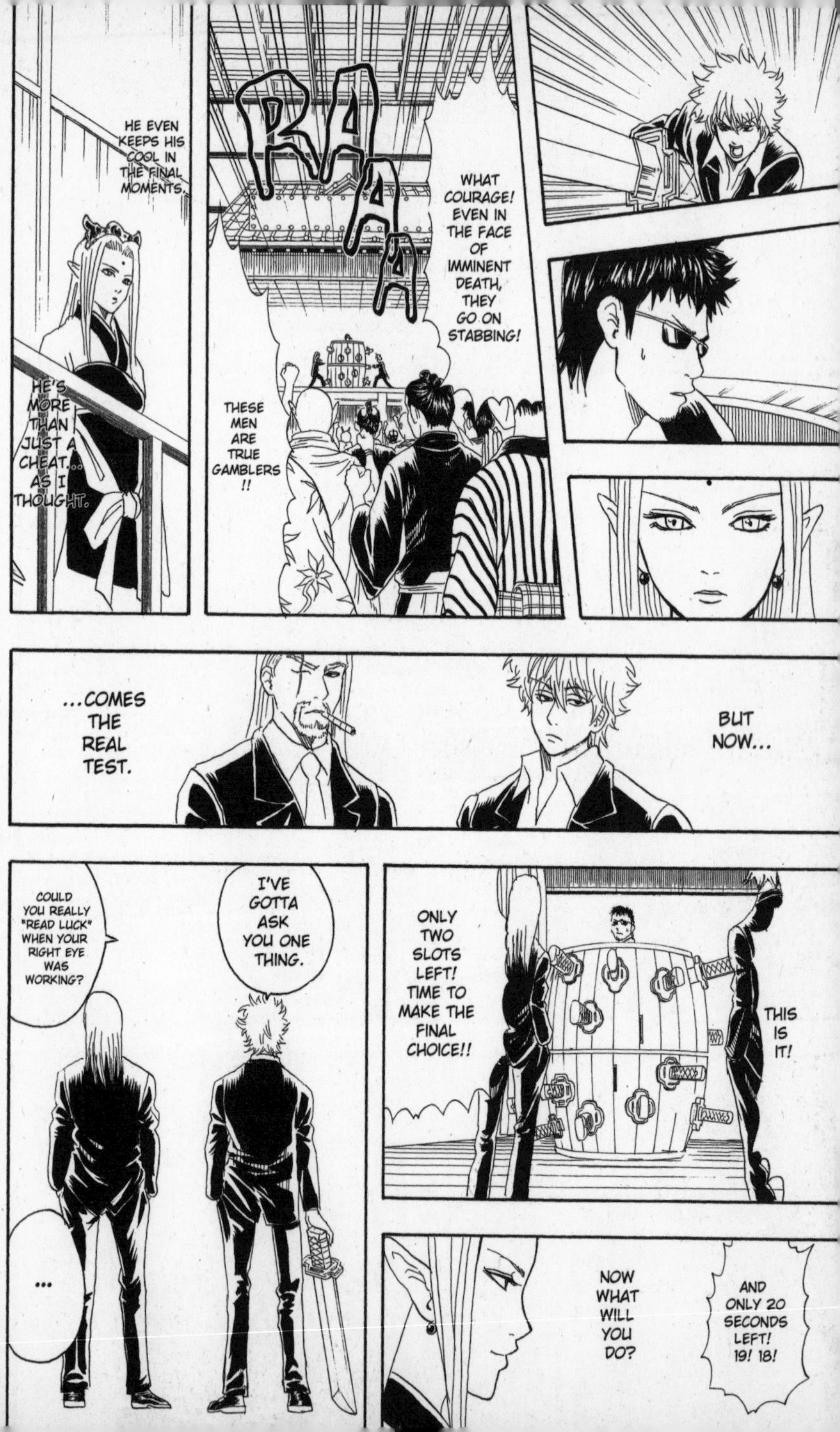
RAAA
WHAT COURAGE! EVEN IN THE FACE OF IMMINENT DEATH, THEY GO ON STABBING!
THESE MEN ARE TRUE GAMBLERS!!
HE EVEN KEEPS HIS COOL IN THE FINAL MOMENTS.
HE'S MORE THAN JUST A CHEAT... AS I THOUGHT.
BUT NOW...
...COMES THE REAL TEST.
THIS IS IT!
ONLY TWO SLOTS LEFT! TIME TO MAKE THE FINAL CHOICE!!
AND ONLY 20 SECONDS LEFT! 19! 18!
NOW WHAT WILL YOU DO?
I'VE GOTTA ASK YOU ONE THING.
COULD YOU REALLY "READ LUCK" WHEN YOUR RIGHT EYE WAS WORKING?
...

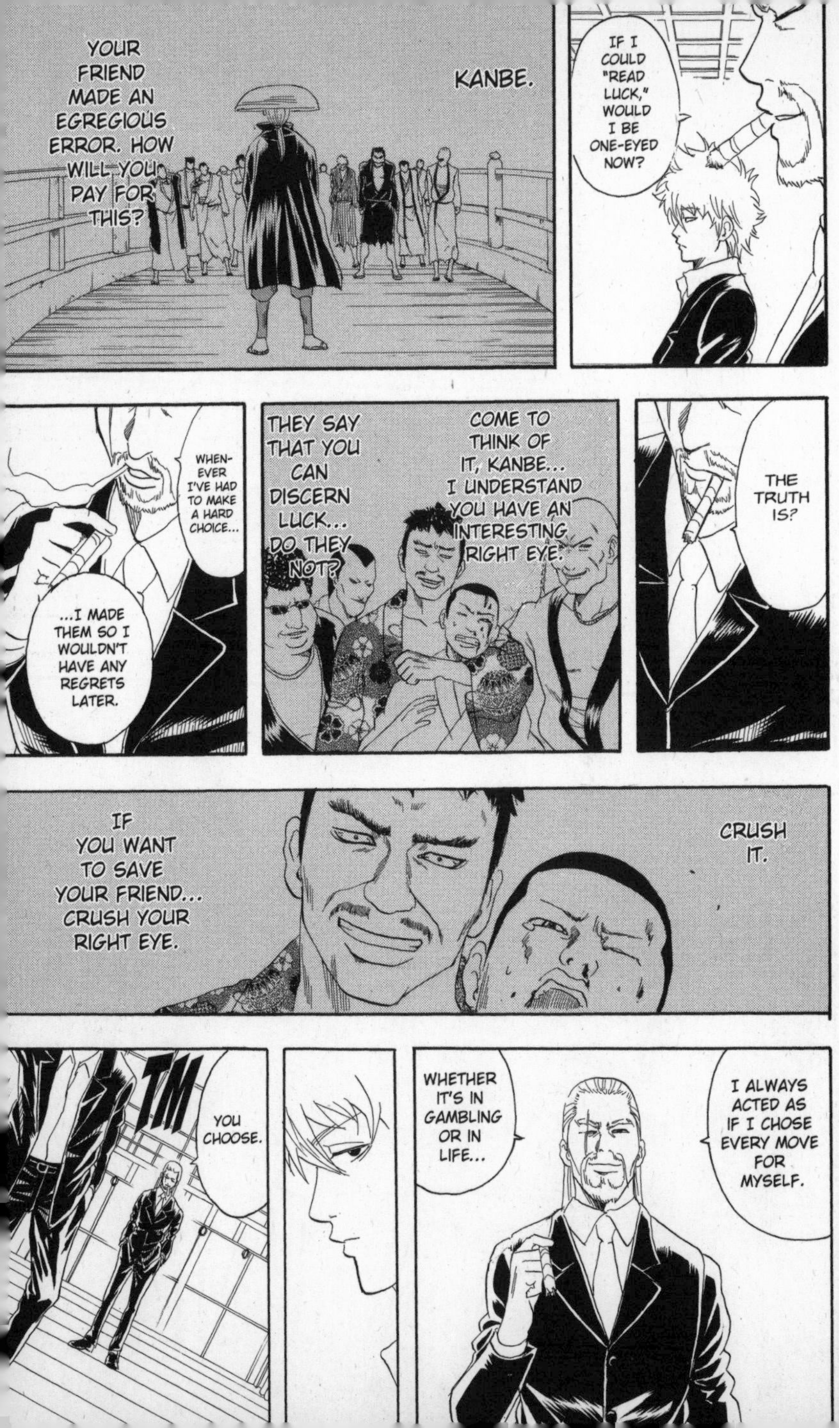
IF I COULD "READ LUCK," WOULD I BE ONE-EYED NOW?
KANBE.
YOUR FRIEND MADE AN EGREGIOUS ERROR. HOW WILL YOU PAY FOR THIS?
THE TRUTH IS?
COME TO THINK OF IT, KANBE... I UNDERSTAND YOU HAVE AN INTERESTING RIGHT EYE.
THEY SAY THAT YOU CAN DISCERN LUCK... DO THEY NOT?
WHEN-EVER I'VE HAD TO MAKE A HARD CHOICE...
...I MADE THEM SO I WOULDN'T HAVE ANY REGRETS LATER.
CRUSH IT.
IF YOU WANT TO SAVE YOUR FRIEND... CRUSH YOUR RIGHT EYE.
I ALWAYS ACTED AS IF I CHOSE EVERY MOVE FOR MYSELF.
WHETHER IT'S IN GAMBLING OR IN LIFE...
TM
YOU CHOOSE.

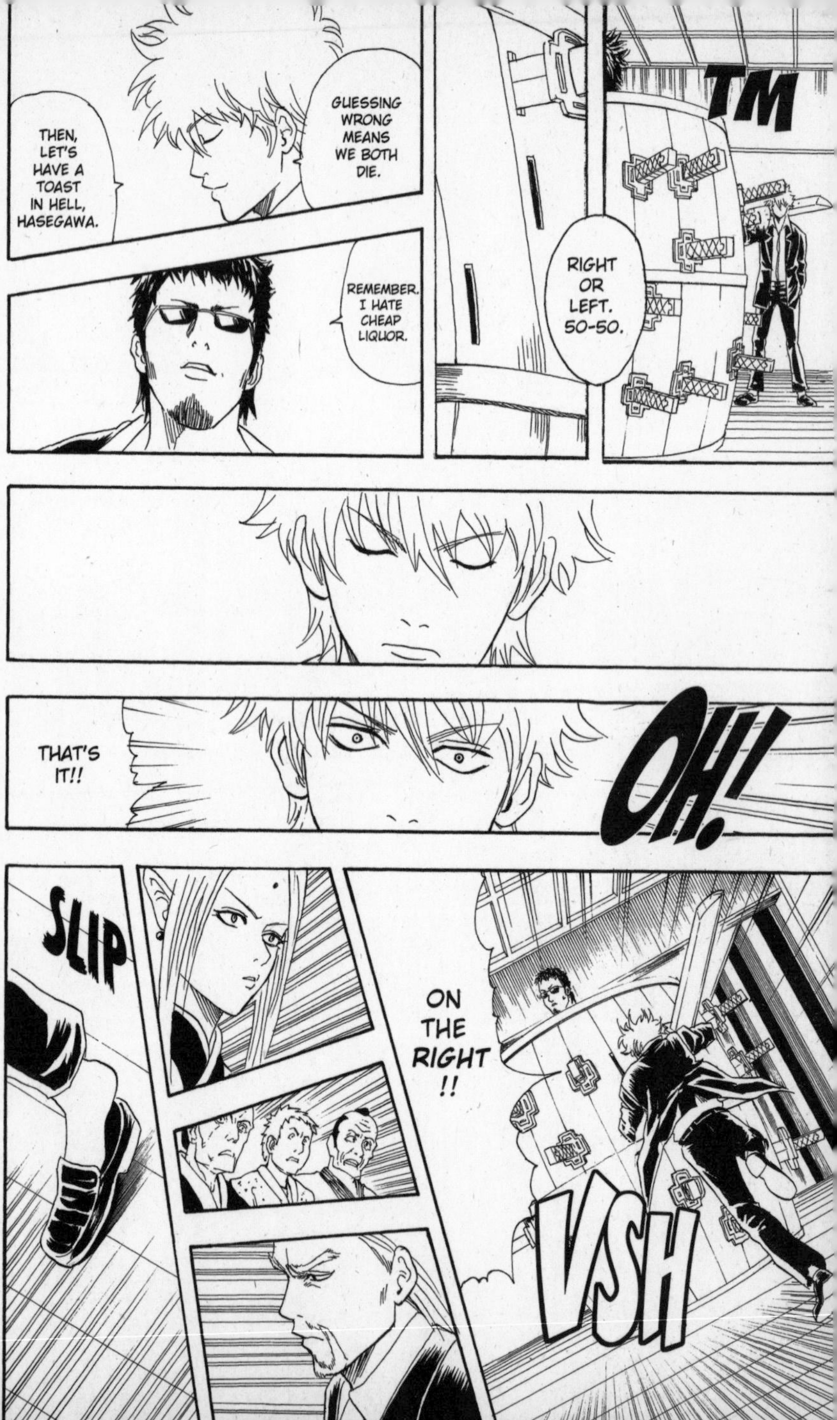
TM
RIGHT OR LEFT. 50-50.
GUESSING WRONG MEANS WE BOTH DIE.
THEN, LET'S HAVE A TOAST IN HELL, HASEGAWA.
REMEMBER. I HATE CHEAP LIQUOR.
OH!
THAT'S IT!!
ON THE RIGHT!!
VSH
SLIP

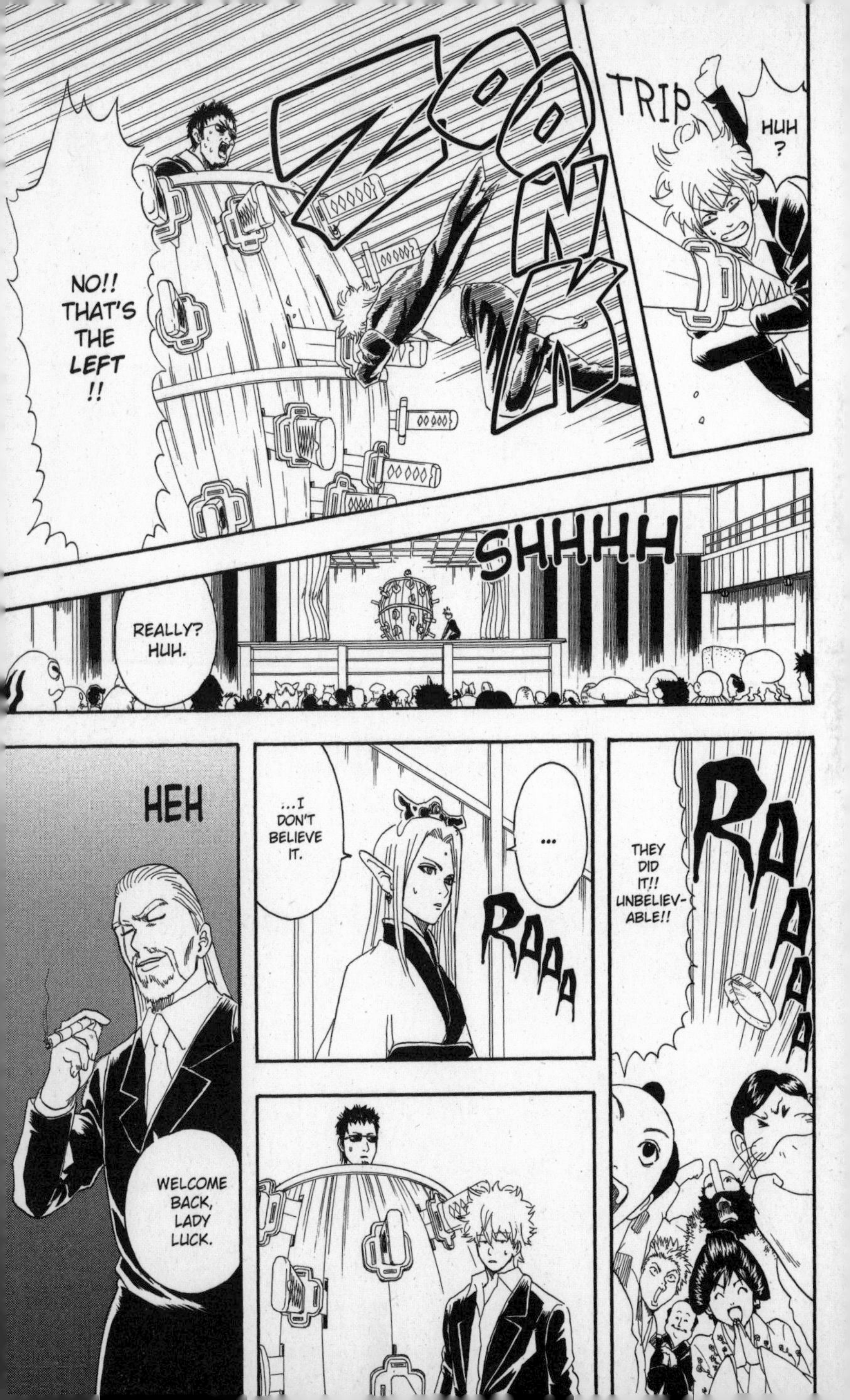
TRIP
HUH?
ZOOONK
NO!! THAT'S THE LEFT!!
SHHHH
REALLY? HUH.
RAAAAA
THEY DID IT!! UNBELIEV-ABLE!!
...
RAAAA
...I DON'T BELIEVE IT.
HEH
WELCOME BACK, LADY LUCK.

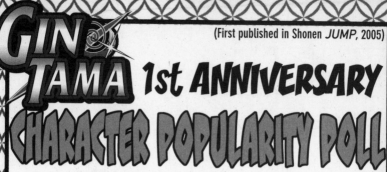

(First published in Shonen *JUMP*, 2005)

GIN TAMA 1st ANNIVERSARY CHARACTER POPULARITY POLL

1st	Gintoki Sakata	2632 votes
2nd	Sogo Okita	1515 votes
3rd	Toshiro Hijikata	1512 votes
4th	Shinsuke Takasugi	1500 votes
5th	Sagaru Yamazaki	1458 votes
6th	Kotaro Katsura	1291 votes
7th	Kagura	878 votes
8th	Shinpachi Shimura	873 votes
9th	Tatsuma Sakamoto	679 votes
10th	Isao Kondo	543 votes
11th	Elizabeth	374 votes
12th	Otae Shimura	350 votes
13th	Taizo Hasegawa	332 votes
14th	Hideaki Sorachi	285 votes
15th	Mutsu	284 votes
16th	Sadaharu	280 votes
17th	AyanoTerada(Otose)	188 votes
18th	Prince Hata	174 votes
19th	Jastaway	172 votes
20th	Ayame Sarutobi	168 votes
21st	Kimiko (Hammy)	137 votes
22nd	Catherine	133 votes
23rd	Katakuriko Matsudaira	132 votes
24th	Ebina	128 votes
25th	Editor: Onishi	127 votes
26th	Musashi	125 votes
27th	Zurako	121 votes
27th	Pako	121 votes
29th	Saburo Hiraga	117 votes
30th	Tatsuri	115 votes

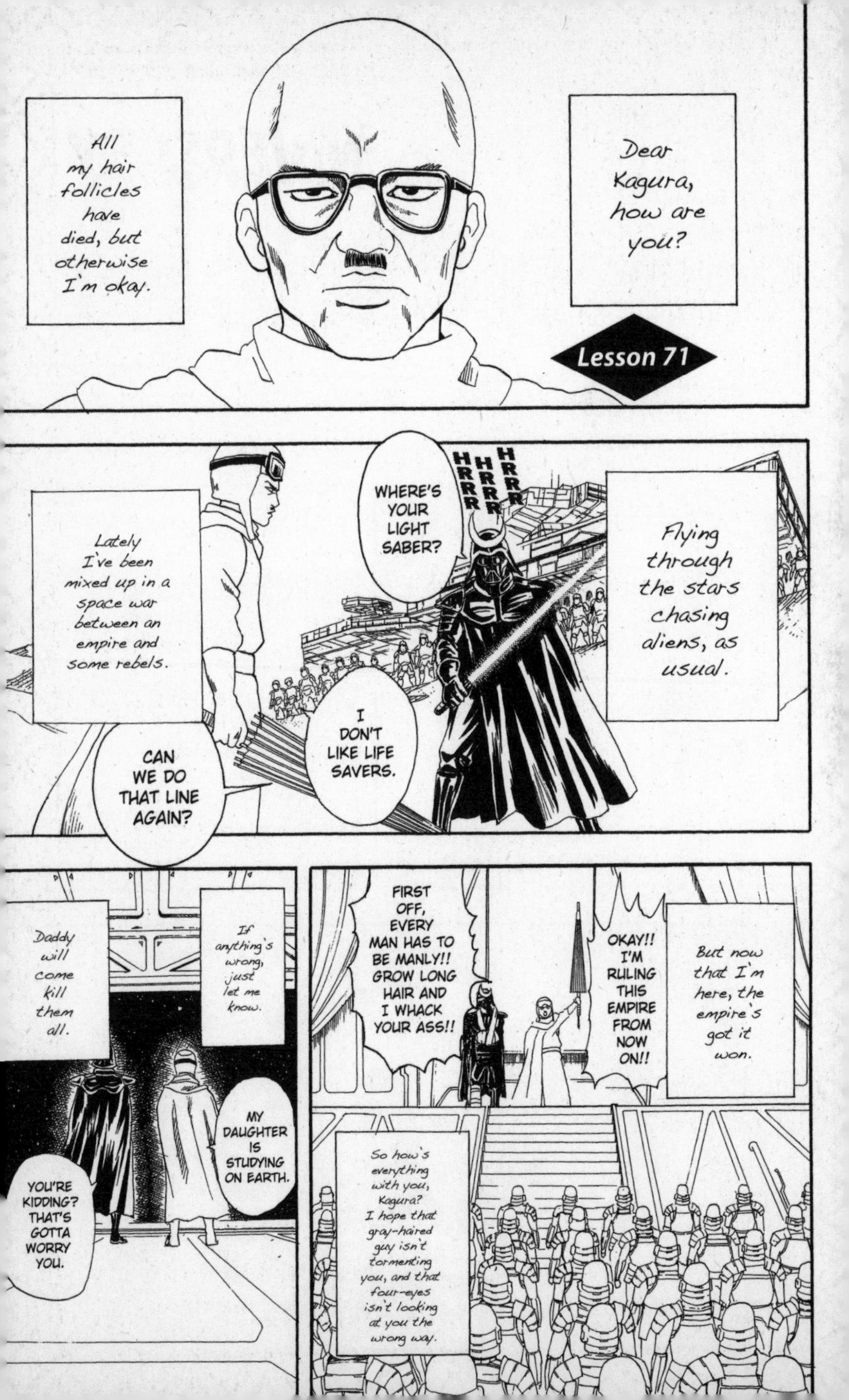
Dear Kagura, how are you?
Lesson 71
All my hair follicles have died, but otherwise I'm okay.
Flying through the stars chasing aliens, as usual.
HRRR HRRR HRRR
WHERE'S YOUR LIGHT SABER?
Lately I've been mixed up in a space war between an empire and some rebels.
I DON'T LIKE LIFE SAVERS.
CAN WE DO THAT LINE AGAIN?
But now that I'm here, the empire's got it won.
OKAY!! I'M RULING THIS EMPIRE FROM NOW ON!!
FIRST OFF, EVERY MAN HAS TO BE MANLY!! GROW LONG HAIR AND I WHACK YOUR ASS!!
So how's everything with you, Kagura? I hope that gray-haired guy isn't tormenting you, and that four-eyes isn't looking at you the wrong way.
If anything's wrong, just let me know.
Daddy will come kill them all.
MY DAUGHTER IS STUDYING ON EARTH.
YOU'RE KIDDING? THAT'S GOTTA WORRY YOU.

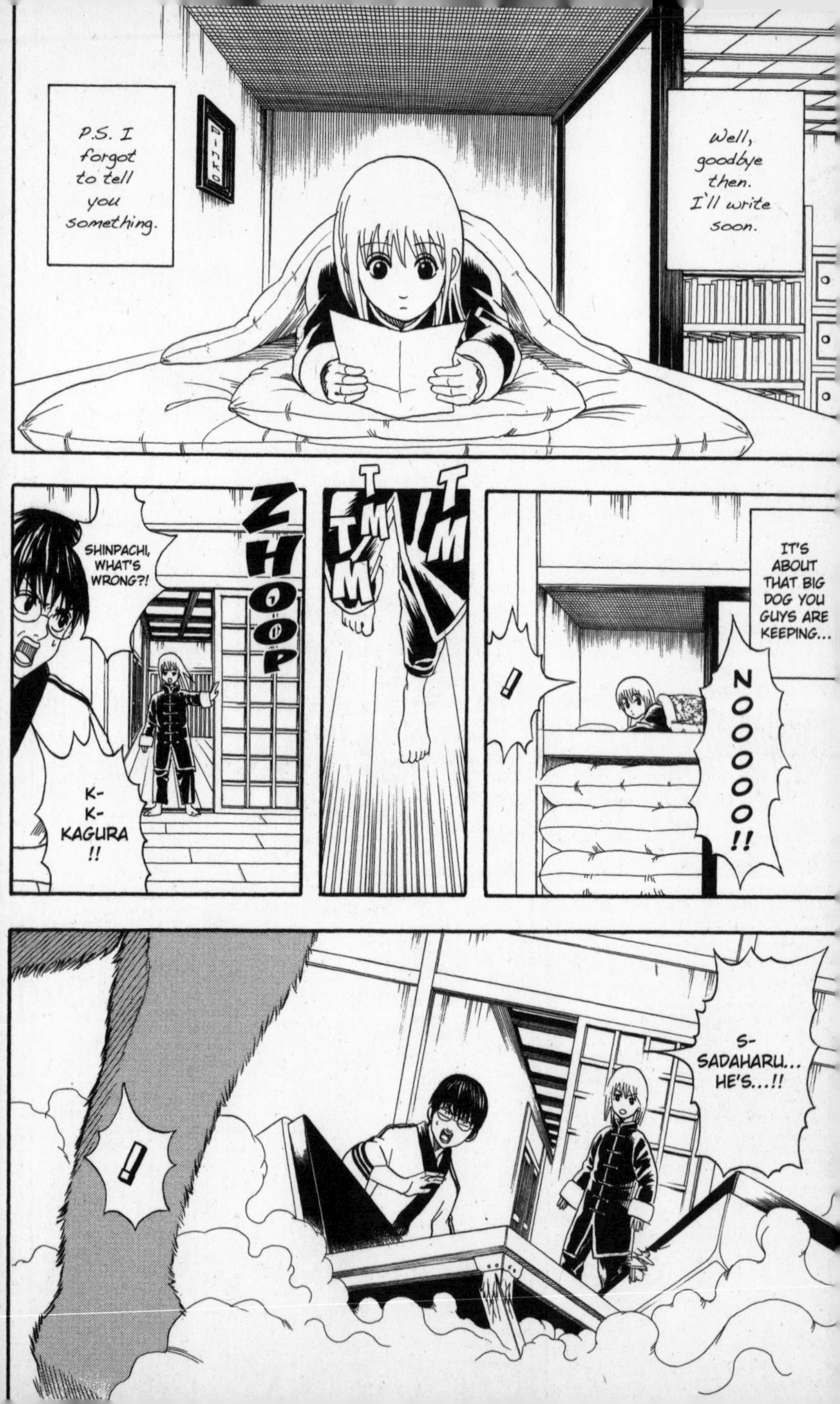
Well, goodbye then. I'll write soon.
P.S. I forgot to tell you something.
IT'S ABOUT THAT BIG DOG YOU GUYS ARE KEEPING...
!
NOOOOOO!!
TMTM TMTM
ZHOOP
SHINPACHI, WHAT'S WRONG?!
K-K-KAGURA!!
S-SADAHARU... HE'S...!!
!

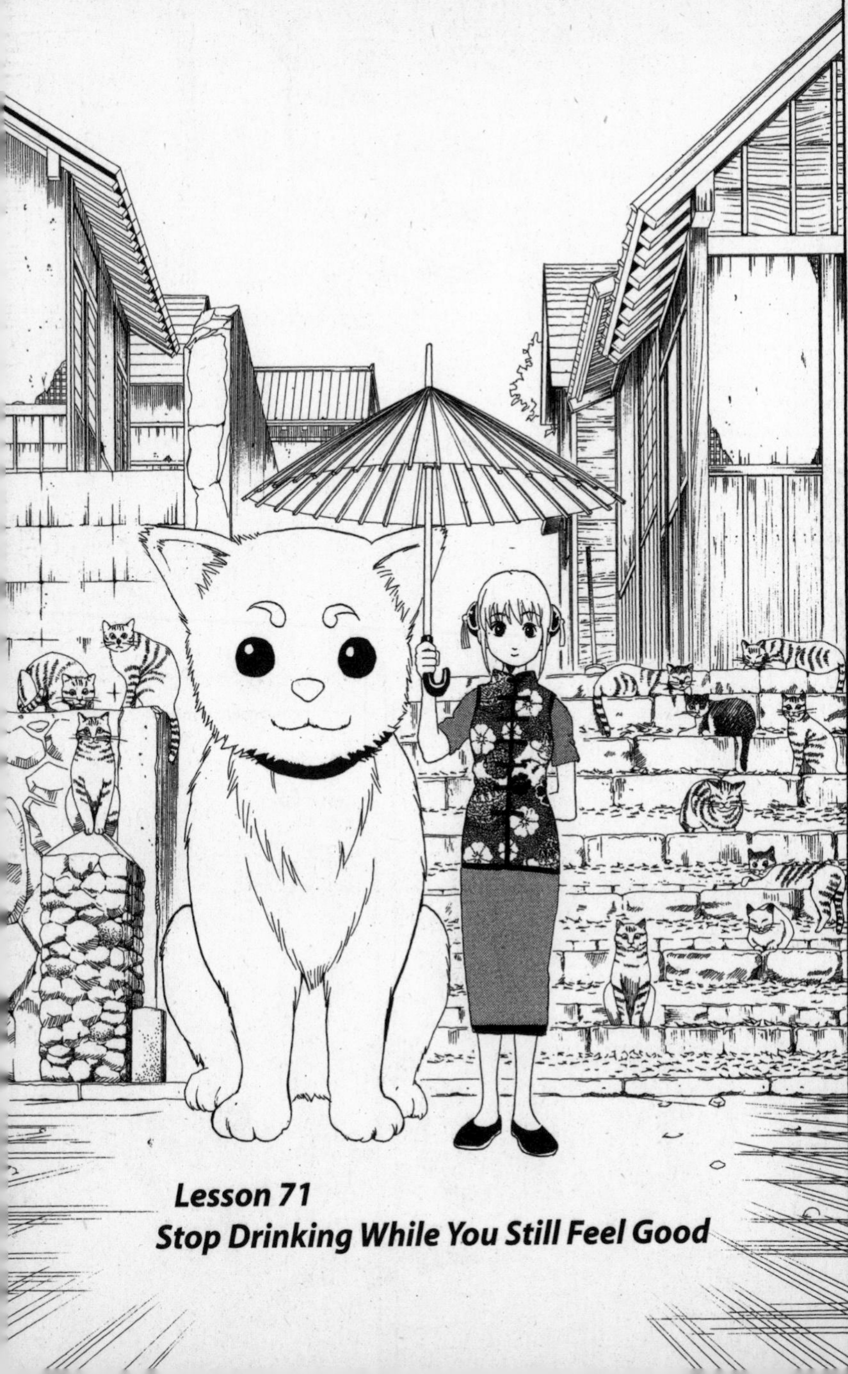

Lesson 71
Stop Drinking While You Still Feel Good

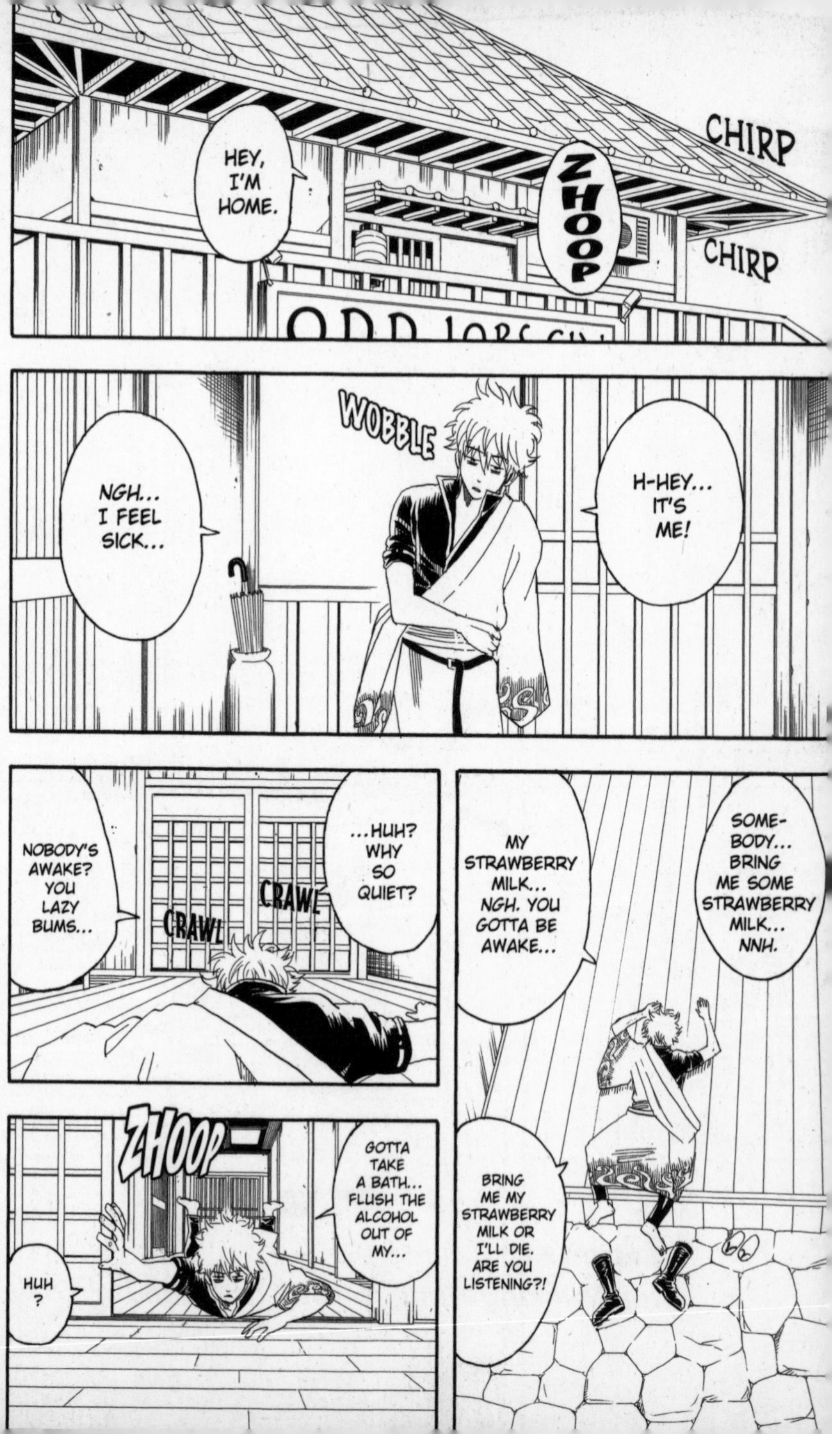
CHIRP
CHIRP
ZHOOP
HEY, I'M HOME.
H-HEY... IT'S ME!
WOBBLE
NGH... I FEEL SICK...
SOME-BODY... BRING ME SOME STRAWBERRY MILK... NNH.
MY STRAWBERRY MILK... NGH. YOU GOTTA BE AWAKE...
BRING ME MY STRAWBERRY MILK OR I'LL DIE. ARE YOU LISTENING?!
...HUH? WHY SO QUIET?
CRAWL
CRAWL
NOBODY'S AWAKE? YOU LAZY BUMS...
GOTTA TAKE A BATH... FLUSH THE ALCOHOL OUT OF MY...
ZHOOP
HUH?

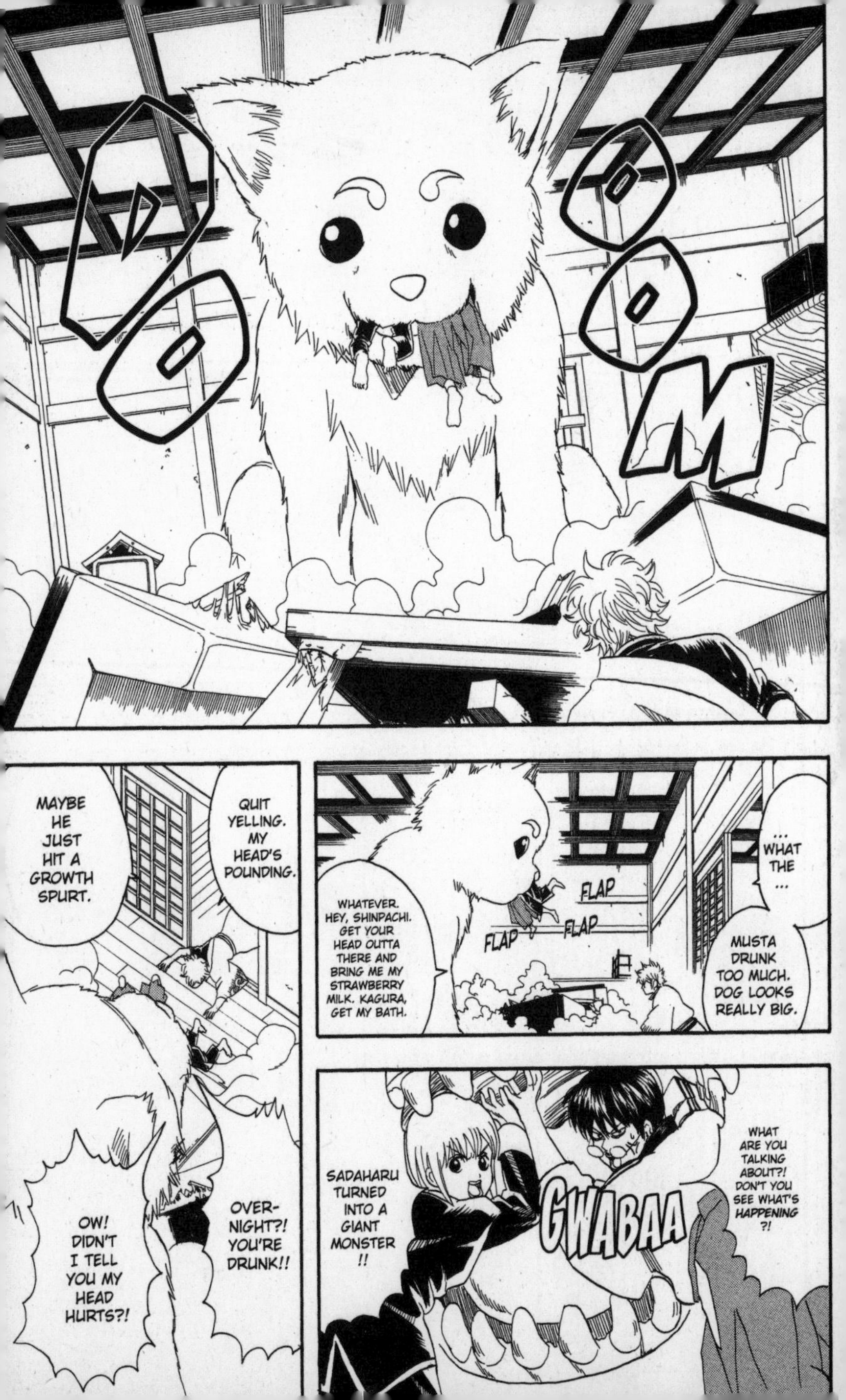
DOOOM
... WHAT THE ...
MUSTA DRUNK TOO MUCH. DOG LOOKS REALLY BIG.
FLAP
FLAP
FLAP
WHATEVER. HEY, SHINPACHI. GET YOUR HEAD OUTTA THERE AND BRING ME MY STRAWBERRY MILK. KAGURA, GET MY BATH.
WHAT ARE YOU TALKING ABOUT?! DON'T YOU SEE WHAT'S HAPPENING ?!
GWABAA
SADAHARU TURNED INTO A GIANT MONSTER !!
QUIT YELLING. MY HEAD'S POUNDING.
MAYBE HE JUST HIT A GROWTH SPURT.
OVER-NIGHT?! YOU'RE DRUNK!!
OW! DIDN'T I TELL YOU MY HEAD HURTS?!

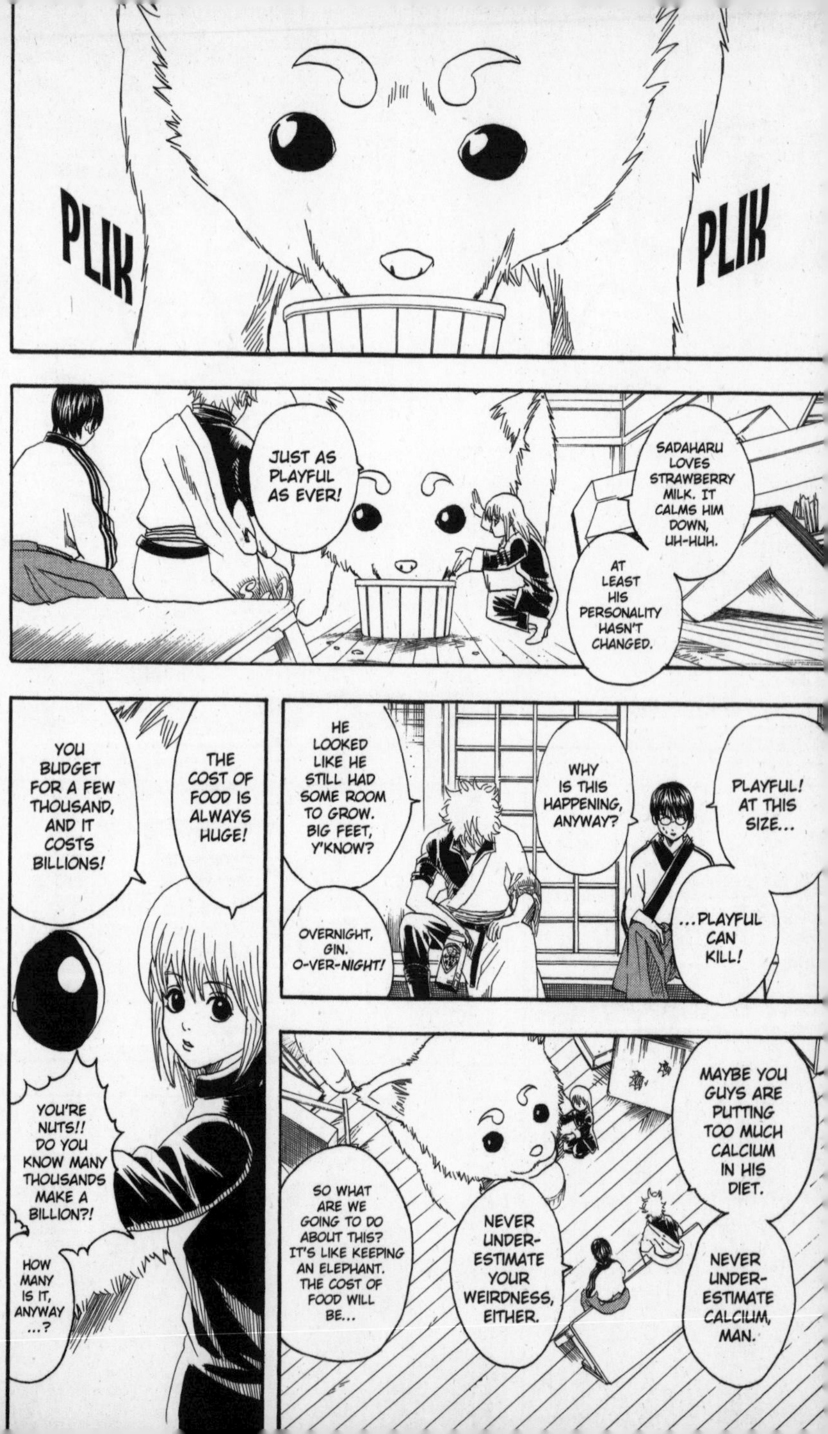
PLIK
PLIK
SADAHARU LOVES STRAWBERRY MILK. IT CALMS HIM DOWN, UH-HUH.
AT LEAST HIS PERSONALITY HASN'T CHANGED.
JUST AS PLAYFUL AS EVER!
PLAYFUL! AT THIS SIZE...
...PLAYFUL CAN KILL!
WHY IS THIS HAPPENING, ANYWAY?
HE LOOKED LIKE HE STILL HAD SOME ROOM TO GROW. BIG FEET, Y'KNOW?
OVERNIGHT, GIN. O-VER-NIGHT!
MAYBE YOU GUYS ARE PUTTING TOO MUCH CALCIUM IN HIS DIET.
NEVER UNDER-ESTIMATE CALCIUM, MAN.
NEVER UNDER-ESTIMATE YOUR WEIRDNESS, EITHER.
SO WHAT ARE WE GOING TO DO ABOUT THIS? IT'S LIKE KEEPING AN ELEPHANT. THE COST OF FOOD WILL BE...
THE COST OF FOOD IS ALWAYS HUGE!
YOU BUDGET FOR A FEW THOUSAND, AND IT COSTS BILLIONS!
YOU'RE NUTS!! DO YOU KNOW MANY THOUSANDS MAKE A BILLION?!
HOW MANY IS IT, ANYWAY ...?

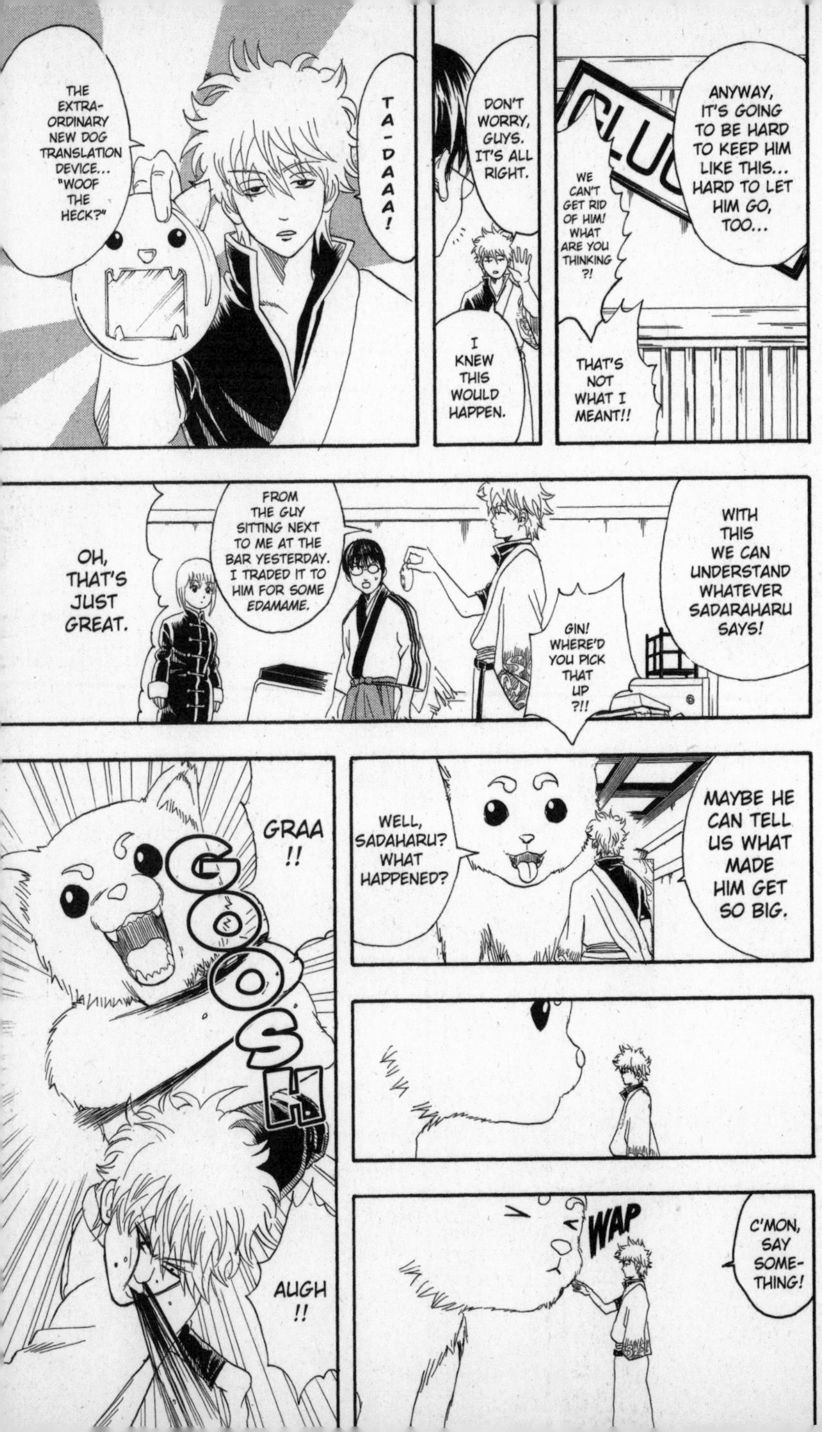
ANYWAY, IT'S GOING TO BE HARD TO KEEP HIM LIKE THIS... HARD TO LET HIM GO, TOO...
WE CAN'T GET RID OF HIM! WHAT ARE YOU THINKING ?!
THAT'S NOT WHAT I MEANT!!
DON'T WORRY, GUYS. IT'S ALL RIGHT.
I KNEW THIS WOULD HAPPEN.
TA-DAAAA!
THE EXTRA-ORDINARY NEW DOG TRANSLATION DEVICE... "WOOF THE HECK?"
WITH THIS WE CAN UNDERSTAND WHATEVER SADARAHARU SAYS!
GIN! WHERE'D YOU PICK THAT UP ?!!
FROM THE GUY SITTING NEXT TO ME AT THE BAR YESTERDAY. I TRADED IT TO HIM FOR SOME EDAMAME.
OH, THAT'S JUST GREAT.
MAYBE HE CAN TELL US WHAT MADE HIM GET SO BIG.
WELL, SADAHARU? WHAT HAPPENED?
C'MON, SAY SOME-THING!
WAP
GRAA !!
GOOOSH
AUGH !!

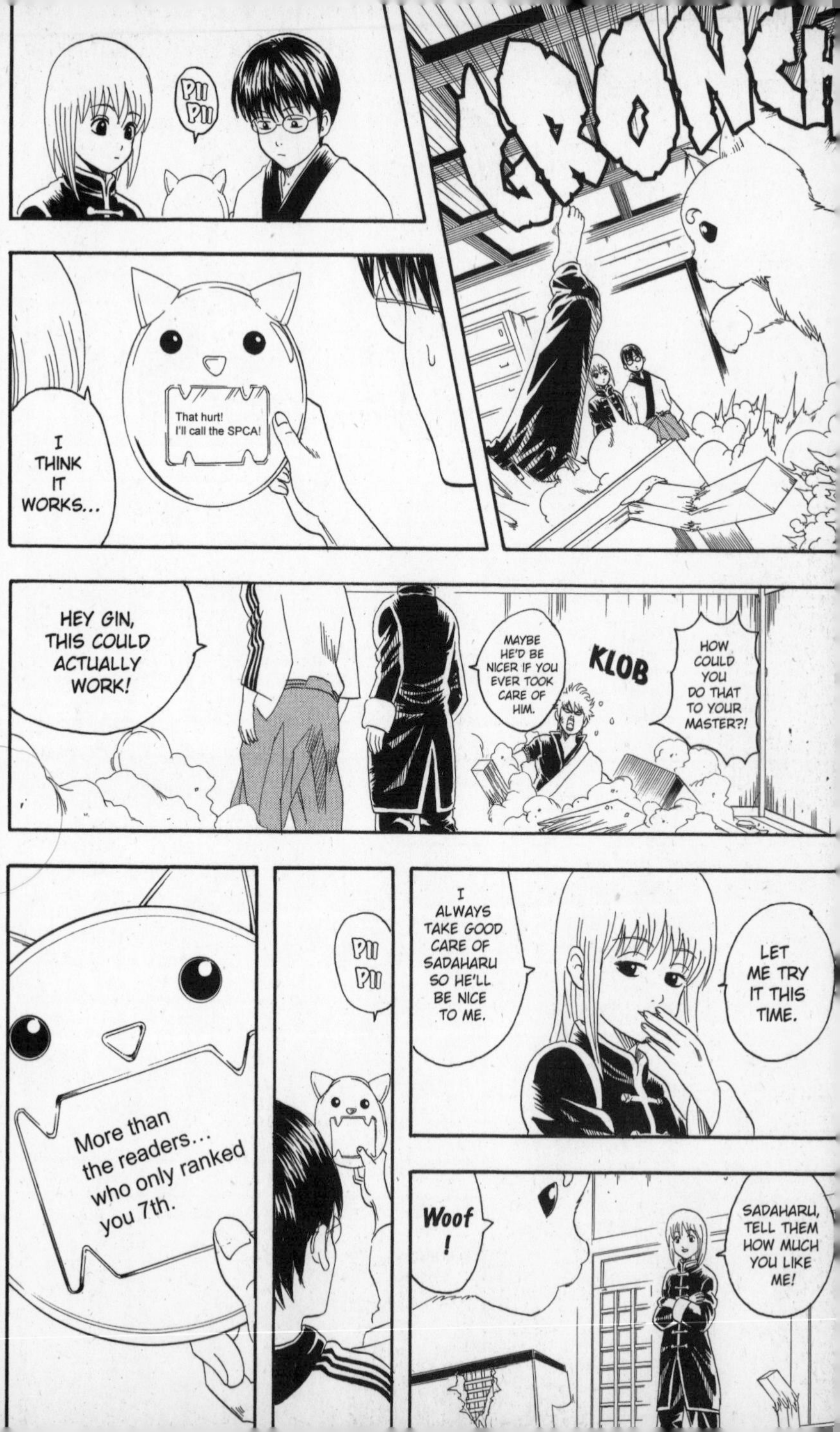
CRONK
PII PII
That hurt! I'll call the SPCA!
I THINK IT WORKS...
HOW COULD YOU DO THAT TO YOUR MASTER?!
KLOB
MAYBE HE'D BE NICER IF YOU EVER TOOK CARE OF HIM.
HEY GIN, THIS COULD ACTUALLY WORK!
LET ME TRY IT THIS TIME.
I ALWAYS TAKE GOOD CARE OF SADAHARU SO HE'LL BE NICE TO ME.
SADAHARU, TELL THEM HOW MUCH YOU LIKE ME!
Woof!
PII PII
More than the readers... who only ranked you 7th.

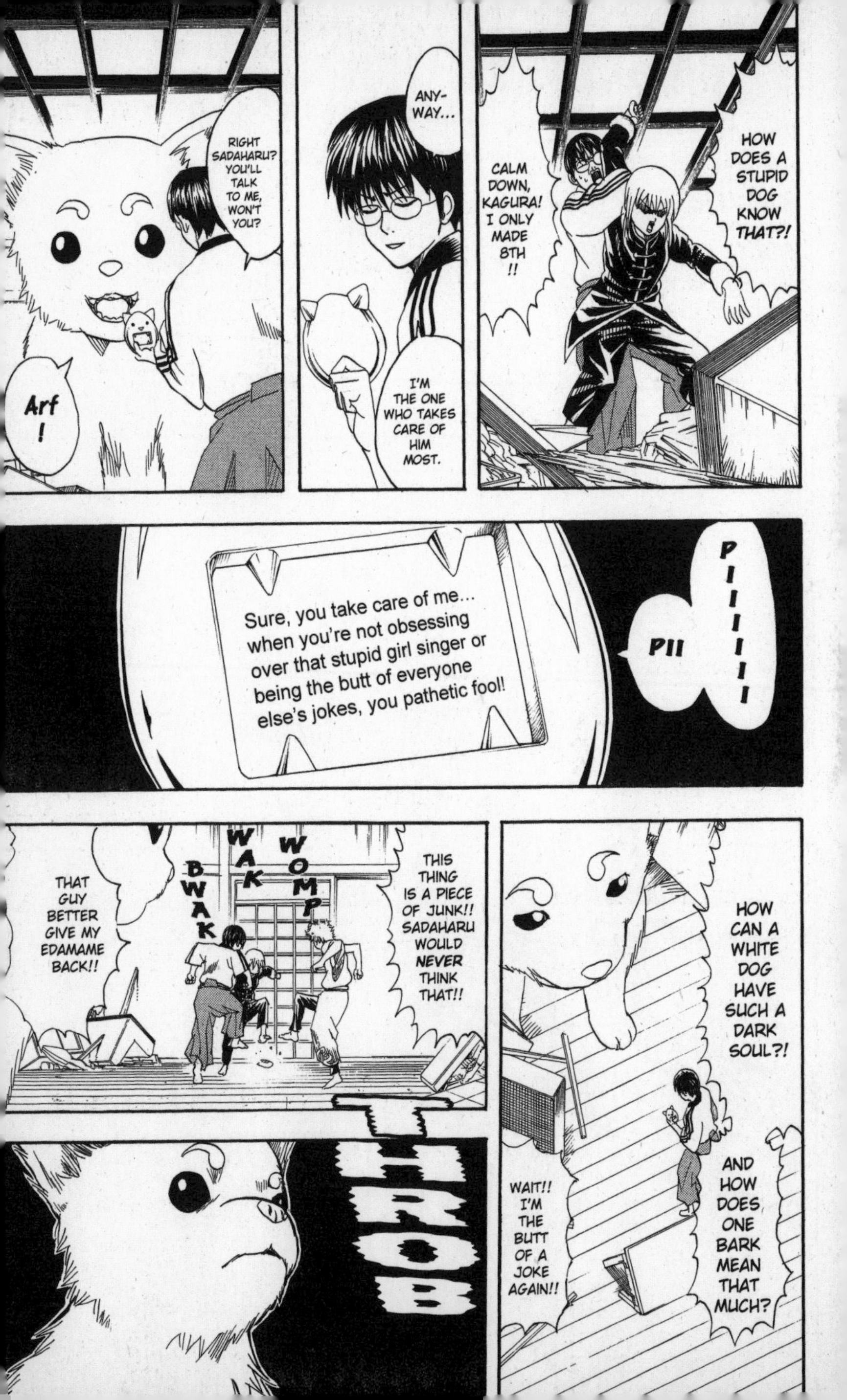
HOW DOES A STUPID DOG KNOW THAT?!
CALM DOWN, KAGURA! I ONLY MADE 8TH !!
ANY-WAY...
I'M THE ONE WHO TAKES CARE OF HIM MOST.
RIGHT SADAHARU? YOU'LL TALK TO ME, WON'T YOU?
Arf !
PIIIIIIII
PII
Sure, you take care of me... when you're not obsessing over that stupid girl singer or being the butt of everyone else's jokes, you pathetic fool!
HOW CAN A WHITE DOG HAVE SUCH A DARK SOUL?!
AND HOW DOES ONE BARK MEAN THAT MUCH?
WAIT!! I'M THE BUTT OF A JOKE AGAIN!!
THIS THING IS A PIECE OF JUNK!! SADAHARU WOULD NEVER THINK THAT!!
WOMP
WAK
BWAK
THAT GUY BETTER GIVE MY EDAMAME BACK!!
THROB

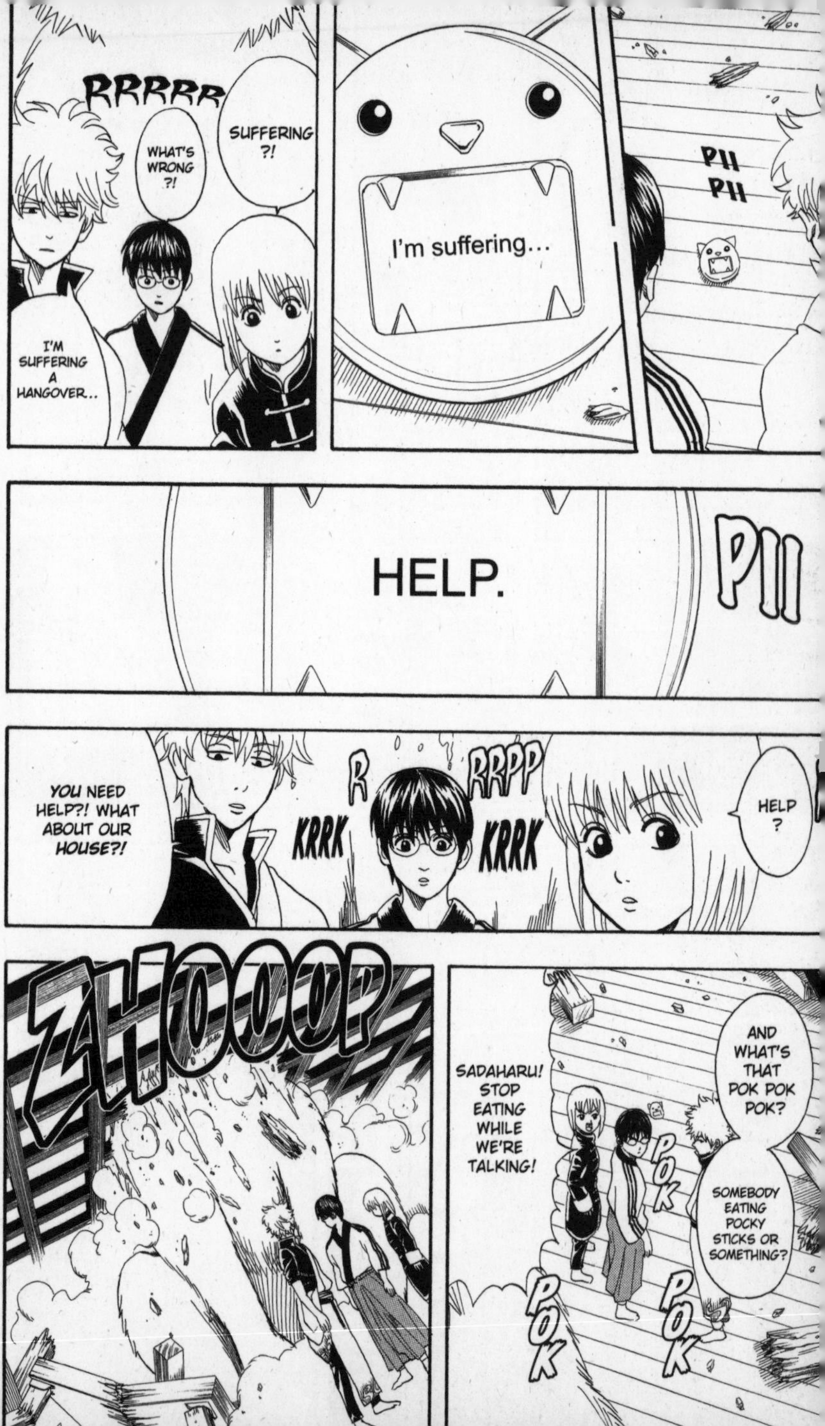
PH PH
I'm suffering…
SUFFERING ?!
RRRRR
WHAT'S WRONG ?!
I'M SUFFERING A HANGOVER...
PII
HELP.
HELP ?
RRPP
KRRK
R
KRRK
YOU NEED HELP?! WHAT ABOUT OUR HOUSE?!
AND WHAT'S THAT POK POK POK?
SOMEBODY EATING POCKY STICKS OR SOMETHING?
POK
POK
SADAHARU! STOP EATING WHILE WE'RE TALKING!
POK
ZHOOOOP

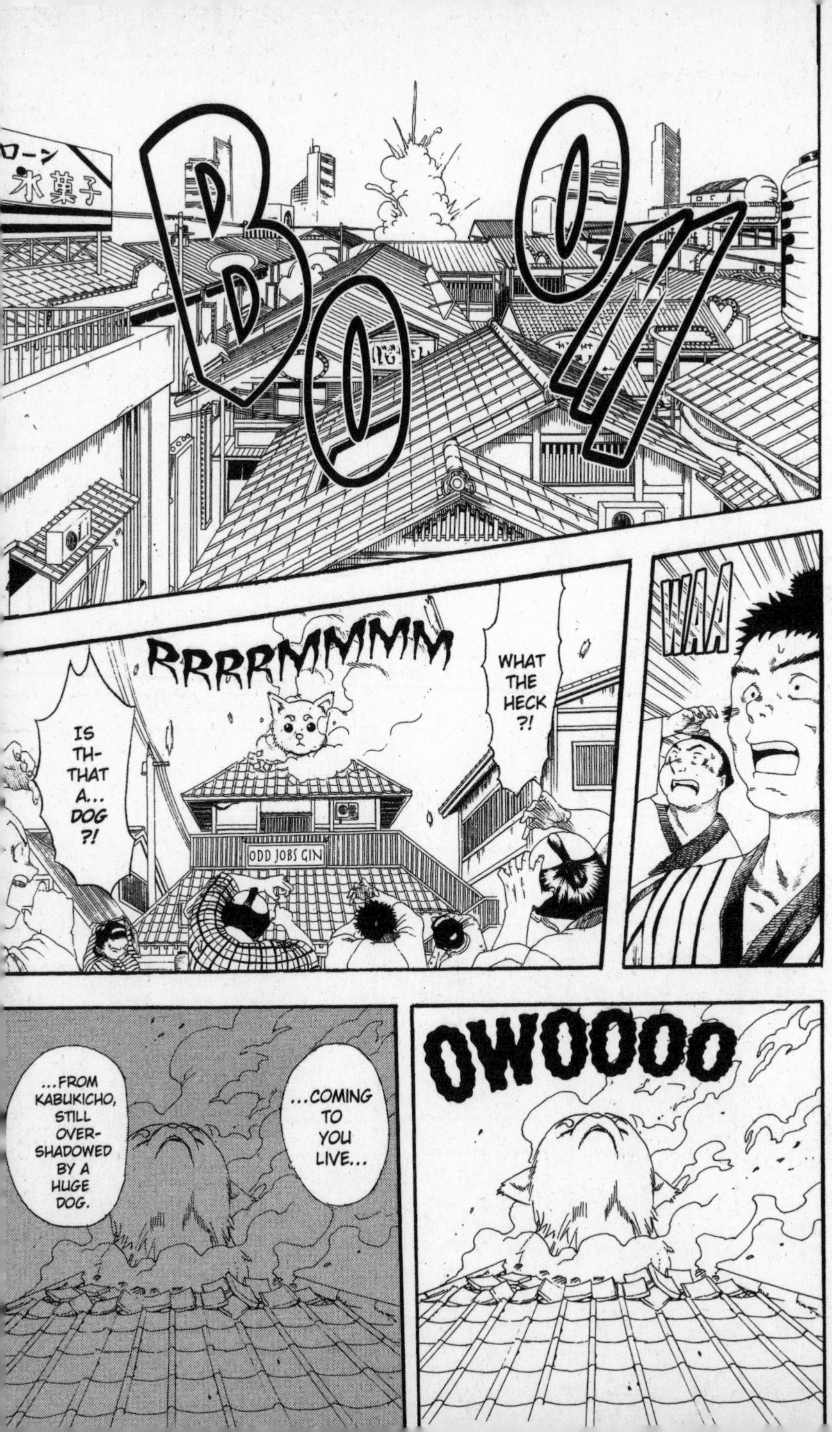
BOOM
ローン
氷菓子
WAA
RRRRMMMM
WHAT THE HECK?!
IS TH-THAT A... DOG?!
ODD JOBS GIN
OWOOOO
...COMING TO YOU LIVE...
...FROM KABUKICHO, STILL OVER-SHADOWED BY A HUGE DOG.

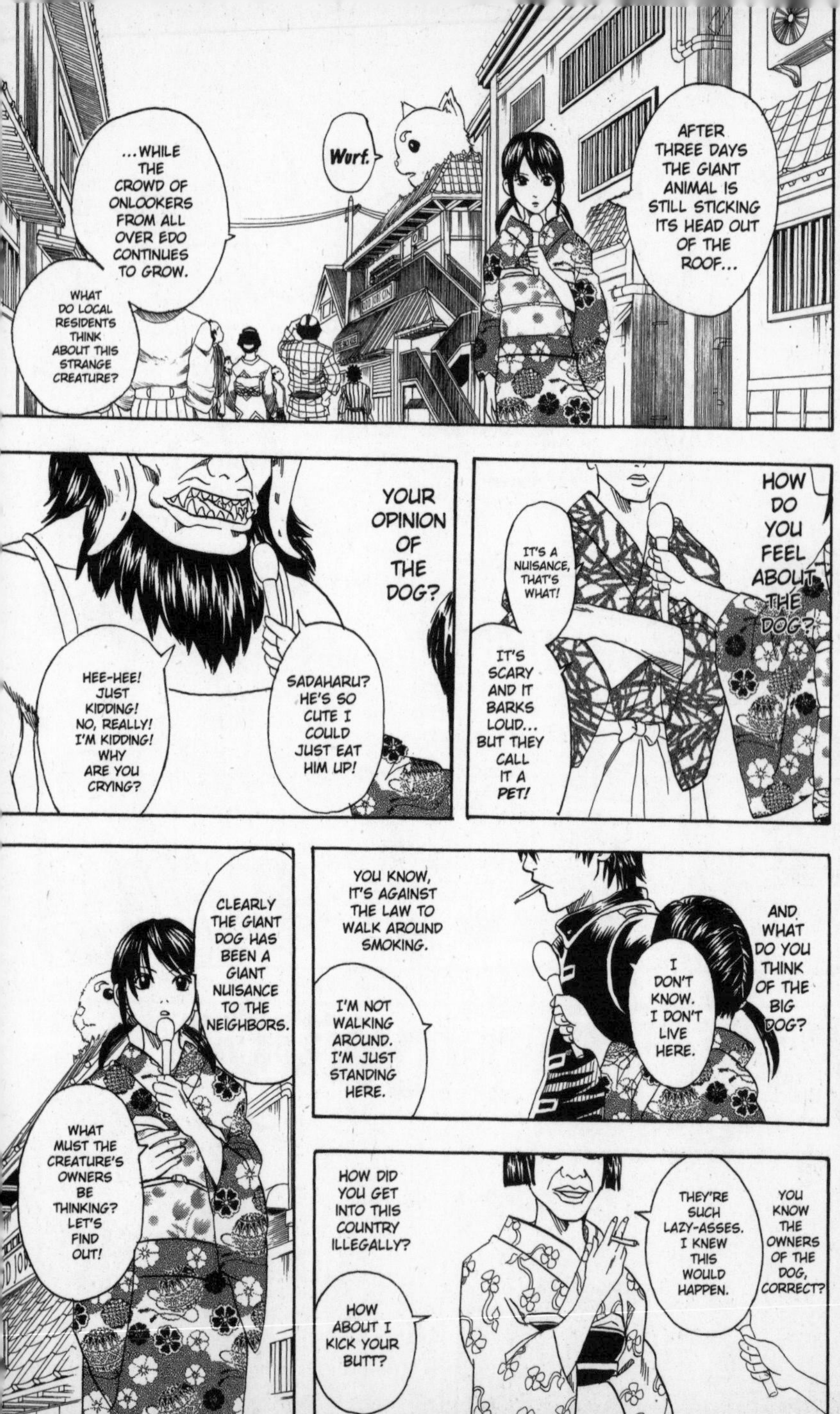
AFTER THREE DAYS THE GIANT ANIMAL IS STILL STICKING ITS HEAD OUT OF THE ROOF...
Wurf.
...WHILE THE CROWD OF ONLOOKERS FROM ALL OVER EDO CONTINUES TO GROW.
WHAT DO LOCAL RESIDENTS THINK ABOUT THIS STRANGE CREATURE?
HOW DO YOU FEEL ABOUT THE DOG?
IT'S A NUISANCE, THAT'S WHAT!
IT'S SCARY AND IT BARKS LOUD... BUT THEY CALL IT A PET!
YOUR OPINION OF THE DOG?
SADAHARU? HE'S SO CUTE I COULD JUST EAT HIM UP!
HEE-HEE! JUST KIDDING! NO, REALLY! I'M KIDDING! WHY ARE YOU CRYING?
AND WHAT DO YOU THINK OF THE BIG DOG?
I DON'T KNOW. I DON'T LIVE HERE.
YOU KNOW, IT'S AGAINST THE LAW TO WALK AROUND SMOKING.
I'M NOT WALKING AROUND. I'M JUST STANDING HERE.
YOU KNOW THE OWNERS OF THE DOG, CORRECT?
THEY'RE SUCH LAZY-ASSES. I KNEW THIS WOULD HAPPEN.
HOW DID YOU GET INTO THIS COUNTRY ILLEGALLY?
HOW ABOUT I KICK YOUR BUTT?
CLEARLY THE GIANT DOG HAS BEEN A GIANT NUISANCE TO THE NEIGHBORS.
WHAT MUST THE CREATURE'S OWNERS BE THINKING? LET'S FIND OUT!

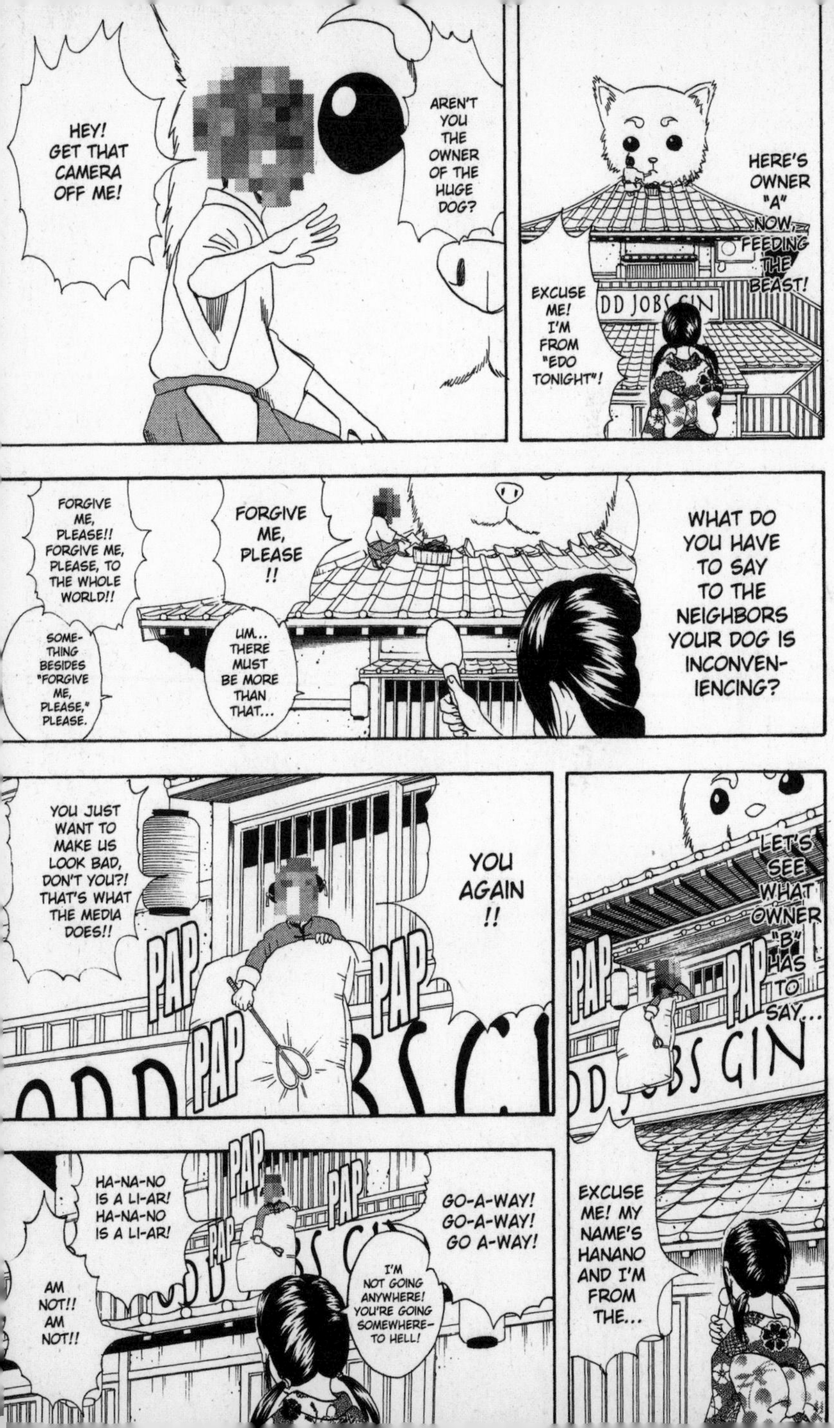
HERE'S OWNER "A" NOW, FEEDING THE BEAST!
DD JOBS GIN
EXCUSE ME! I'M FROM "EDO TONIGHT"!
AREN'T YOU THE OWNER OF THE HUGE DOG?
HEY! GET THAT CAMERA OFF ME!
WHAT DO YOU HAVE TO SAY TO THE NEIGHBORS YOUR DOG IS INCONVENIENCING?
FORGIVE ME, PLEASE!!
UM... THERE MUST BE MORE THAN THAT...
FORGIVE ME, PLEASE!! FORGIVE ME, PLEASE, TO THE WHOLE WORLD!!
SOMETHING BESIDES "FORGIVE ME, PLEASE," PLEASE.
LET'S SEE WHAT OWNER "B" HAS TO SAY...
PAP
PAP
DD JOBS GIN
EXCUSE ME! MY NAME'S HANANO AND I'M FROM THE...
YOU AGAIN!!
PAP
PAP
YOU JUST WANT TO MAKE US LOOK BAD, DON'T YOU?! THAT'S WHAT THE MEDIA DOES!!
PAP
GO-A-WAY! GO-A-WAY! GO A-WAY!
I'M NOT GOING ANYWHERE! YOU'RE GOING SOMEWHERE—TO HELL!
PAP
PAP
HA-NA-NO IS A LI-AR! HA-NA-NO IS A LI-AR!
PAP
AM NOT!! AM NOT!!

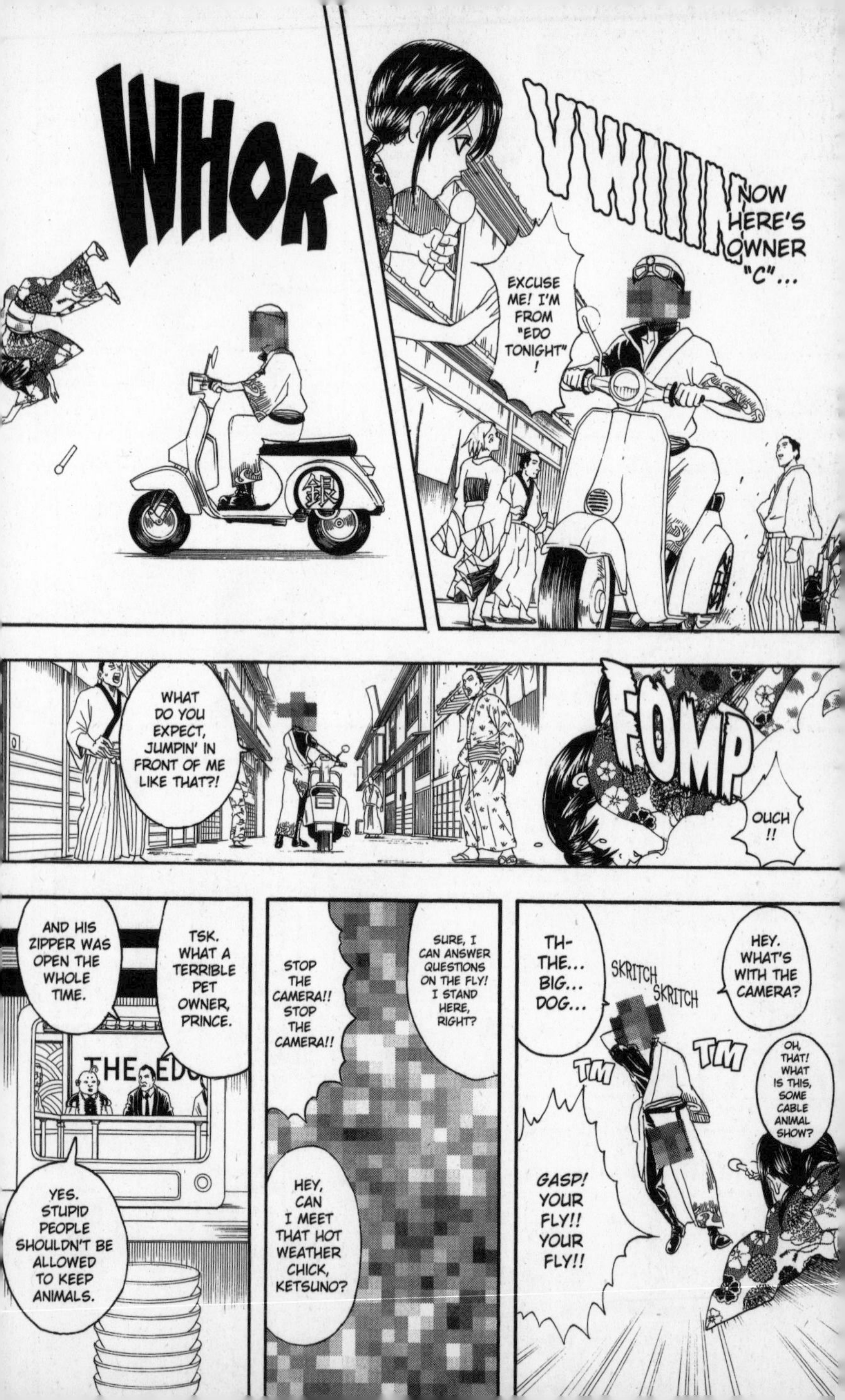
VWIIIN
NOW HERE'S OWNER "C"...
EXCUSE ME! I'M FROM "EDO TONIGHT"!
WHOK
FOMP
OUCH!!
WHAT DO YOU EXPECT, JUMPIN' IN FRONT OF ME LIKE THAT?!
HEY. WHAT'S WITH THE CAMERA?
OH, THAT! WHAT IS THIS, SOME CABLE ANIMAL SHOW?
TH-THE... BIG... DOG...
SKRITCH SKRITCH
TM TM
GASP! YOUR FLY!! YOUR FLY!!
SURE, I CAN ANSWER QUESTIONS ON THE FLY! I STAND HERE, RIGHT?
STOP THE CAMERA!! STOP THE CAMERA!!
HEY, CAN I MEET THAT HOT WEATHER CHICK, KETSUNO?
TSK. WHAT A TERRIBLE PET OWNER, PRINCE.
AND HIS ZIPPER WAS OPEN THE WHOLE TIME.
YES. STUPID PEOPLE SHOULDN'T BE ALLOWED TO KEEP ANIMALS.

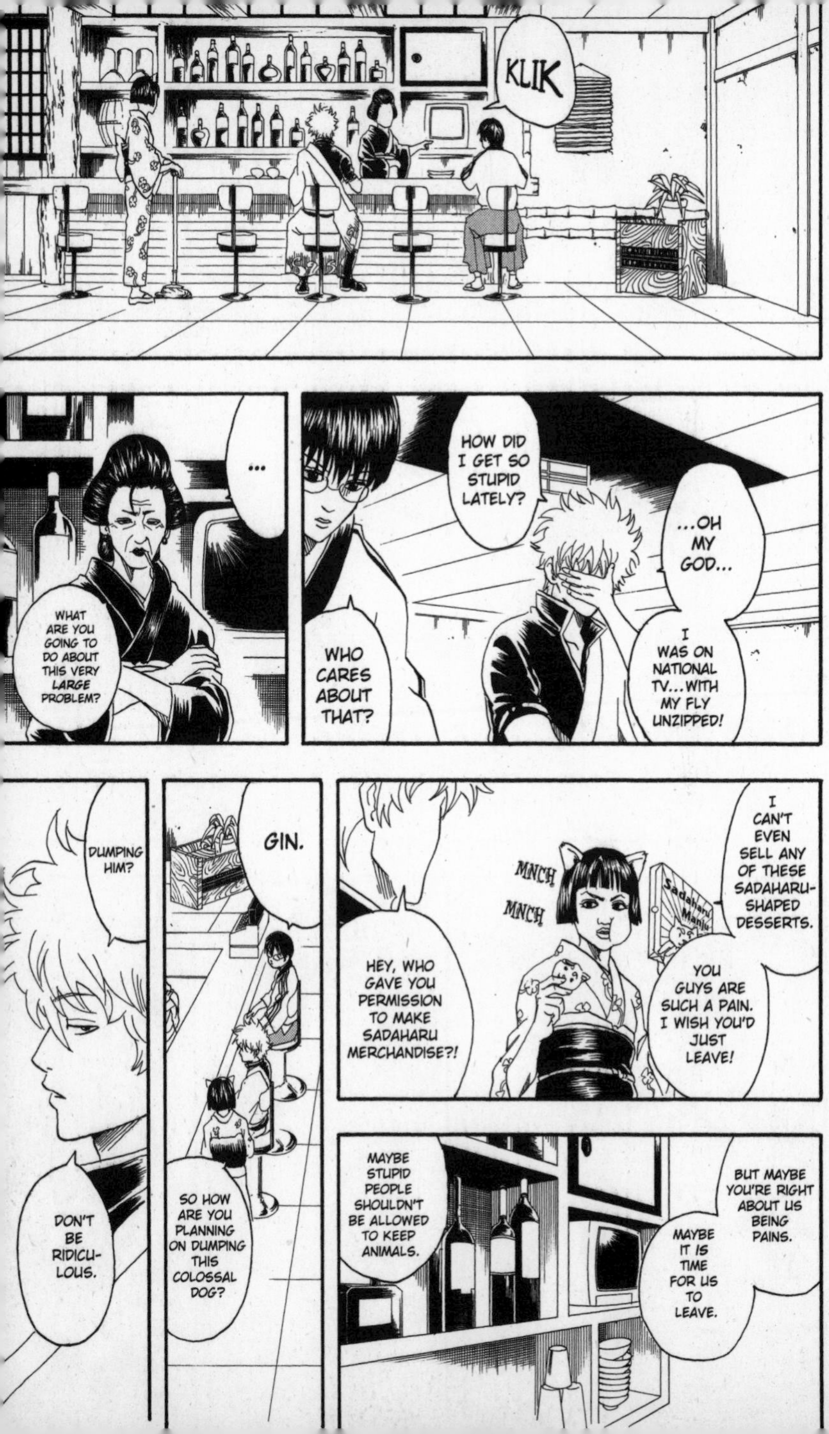
KLIK
HOW DID I GET SO STUPID LATELY?
...OH MY GOD...
I WAS ON NATIONAL TV...WITH MY FLY UNZIPPED!
WHO CARES ABOUT THAT?
...
WHAT ARE YOU GOING TO DO ABOUT THIS VERY LARGE PROBLEM?
I CAN'T EVEN SELL ANY OF THESE SADAHARU-SHAPED DESSERTS.
Sadaharu Manju
MNCH
MNCH
YOU GUYS ARE SUCH A PAIN. I WISH YOU'D JUST LEAVE!
HEY, WHO GAVE YOU PERMISSION TO MAKE SADAHARU MERCHANDISE?!
BUT MAYBE YOU'RE RIGHT ABOUT US BEING PAINS.
MAYBE IT IS TIME FOR US TO LEAVE.
MAYBE STUPID PEOPLE SHOULDN'T BE ALLOWED TO KEEP ANIMALS.
GIN.
SO HOW ARE YOU PLANNING ON DUMPING THIS COLOSSAL DOG?
DUMPING HIM?
DON'T BE RIDICULOUS.

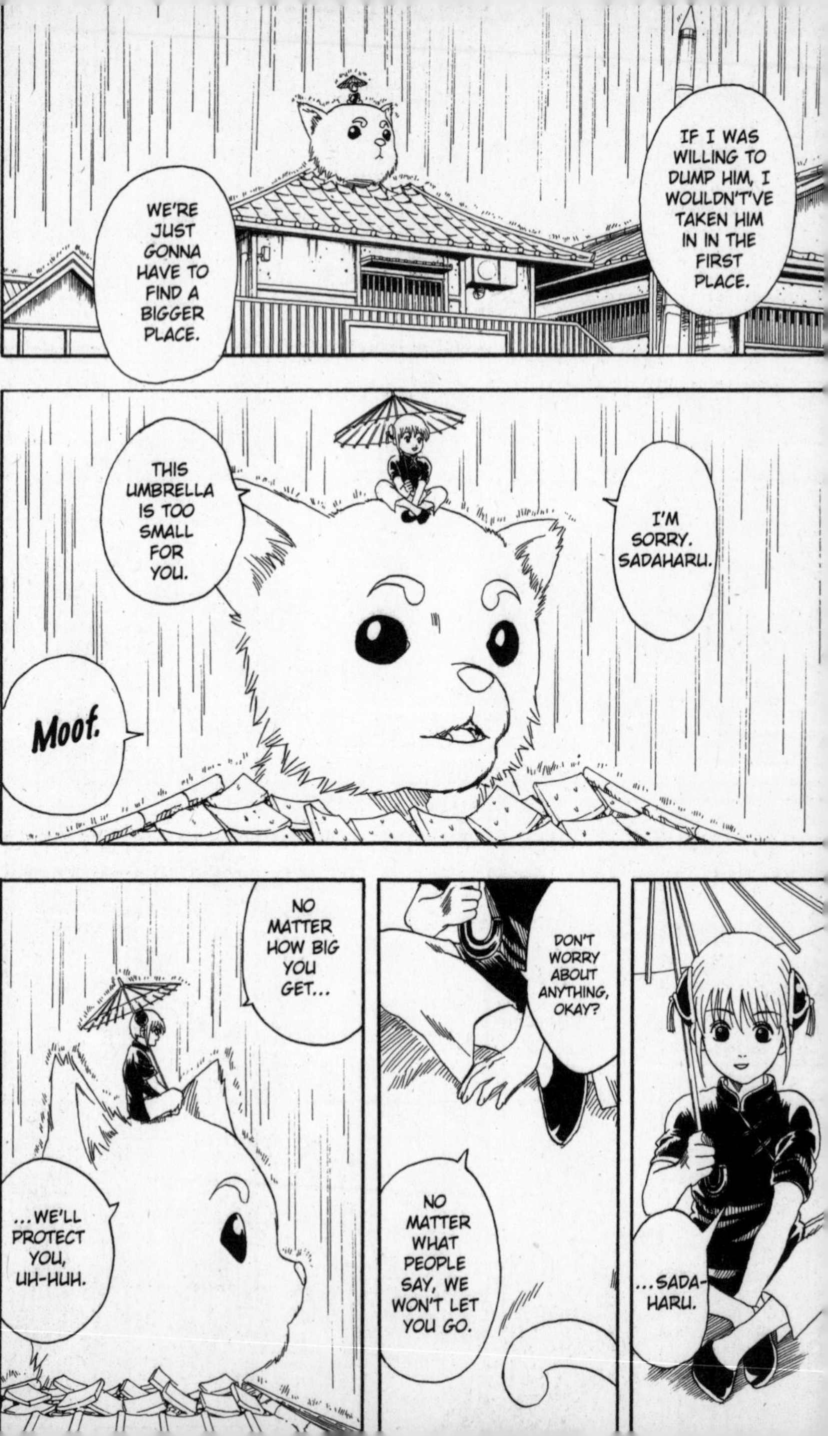
IF I WAS WILLING TO DUMP HIM, I WOULDN'T'VE TAKEN HIM IN IN THE FIRST PLACE.
WE'RE JUST GONNA HAVE TO FIND A BIGGER PLACE.
I'M SORRY. SADAHARU.
THIS UMBRELLA IS TOO SMALL FOR YOU.
Moof.
...SADA-HARU.
DON'T WORRY ABOUT ANYTHING, OKAY?
NO MATTER WHAT PEOPLE SAY, WE WON'T LET YOU GO.
NO MATTER HOW BIG YOU GET...
...WE'LL PROTECT YOU, UH-HUH.

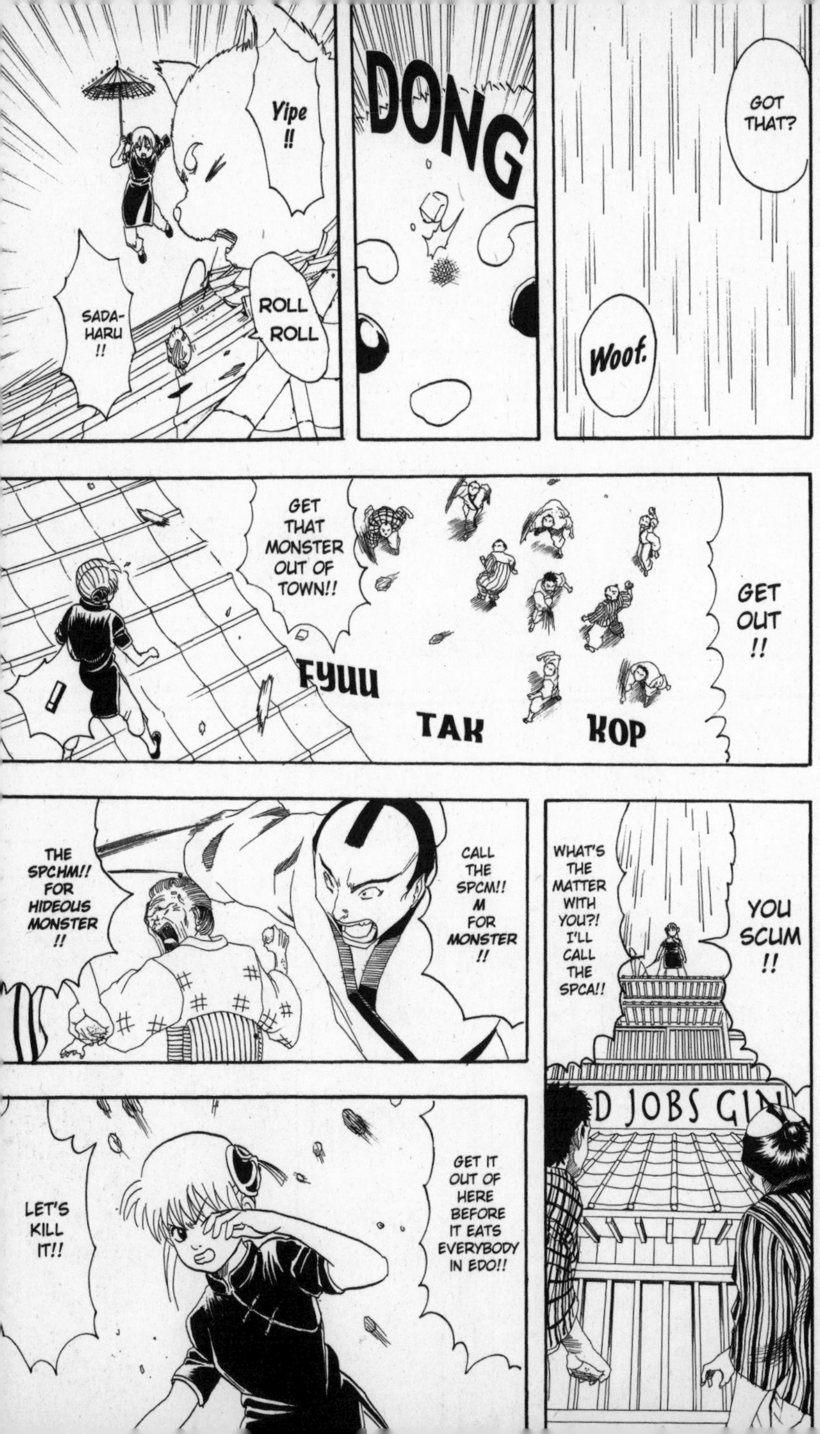
GOT THAT?
Woof.
DONG
Yipe !!
ROLL ROLL
SADA-HARU !!
GET OUT !!
GET THAT MONSTER OUT OF TOWN!!
KOP
TAK
FYUU
YOU SCUM !!
WHAT'S THE MATTER WITH YOU?! I'LL CALL THE SPCA!!
D JOBS GIN
CALL THE SPCM!! M FOR MONSTER !!
THE SPCHM!! FOR HIDEOUS MONSTER !!
GET IT OUT OF HERE BEFORE IT EATS EVERYBODY IN EDO!!
LET'S KILL IT!!

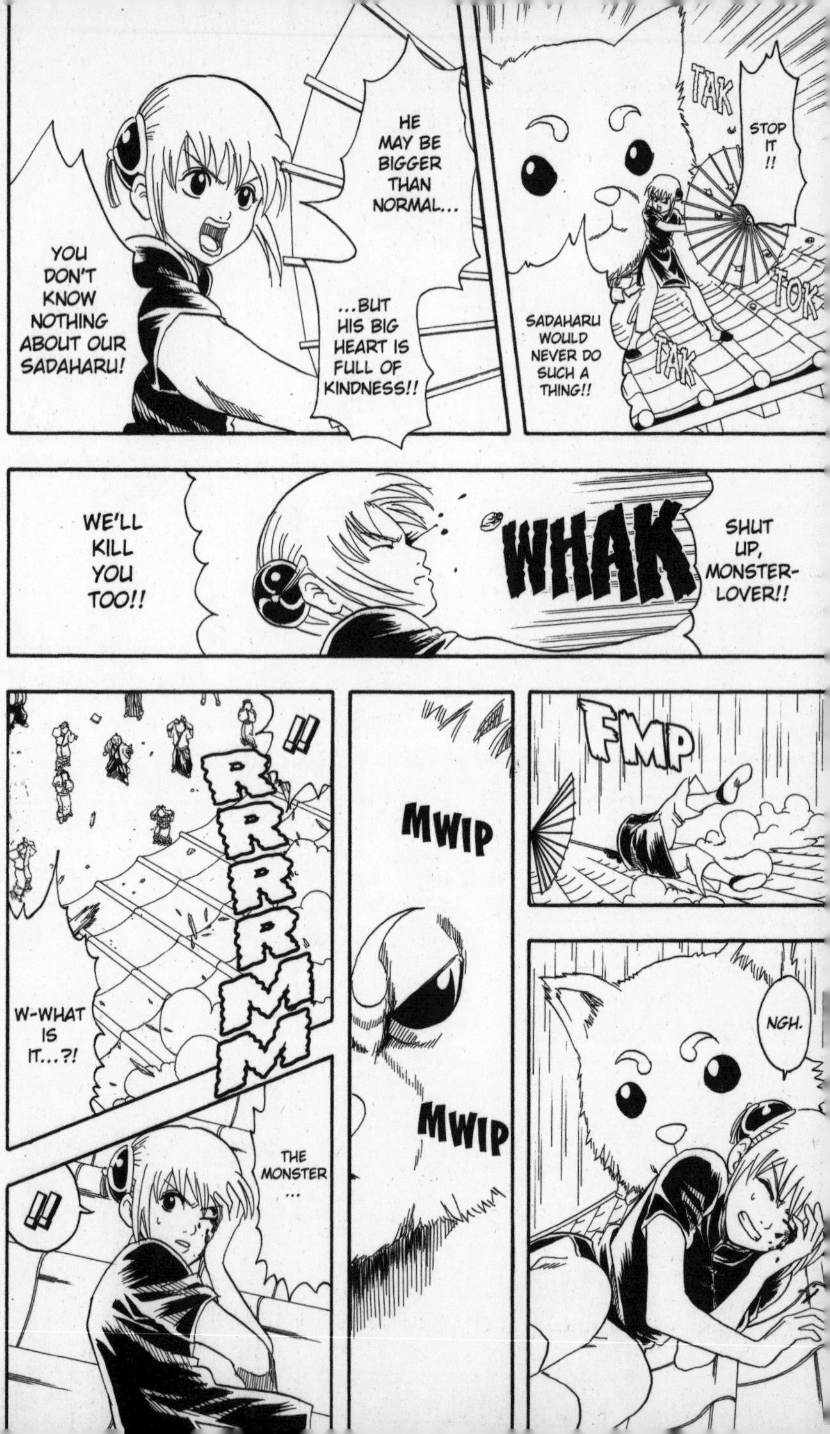
TAK
STOP IT!!
TOK
TAK
SADAHARU WOULD NEVER DO SUCH A THING!!
HE MAY BE BIGGER THAN NORMAL...
...BUT HIS BIG HEART IS FULL OF KINDNESS!!
YOU DON'T KNOW NOTHING ABOUT OUR SADAHARU!
SHUT UP, MONSTER-LOVER!!
WHAK
WE'LL KILL YOU TOO!!
FMP
NGH.
MWIP
MWIP
!!
RRRRMMM
W-WHAT IS IT...?!
THE MONSTER...
!!

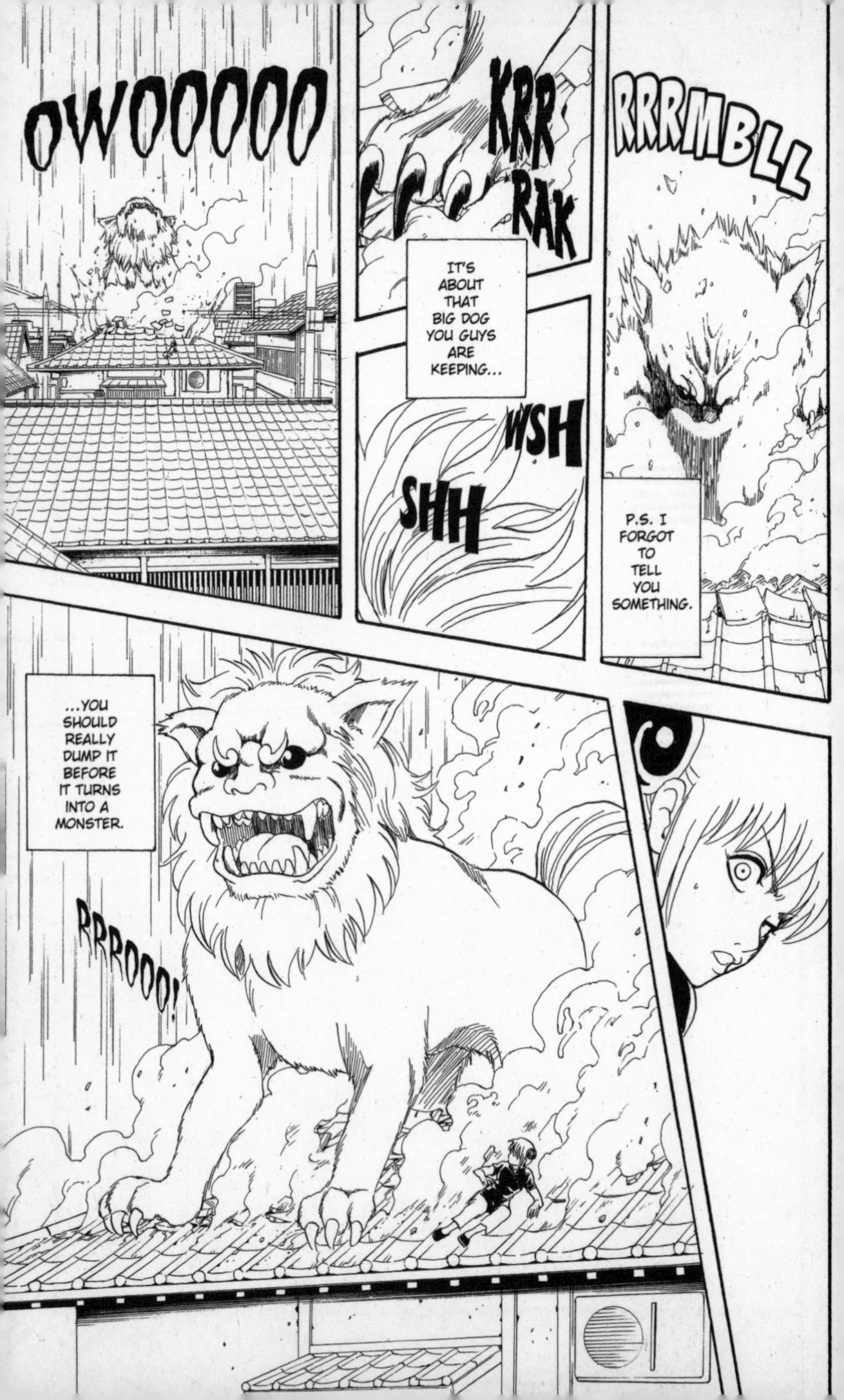
RRRMBLL
P.S. I FORGOT TO TELL YOU SOMETHING.
KRR RAK
IT'S ABOUT THAT BIG DOG YOU GUYS ARE KEEPING...
WSH
SHH
OWOOOOO
...YOU SHOULD REALLY DUMP IT BEFORE IT TURNS INTO A MONSTER.
RRROOO!

Sorachi's Q&A Corner #19

<From Mogutan-san of Osaka.>

Is Tasuke, Hamko's boyfriend, also Mamushi's son? What happened to Hamko and Tasuke after?

<Answer>

You're right, Mogutan. Tasuke, the son of Mamushi, is the same as Tasuke, Hamko's boyfriend. Now that Mamushi has been arrested, he went straight and is now working as a steeplejack. Hamko got obsessed with dieting and managed to lose 65 pounds in two months, but she's still butt-ugly. By the way, they're not dating anymore. They broke up. You know how it goes.

(Q&A #20 is on page 126)

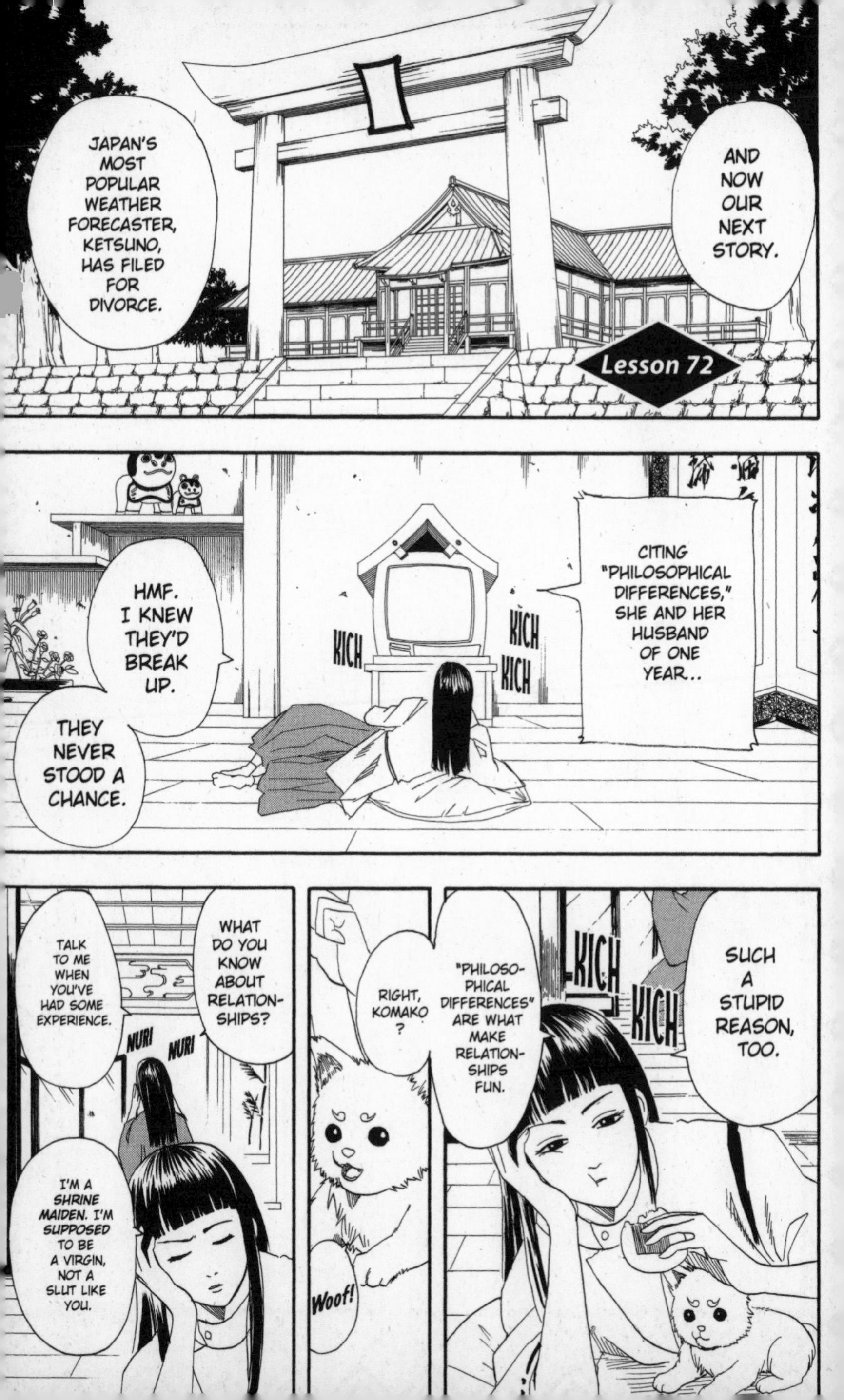
AND NOW OUR NEXT STORY.
Lesson 72
JAPAN'S MOST POPULAR WEATHER FORECASTER, KETSUNO, HAS FILED FOR DIVORCE.
CITING "PHILOSOPHICAL DIFFERENCES," SHE AND HER HUSBAND OF ONE YEAR...
KICH KICH
KICH
HMF. I KNEW THEY'D BREAK UP.
THEY NEVER STOOD A CHANCE.
SUCH A STUPID REASON, TOO.
KICH KICH
"PHILOSO-PHICAL DIFFERENCES" ARE WHAT MAKE RELATION-SHIPS FUN.
RIGHT, KOMAKO?
Woof!
WHAT DO YOU KNOW ABOUT RELATION-SHIPS?
TALK TO ME WHEN YOU'VE HAD SOME EXPERIENCE.
NURI NURI
I'M A SHRINE MAIDEN. I'M SUPPOSED TO BE A VIRGIN, NOT A SLUT LIKE YOU.

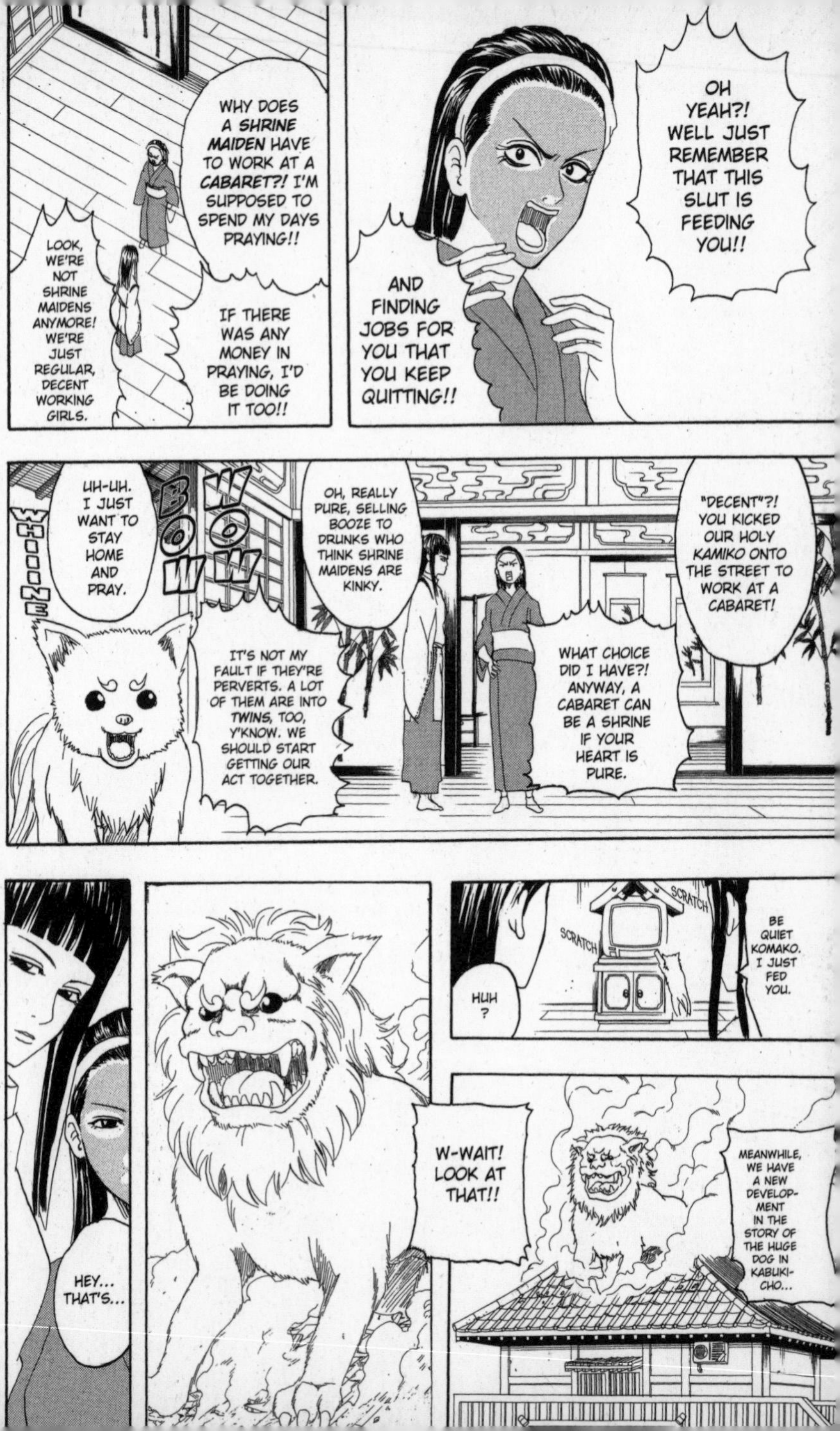
OH YEAH?! WELL JUST REMEMBER THAT THIS SLUT IS FEEDING YOU!!
AND FINDING JOBS FOR YOU THAT YOU KEEP QUITTING!!
WHY DOES A SHRINE MAIDEN HAVE TO WORK AT A CABARET?! I'M SUPPOSED TO SPEND MY DAYS PRAYING!!
IF THERE WAS ANY MONEY IN PRAYING, I'D BE DOING IT TOO!!
LOOK, WE'RE NOT SHRINE MAIDENS ANYMORE! WE'RE JUST REGULAR, DECENT WORKING GIRLS.
"DECENT"?! YOU KICKED OUR HOLY KAMIKO ONTO THE STREET TO WORK AT A CABARET!
WHAT CHOICE DID I HAVE?! ANYWAY, A CABARET CAN BE A SHRINE IF YOUR HEART IS PURE.
OH, REALLY PURE, SELLING BOOZE TO DRUNKS WHO THINK SHRINE MAIDENS ARE KINKY.
IT'S NOT MY FAULT IF THEY'RE PERVERTS. A LOT OF THEM ARE INTO TWINS, TOO, Y'KNOW. WE SHOULD START GETTING OUR ACT TOGETHER.
BOW WOW
UH-UH. I JUST WANT TO STAY HOME AND PRAY.
WHIIIINE
SCRATCH
SCRATCH
BE QUIET KOMAKO. I JUST FED YOU.
HUH ?
MEANWHILE, WE HAVE A NEW DEVELOPMENT IN THE STORY OF THE HUGE DOG IN KABUKI-CHO...
W-WAIT! LOOK AT THAT!!
HEY... THAT'S...

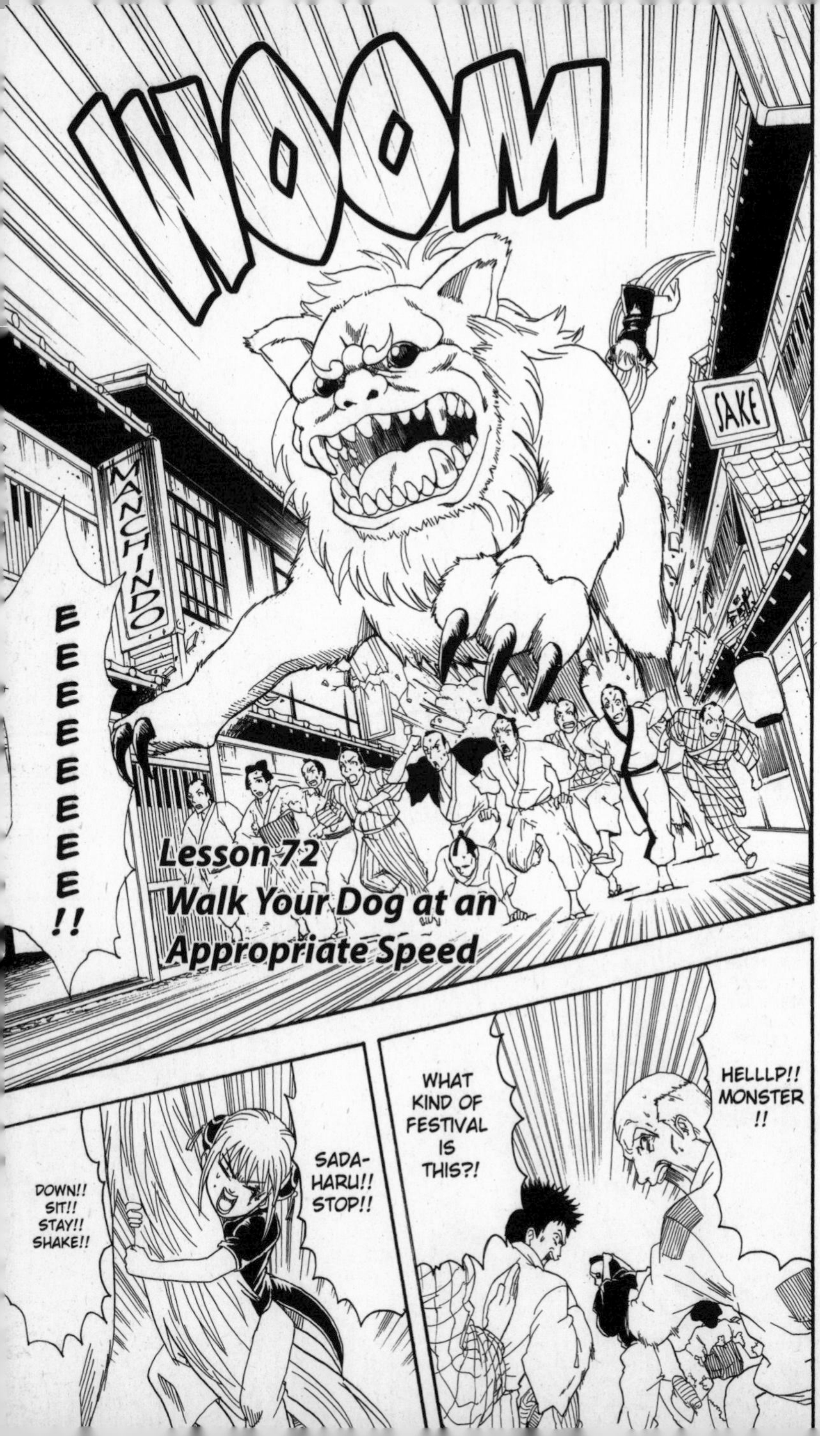
WOOM
SAKE
MANCHINDO
EEEEEEEEEEE!!
Lesson 72
Walk Your Dog at an Appropriate Speed
HELLLP!! MONSTER!!
WHAT KIND OF FESTIVAL IS THIS?!
SADA-HARU!! STOP!!
DOWN!! SIT!! STAY!! SHAKE!!

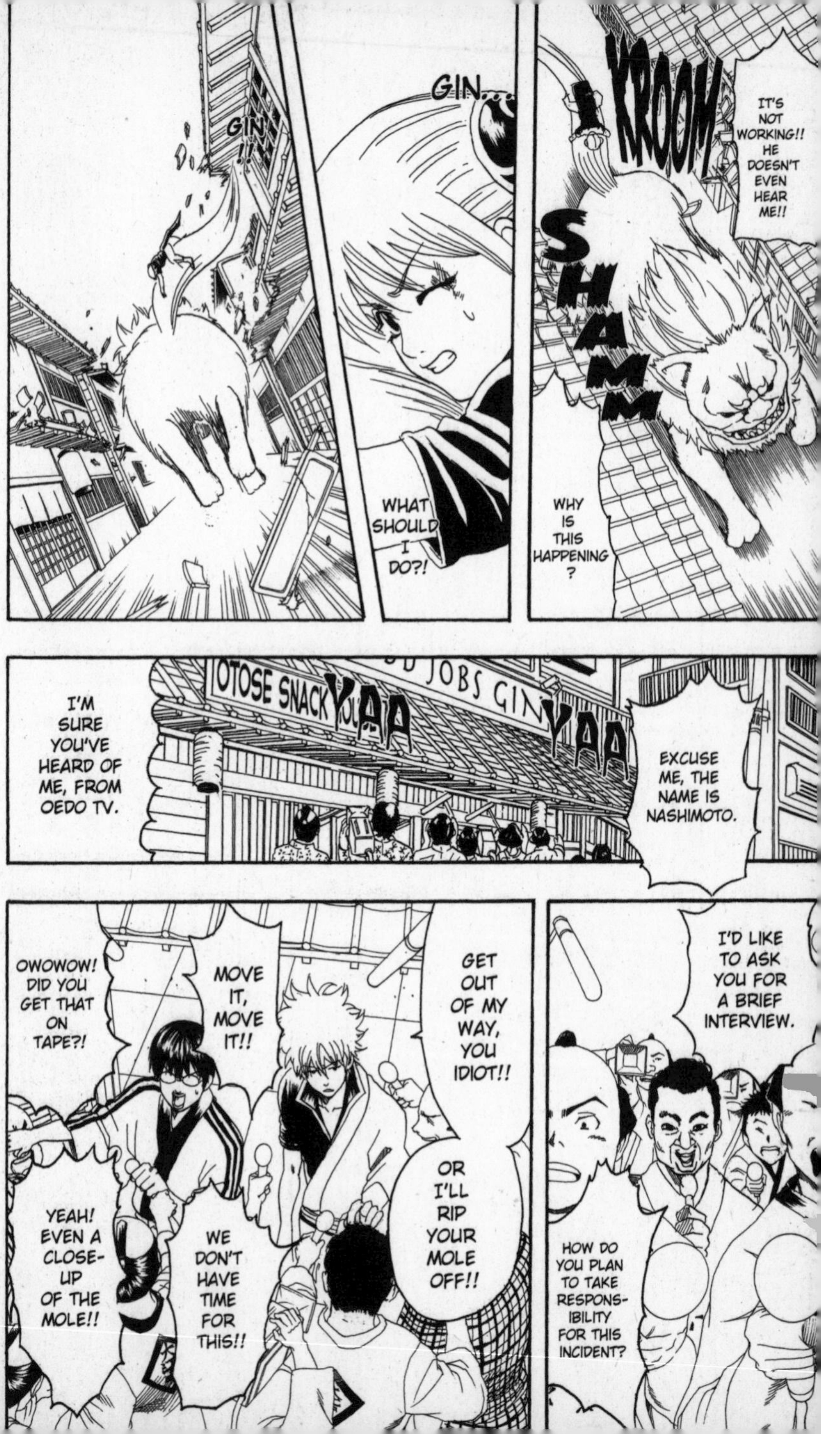
KROOM
IT'S NOT WORKING!! HE DOESN'T EVEN HEAR ME!!
SHAMM
WHY IS THIS HAPPENING?
GIN...
WHAT SHOULD I DO?!
GIN!!
EXCUSE ME, THE NAME IS NASHIMOTO.
YAA
JOBS GIN
YAA
OTOSE SNACK
I'M SURE YOU'VE HEARD OF ME, FROM OEDO TV.
I'D LIKE TO ASK YOU FOR A BRIEF INTERVIEW.
HOW DO YOU PLAN TO TAKE RESPONSIBILITY FOR THIS INCIDENT?
GET OUT OF MY WAY, YOU IDIOT!!
OR I'LL RIP YOUR MOLE OFF!!
MOVE IT, MOVE IT!!
WE DON'T HAVE TIME FOR THIS!!
OWOWOW! DID YOU GET THAT ON TAPE?!
YEAH! EVEN A CLOSE-UP OF THE MOLE!!

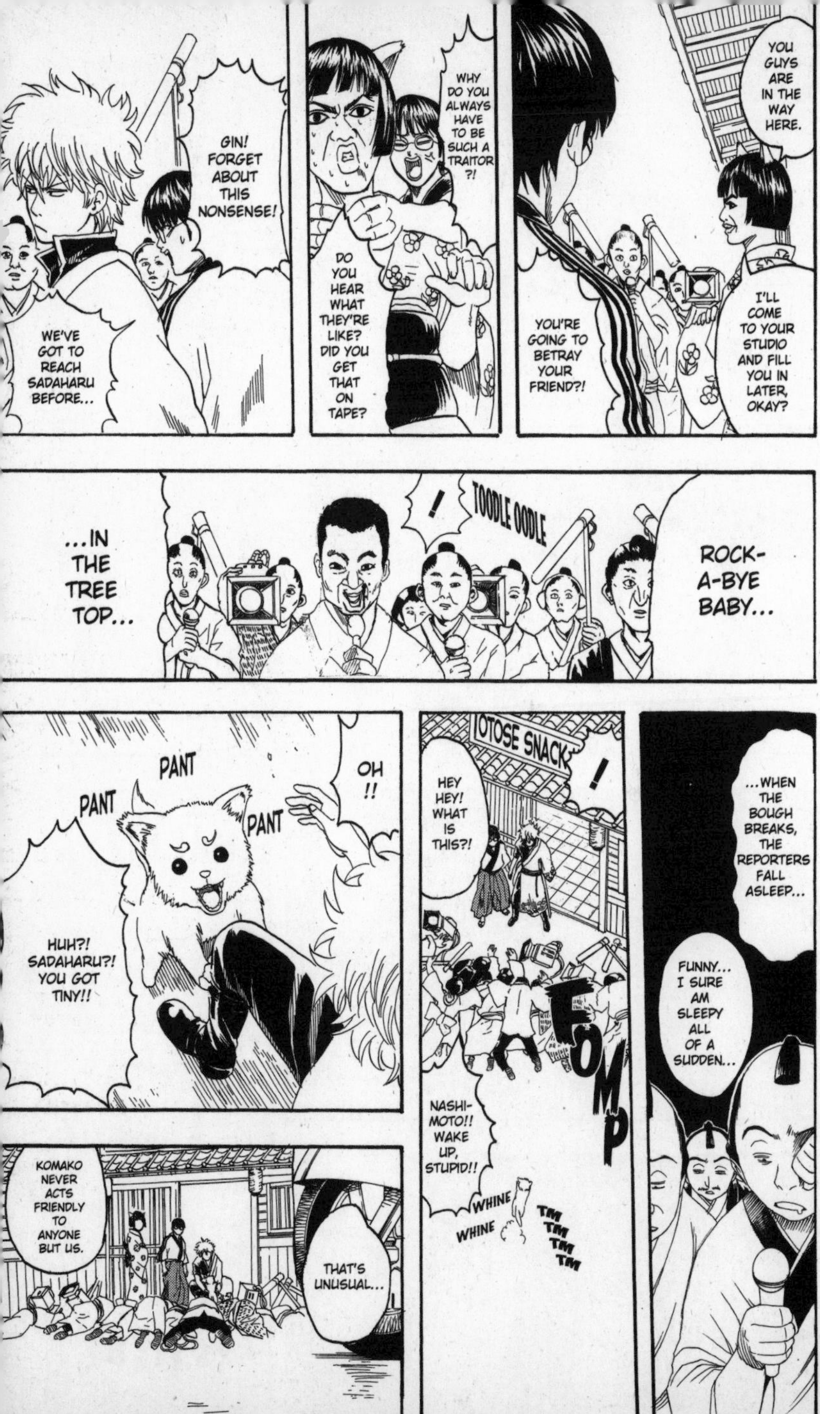
YOU GUYS ARE IN THE WAY HERE.
I'LL COME TO YOUR STUDIO AND FILL YOU IN LATER, OKAY?
YOU'RE GOING TO BETRAY YOUR FRIEND?!
WHY DO YOU ALWAYS HAVE TO BE SUCH A TRAITOR?!
DO YOU HEAR WHAT THEY'RE LIKE? DID YOU GET THAT ON TAPE?
GIN! FORGET ABOUT THIS NONSENSE!
WE'VE GOT TO REACH SADAHARU BEFORE...
ROCK-A-BYE BABY...
TOODLE OODLE
!
...IN THE TREE TOP...
...WHEN THE BOUGH BREAKS, THE REPORTERS FALL ASLEEP...
FUNNY... I SURE AM SLEEPY ALL OF A SUDDEN...
OTOSE SNACK
!
HEY HEY! WHAT IS THIS?!
FOMP
NASHI-MOTO!! WAKE UP, STUPID!!
WHINE
WHINE
TM TM TM TM
OH !!
PANT
PANT
PANT
HUH?! SADAHARU?! YOU GOT TINY!!
KOMAKO NEVER ACTS FRIENDLY TO ANYONE BUT US.
THAT'S UNUSUAL...

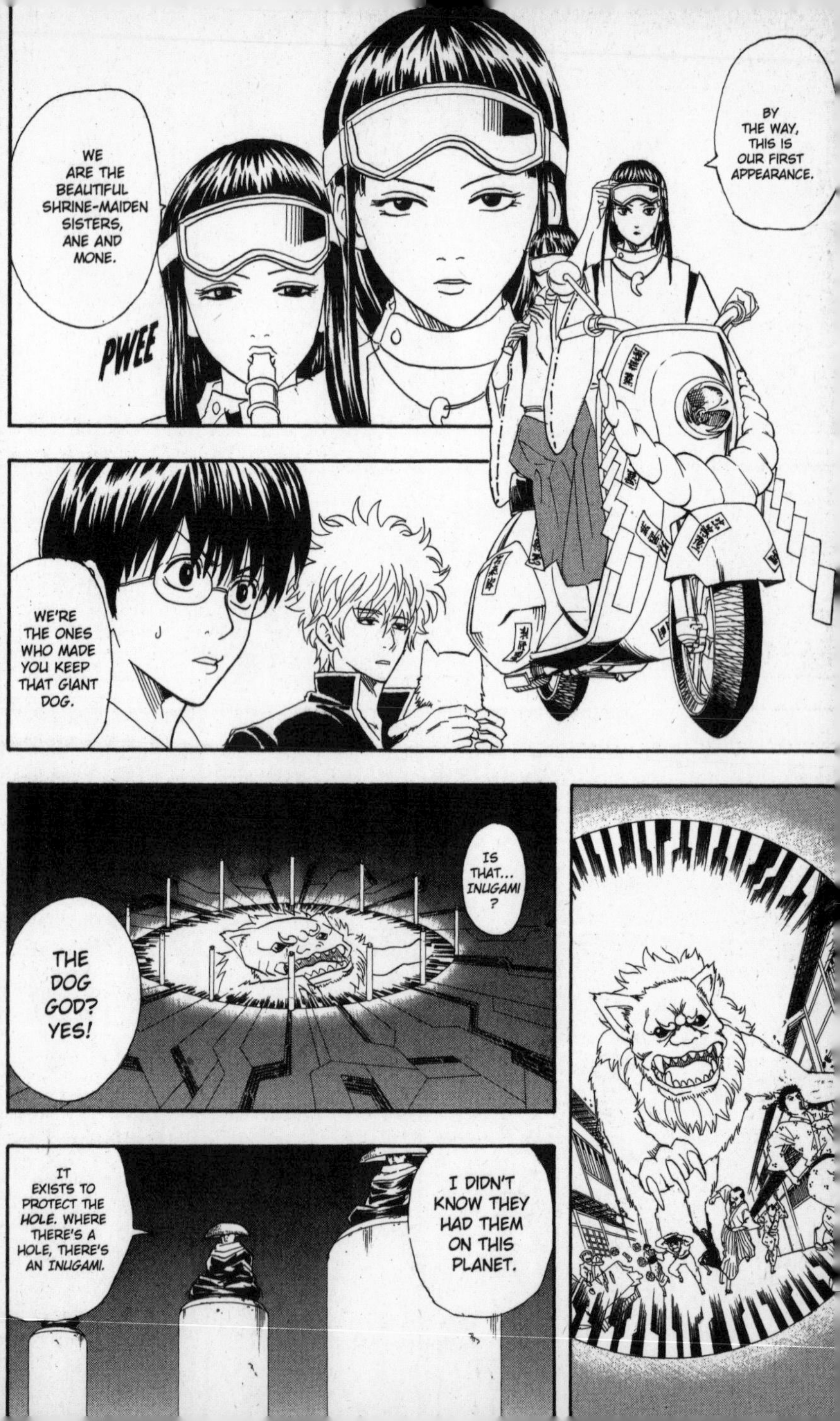
BY THE WAY, THIS IS OUR FIRST APPEARANCE.
WE ARE THE BEAUTIFUL SHRINE-MAIDEN SISTERS, ANE AND MONE.
PWEE
WE'RE THE ONES WHO MADE YOU KEEP THAT GIANT DOG.
IS THAT... INUGAMI ?
THE DOG GOD? YES!
I DIDN'T KNOW THEY HAD THEM ON THIS PLANET.
IT EXISTS TO PROTECT THE HOLE. WHERE THERE'S A HOLE, THERE'S AN INUGAMI.

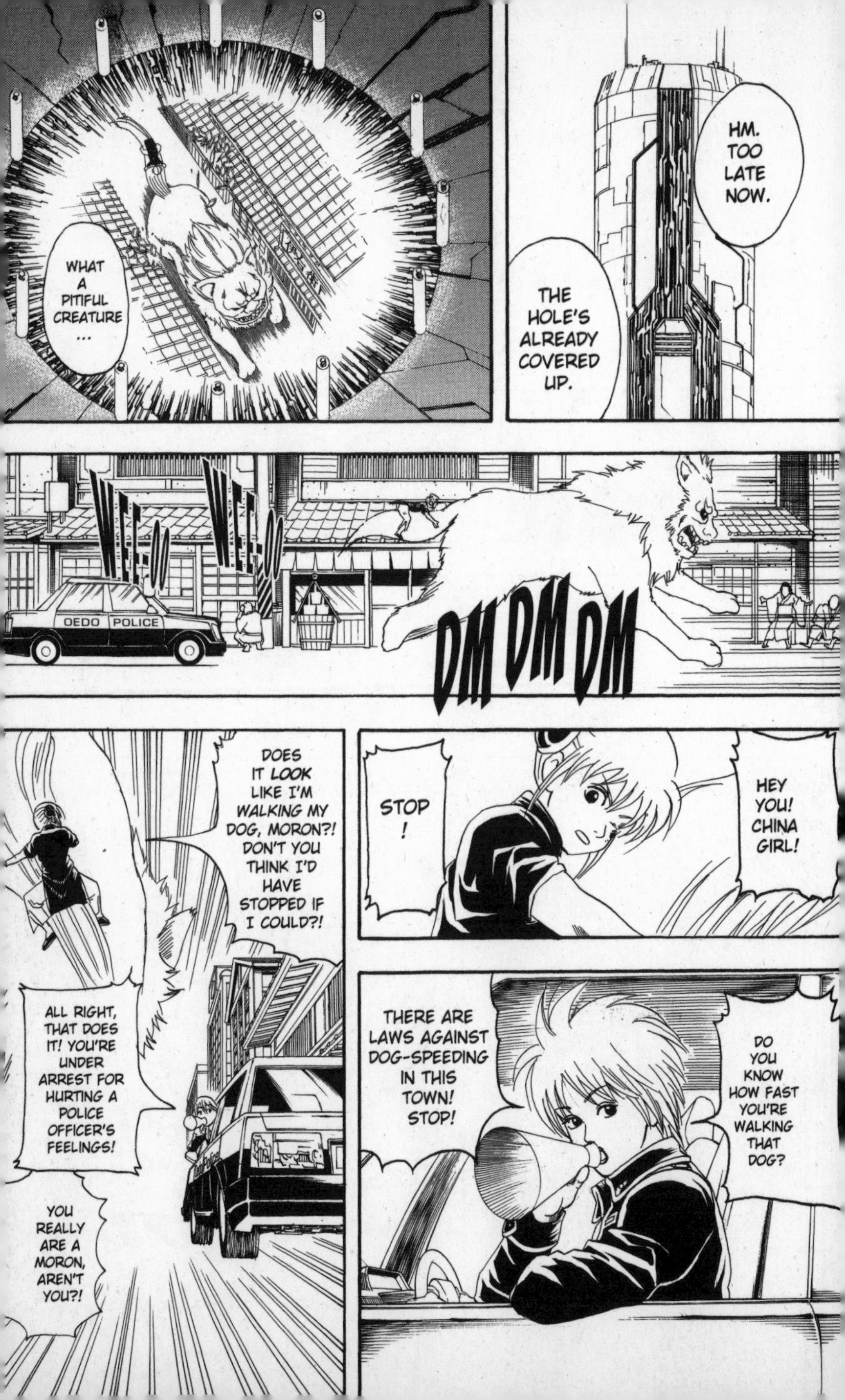
HM. TOO LATE NOW.
THE HOLE'S ALREADY COVERED UP.
WHAT A PITIFUL CREATURE ...
WEE-OO
WEE-OO
DM DM DM
HEY YOU! CHINA GIRL!
STOP!
DO YOU KNOW HOW FAST YOU'RE WALKING THAT DOG?
THERE ARE LAWS AGAINST DOG-SPEEDING IN THIS TOWN! STOP!
DOES IT LOOK LIKE I'M WALKING MY DOG, MORON?! DON'T YOU THINK I'D HAVE STOPPED IF I COULD?!
ALL RIGHT, THAT DOES IT! YOU'RE UNDER ARREST FOR HURTING A POLICE OFFICER'S FEELINGS!
YOU REALLY ARE A MORON, AREN'T YOU?!
OEDO POLICE

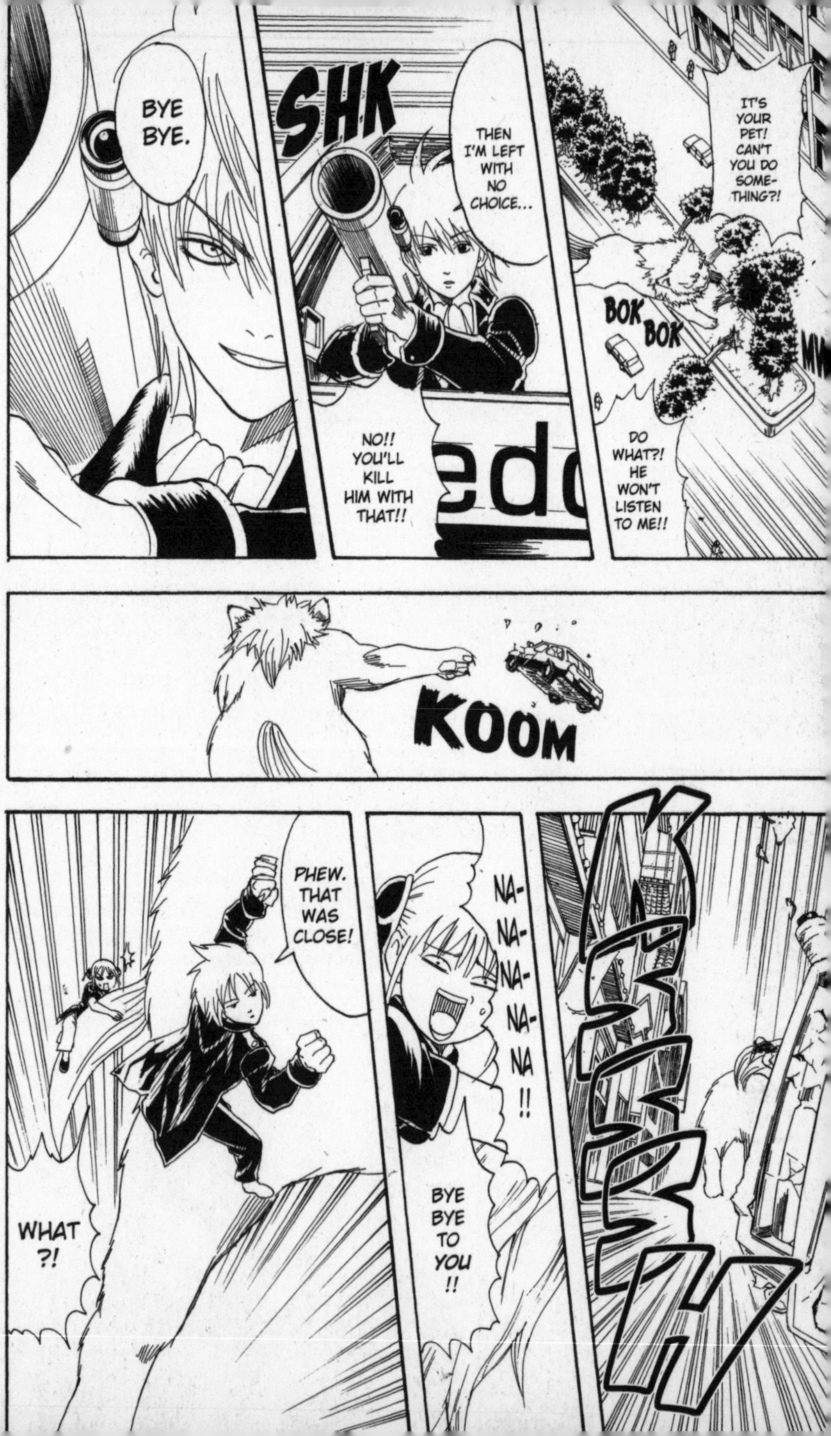
IT'S YOUR PET! CAN'T YOU DO SOMETHING?!
BOK BOK
DO WHAT?! HE WON'T LISTEN TO ME!!
SHK
THEN I'M LEFT WITH NO CHOICE...
NO!! YOU'LL KILL HIM WITH THAT!!
BYE BYE.
KOOM
NA-NA-NA-NA-NA!!
BYE BYE TO YOU!!
PHEW. THAT WAS CLOSE!
WHAT?!

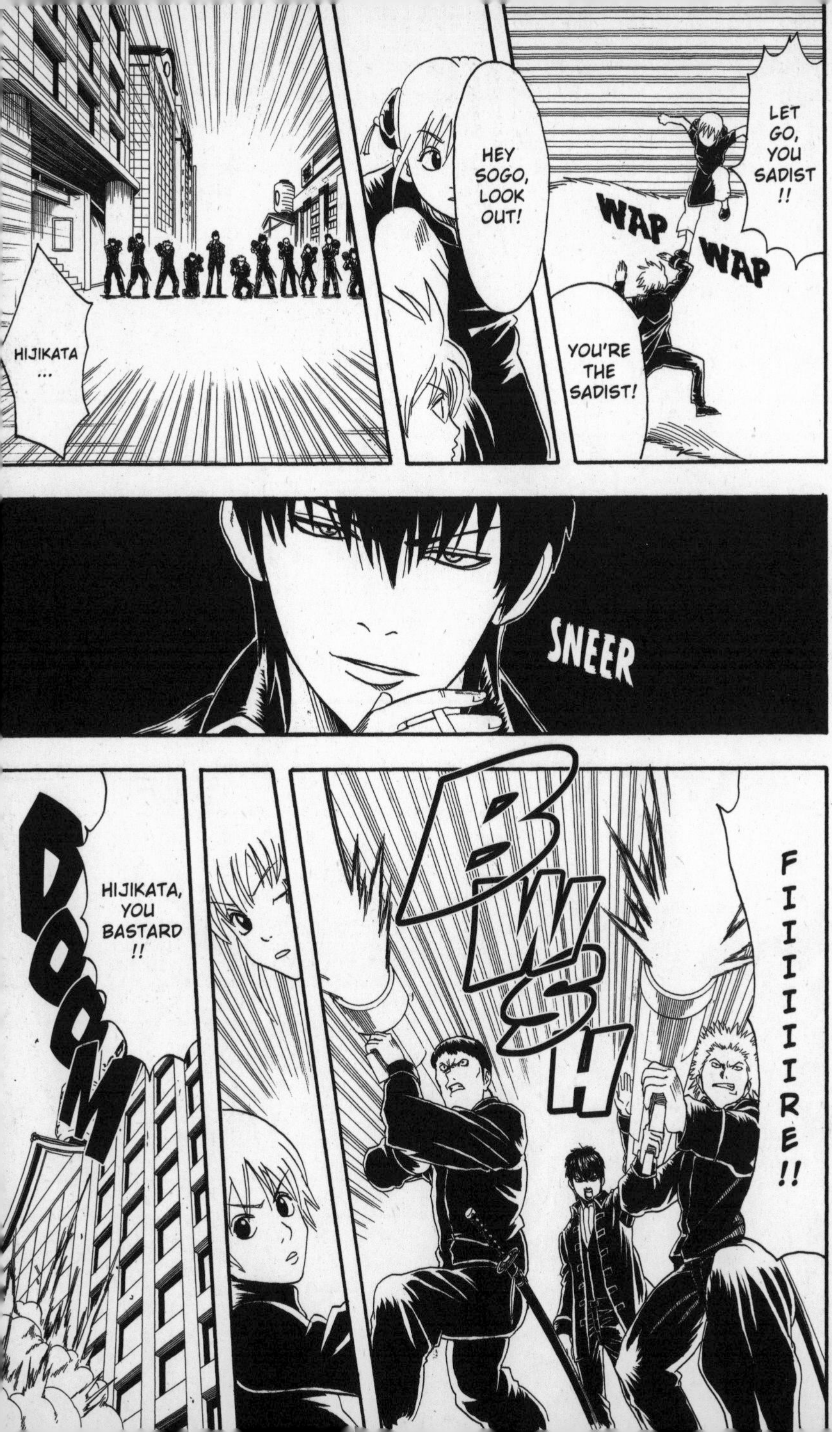
LET GO, YOU SADIST!!
WAP WAP
YOU'RE THE SADIST!
HEY SOGO, LOOK OUT!
HIJIKATA...
SNEER
FIIIIIIRE!!
BWSH
HIJIKATA, YOU BASTARD!!
DOOOM

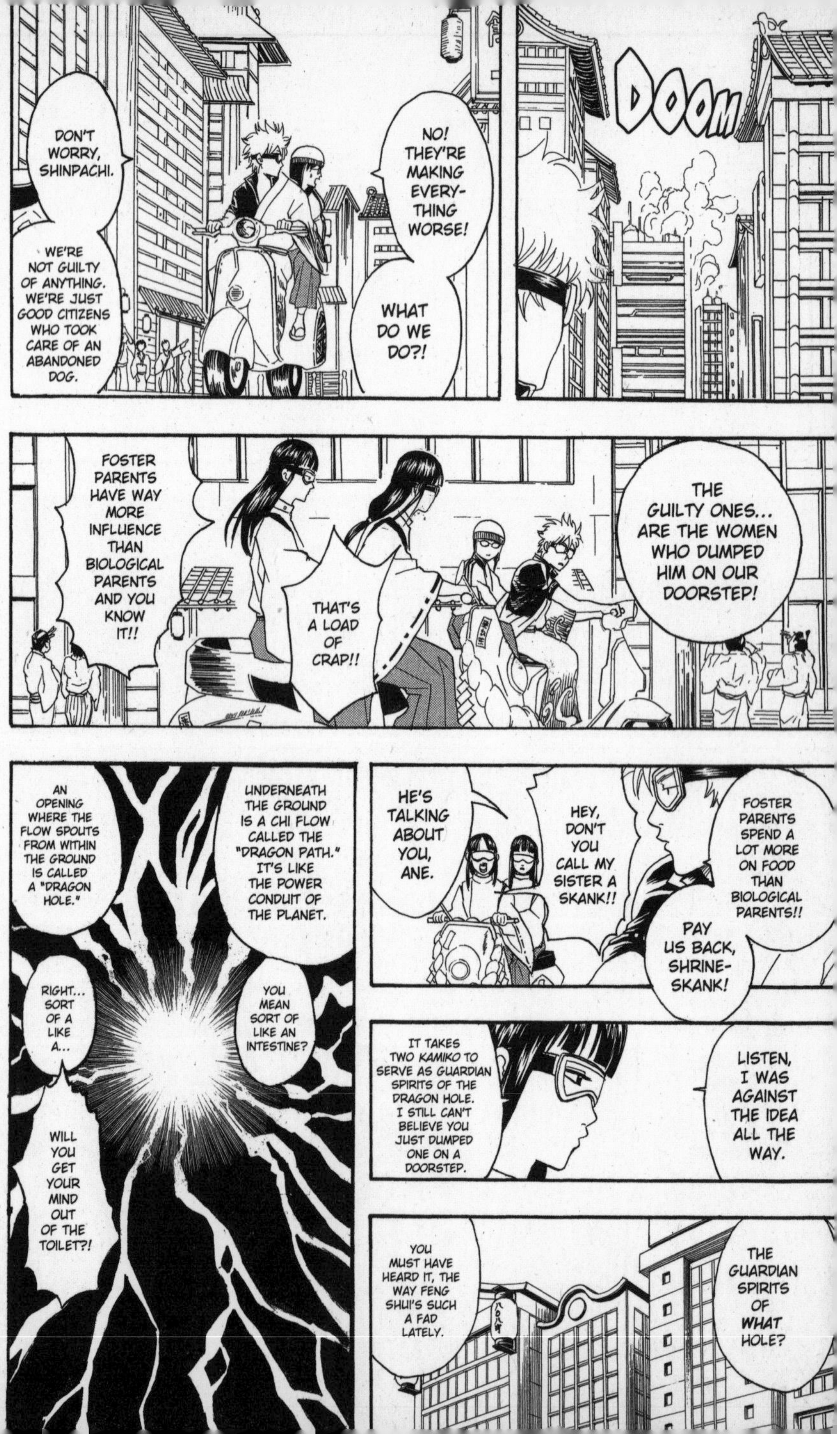
DOOM
NO! THEY'RE MAKING EVERYTHING WORSE!
WHAT DO WE DO?!
DON'T WORRY, SHINPACHI.
WE'RE NOT GUILTY OF ANYTHING. WE'RE JUST GOOD CITIZENS WHO TOOK CARE OF AN ABANDONED DOG.
THE GUILTY ONES... ARE THE WOMEN WHO DUMPED HIM ON OUR DOORSTEP!
THAT'S A LOAD OF CRAP!!
FOSTER PARENTS HAVE WAY MORE INFLUENCE THAN BIOLOGICAL PARENTS AND YOU KNOW IT!!
FOSTER PARENTS SPEND A LOT MORE ON FOOD THAN BIOLOGICAL PARENTS!!
PAY US BACK, SHRINE-SKANK!
HEY, DON'T YOU CALL MY SISTER A SKANK!!
HE'S TALKING ABOUT YOU, ANE.
LISTEN, I WAS AGAINST THE IDEA ALL THE WAY.
IT TAKES TWO KAMIKO TO SERVE AS GUARDIAN SPIRITS OF THE DRAGON HOLE. I STILL CAN'T BELIEVE YOU JUST DUMPED ONE ON A DOORSTEP.
THE GUARDIAN SPIRITS OF WHAT HOLE?
YOU MUST HAVE HEARD IT, THE WAY FENG SHUI'S SUCH A FAD LATELY.
UNDERNEATH THE GROUND IS A CHI FLOW CALLED THE "DRAGON PATH." IT'S LIKE THE POWER CONDUIT OF THE PLANET.
AN OPENING WHERE THE FLOW SPOUTS FROM WITHIN THE GROUND IS CALLED A "DRAGON HOLE."
YOU MEAN SORT OF LIKE AN INTESTINE?
RIGHT... SORT OF A LIKE A...
WILL YOU GET YOUR MIND OUT OF THE TOILET?!

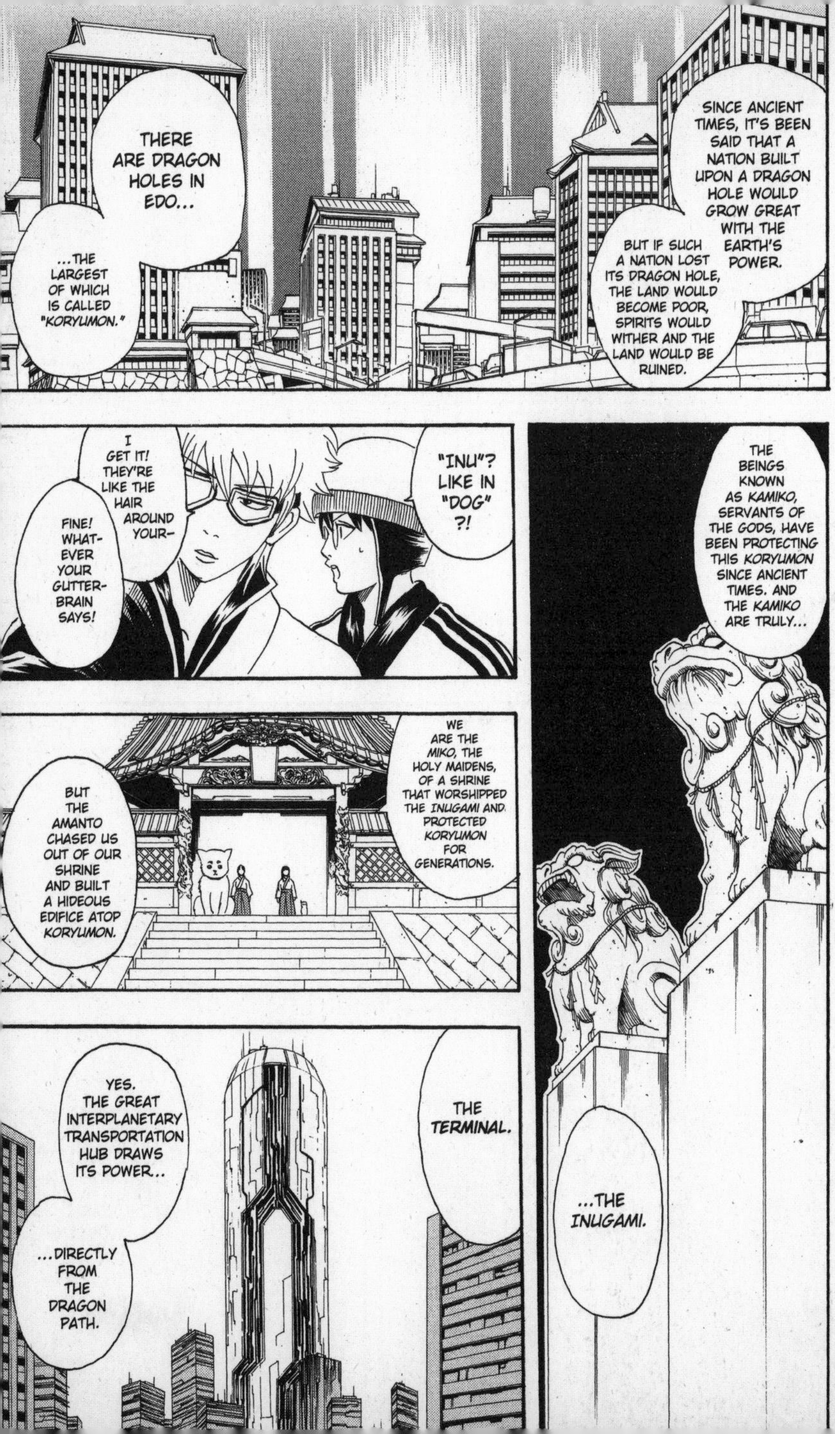
SINCE ANCIENT TIMES, IT'S BEEN SAID THAT A NATION BUILT UPON A DRAGON HOLE WOULD GROW GREAT WITH THE EARTH'S POWER.
BUT IF SUCH A NATION LOST ITS DRAGON HOLE, THE LAND WOULD BECOME POOR, SPIRITS WOULD WITHER AND THE LAND WOULD BE RUINED.
THERE ARE DRAGON HOLES IN EDO...
...THE LARGEST OF WHICH IS CALLED "KORYUMON."
THE BEINGS KNOWN AS KAMIKO, SERVANTS OF THE GODS, HAVE BEEN PROTECTING THIS KORYUMON SINCE ANCIENT TIMES. AND THE KAMIKO ARE TRULY...
...THE INUGAMI.
"INU"? LIKE IN "DOG" ?!
I GET IT! THEY'RE LIKE THE HAIR AROUND YOUR-
FINE! WHATEVER YOUR GUTTER-BRAIN SAYS!
WE ARE THE MIKO, THE HOLY MAIDENS, OF A SHRINE THAT WORSHIPPED THE INUGAMI AND PROTECTED KORYUMON FOR GENERATIONS.
BUT THE AMANTO CHASED US OUT OF OUR SHRINE AND BUILT A HIDEOUS EDIFICE ATOP KORYUMON.
THE TERMINAL.
YES. THE GREAT INTERPLANETARY TRANSPORTATION HUB DRAWS ITS POWER...
...DIRECTLY FROM THE DRAGON PATH.

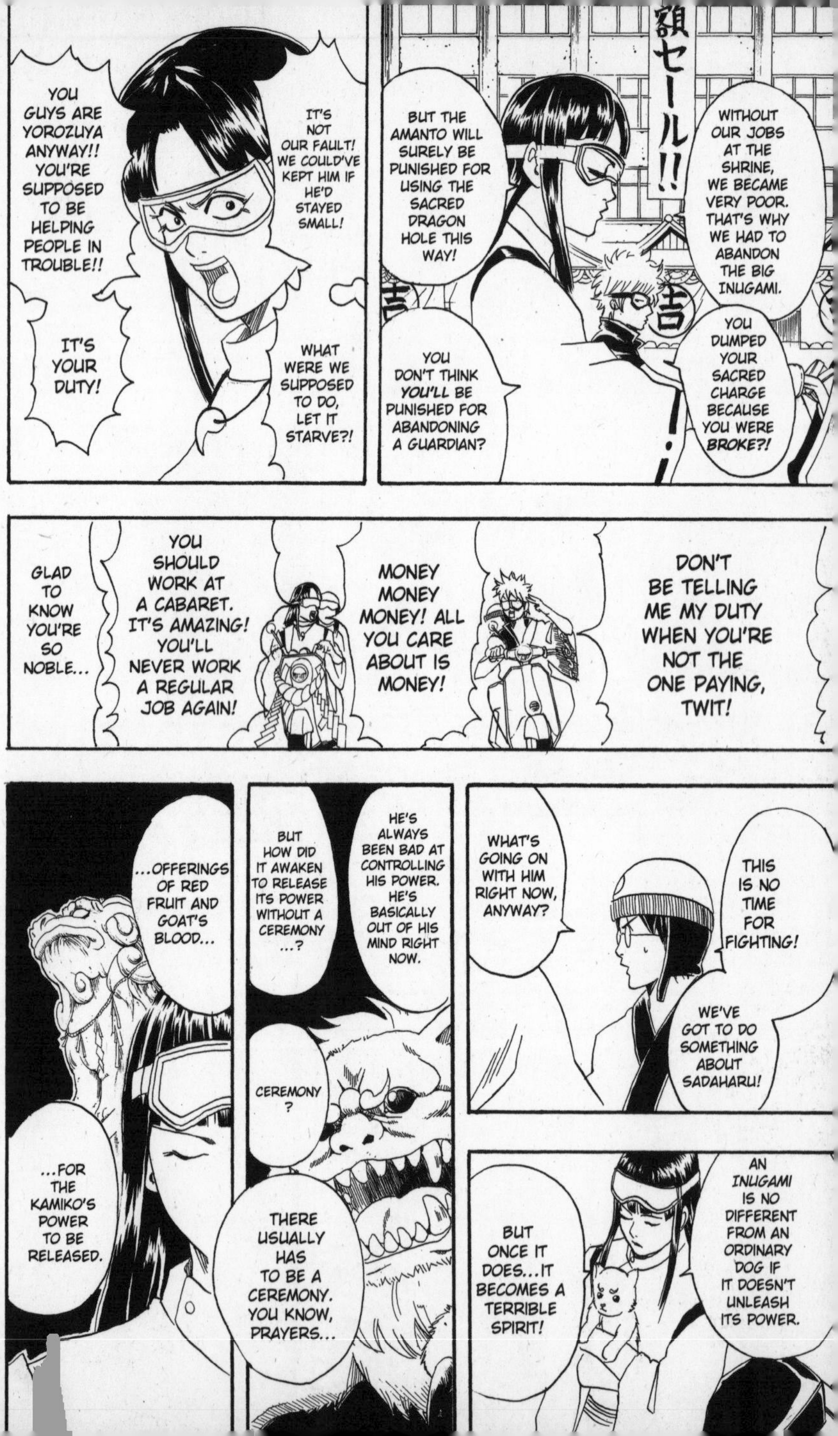

WITHOUT OUR JOBS AT THE SHRINE, WE BECAME VERY POOR. THAT'S WHY WE HAD TO ABANDON THE BIG INUGAMI.
額セール!!
YOU DUMPED YOUR SACRED CHARGE BECAUSE YOU WERE BROKE?!
BUT THE AMANTO WILL SURELY BE PUNISHED FOR USING THE SACRED DRAGON HOLE THIS WAY!
YOU DON'T THINK YOU'LL BE PUNISHED FOR ABANDONING A GUARDIAN?
IT'S NOT OUR FAULT! WE COULD'VE KEPT HIM IF HE'D STAYED SMALL!
WHAT WERE WE SUPPOSED TO DO, LET IT STARVE?!
YOU GUYS ARE YOROZUYA ANYWAY!! YOU'RE SUPPOSED TO BE HELPING PEOPLE IN TROUBLE!!
IT'S YOUR DUTY!
DON'T BE TELLING ME MY DUTY WHEN YOU'RE NOT THE ONE PAYING, TWIT!
MONEY MONEY MONEY! ALL YOU CARE ABOUT IS MONEY!
YOU SHOULD WORK AT A CABARET. IT'S AMAZING! YOU'LL NEVER WORK A REGULAR JOB AGAIN!
GLAD TO KNOW YOU'RE SO NOBLE...
THIS IS NO TIME FOR FIGHTING!
WE'VE GOT TO DO SOMETHING ABOUT SADAHARU!
WHAT'S GOING ON WITH HIM RIGHT NOW, ANYWAY?
AN INUGAMI IS NO DIFFERENT FROM AN ORDINARY DOG IF IT DOESN'T UNLEASH ITS POWER.
BUT ONCE IT DOES... IT BECOMES A TERRIBLE SPIRIT!
HE'S ALWAYS BEEN BAD AT CONTROLLING HIS POWER. HE'S BASICALLY OUT OF HIS MIND RIGHT NOW.
BUT HOW DID IT AWAKEN TO RELEASE ITS POWER WITHOUT A CEREMONY...?
CEREMONY?
THERE USUALLY HAS TO BE A CEREMONY. YOU KNOW, PRAYERS...
...OFFERINGS OF RED FRUIT AND GOAT'S BLOOD...
...FOR THE KAMIKO'S POWER TO BE RELEASED.

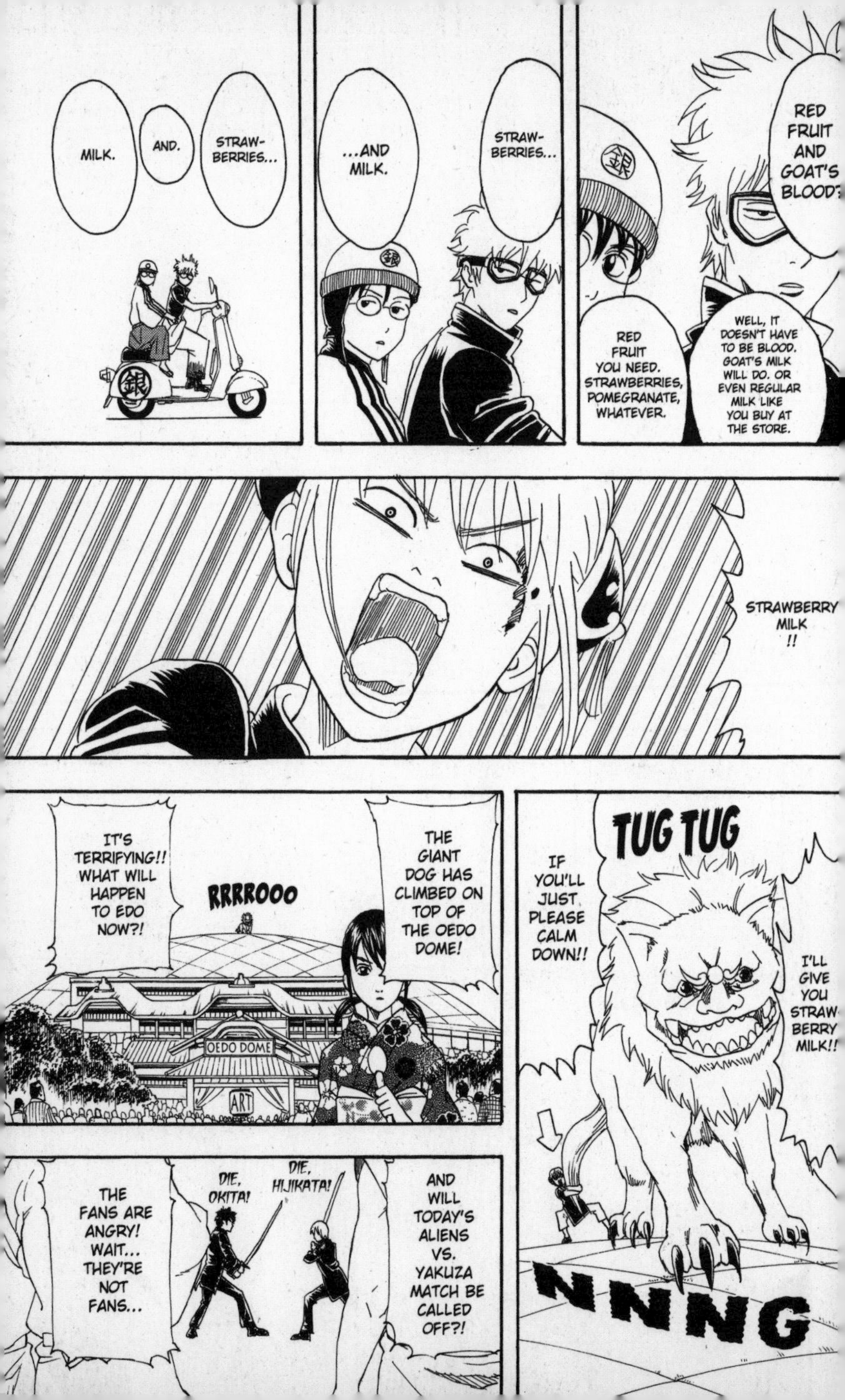
RED FRUIT AND GOAT'S BLOOD?
WELL, IT DOESN'T HAVE TO BE BLOOD. GOAT'S MILK WILL DO. OR EVEN REGULAR MILK LIKE YOU BUY AT THE STORE.
RED FRUIT YOU NEED. STRAWBERRIES, POMEGRANATE, WHATEVER.
STRAW-BERRIES...
...AND MILK.
STRAW-BERRIES...
AND.
MILK.
STRAWBERRY MILK !!
TUG TUG
I'LL GIVE YOU STRAW BERRY MILK!!
IF YOU'LL JUST PLEASE CALM DOWN!!
NNNG
THE GIANT DOG HAS CLIMBED ON TOP OF THE OEDO DOME!
RRRROOO
IT'S TERRIFYING!! WHAT WILL HAPPEN TO EDO NOW?!
OEDO DOME
ART
AND WILL TODAY'S ALIENS VS. YAKUZA MATCH BE CALLED OFF?!
DIE, HIJIKATA!
DIE, OKITA!
THE FANS ARE ANGRY! WAIT... THEY'RE NOT FANS...

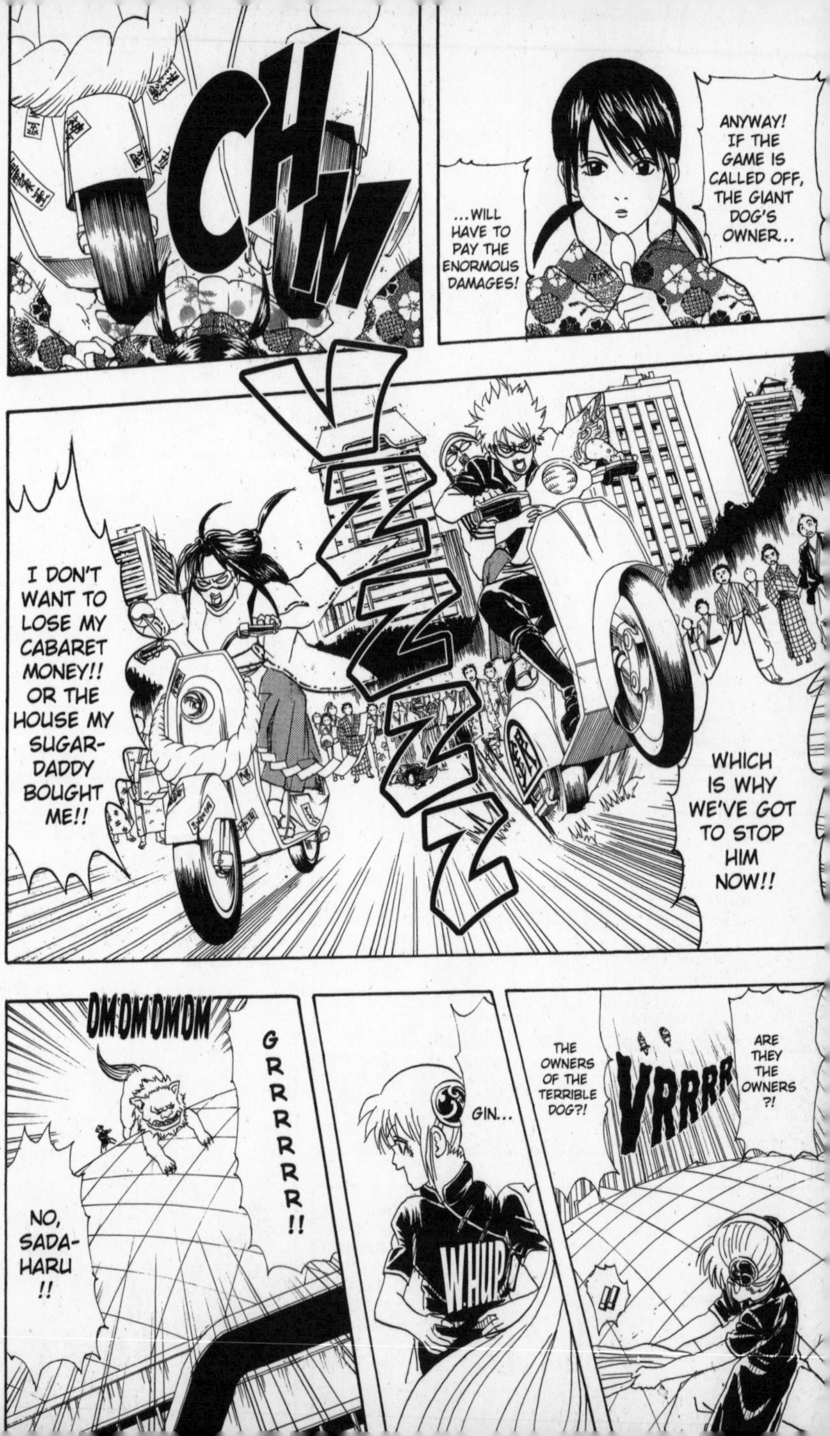
ANYWAY! IF THE GAME IS CALLED OFF, THE GIANT DOG'S OWNER...
...WILL HAVE TO PAY THE ENORMOUS DAMAGES!
CHW
WHICH IS WHY WE'VE GOT TO STOP HIM NOW!!
I DON'T WANT TO LOSE MY CABARET MONEY!! OR THE HOUSE MY SUGAR-DADDY BOUGHT ME!!
ARE THEY THE OWNERS ?!
VRRRR
THE OWNERS OF THE TERRIBLE DOG?!
!!
GIN...
WHUP
DMDMDMDM
GRRRRRR!!
NO, SADA-HARU !!

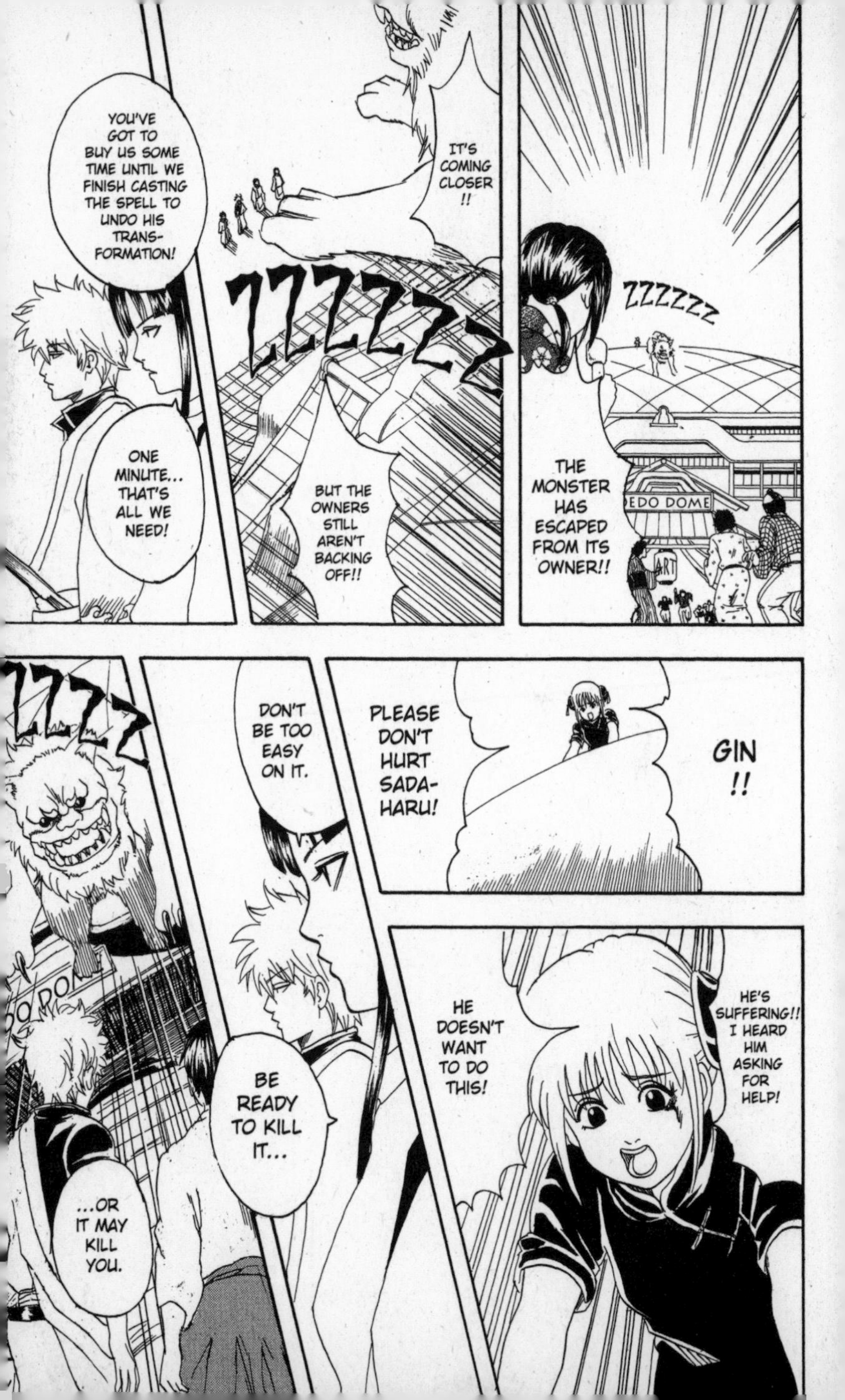
ZZZZZZ
EDO DOME
ART
THE MONSTER HAS ESCAPED FROM ITS OWNER!!
IT'S COMING CLOSER !!
ZZZZZZZ
BUT THE OWNERS STILL AREN'T BACKING OFF!!
YOU'VE GOT TO BUY US SOME TIME UNTIL WE FINISH CASTING THE SPELL TO UNDO HIS TRANS-FORMATION!
ONE MINUTE... THAT'S ALL WE NEED!
GIN !!
PLEASE DON'T HURT SADA-HARU!
HE'S SUFFERING!! I HEARD HIM ASKING FOR HELP!
HE DOESN'T WANT TO DO THIS!
DON'T BE TOO EASY ON IT.
BE READY TO KILL IT...
ZZZZ
...OR IT MAY KILL YOU.

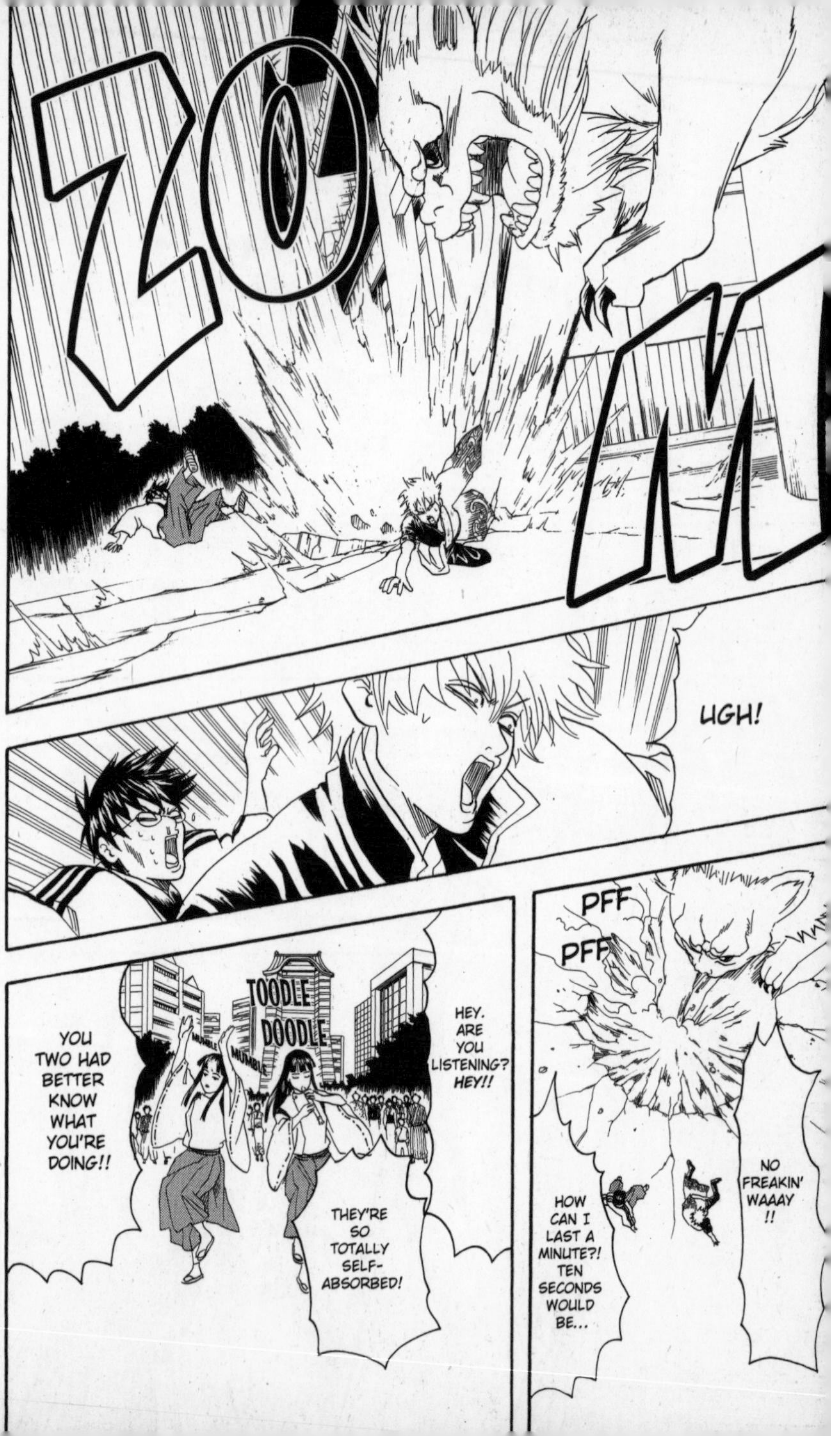
ZOM
UGH!
PFF
PFF
NO FREAKIN' WAAAY!!
HOW CAN I LAST A MINUTE?! TEN SECONDS WOULD BE...
HEY. ARE YOU LISTENING? HEY!!
TOODLE DOODLE
MUMBLE
MUMBLE
YOU TWO HAD BETTER KNOW WHAT YOU'RE DOING!!
THEY'RE SO TOTALLY SELF-ABSORBED!

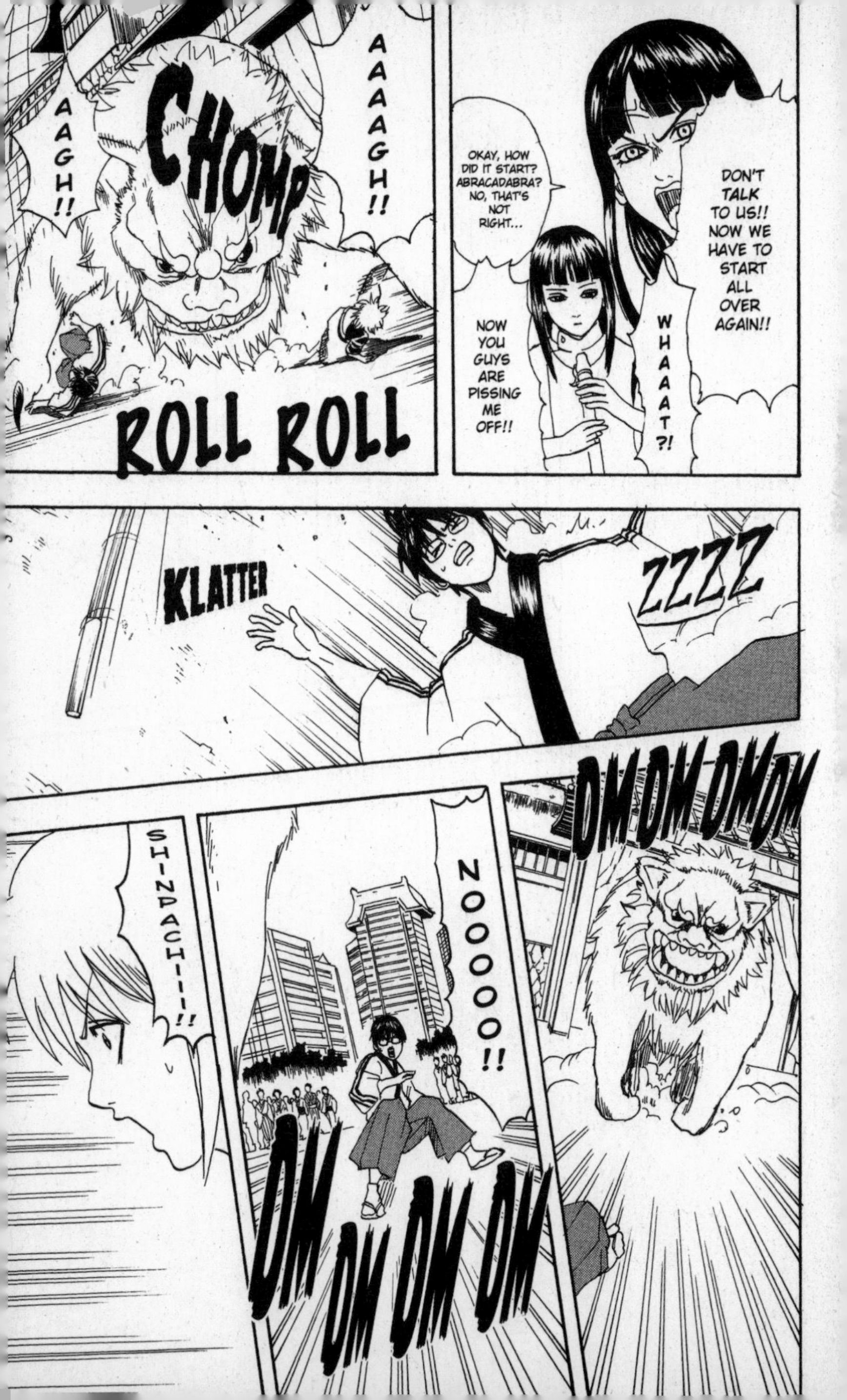

DON'T TALK TO US!! NOW WE HAVE TO START ALL OVER AGAIN!!
OKAY, HOW DID IT START? ABRACADABRA? NO, THAT'S NOT RIGHT...
WHAAAAT?!
NOW YOU GUYS ARE PISSING ME OFF!!
AAAAAGH!!
CHOMP
AAGH!!
ROLL ROLL
ZZZZ
KLATTER
DM DM DMDM
NOOOOOO!!
DM DM DM DM
SHINPACHIII!!

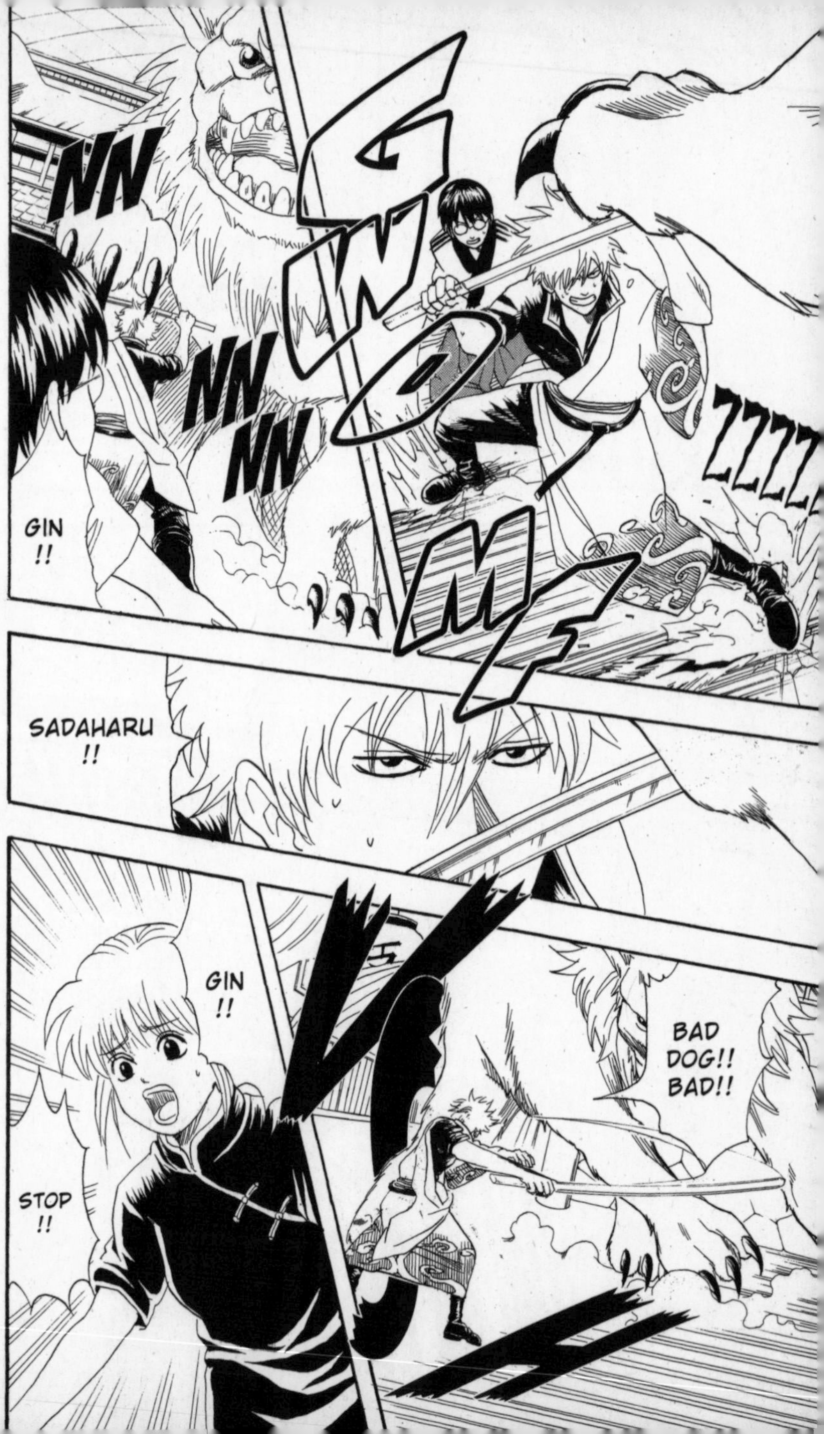
ZZZZ
GWOMF
NN
NN NN
GIN !!
SADAHARU !!
BAD DOG!! BAD!!
GIN !!
STOP !!

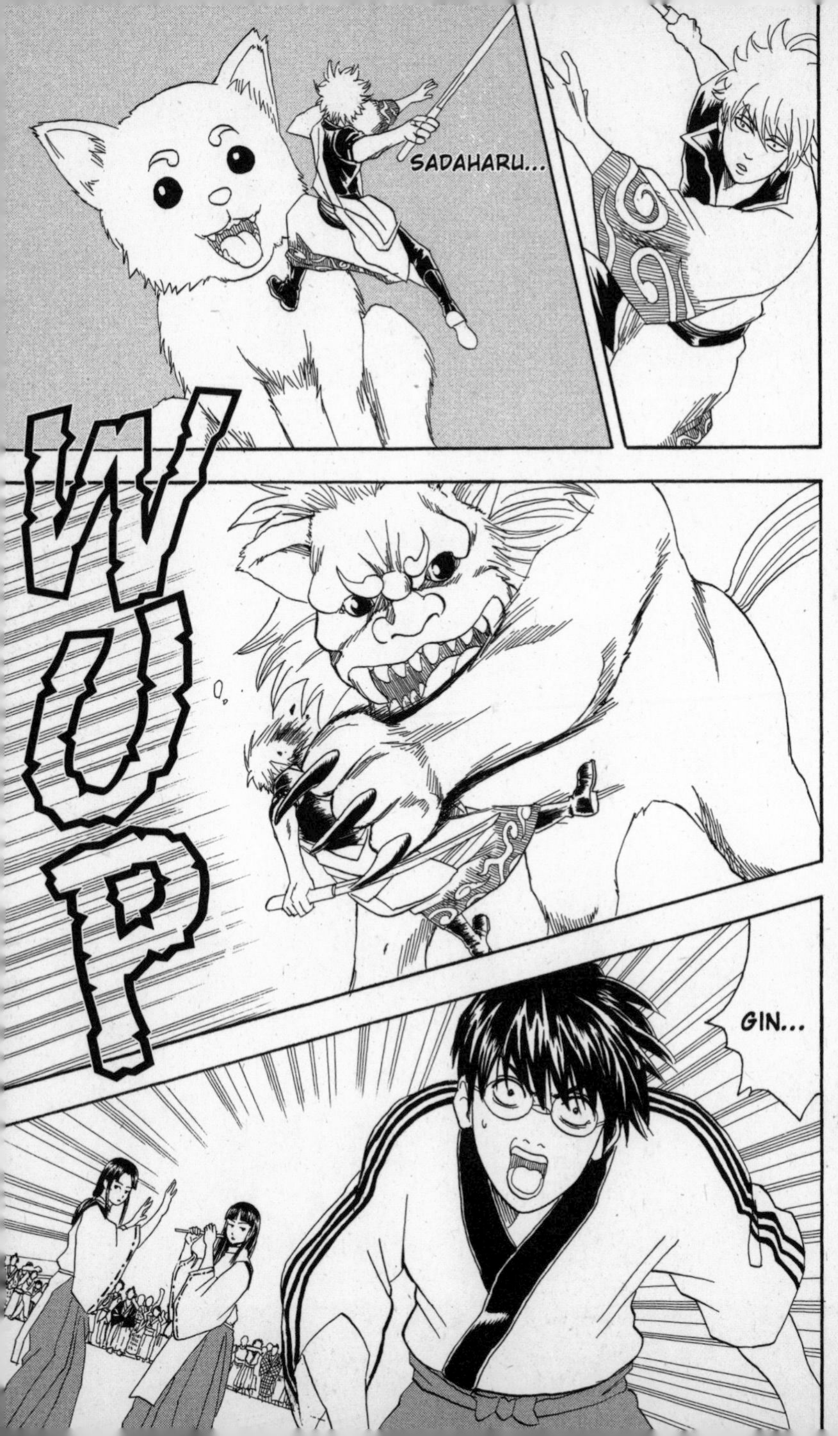
SADAHARU...
WUP
GIN...

Lesson 73
One Bark Is Sweeter than a Million Songs

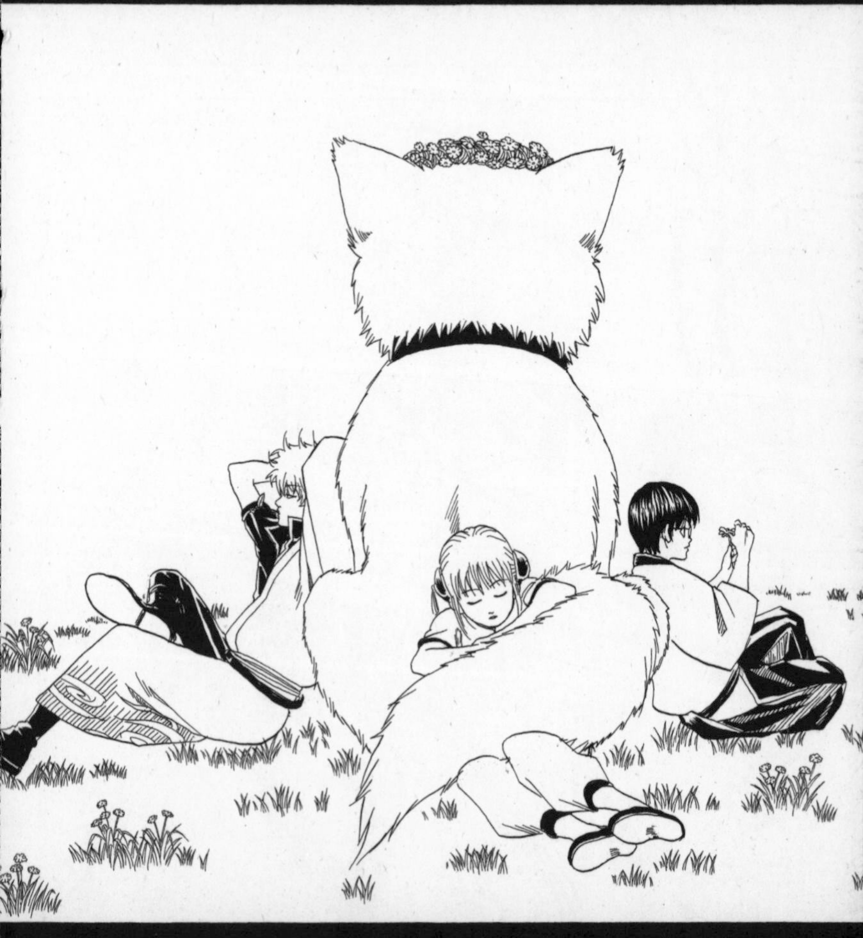

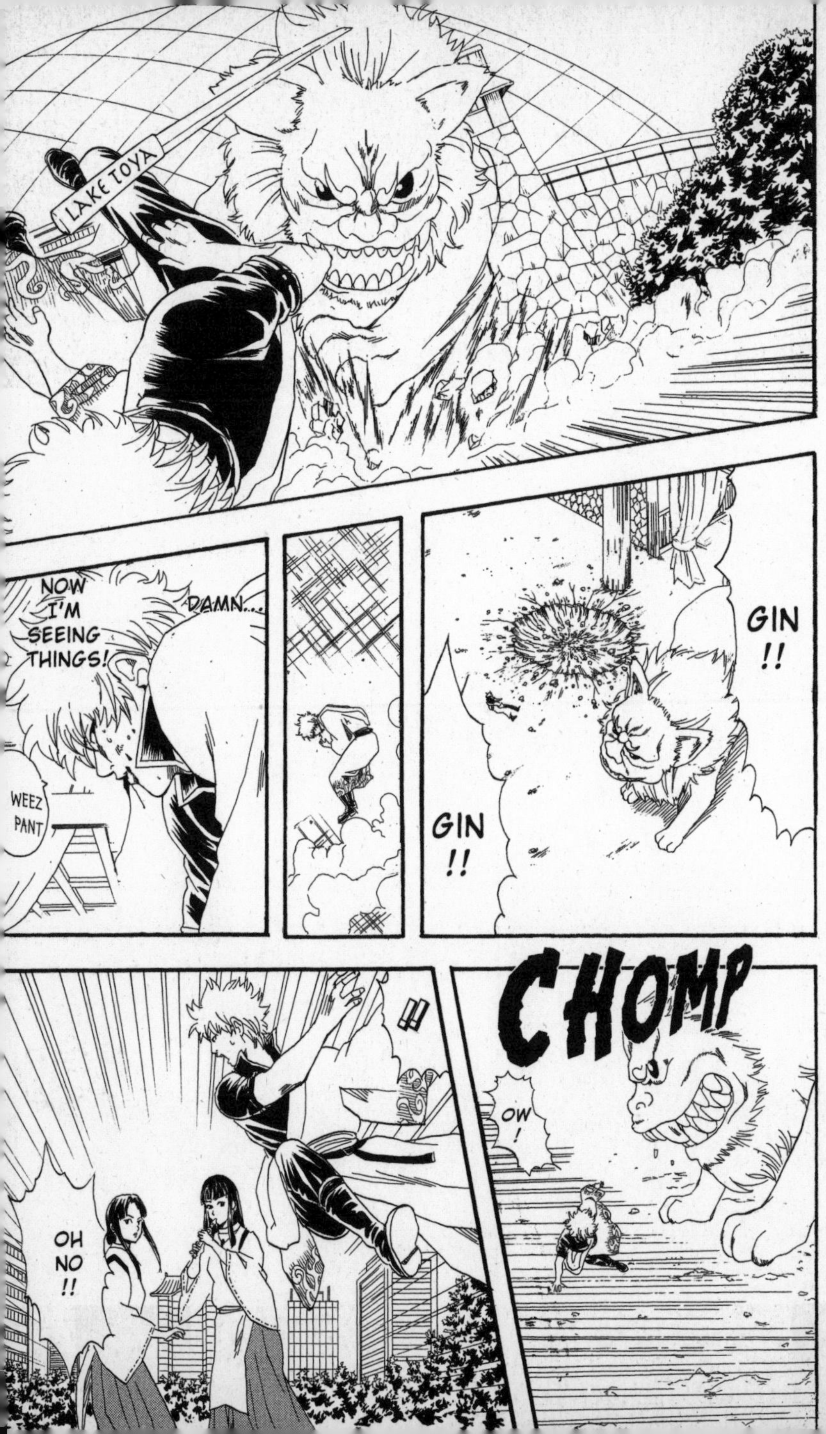
LAKE TOYA
GIN !!
GIN !!
DAMN...
NOW I'M SEEING THINGS!
WEEZ PANT
CHOMP
OW!
!!
OH NO !!

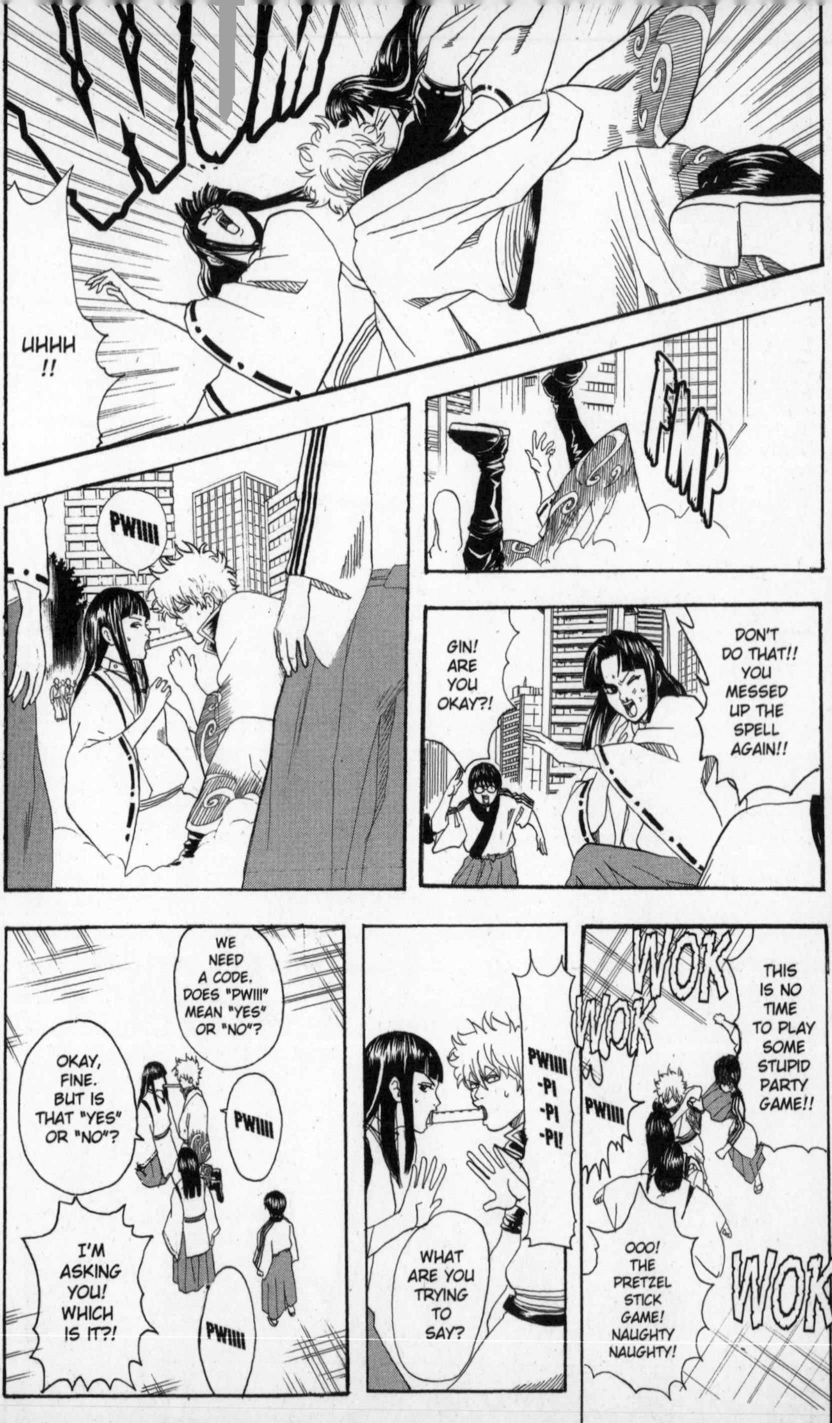

UHHH !!
FMP
PWIIII
DON'T DO THAT!! YOU MESSED UP THE SPELL AGAIN!!
GIN! ARE YOU OKAY?!
WOK
WOK
THIS IS NO TIME TO PLAY SOME STUPID PARTY GAME!!
PWIIII
OOO! THE PRETZEL STICK GAME! NAUGHTY NAUGHTY!
WOK
PWIIII -PI -PI -PI!
WHAT ARE YOU TRYING TO SAY?
WE NEED A CODE. DOES "PWIII" MEAN "YES" OR "NO"?
PWIIII
OKAY, FINE. BUT IS THAT "YES" OR "NO"?
I'M ASKING YOU! WHICH IS IT?!
PWIIII

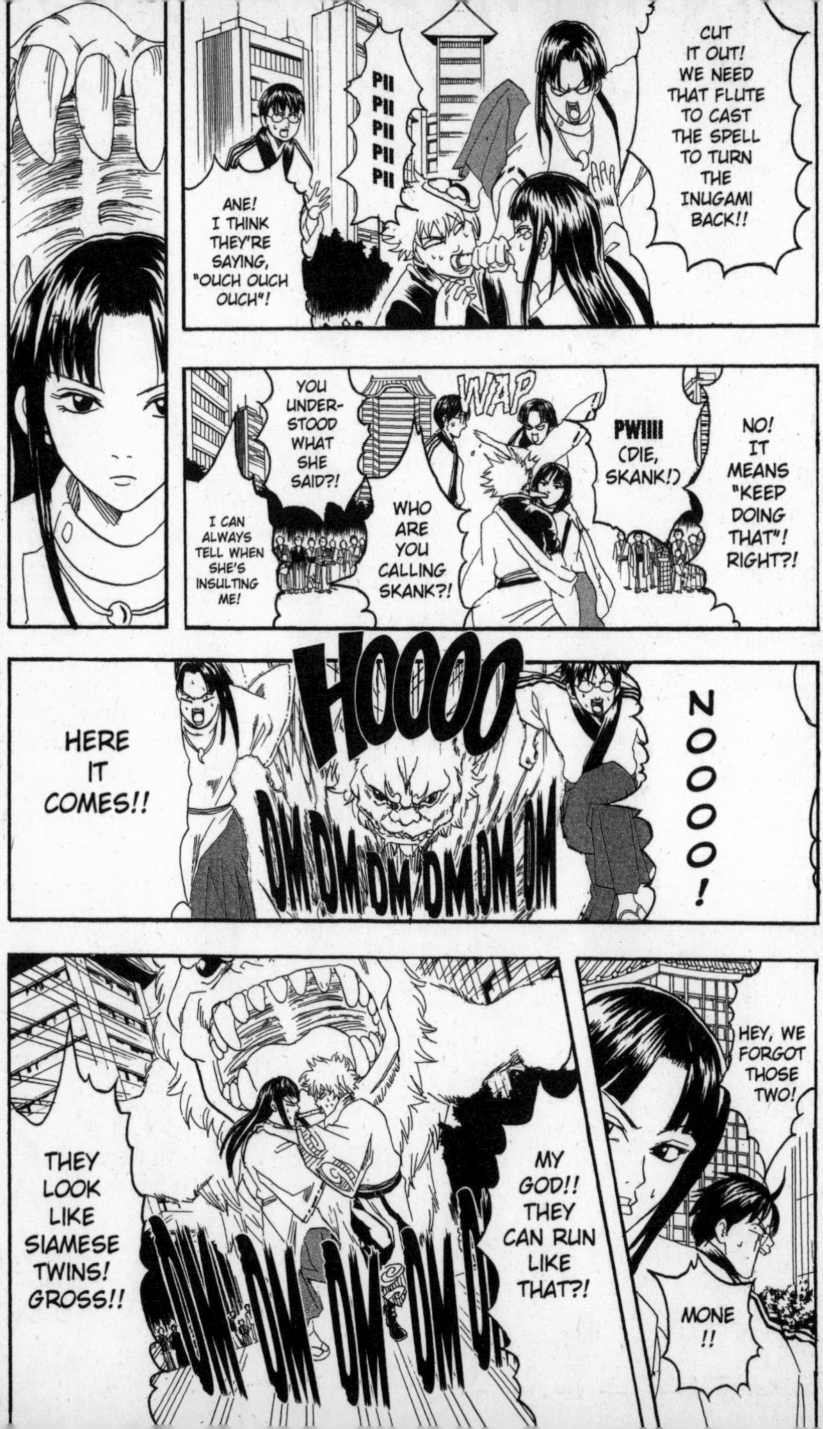
CUT IT OUT! WE NEED THAT FLUTE TO CAST THE SPELL TO TURN THE INUGAMI BACK!!
PII PII PII PII PII
ANE! I THINK THEY'RE SAYING, "OUCH OUCH OUCH"!
NO! IT MEANS "KEEP DOING THAT"! RIGHT?!
PWIIII (DIE, SKANK!)
WAP
YOU UNDER-STOOD WHAT SHE SAID?!
WHO ARE YOU CALLING SKANK?!
I CAN ALWAYS TELL WHEN SHE'S INSULTING ME!
NOOOOO!
HOOOO
DM DM DM DM DM DM
HERE IT COMES!!
HEY, WE FORGOT THOSE TWO!
MONE !!
MY GOD!! THEY CAN RUN LIKE THAT?!
DM DM DM DM
THEY LOOK LIKE SIAMESE TWINS! GROSS!!

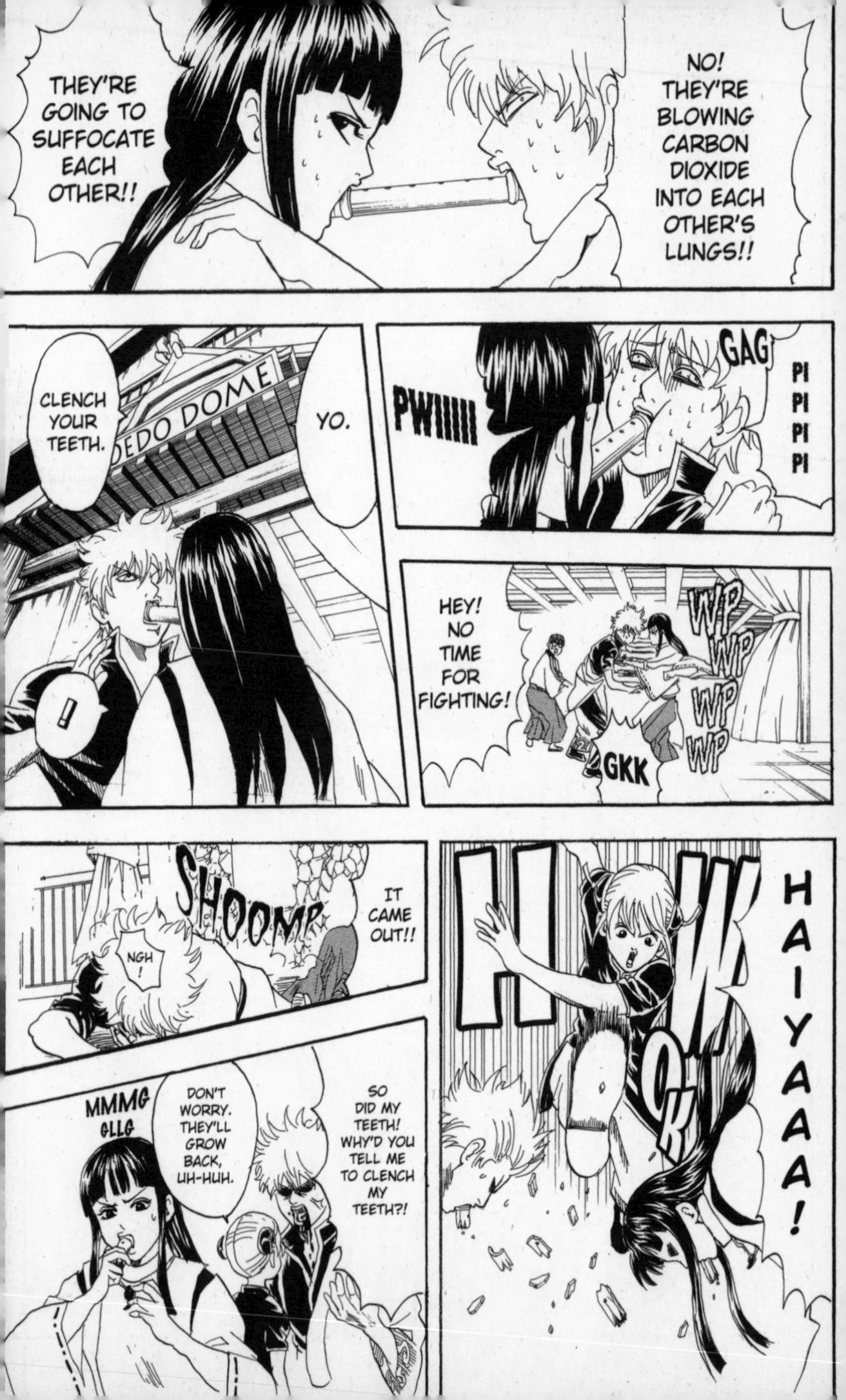
NO! THEY'RE BLOWING CARBON DIOXIDE INTO EACH OTHER'S LUNGS!!
THEY'RE GOING TO SUFFOCATE EACH OTHER!!
GAG
PI PI PI PI
PWIIIII
HEY! NO TIME FOR FIGHTING!
WP WP WP WP
GKK
YO.
CLENCH YOUR TEETH.
EDO DOME
!
HAIYAAAA!
HWOK
IT CAME OUT!!
SHOOMP
NGH!
SO DID MY TEETH! WHY'D YOU TELL ME TO CLENCH MY TEETH?!
DON'T WORRY. THEY'LL GROW BACK, UH-HUH.
MMMG GLLG

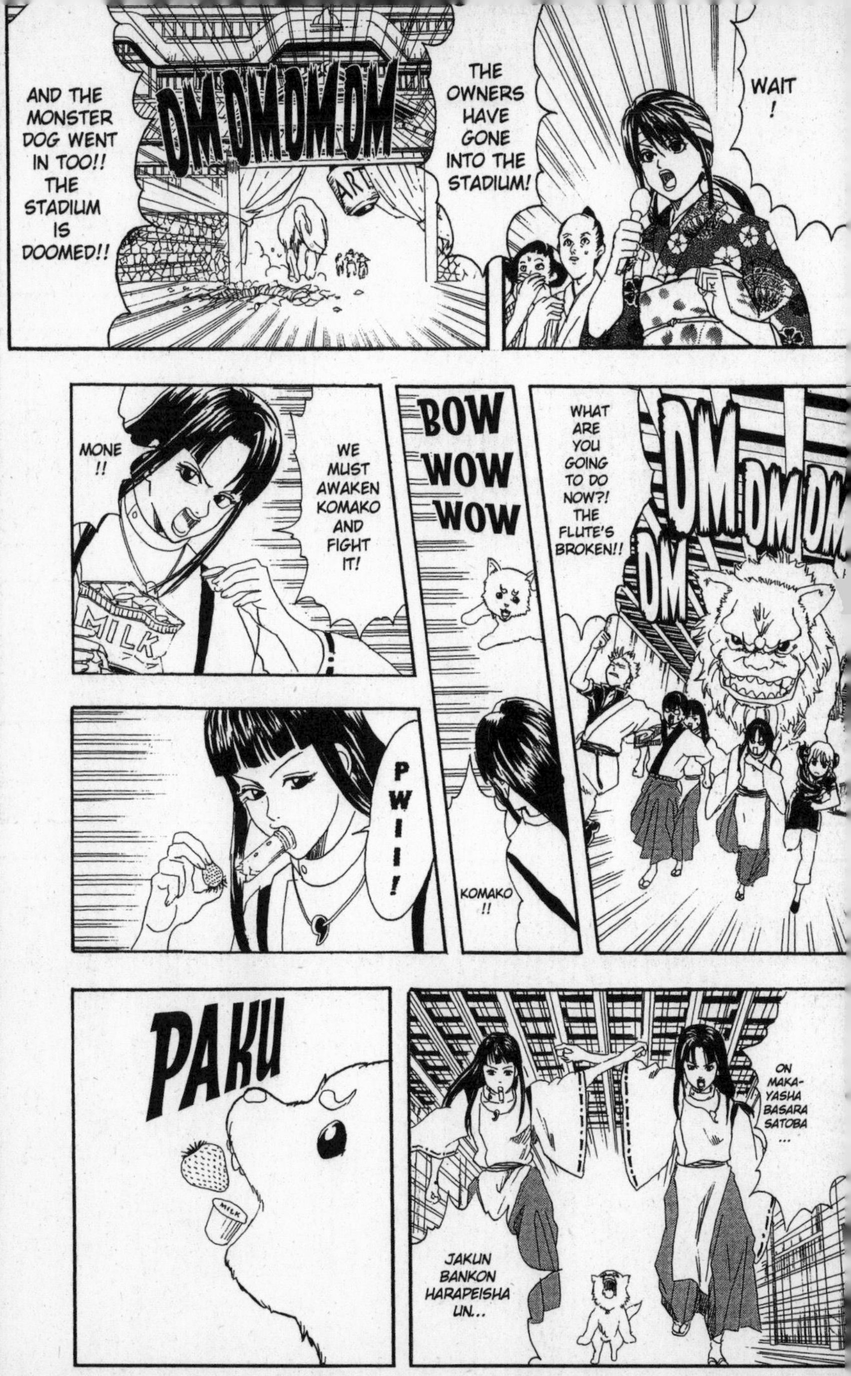
WAIT!
THE OWNERS HAVE GONE INTO THE STADIUM!
AND THE MONSTER DOG WENT IN TOO!! THE STADIUM IS DOOMED!!
DMDMOMOM
ART
DM DM DM OM
WHAT ARE YOU GOING TO DO NOW?! THE FLUTE'S BROKEN!!
BOW WOW WOW
KOMAKO!!
WE MUST AWAKEN KOMAKO AND FIGHT IT!
MONE!!
MILK
PWIII!
ON MAKA-YASHA BASARA SATOBA...
JAKUN BANKON HARAPEISHA UN...
PAKU
MILK

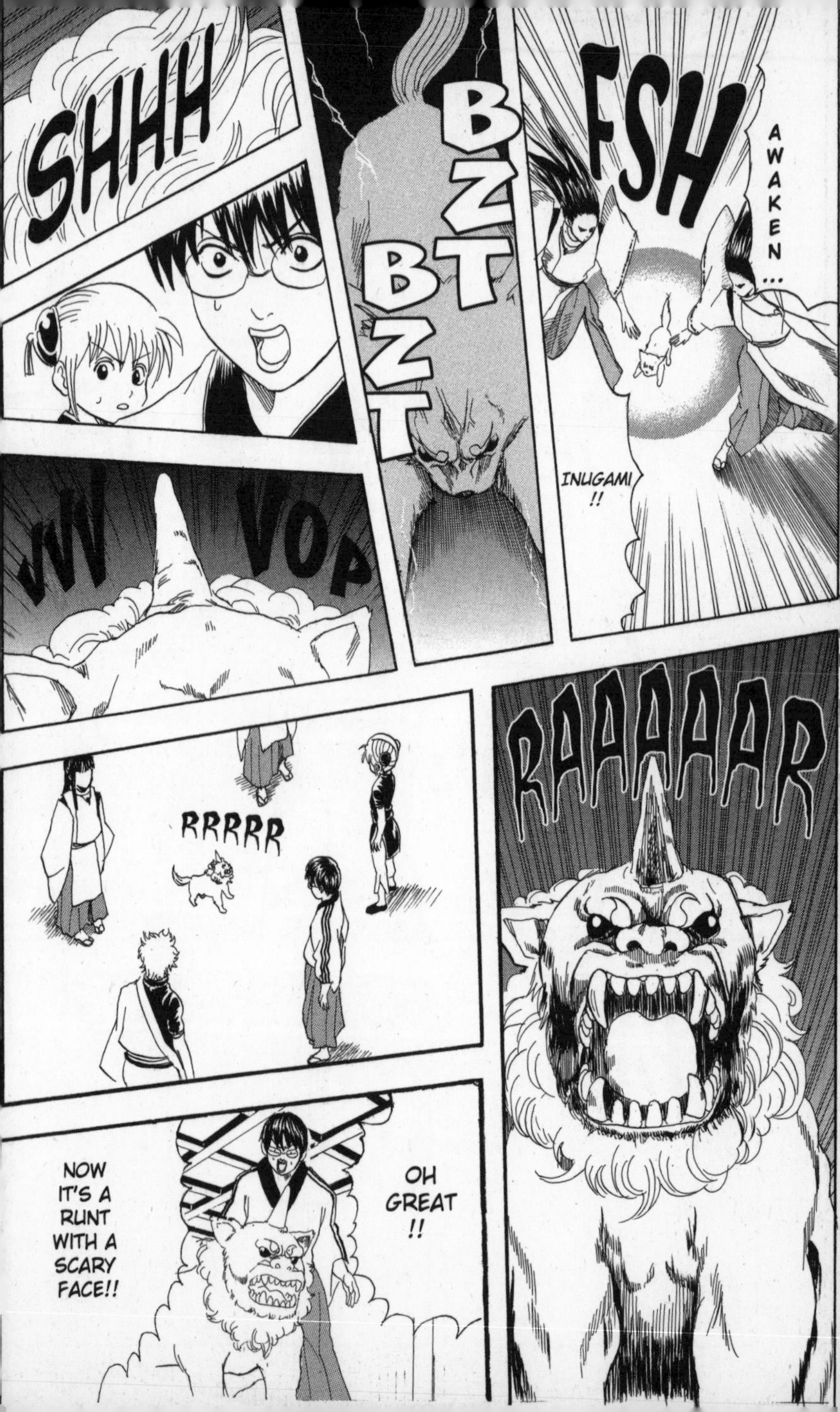
AWAKEN...
FSH
INUGAMI!!
BZT
BZT
SHHH
VOP
RAAAAAR
RRRRR
OH GREAT!!
NOW IT'S A RUNT WITH A SCARY FACE!!

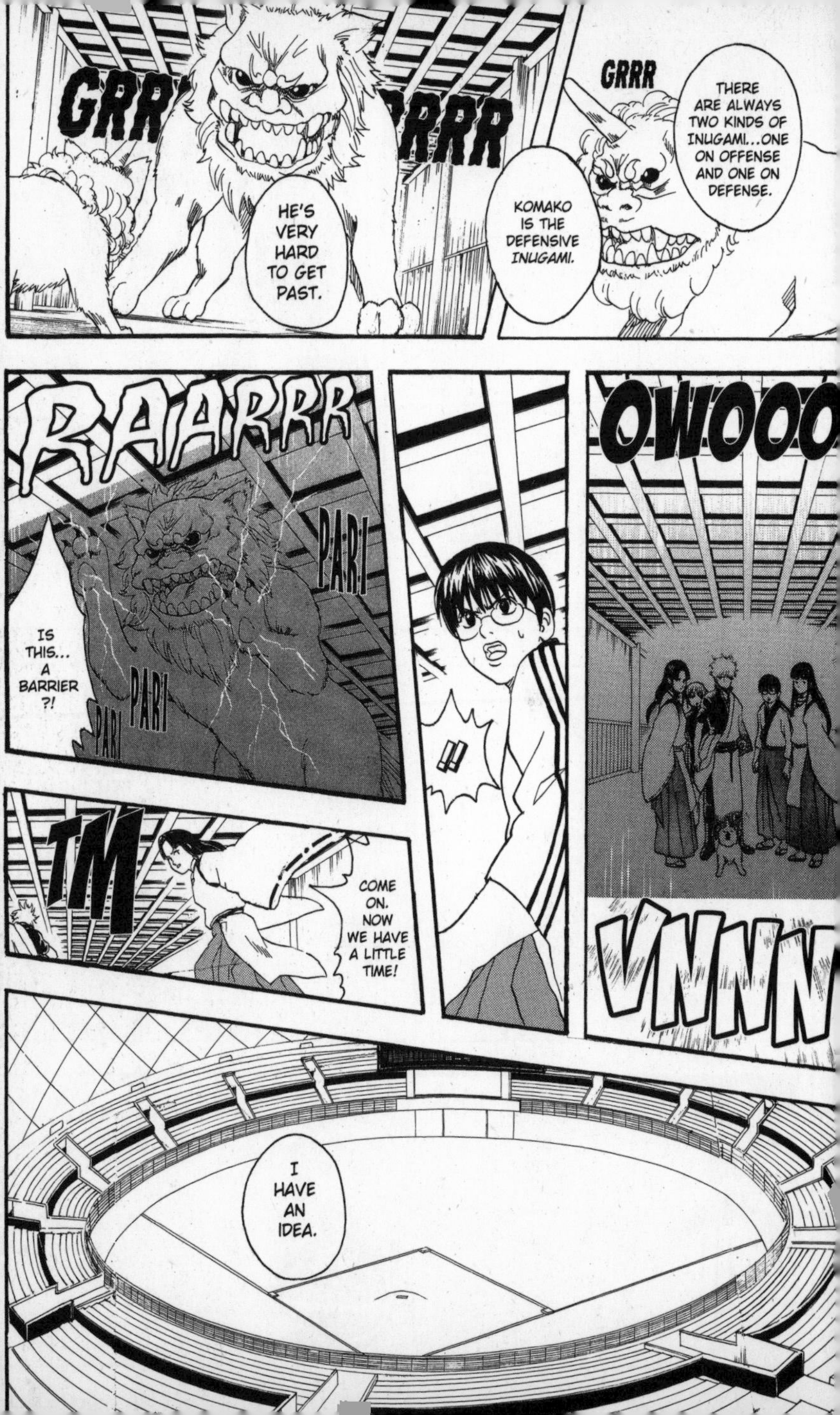
GRRR
THERE ARE ALWAYS TWO KINDS OF INUGAMI...ONE ON OFFENSE AND ONE ON DEFENSE.
KOMAKO IS THE DEFENSIVE INUGAMI.
GRR
RRRR
HE'S VERY HARD TO GET PAST.
OWOOO
VNNN
!!
RAARRR
PARI
PARI
PARI
IS THIS... A BARRIER?!
TM
COME ON. NOW WE HAVE A LITTLE TIME!
I HAVE AN IDEA.

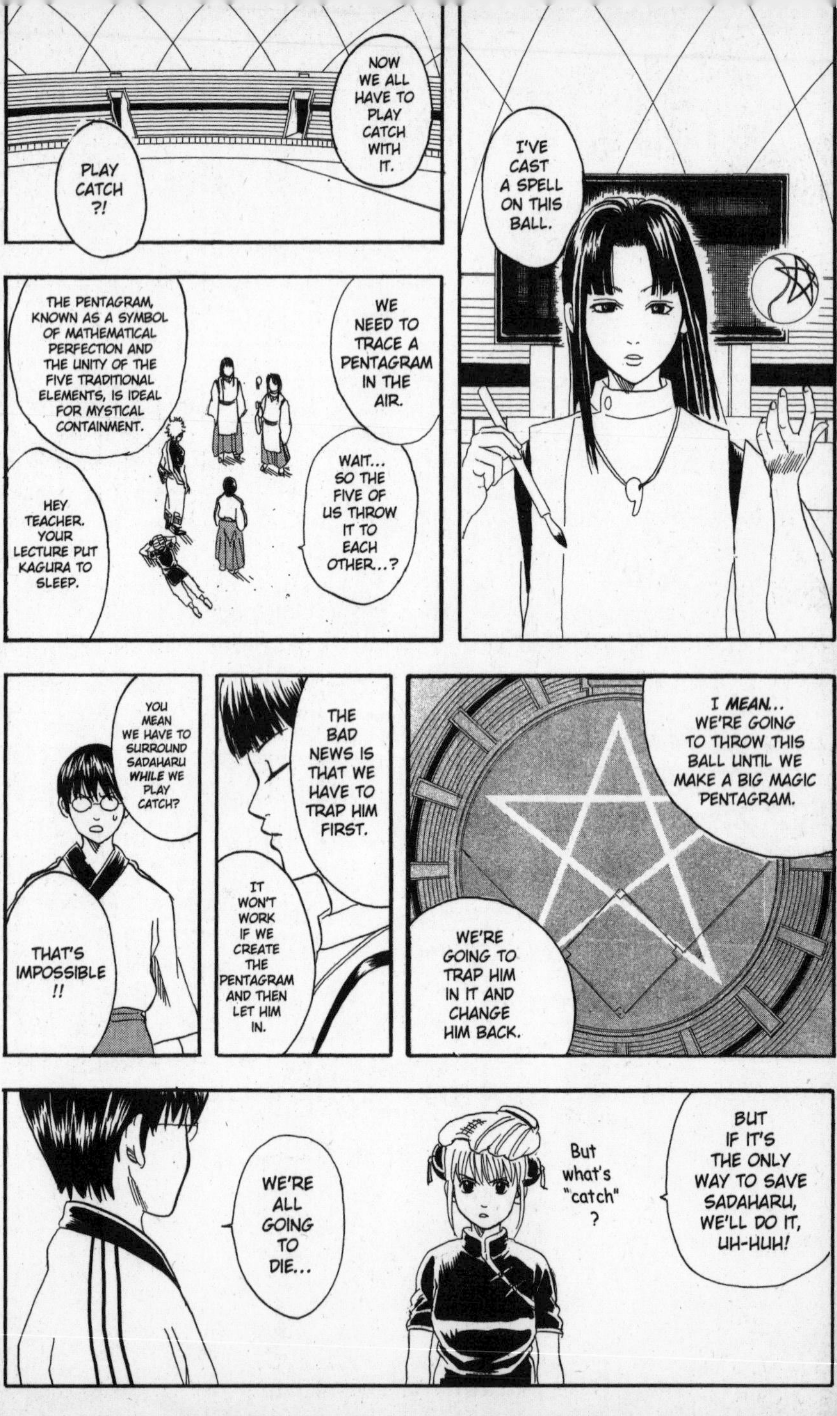
I'VE CAST A SPELL ON THIS BALL.
NOW WE ALL HAVE TO PLAY CATCH WITH IT.
PLAY CATCH ?!
WE NEED TO TRACE A PENTAGRAM IN THE AIR.
THE PENTAGRAM, KNOWN AS A SYMBOL OF MATHEMATICAL PERFECTION AND THE UNITY OF THE FIVE TRADITIONAL ELEMENTS, IS IDEAL FOR MYSTICAL CONTAINMENT.
WAIT... SO THE FIVE OF US THROW IT TO EACH OTHER...?
HEY TEACHER. YOUR LECTURE PUT KAGURA TO SLEEP.
I *MEAN*... WE'RE GOING TO THROW THIS BALL UNTIL WE MAKE A BIG MAGIC PENTAGRAM.
WE'RE GOING TO TRAP HIM IN IT AND CHANGE HIM BACK.
THE BAD NEWS IS THAT WE HAVE TO TRAP HIM FIRST.
IT WON'T WORK IF WE CREATE THE PENTAGRAM AND THEN LET HIM IN.
YOU MEAN WE HAVE TO SURROUND SADAHARU *WHILE* WE PLAY CATCH?
THAT'S IMPOSSIBLE !!
BUT IF IT'S THE ONLY WAY TO SAVE SADAHARU, WE'LL DO IT, UH-HUH!
But what's "catch" ?
WE'RE ALL GOING TO DIE...

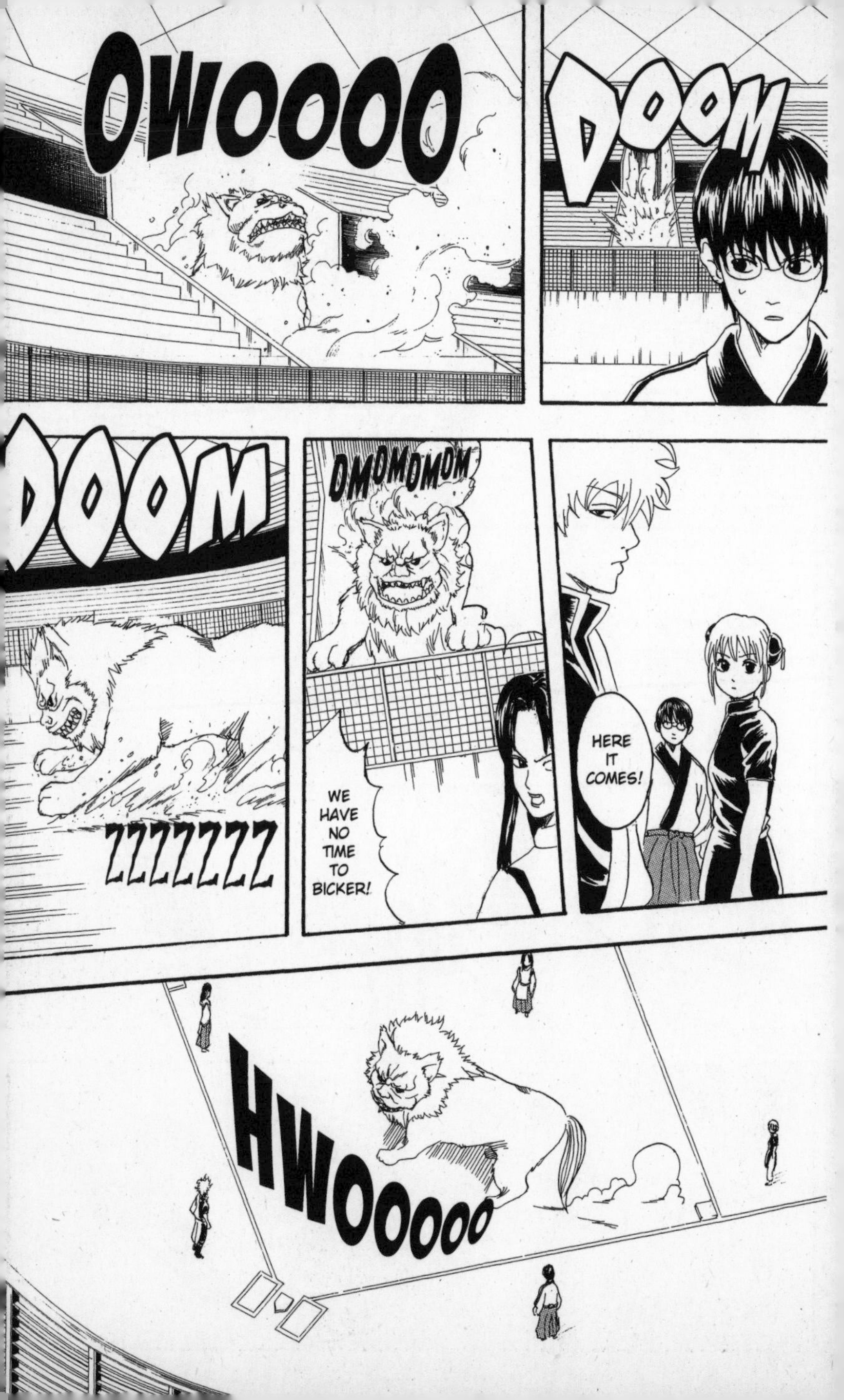
DOOM
OWOOOO
HERE IT COMES!
DMOMDMDM
WE HAVE NO TIME TO BICKER!
DOOM
ZZZZZZZ
HWOOOOO

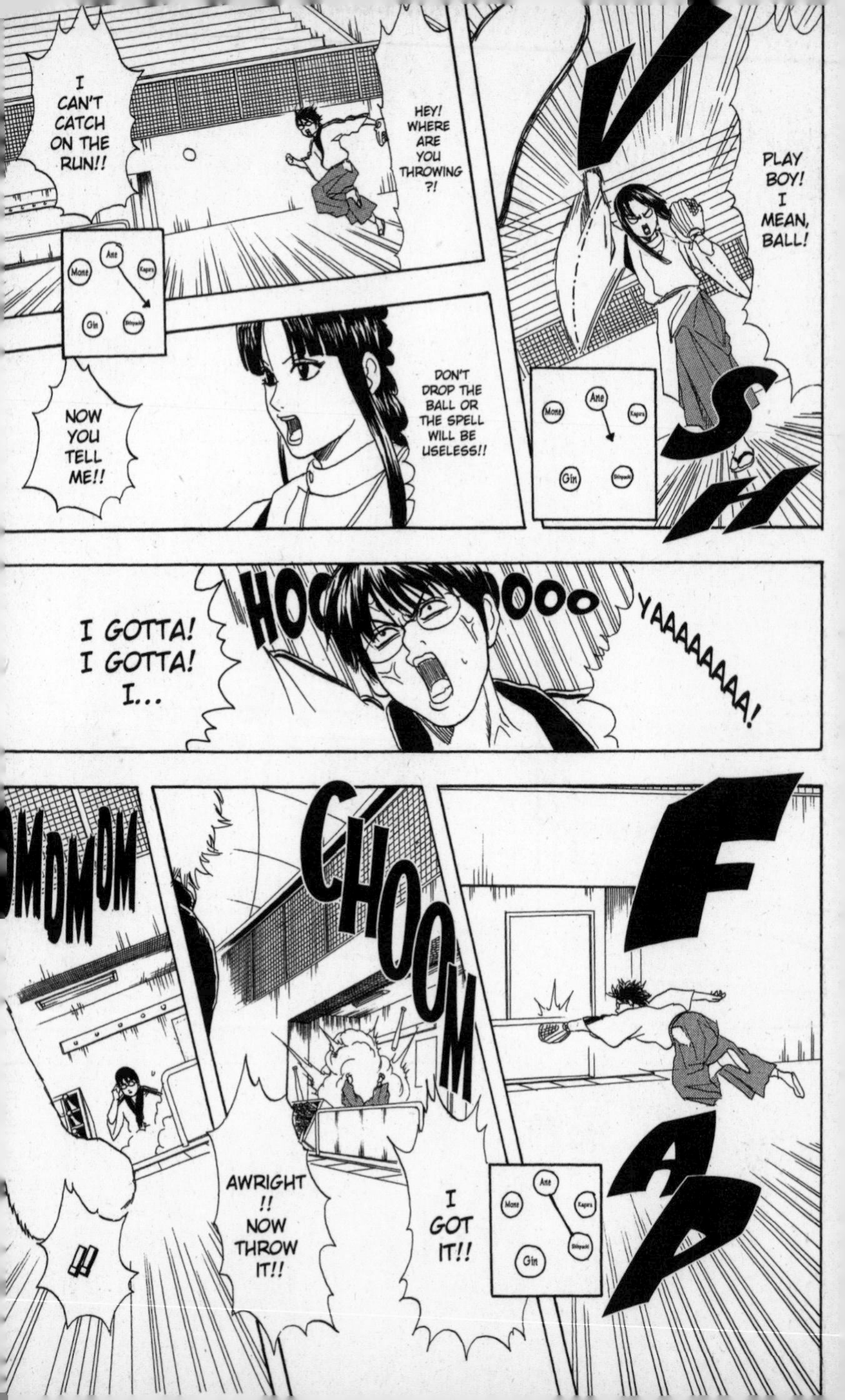
VSH
PLAY BOY! I MEAN, BALL!
Ane
Mone
Kagura
Gin
Shinpachi
HEY! WHERE ARE YOU THROWING?!
I CAN'T CATCH ON THE RUN!!
Ane
Mone
Kagura
Gin
Shinpachi
DON'T DROP THE BALL OR THE SPELL WILL BE USELESS!!
NOW YOU TELL ME!!
YAAAAAAAAA!
I GOTTA! I GOTTA! I...
FWAP
I GOT IT!!
Ane
Mone
Kagura
Gin
Shinpachi
CHOOM
AWRIGHT!! NOW THROW IT!!
!!

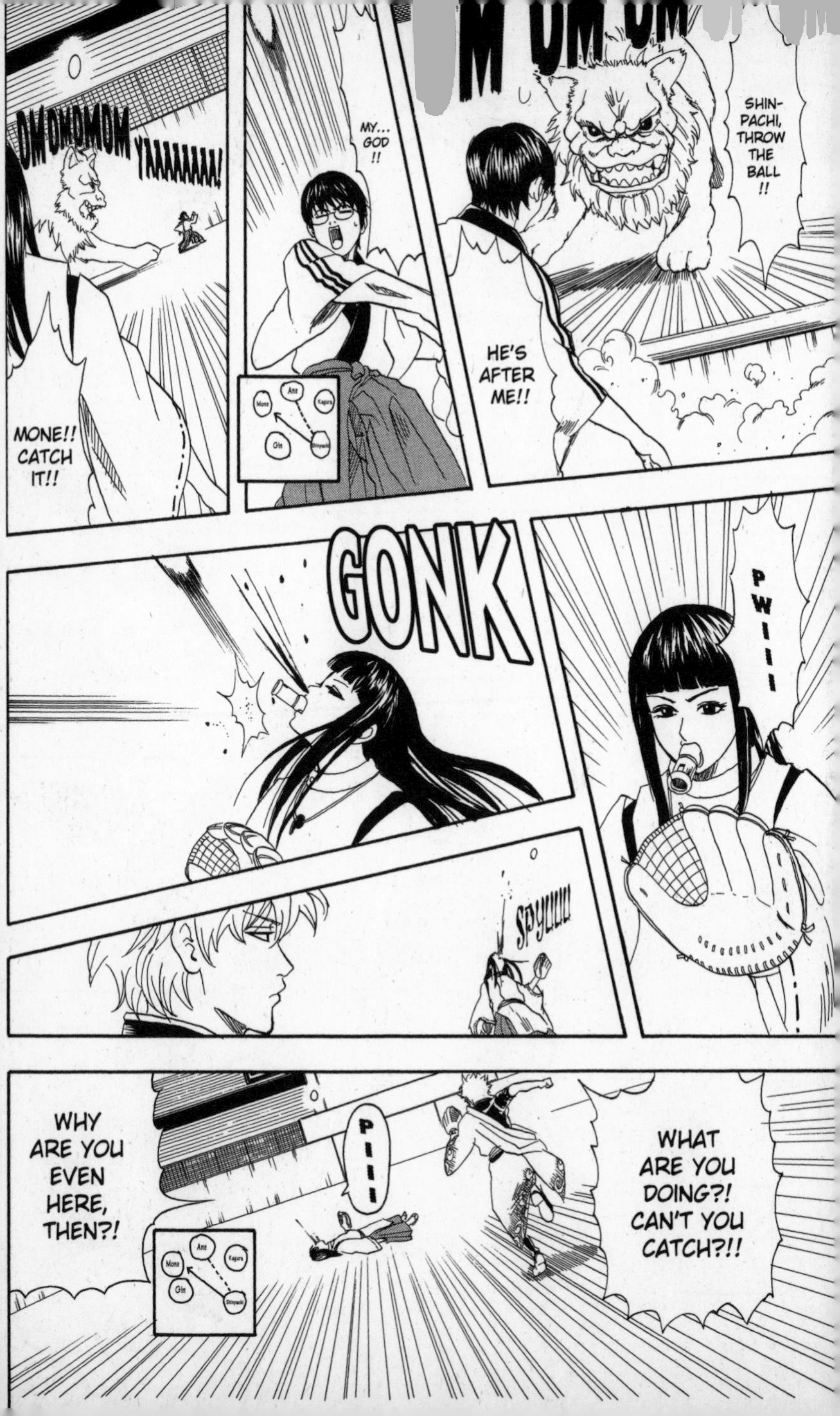
M UM UM
SHIN-PACHI, THROW THE BALL!!
HE'S AFTER ME!!
MY... GOD!!
Ane
Kagura
Mone
Gin
Shinpachi
OMOMOMOM
YAAAAAAAA!
MONE!! CATCH IT!!
PWIII
GONK
SPYUUU
WHAT ARE YOU DOING?! CAN'T YOU CATCH?!!
PIII
WHY ARE YOU EVEN HERE, THEN?!
Ane
Kagura
Mone
Gin
Shinpachi

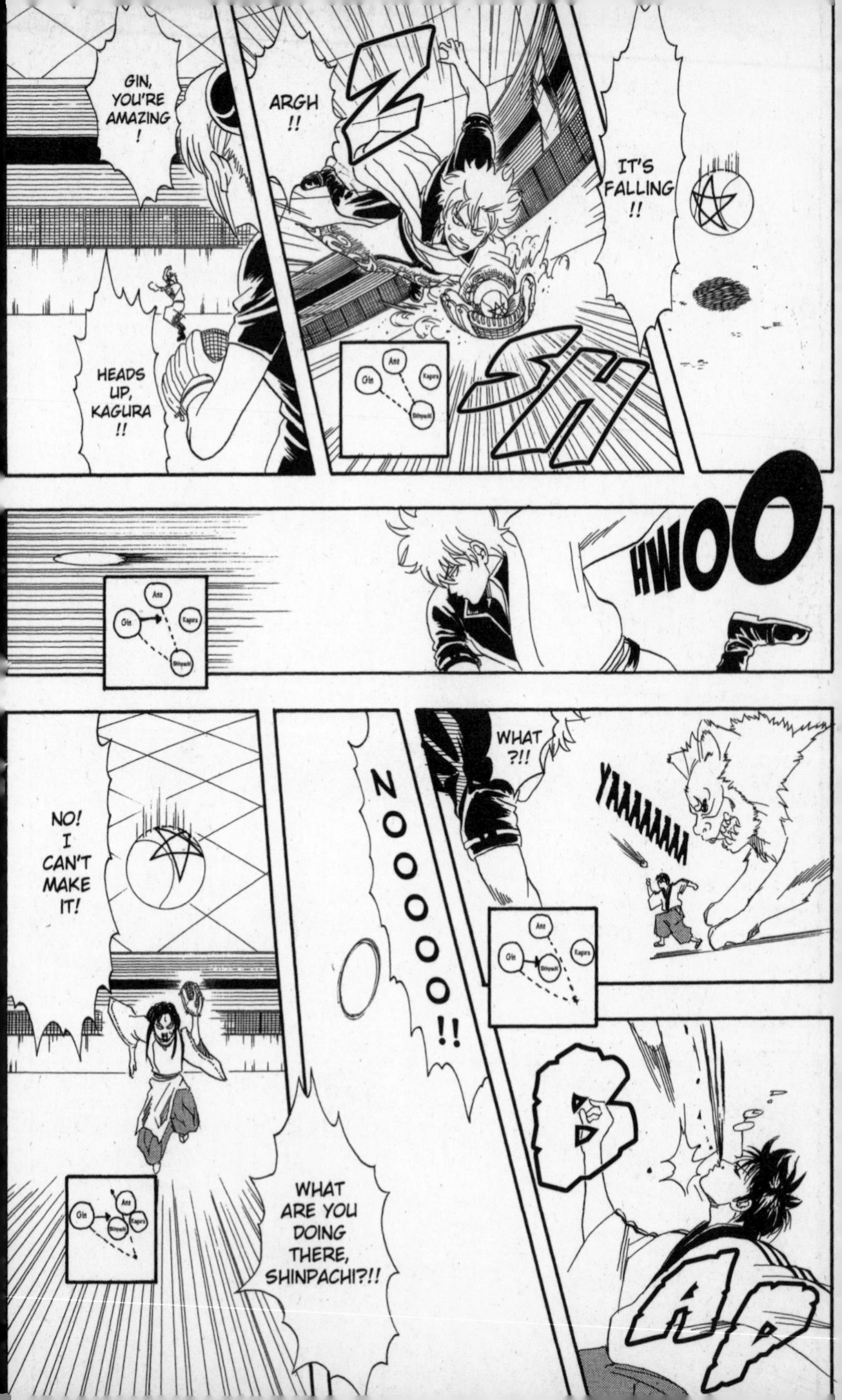
IT'S FALLING!!
ARGH!!
Z
Ane
Gin
Kagura
Shinpachi
SH
GIN, YOU'RE AMAZING!
HEADS UP, KAGURA!!
HWOO
Ane
Gin
Kagura
Shinpachi
WHAT?!!
YAAAAAAAA
Ane
Gin
Kagura
Shinpachi
G
AP
NOOOOOO!!
WHAT ARE YOU DOING THERE, SHINPACHI?!!
NO! I CAN'T MAKE IT!
Ane
Gin
Kagura
Shinpachi

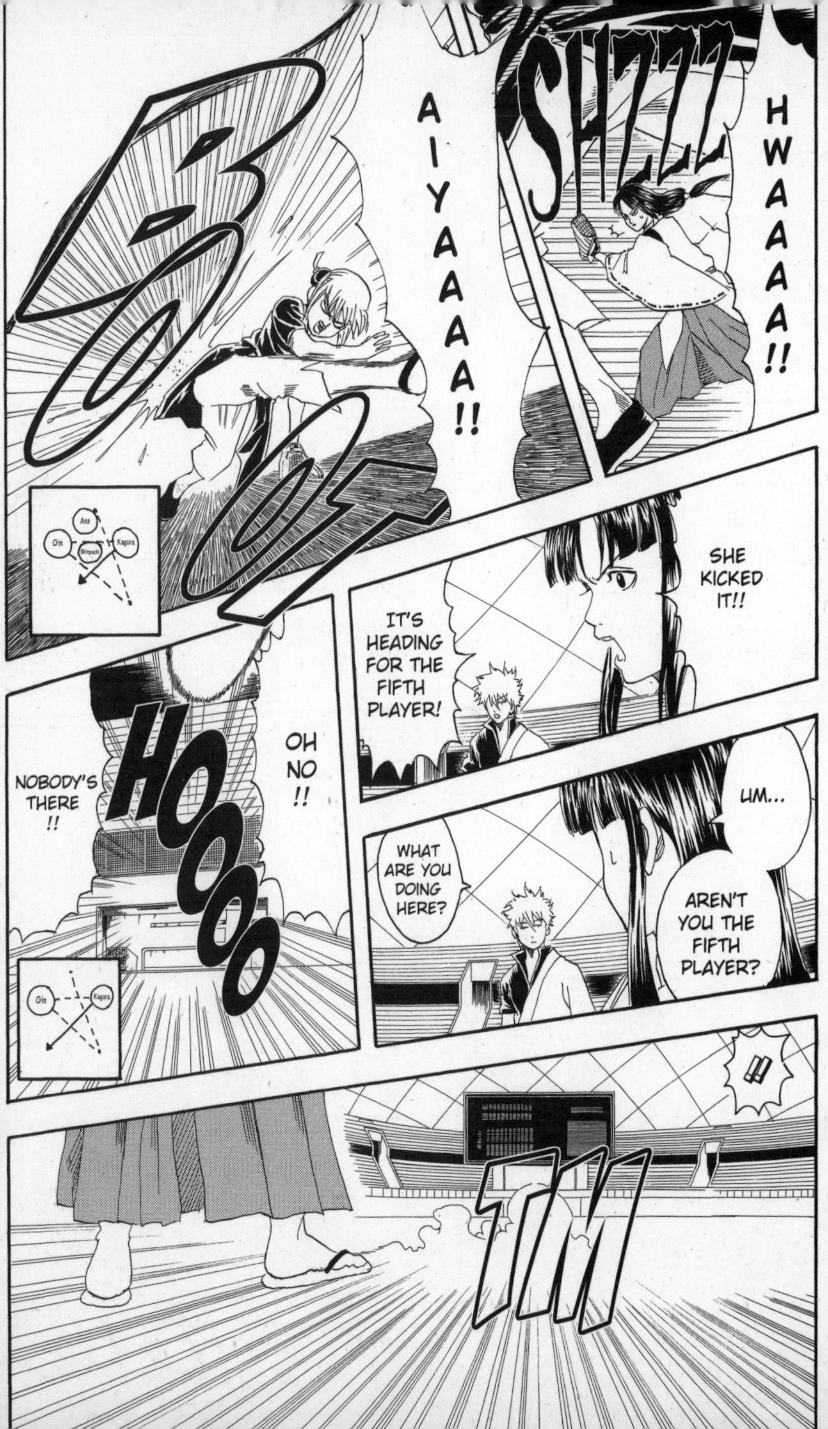
SHZZZ
HWAAAAA!!
AIYAAAAA!!
Ane
Gin
Shinpachi
Kagura
SHE KICKED IT!!
IT'S HEADING FOR THE FIFTH PLAYER!
UM...
AREN'T YOU THE FIFTH PLAYER?
WHAT ARE YOU DOING HERE?
HOOOO
OH NO!!
NOBODY'S THERE!!
Gin
Kagura
!!
TM

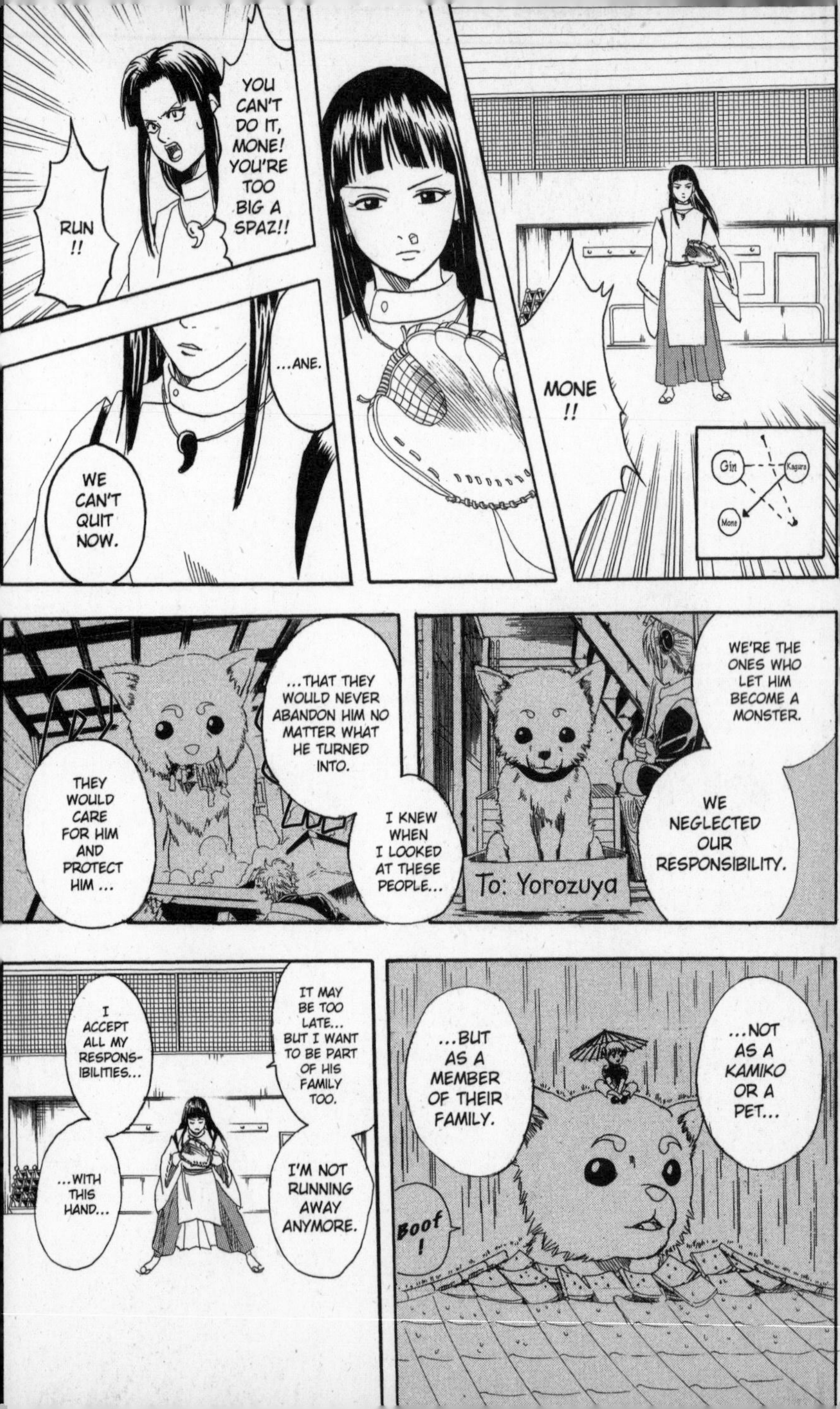
MONE !!
Gin
Kagura
Mone
YOU CAN'T DO IT, MONE! YOU'RE TOO BIG A SPAZ!!
RUN !!
...ANE.
WE CAN'T QUIT NOW.
WE'RE THE ONES WHO LET HIM BECOME A MONSTER.
WE NEGLECTED OUR RESPONSIBILITY.
To: Yorozuya
I KNEW WHEN I LOOKED AT THESE PEOPLE...
...THAT THEY WOULD NEVER ABANDON HIM NO MATTER WHAT HE TURNED INTO.
THEY WOULD CARE FOR HIM AND PROTECT HIM...
...NOT AS A KAMIKO OR A PET...
...BUT AS A MEMBER OF THEIR FAMILY.
Boof !
IT MAY BE TOO LATE... BUT I WANT TO BE PART OF HIS FAMILY TOO.
I ACCEPT ALL MY RESPONSIBILITIES...
I'M NOT RUNNING AWAY ANYMORE.
...WITH THIS HAND...

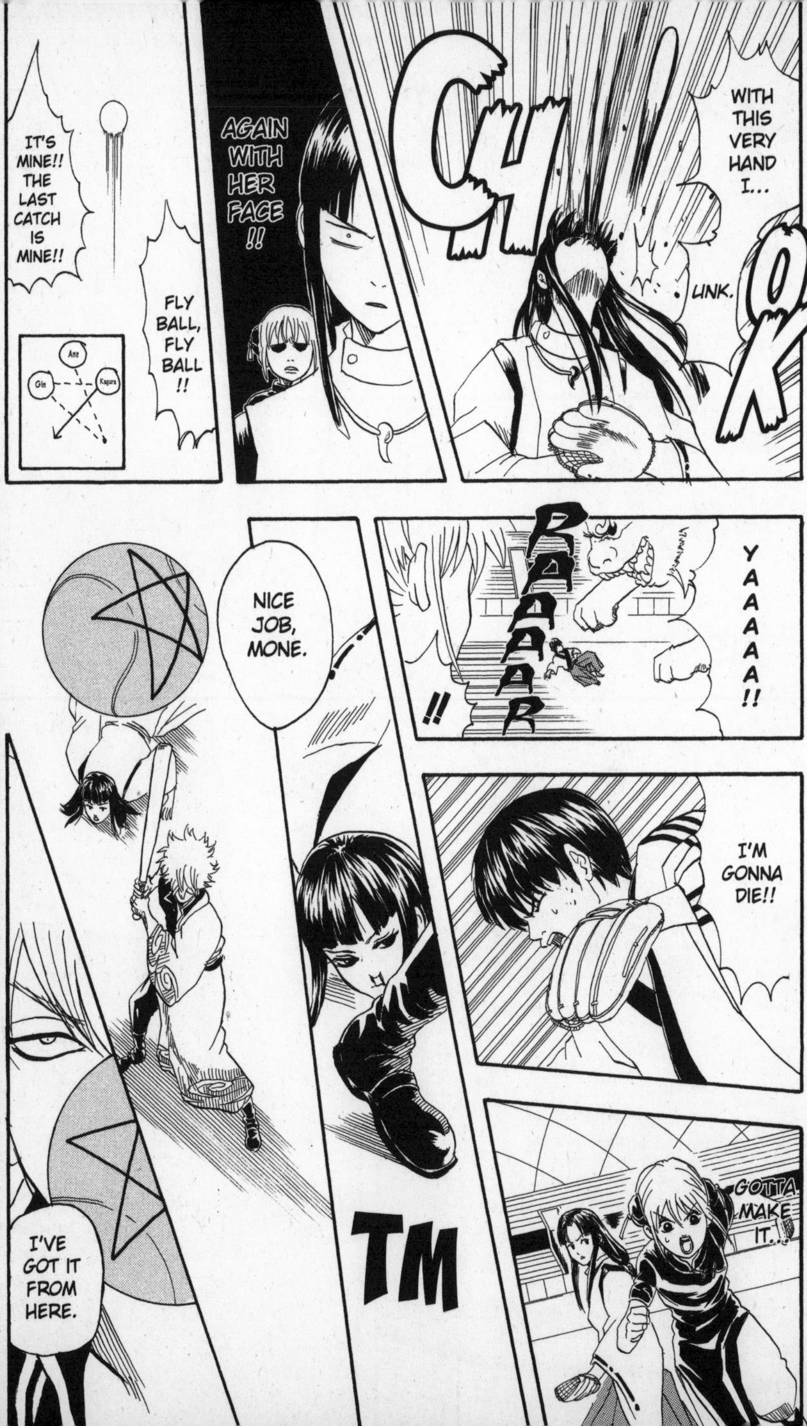
WITH THIS VERY HAND I...
CH
UNK.
AGAIN WITH HER FACE!!
FLY BALL, FLY BALL!!
IT'S MINE!! THE LAST CATCH IS MINE!!
Ane
Gin
Kagura
YAAAAAA!!
RAAAAAR
!!
I'M GONNA DIE!!
GOTTA MAKE IT...!
NICE JOB, MONE.
TM
I'VE GOT IT FROM HERE.

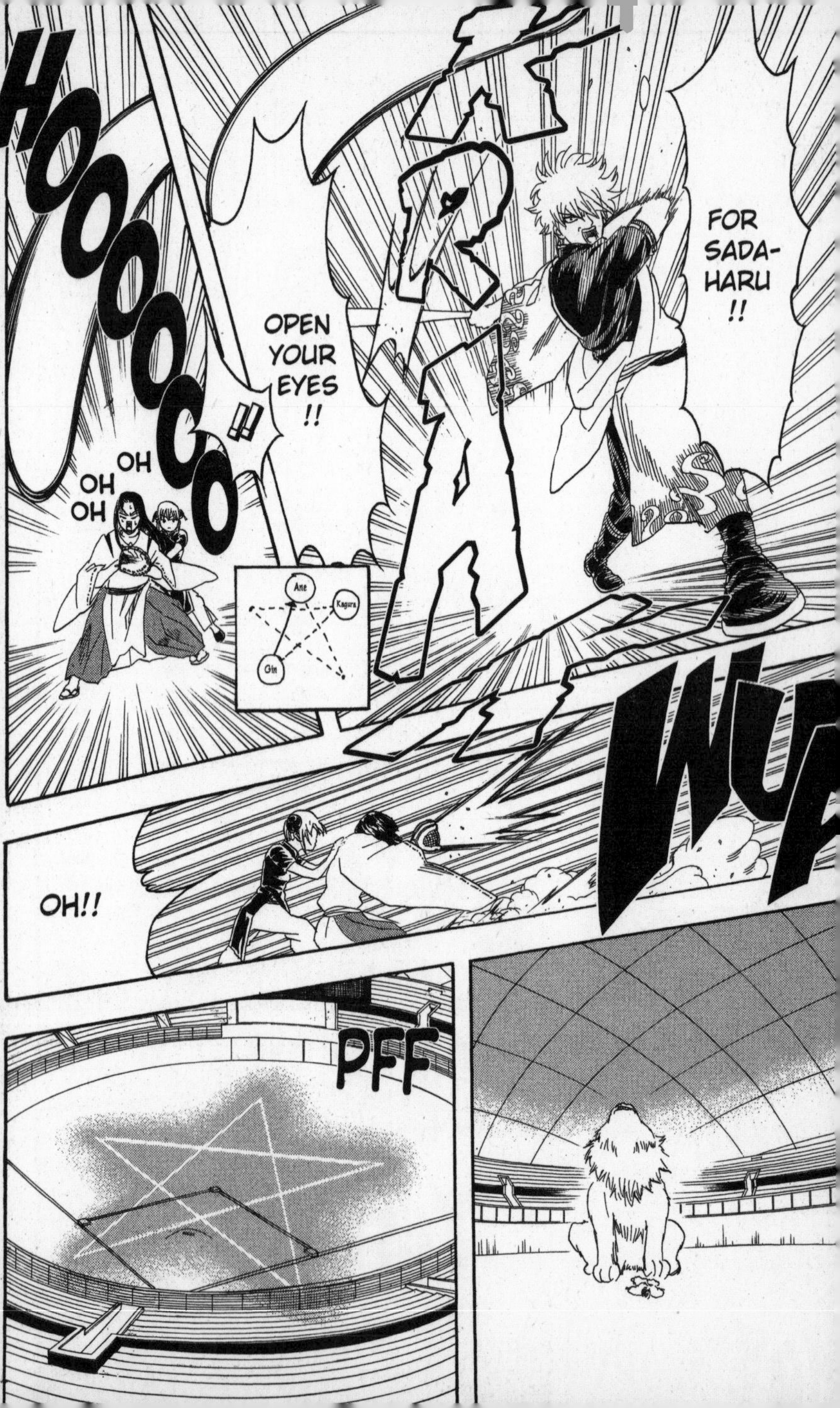
FOR SADA-HARU!!
OPEN YOUR EYES!!
HOOOOOOOO!!
OH OH OH
Ane
Kagura
Gin
WUP
OH!!
PFF

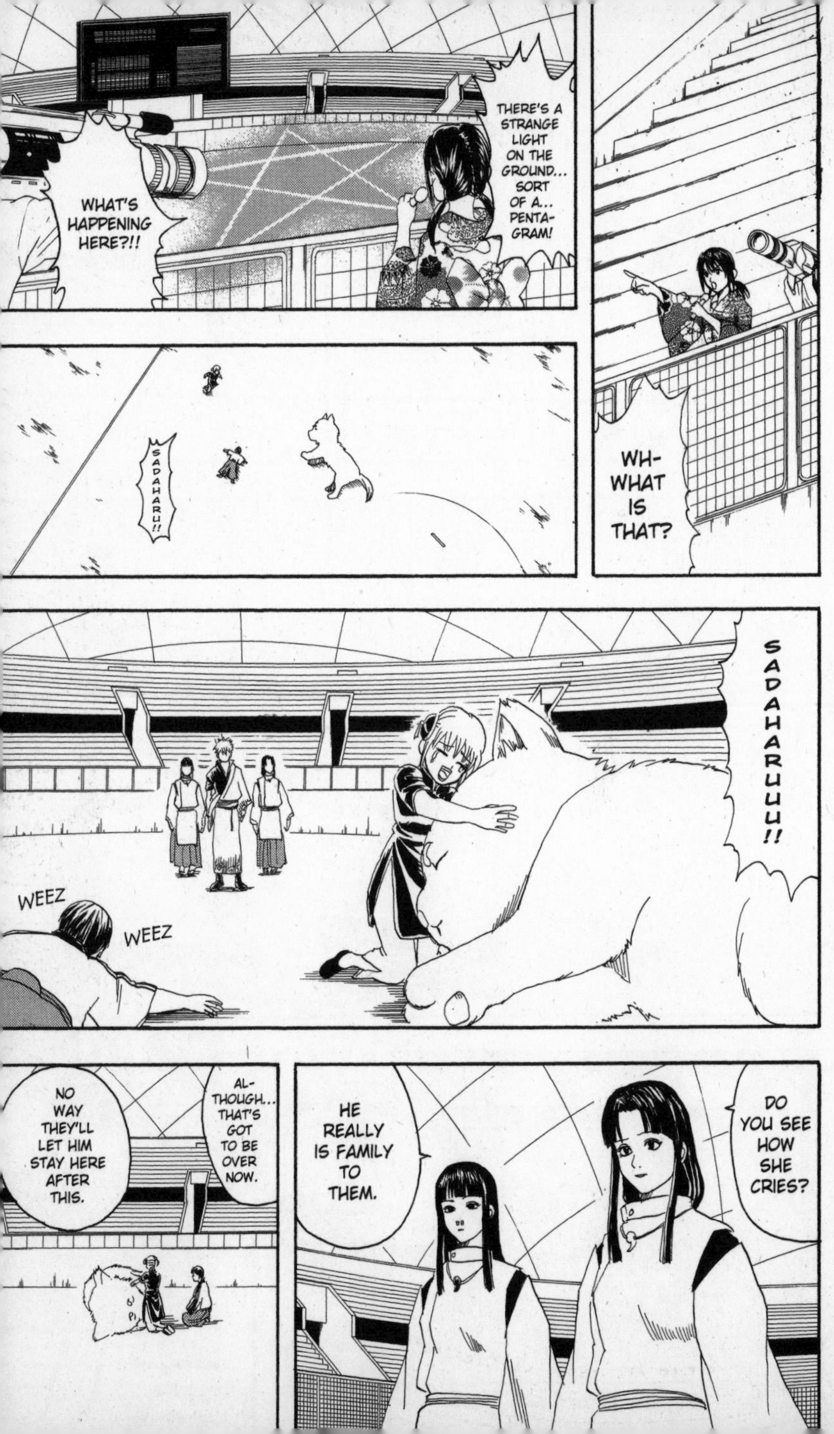
WH-WHAT IS THAT?
THERE'S A STRANGE LIGHT ON THE GROUND... SORT OF A... PENTAGRAM!
WHAT'S HAPPENING HERE?!!
SADAHARU!!
SADAHARUUUU!!
WEEZ
WEEZ
DO YOU SEE HOW SHE CRIES?
HE REALLY IS FAMILY TO THEM.
ALTHOUGH... THAT'S GOT TO BE OVER NOW.
NO WAY THEY'LL LET HIM STAY HERE AFTER THIS.

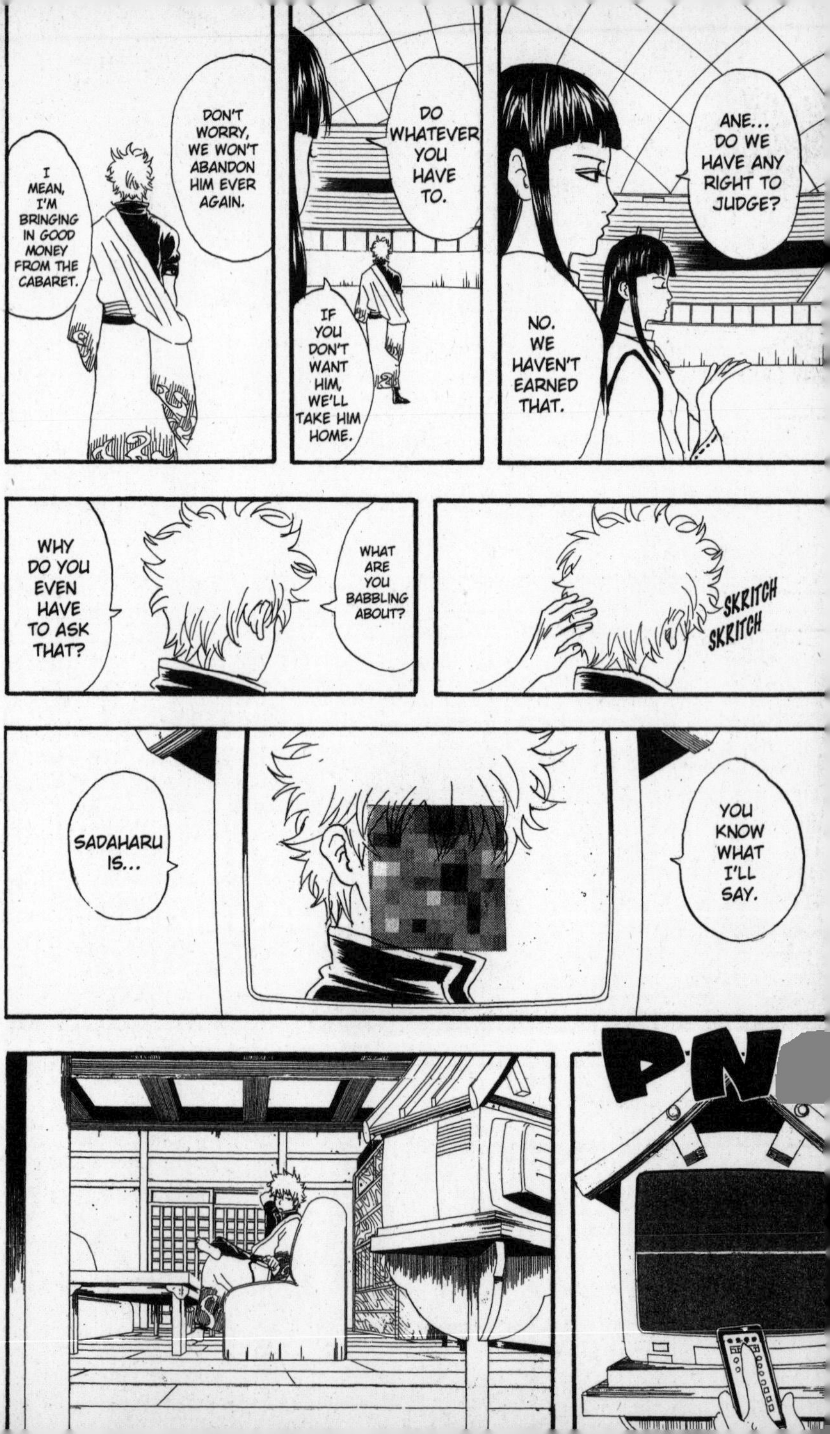
ANE... DO WE HAVE ANY RIGHT TO JUDGE?
NO. WE HAVEN'T EARNED THAT.
DO WHATEVER YOU HAVE TO.
IF YOU DON'T WANT HIM, WE'LL TAKE HIM HOME.
DON'T WORRY, WE WON'T ABANDON HIM EVER AGAIN.
I MEAN, I'M BRINGING IN GOOD MONEY FROM THE CABARET.
SKRITCH SKRITCH
WHAT ARE YOU BABBLING ABOUT?
WHY DO YOU EVEN HAVE TO ASK THAT?
YOU KNOW WHAT I'LL SAY.
SADAHARU IS...
PN

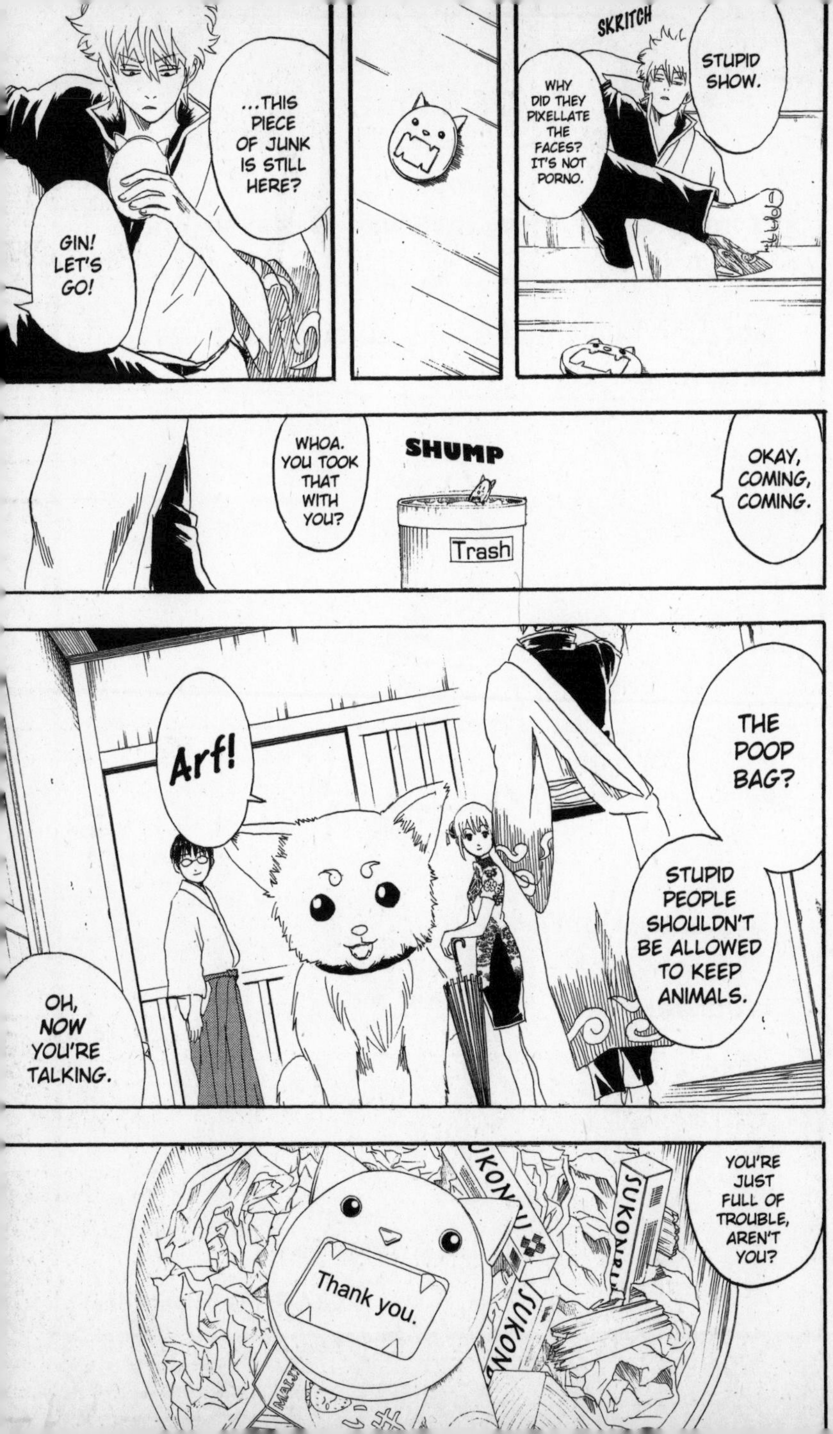
SKRITCH
STUPID SHOW.
WHY DID THEY PIXELLATE THE FACES? IT'S NOT PORNO.
...THIS PIECE OF JUNK IS STILL HERE?
GIN! LET'S GO!
OKAY, COMING, COMING.
SHUMP
Trash
WHOA. YOU TOOK THAT WITH YOU?
THE POOP BAG?
STUPID PEOPLE SHOULDN'T BE ALLOWED TO KEEP ANIMALS.
Arf!
OH, NOW YOU'RE TALKING.
YOU'RE JUST FULL OF TROUBLE, AREN'T YOU?
Thank you.

Sorachi's Q&A Corner #20

<From "Did-You-Know-That-Snot-Is-Melted-Brains"? of Tokyo>

Sorachi, I invented a new autograph for you! Please use it!

It's easy, right?

<Answer>

Why does it spiral like poop?

(Q&A #21 is on page 146)

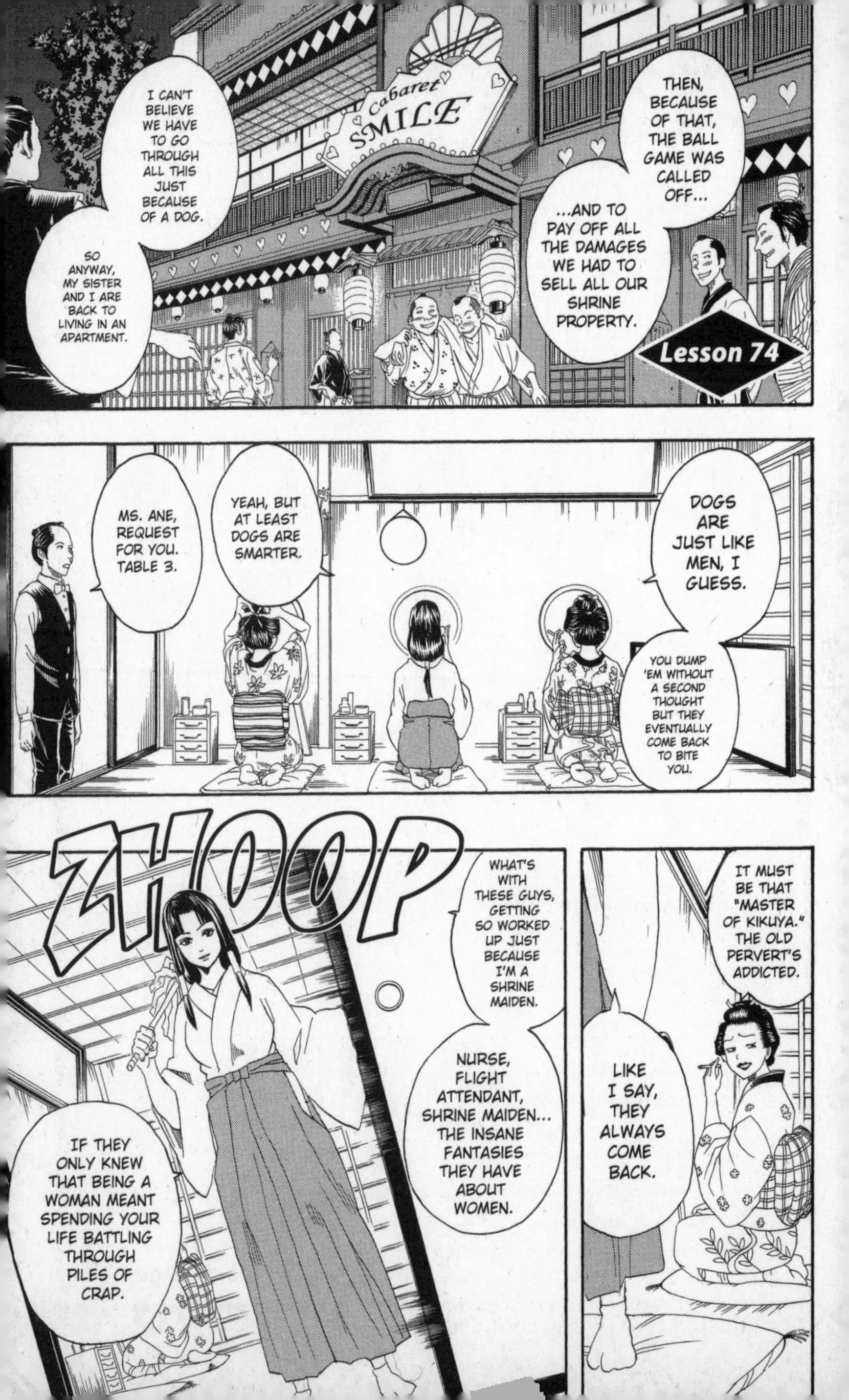
THEN, BECAUSE OF THAT, THE BALL GAME WAS CALLED OFF...
...AND TO PAY OFF ALL THE DAMAGES WE HAD TO SELL ALL OUR SHRINE PROPERTY.
I CAN'T BELIEVE WE HAVE TO GO THROUGH ALL THIS JUST BECAUSE OF A DOG.
SO ANYWAY, MY SISTER AND I ARE BACK TO LIVING IN AN APARTMENT.
Cabaret SMILE
Lesson 74
DOGS ARE JUST LIKE MEN, I GUESS.
YOU DUMP 'EM WITHOUT A SECOND THOUGHT BUT THEY EVENTUALLY COME BACK TO BITE YOU.
YEAH, BUT AT LEAST DOGS ARE SMARTER.
MS. ANE, REQUEST FOR YOU. TABLE 3.
IT MUST BE THAT "MASTER OF KIKUYA." THE OLD PERVERT'S ADDICTED.
LIKE I SAY, THEY ALWAYS COME BACK.
ZHOOP
WHAT'S WITH THESE GUYS, GETTING SO WORKED UP JUST BECAUSE I'M A SHRINE MAIDEN.
NURSE, FLIGHT ATTENDANT, SHRINE MAIDEN... THE INSANE FANTASIES THEY HAVE ABOUT WOMEN.
IF THEY ONLY KNEW THAT BEING A WOMAN MEANT SPENDING YOUR LIFE BATTLING THROUGH PILES OF CRAP.

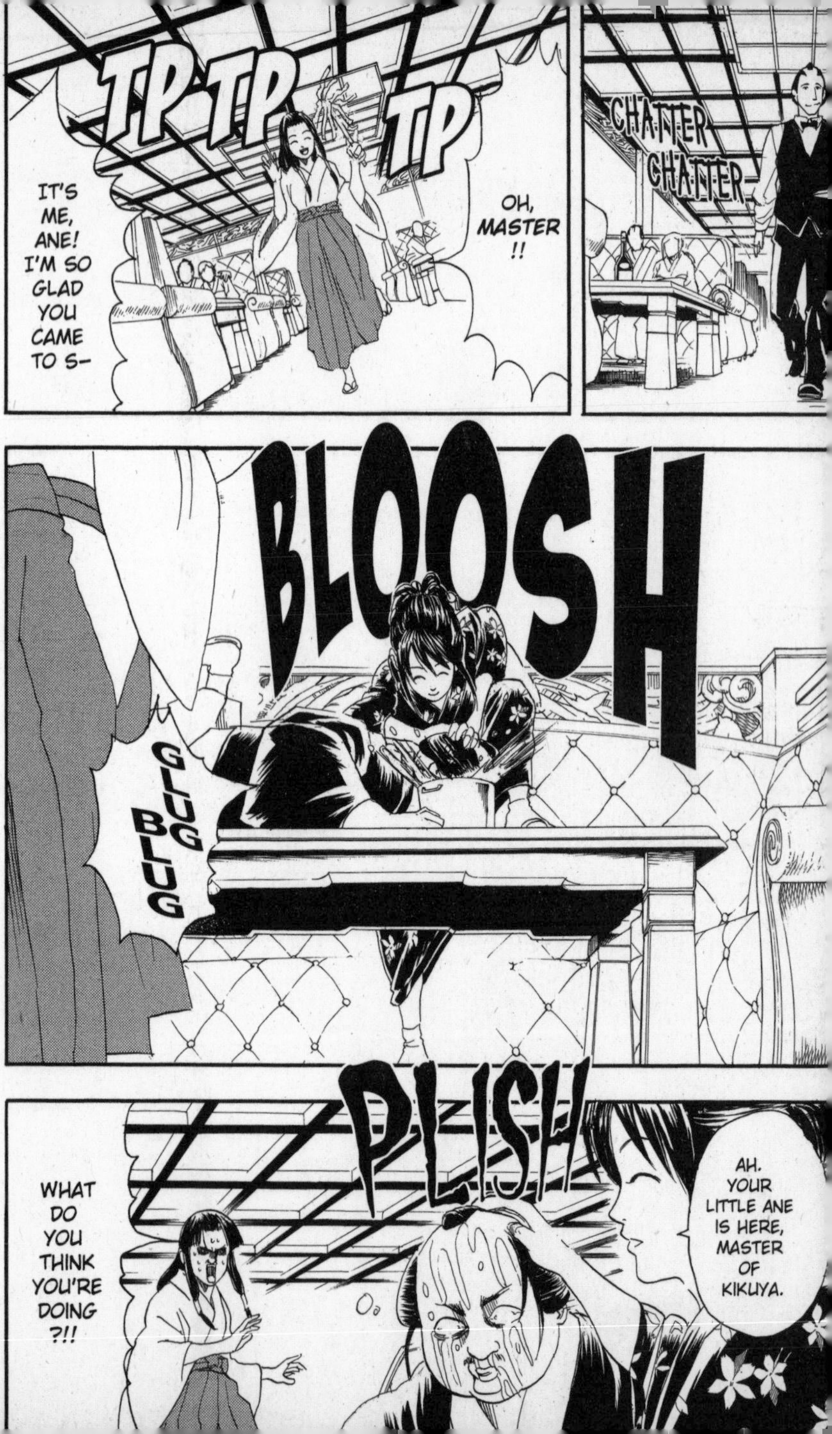
CHATTER
CHATTER
TP TP TP
OH, MASTER!!
IT'S ME, ANE! I'M SO GLAD YOU CAME TO S—
BLOOSH
GLUG BLUG
PLISH
AH. YOUR LITTLE ANE IS HERE, MASTER OF KIKUYA.
WHAT DO YOU THINK YOU'RE DOING?!!

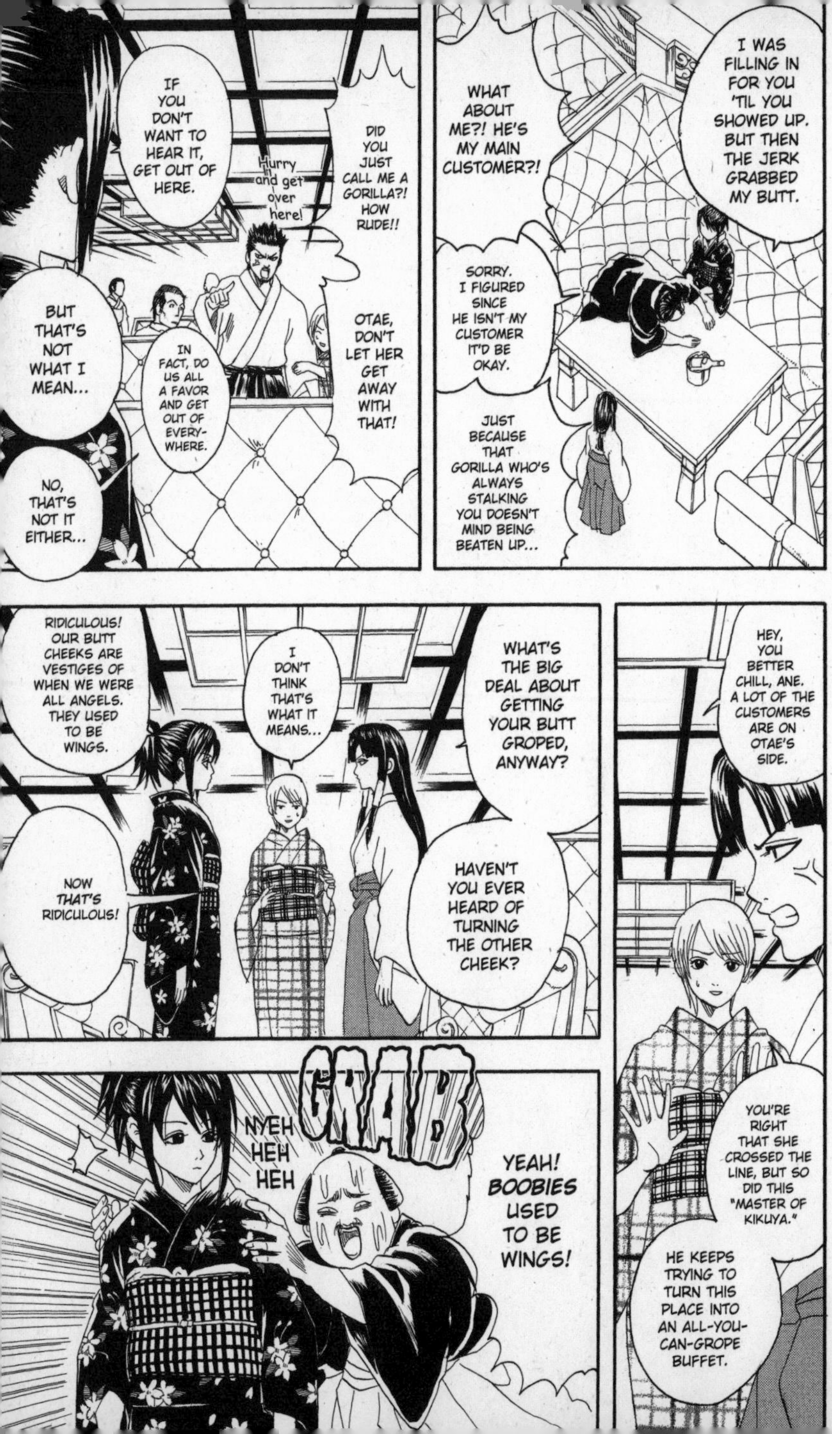
I WAS FILLING IN FOR YOU 'TIL YOU SHOWED UP. BUT THEN THE JERK GRABBED MY BUTT.
WHAT ABOUT ME?! HE'S MY MAIN CUSTOMER?!
SORRY. I FIGURED SINCE HE ISN'T MY CUSTOMER IT'D BE OKAY.
JUST BECAUSE THAT GORILLA WHO'S ALWAYS STALKING YOU DOESN'T MIND BEING BEATEN UP...
DID YOU JUST CALL ME A GORILLA?! HOW RUDE!!
IF YOU DON'T WANT TO HEAR IT, GET OUT OF HERE.
Hurry and get over here!
OTAE, DON'T LET HER GET AWAY WITH THAT!
IN FACT, DO US ALL A FAVOR AND GET OUT OF EVERYWHERE.
BUT THAT'S NOT WHAT I MEAN...
NO, THAT'S NOT IT EITHER...
HEY, YOU BETTER CHILL, ANE. A LOT OF THE CUSTOMERS ARE ON OTAE'S SIDE.
YOU'RE RIGHT THAT SHE CROSSED THE LINE, BUT SO DID THIS "MASTER OF KIKUYA."
HE KEEPS TRYING TO TURN THIS PLACE INTO AN ALL-YOU-CAN-GROPE BUFFET.
WHAT'S THE BIG DEAL ABOUT GETTING YOUR BUTT GROPED, ANYWAY?
HAVEN'T YOU EVER HEARD OF TURNING THE OTHER CHEEK?
I DON'T THINK THAT'S WHAT IT MEANS...
RIDICULOUS! OUR BUTT CHEEKS ARE VESTIGES OF WHEN WE WERE ALL ANGELS. THEY USED TO BE WINGS.
NOW THAT'S RIDICULOUS!
YEAH! BOOBIES USED TO BE WINGS!
GRAB
NYEH HEH HEH

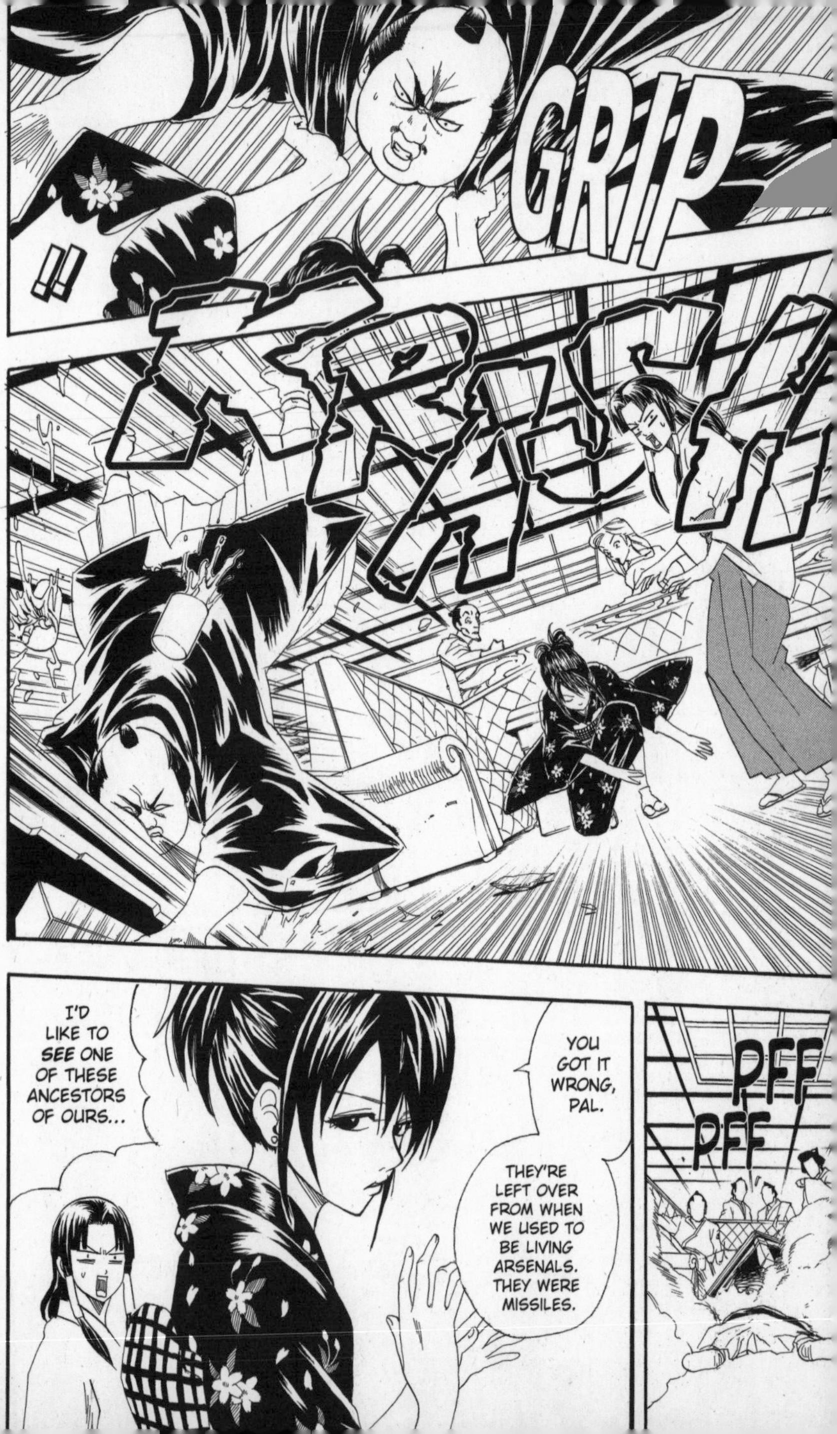
GRIP
!!
PFF
PFF
I'D LIKE TO SEE ONE OF THESE ANCESTORS OF OURS...
YOU GOT IT WRONG, PAL.
THEY'RE LEFT OVER FROM WHEN WE USED TO BE LIVING ARSENALS. THEY WERE MISSILES.

Lesson 74
Adults Only. We Wouldn't Want Anyone Immature in Here...

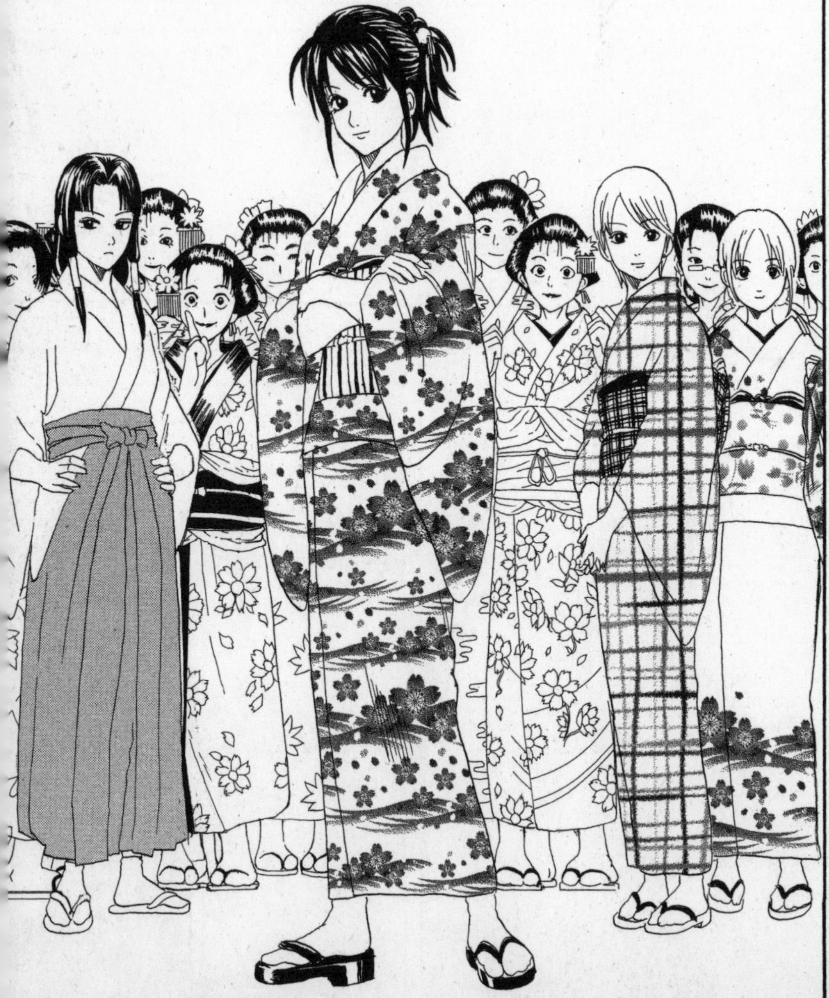

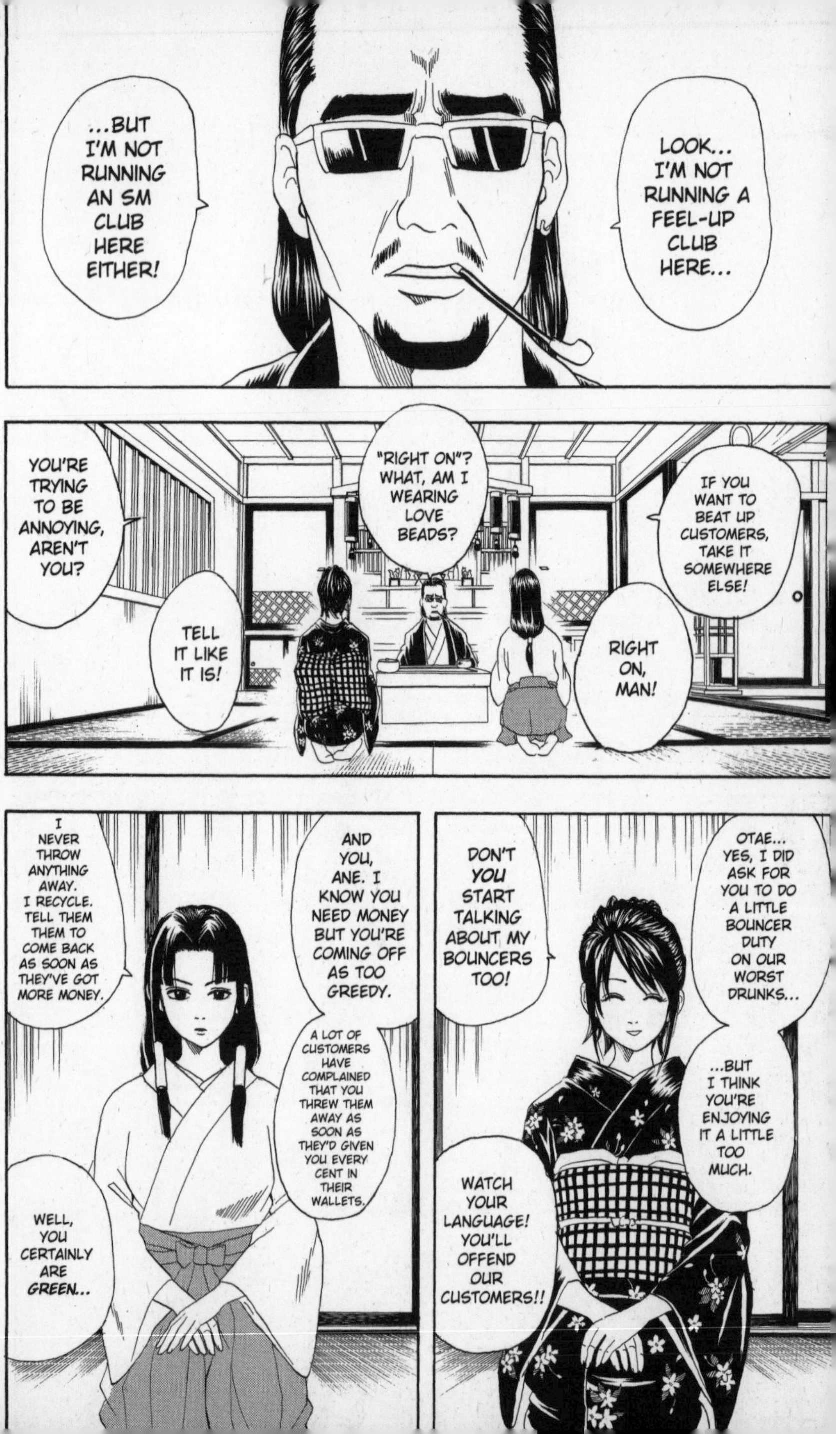
LOOK... I'M NOT RUNNING A FEEL-UP CLUB HERE...
...BUT I'M NOT RUNNING AN SM CLUB HERE EITHER!
IF YOU WANT TO BEAT UP CUSTOMERS, TAKE IT SOMEWHERE ELSE!
RIGHT ON, MAN!
"RIGHT ON"? WHAT, AM I WEARING LOVE BEADS?
YOU'RE TRYING TO BE ANNOYING, AREN'T YOU?
TELL IT LIKE IT IS!
OTAE... YES, I DID ASK FOR YOU TO DO A LITTLE BOUNCER DUTY ON OUR WORST DRUNKS...
...BUT I THINK YOU'RE ENJOYING IT A LITTLE TOO MUCH.
DON'T YOU START TALKING ABOUT MY BOUNCERS TOO!
WATCH YOUR LANGUAGE! YOU'LL OFFEND OUR CUSTOMERS!!
AND YOU, ANE. I KNOW YOU NEED MONEY BUT YOU'RE COMING OFF AS TOO GREEDY.
A LOT OF CUSTOMERS HAVE COMPLAINED THAT YOU THREW THEM AWAY AS SOON AS THEY'D GIVEN YOU EVERY CENT IN THEIR WALLETS.
I NEVER THROW ANYTHING AWAY. I RECYCLE. TELL THEM THEM TO COME BACK AS SOON AS THEY'VE GOT MORE MONEY.
WELL, YOU CERTAINLY ARE GREEN...

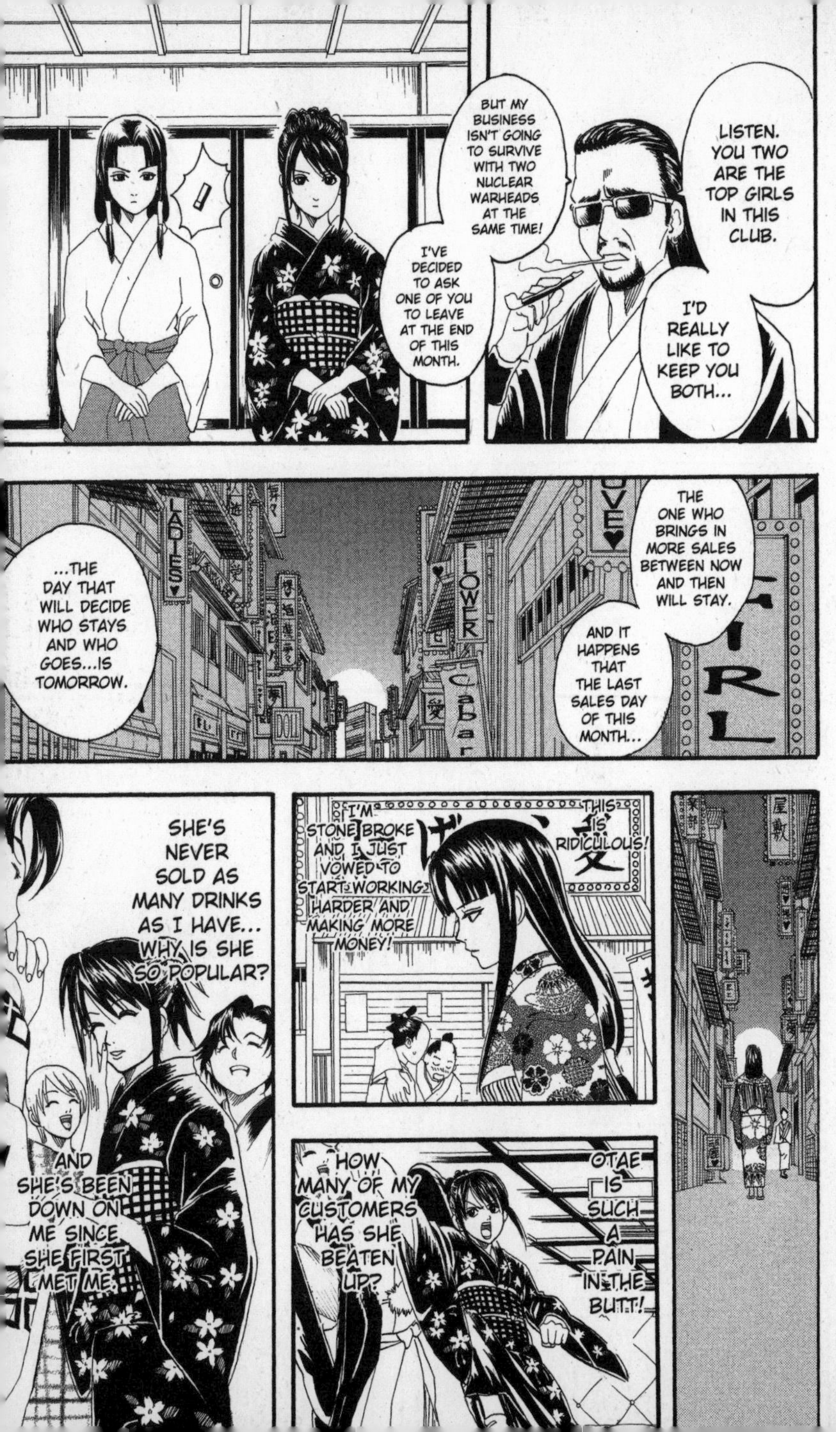
LISTEN. YOU TWO ARE THE TOP GIRLS IN THIS CLUB.
I'D REALLY LIKE TO KEEP YOU BOTH...
BUT MY BUSINESS ISN'T GOING TO SURVIVE WITH TWO NUCLEAR WARHEADS AT THE SAME TIME!
I'VE DECIDED TO ASK ONE OF YOU TO LEAVE AT THE END OF THIS MONTH.
!
THE ONE WHO BRINGS IN MORE SALES BETWEEN NOW AND THEN WILL STAY.
AND IT HAPPENS THAT THE LAST SALES DAY OF THIS MONTH...
...THE DAY THAT WILL DECIDE WHO STAYS AND WHO GOES...IS TOMORROW.
THIS IS RIDICULOUS!
I'M STONE BROKE AND I JUST VOWED TO START WORKING HARDER AND MAKING MORE MONEY!
OTAE IS SUCH A PAIN IN THE BUTT!
HOW MANY OF MY CUSTOMERS HAS SHE BEATEN UP?
SHE'S NEVER SOLD AS MANY DRINKS AS I HAVE... WHY IS SHE SO POPULAR?
AND SHE'S BEEN DOWN ON ME SINCE SHE FIRST MET ME.

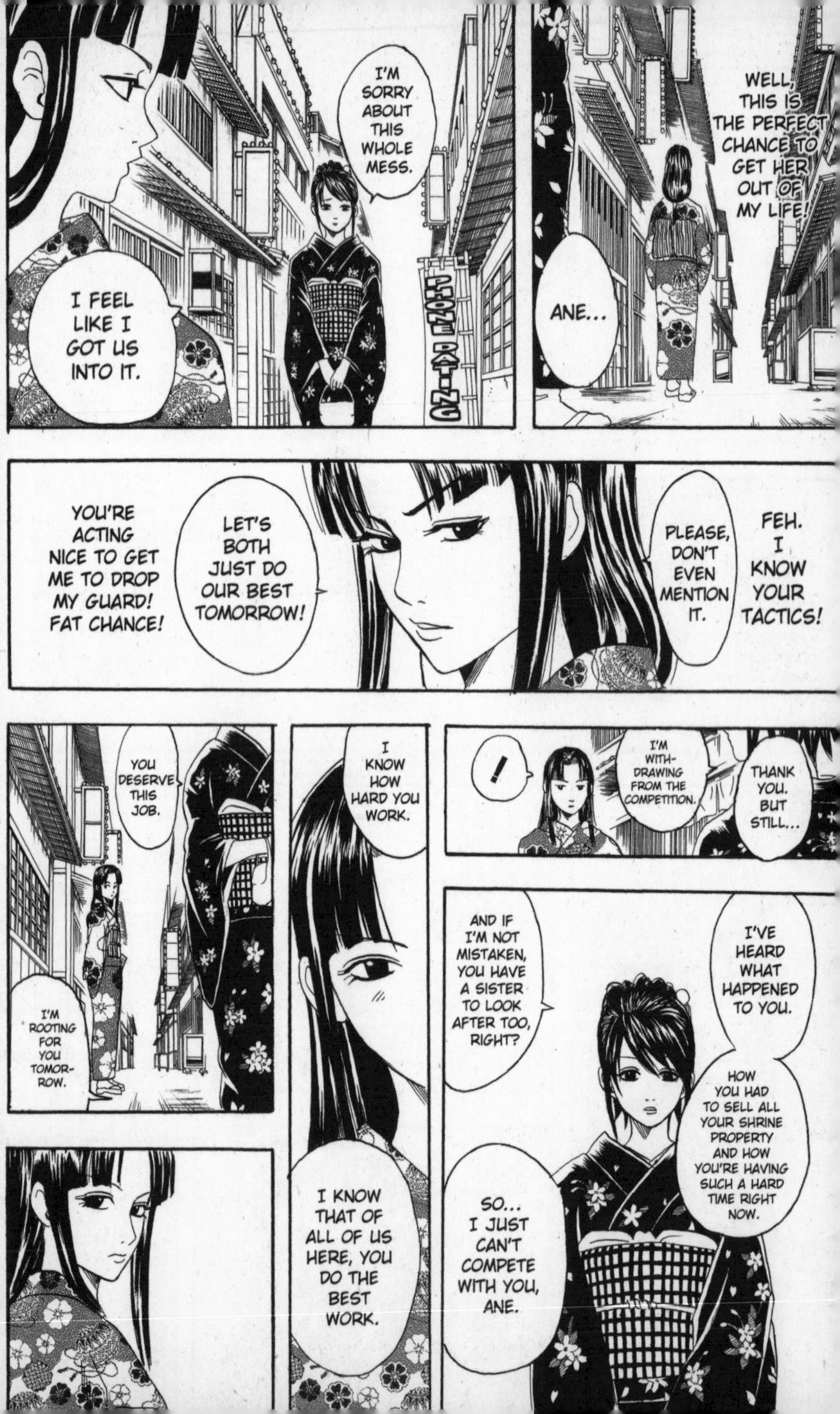

WELL, THIS IS THE PERFECT CHANCE TO GET HER OUT OF MY LIFE!
ANE...
I'M SORRY ABOUT THIS WHOLE MESS.
PHONE DATING
I FEEL LIKE I GOT US INTO IT.
FEH. I KNOW YOUR TACTICS!
PLEASE, DON'T EVEN MENTION IT.
LET'S BOTH JUST DO OUR BEST TOMORROW!
YOU'RE ACTING NICE TO GET ME TO DROP MY GUARD! FAT CHANCE!
THANK YOU. BUT STILL...
I'M WITH-DRAWING FROM THE COMPETITION.
!
I'VE HEARD WHAT HAPPENED TO YOU.
AND IF I'M NOT MISTAKEN, YOU HAVE A SISTER TO LOOK AFTER TOO, RIGHT?
HOW YOU HAD TO SELL ALL YOUR SHRINE PROPERTY AND HOW YOU'RE HAVING SUCH A HARD TIME RIGHT NOW.
SO... I JUST CAN'T COMPETE WITH YOU, ANE.
I KNOW HOW HARD YOU WORK.
I KNOW THAT OF ALL OF US HERE, YOU DO THE BEST WORK.
YOU DESERVE THIS JOB.
I'M ROOTING FOR YOU TOMOR-ROW.

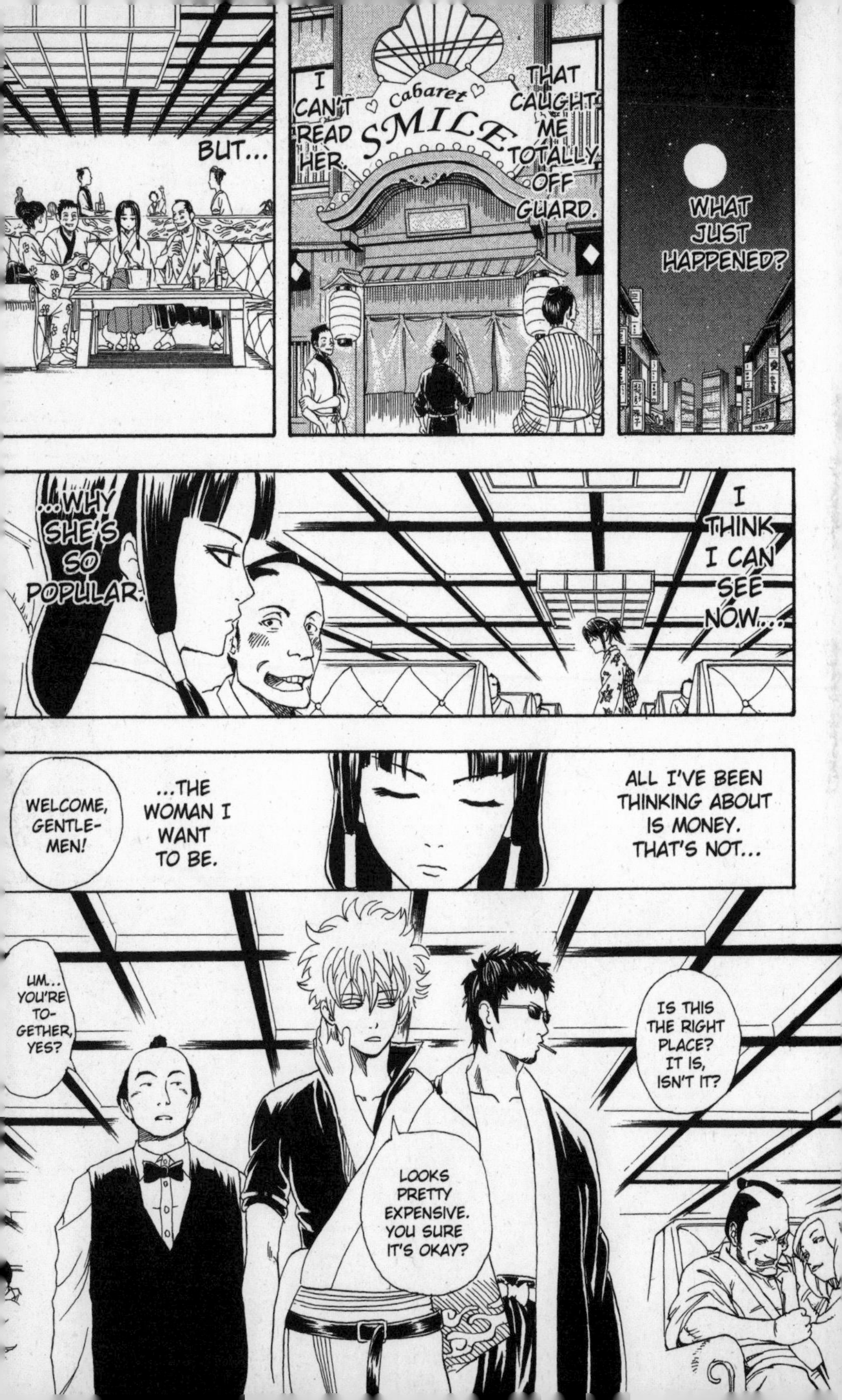
WHAT JUST HAPPENED?
THAT CAUGHT ME TOTALLY OFF GUARD.
I CAN'T READ HER.
Cabaret SMILE
BUT...
I THINK I CAN SEE NOW...
...WHY SHE'S SO POPULAR.
ALL I'VE BEEN THINKING ABOUT IS MONEY. THAT'S NOT...
...THE WOMAN I WANT TO BE.
WELCOME, GENTLE-MEN!
IS THIS THE RIGHT PLACE? IT IS, ISN'T IT?
LOOKS PRETTY EXPENSIVE. YOU SURE IT'S OKAY?
UM... YOU'RE TO-GETHER, YES?

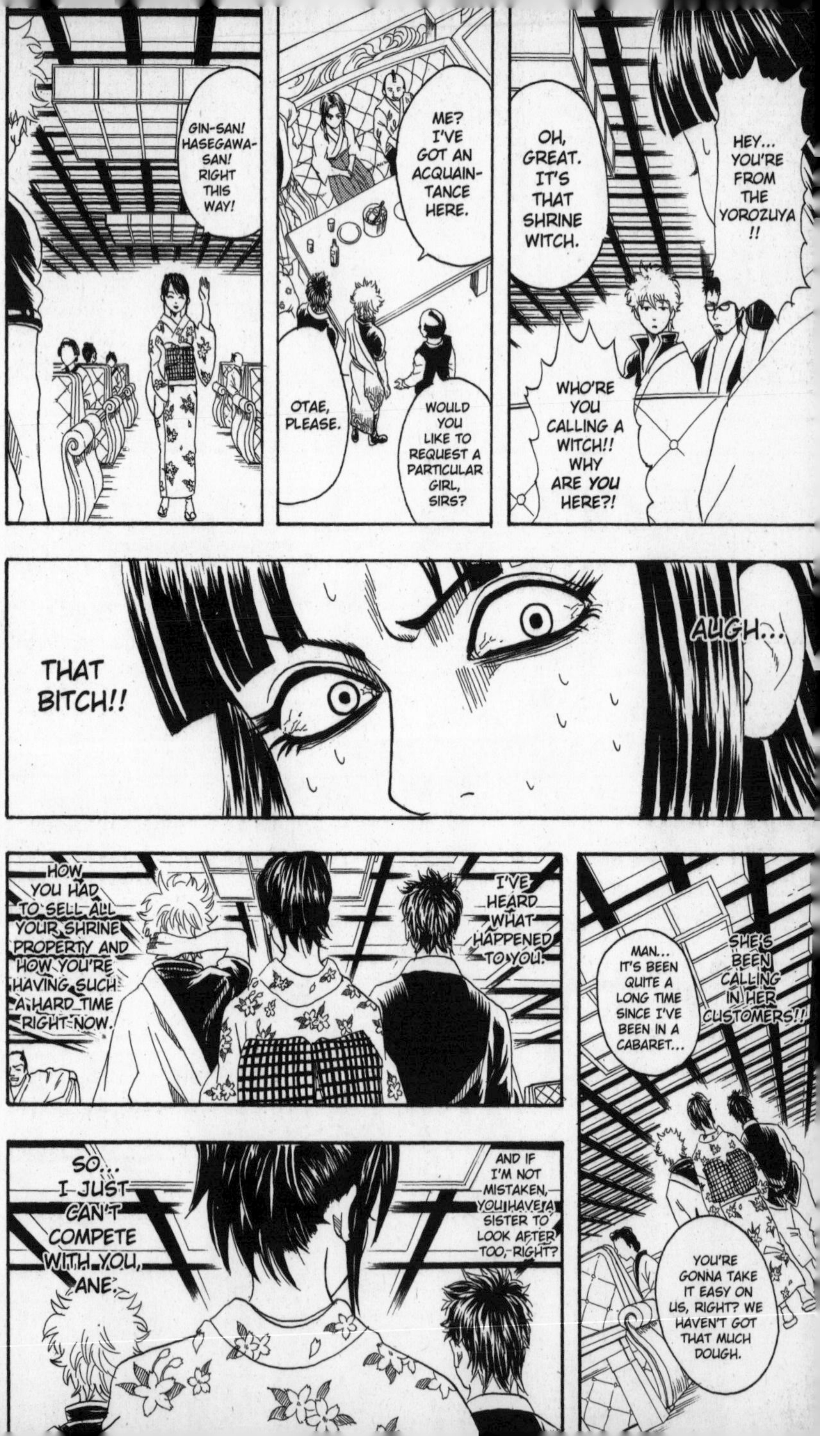
HEY... YOU'RE FROM THE YOROZUYA!!
OH, GREAT. IT'S THAT SHRINE WITCH.
WHO'RE YOU CALLING A WITCH!! WHY ARE YOU HERE?!
ME? I'VE GOT AN ACQUAIN-TANCE HERE.
WOULD YOU LIKE TO REQUEST A PARTICULAR GIRL, SIRS?
OTAE, PLEASE.
GIN-SAN! HASEGAWA-SAN! RIGHT THIS WAY!
AUGH...
THAT BITCH!!
SHE'S BEEN CALLING IN HER CUSTOMERS!!
MAN... IT'S BEEN QUITE A LONG TIME SINCE I'VE BEEN IN A CABARET...
YOU'RE GONNA TAKE IT EASY ON US, RIGHT? WE HAVEN'T GOT THAT MUCH DOUGH.
I'VE HEARD WHAT HAPPENED TO YOU.
HOW YOU HAD TO SELL ALL YOUR SHRINE PROPERTY AND HOW YOU'RE HAVING SUCH A HARD TIME RIGHT NOW.
AND IF I'M NOT MISTAKEN, YOU HAVE A SISTER TO LOOK AFTER TOO, RIGHT?
SO... I JUST CAN'T COMPETE WITH YOU, ANE.

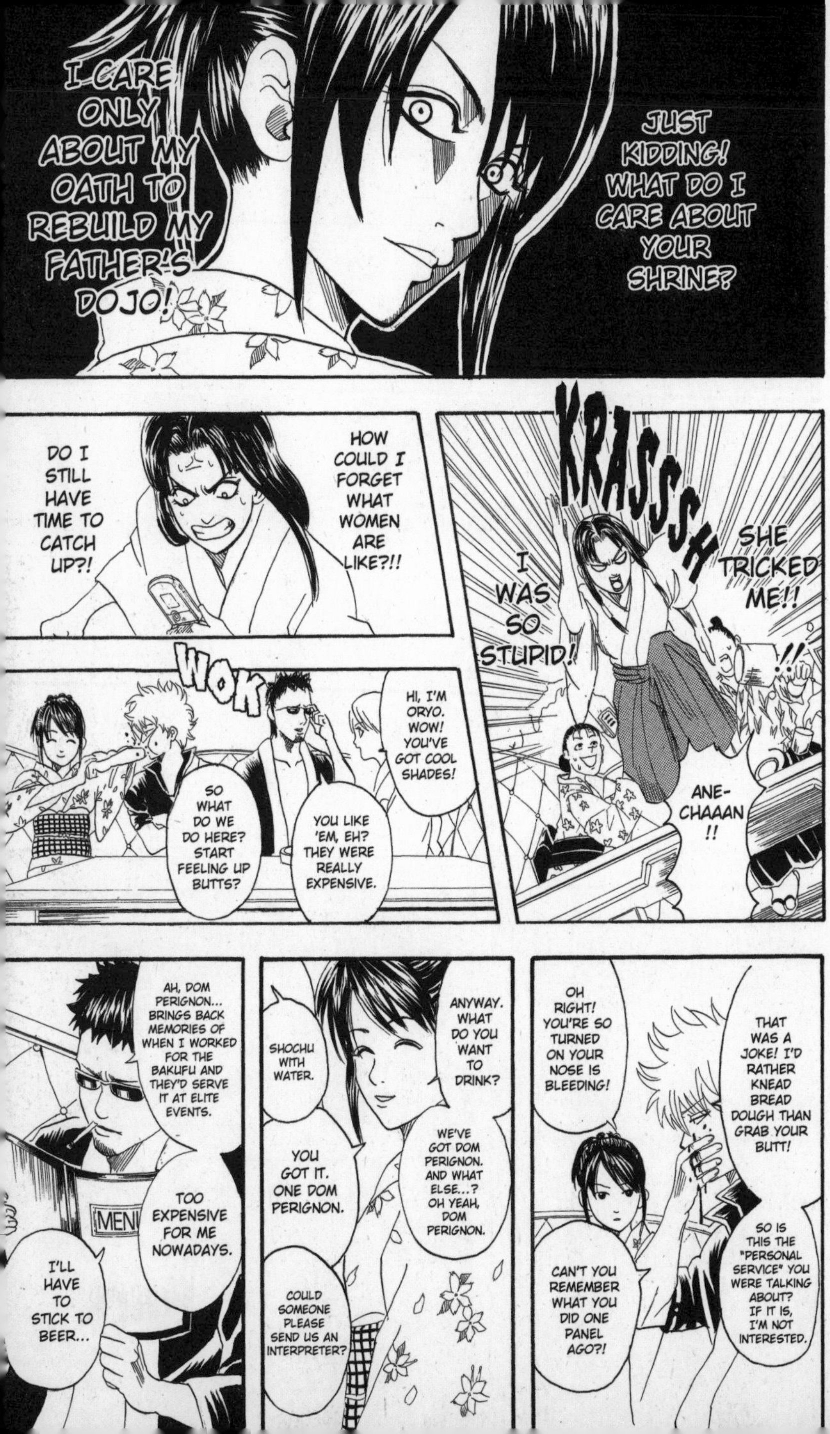
I CARE ONLY ABOUT MY OATH TO REBUILD MY FATHER'S DOJO!
JUST KIDDING! WHAT DO I CARE ABOUT YOUR SHRINE?
KRASSSH
SHE TRICKED ME!!
I WAS SO STUPID!
!!
ANE-CHAAAN!!
HOW COULD I FORGET WHAT WOMEN ARE LIKE?!!
DO I STILL HAVE TIME TO CATCH UP?!
WOK
HI, I'M ORYO. WOW! YOU'VE GOT COOL SHADES!
YOU LIKE 'EM, EH? THEY WERE REALLY EXPENSIVE.
SO WHAT DO WE DO HERE? START FEELING UP BUTTS?
THAT WAS A JOKE! I'D RATHER KNEAD BREAD DOUGH THAN GRAB YOUR BUTT!
OH RIGHT! YOU'RE SO TURNED ON YOUR NOSE IS BLEEDING!
SO IS THIS THE "PERSONAL SERVICE" YOU WERE TALKING ABOUT? IF IT IS, I'M NOT INTERESTED.
CAN'T YOU REMEMBER WHAT YOU DID ONE PANEL AGO?!
ANYWAY. WHAT DO YOU WANT TO DRINK?
SHOCHU WITH WATER.
WE'VE GOT DOM PERIGNON. AND WHAT ELSE...? OH YEAH, DOM PERIGNON.
YOU GOT IT. ONE DOM PERIGNON.
COULD SOMEONE PLEASE SEND US AN INTERPRETER?
AH, DOM PERIGNON... BRINGS BACK MEMORIES OF WHEN I WORKED FOR THE BAKUFU AND THEY'D SERVE IT AT ELITE EVENTS.
MENU
TOO EXPENSIVE FOR ME NOWADAYS.
I'LL HAVE TO STICK TO BEER...

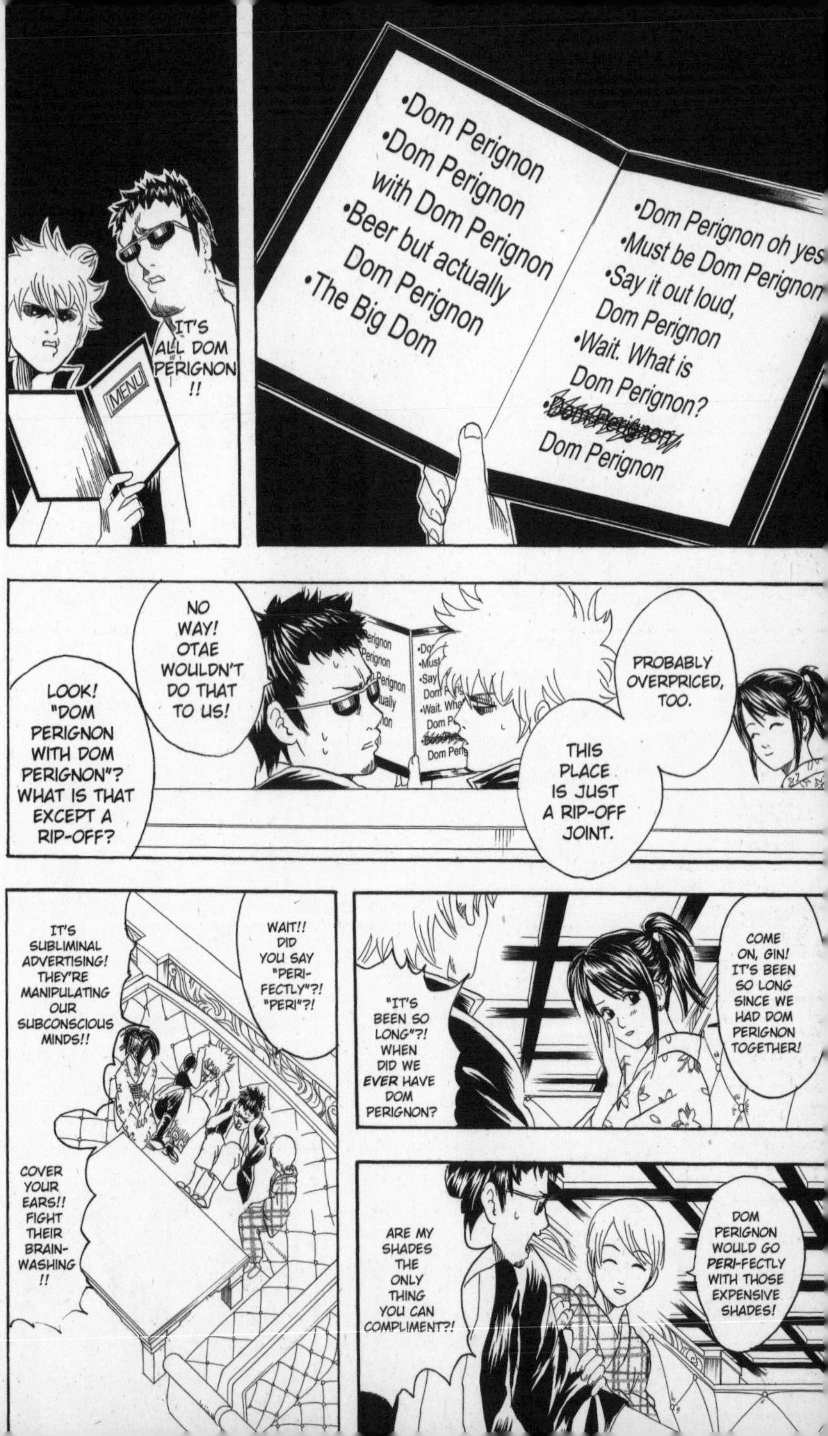

•Dom Perignon
•Dom Perignon with Dom Perignon
•Beer but actually Dom Perignon
•The Big Dom
•Dom Perignon oh yes
•Must be Dom Perignon
•Say it out loud, Dom Perignon
•Wait. What is Dom Perignon?
•~~Dom Perignon~~ Dom Perignon
IT'S ALL DOM PERIGNON !!
MENU
PROBABLY OVERPRICED, TOO.
THIS PLACE IS JUST A RIP-OFF JOINT.
NO WAY! OTAE WOULDN'T DO THAT TO US!
LOOK! "DOM PERIGNON WITH DOM PERIGNON"? WHAT IS THAT EXCEPT A RIP-OFF?
COME ON, GIN! IT'S BEEN SO LONG SINCE WE HAD DOM PERIGNON TOGETHER!
"IT'S BEEN SO LONG"?! WHEN DID WE EVER HAVE DOM PERIGNON?
DOM PERIGNON WOULD GO PERI-FECTLY WITH THOSE EXPENSIVE SHADES!
ARE MY SHADES THE ONLY THING YOU CAN COMPLIMENT?!
WAIT!! DID YOU SAY "PERI-FECTLY"?! "PERI"?!
IT'S SUBLIMINAL ADVERTISING! THEY'RE MANIPULATING OUR SUBCONSCIOUS MINDS!!
COVER YOUR EARS!! FIGHT THEIR BRAIN-WASHING !!

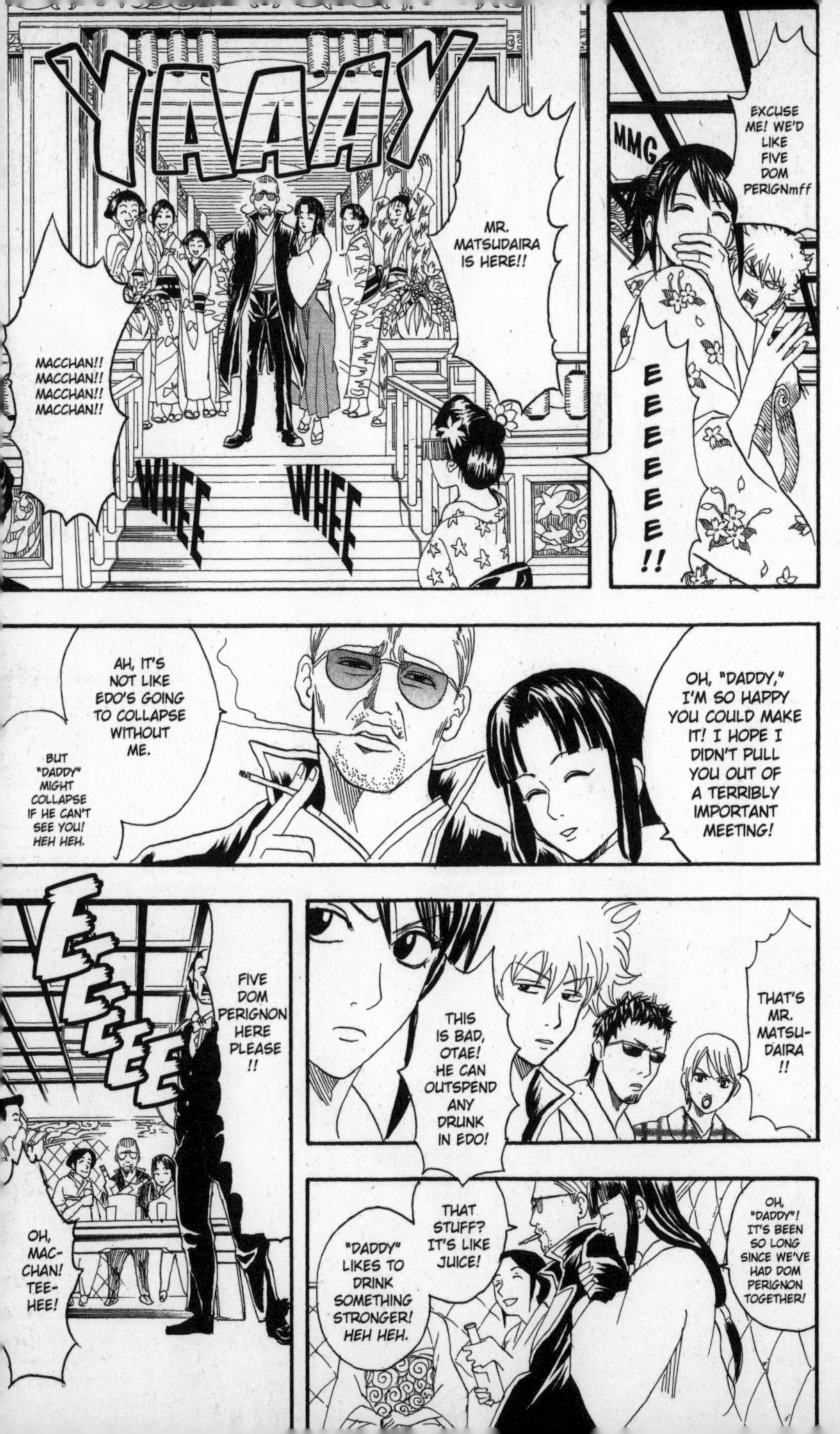
EXCUSE ME! WE'D LIKE FIVE DOM PERIGNmff
MMG
EEEEEE!!
MR. MATSUDAIRA IS HERE!!
YAAAY
MACCHAN!! MACCHAN!! MACCHAN!! MACCHAN!!
WHEE
WHEE
OH, "DADDY," I'M SO HAPPY YOU COULD MAKE IT! I HOPE I DIDN'T PULL YOU OUT OF A TERRIBLY IMPORTANT MEETING!
AH, IT'S NOT LIKE EDO'S GOING TO COLLAPSE WITHOUT ME.
BUT "DADDY" MIGHT COLLAPSE IF HE CAN'T SEE YOU! HEH HEH.
THAT'S MR. MATSU-DAIRA!!
THIS IS BAD, OTAE! HE CAN OUTSPEND ANY DRUNK IN EDO!
OH, "DADDY"! IT'S BEEN SO LONG SINCE WE'VE HAD DOM PERIGNON TOGETHER!
THAT STUFF? IT'S LIKE JUICE!
"DADDY" LIKES TO DRINK SOMETHING STRONGER! HEH HEH.
EEEEE
FIVE DOM PERIGNON HERE PLEASE!!
OH, MAC-CHAN! TEE-HEE!

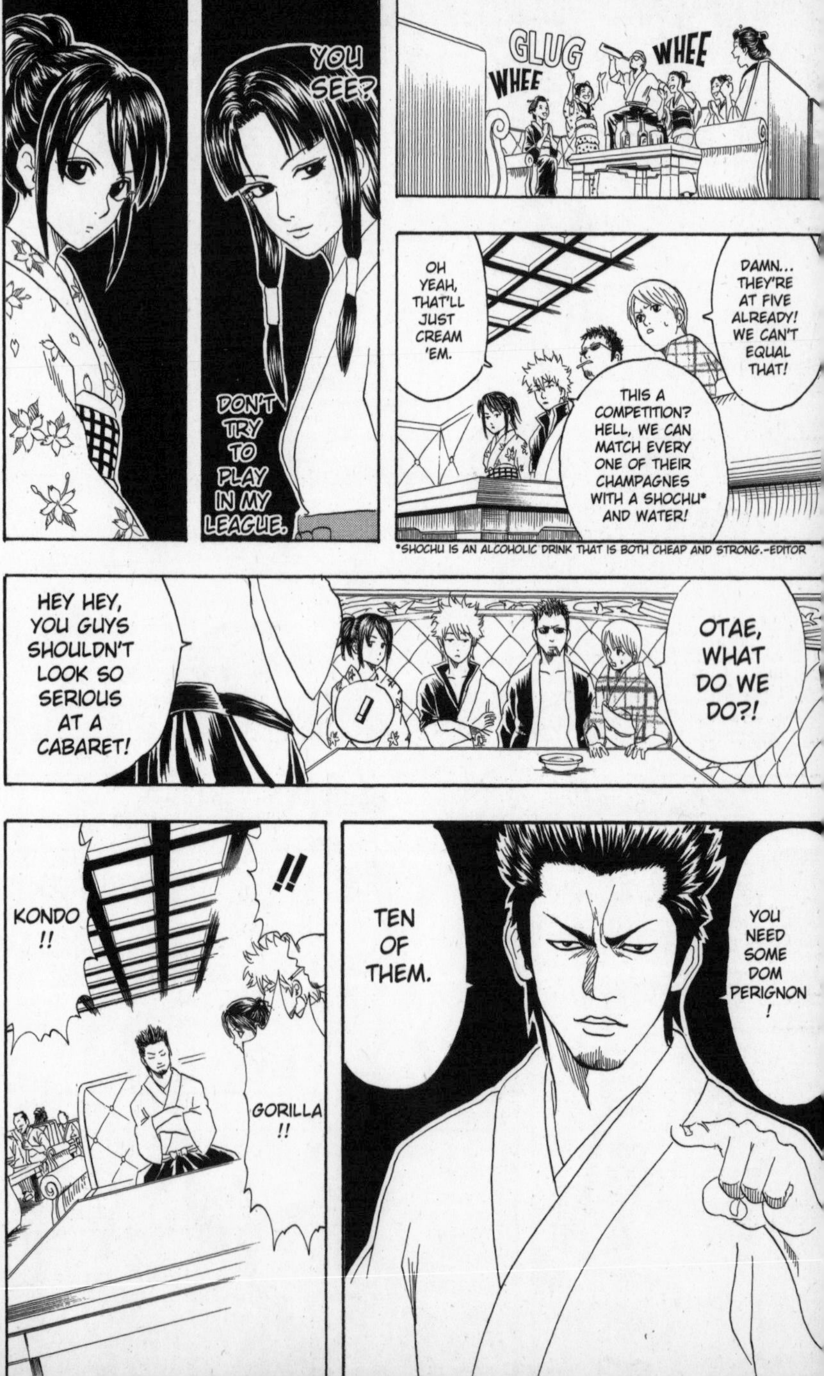
GLUG
WHEE
WHEE
DAMN... THEY'RE AT FIVE ALREADY! WE CAN'T EQUAL THAT!
THIS A COMPETITION? HELL, WE CAN MATCH EVERY ONE OF THEIR CHAMPAGNES WITH A SHOCHU* AND WATER!
OH YEAH, THAT'LL JUST CREAM 'EM.
*SHOCHU IS AN ALCOHOLIC DRINK THAT IS BOTH CHEAP AND STRONG.-EDITOR
YOU SEE?
DON'T TRY TO PLAY IN MY LEAGUE.
OTAE, WHAT DO WE DO?!
!
HEY HEY, YOU GUYS SHOULDN'T LOOK SO SERIOUS AT A CABARET!
YOU NEED SOME DOM PERIGNON!
TEN OF THEM.
!!
KONDO!!
GORILLA!!

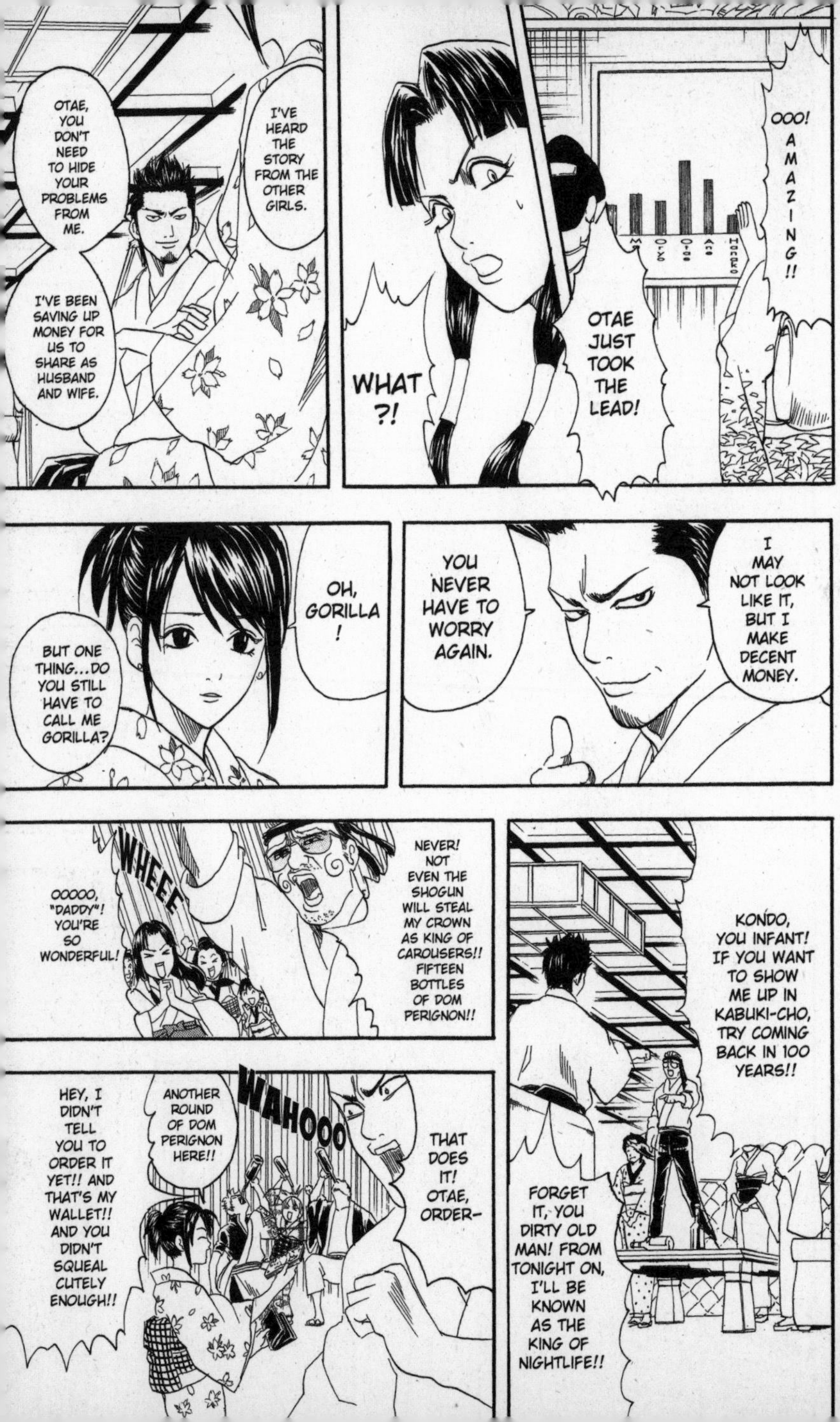
OOO! AMAZING!!
OTAE JUST TOOK THE LEAD!
WHAT?!
I'VE HEARD THE STORY FROM THE OTHER GIRLS.
OTAE, YOU DON'T NEED TO HIDE YOUR PROBLEMS FROM ME.
I'VE BEEN SAVING UP MONEY FOR US TO SHARE AS HUSBAND AND WIFE.
I MAY NOT LOOK LIKE IT, BUT I MAKE DECENT MONEY.
YOU NEVER HAVE TO WORRY AGAIN.
OH, GORILLA!
BUT ONE THING...DO YOU STILL HAVE TO CALL ME GORILLA?
KONDO, YOU INFANT! IF YOU WANT TO SHOW ME UP IN KABUKI-CHO, TRY COMING BACK IN 100 YEARS!!
FORGET IT, YOU DIRTY OLD MAN! FROM TONIGHT ON, I'LL BE KNOWN AS THE KING OF NIGHTLIFE!!
NEVER! NOT EVEN THE SHOGUN WILL STEAL MY CROWN AS KING OF CAROUSERS!! FIFTEEN BOTTLES OF DOM PERIGNON!!
WHEEE
OOOOO, "DADDY"! YOU'RE SO WONDERFUL!
THAT DOES IT! OTAE, ORDER-
WAHOOO
ANOTHER ROUND OF DOM PERIGNON HERE!!
HEY, I DIDN'T TELL YOU TO ORDER IT YET!! AND THAT'S MY WALLET!! AND YOU DIDN'T SQUEAL CUTELY ENOUGH!!

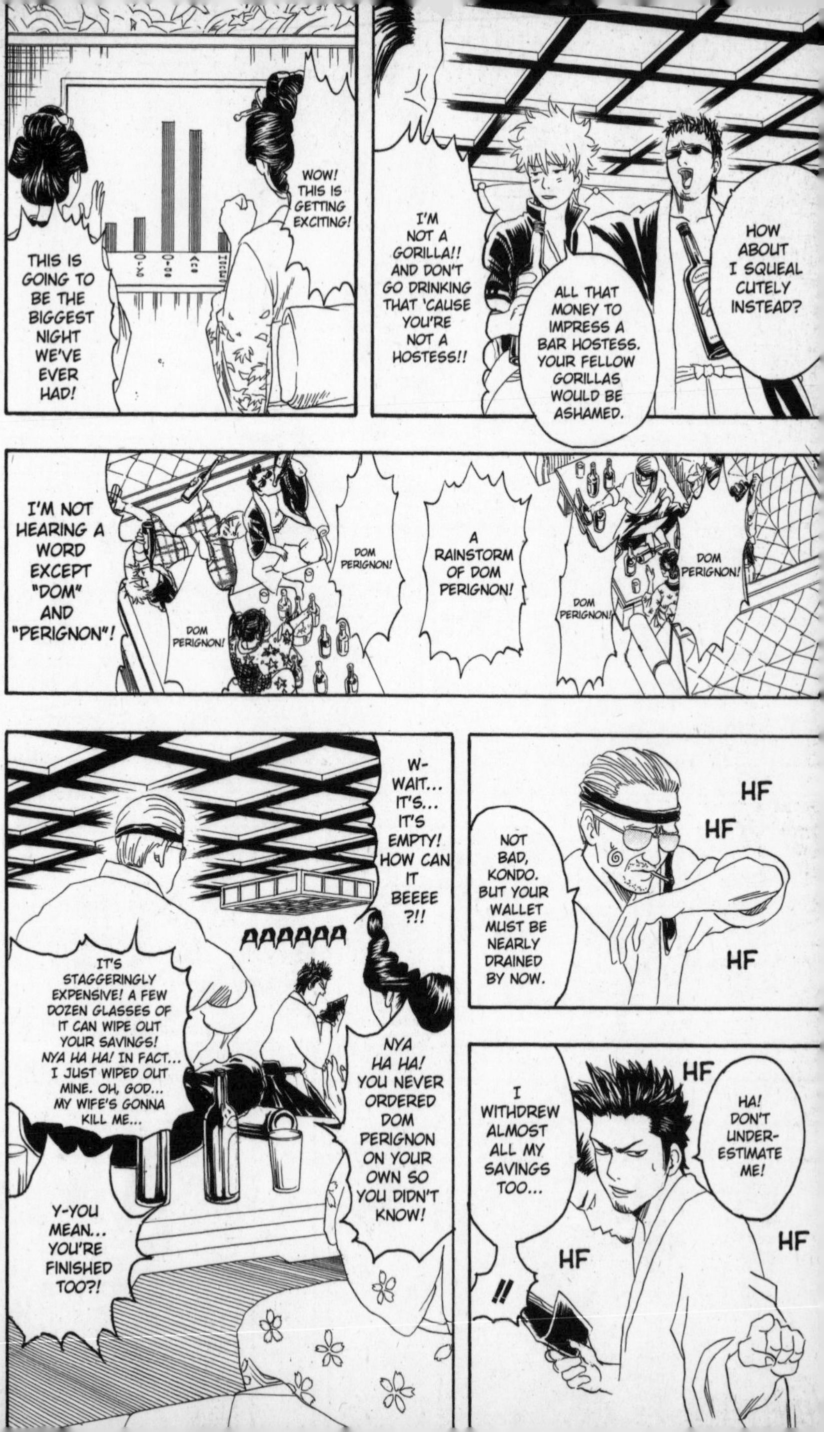
HOW ABOUT I SQUEAL CUTELY INSTEAD?
ALL THAT MONEY TO IMPRESS A BAR HOSTESS. YOUR FELLOW GORILLAS WOULD BE ASHAMED.
I'M NOT A GORILLA!! AND DON'T GO DRINKING THAT 'CAUSE YOU'RE NOT A HOSTESS!!
WOW! THIS IS GETTING EXCITING!
THIS IS GOING TO BE THE BIGGEST NIGHT WE'VE EVER HAD!
DOM PERIGNON!
DOM PERIGNON!
A RAINSTORM OF DOM PERIGNON!
DOM PERIGNON!
I'M NOT HEARING A WORD EXCEPT "DOM" AND "PERIGNON"!
DOM PERIGNON!
HF
HF
NOT BAD, KONDO. BUT YOUR WALLET MUST BE NEARLY DRAINED BY NOW.
HF
HF
HA! DON'T UNDER-ESTIMATE ME!
I WITHDREW ALMOST ALL MY SAVINGS TOO...
HF
HF
!!
W-WAIT... IT'S... IT'S EMPTY! HOW CAN IT BEEEE ?!!
AAAAAA
IT'S STAGGERINGLY EXPENSIVE! A FEW DOZEN GLASSES OF IT CAN WIPE OUT YOUR SAVINGS! NYA HA HA! IN FACT... I JUST WIPED OUT MINE. OH, GOD... MY WIFE'S GONNA KILL ME...
NYA HA HA! YOU NEVER ORDERED DOM PERIGNON ON YOUR OWN SO YOU DIDN'T KNOW!
Y-YOU MEAN... YOU'RE FINISHED TOO?!

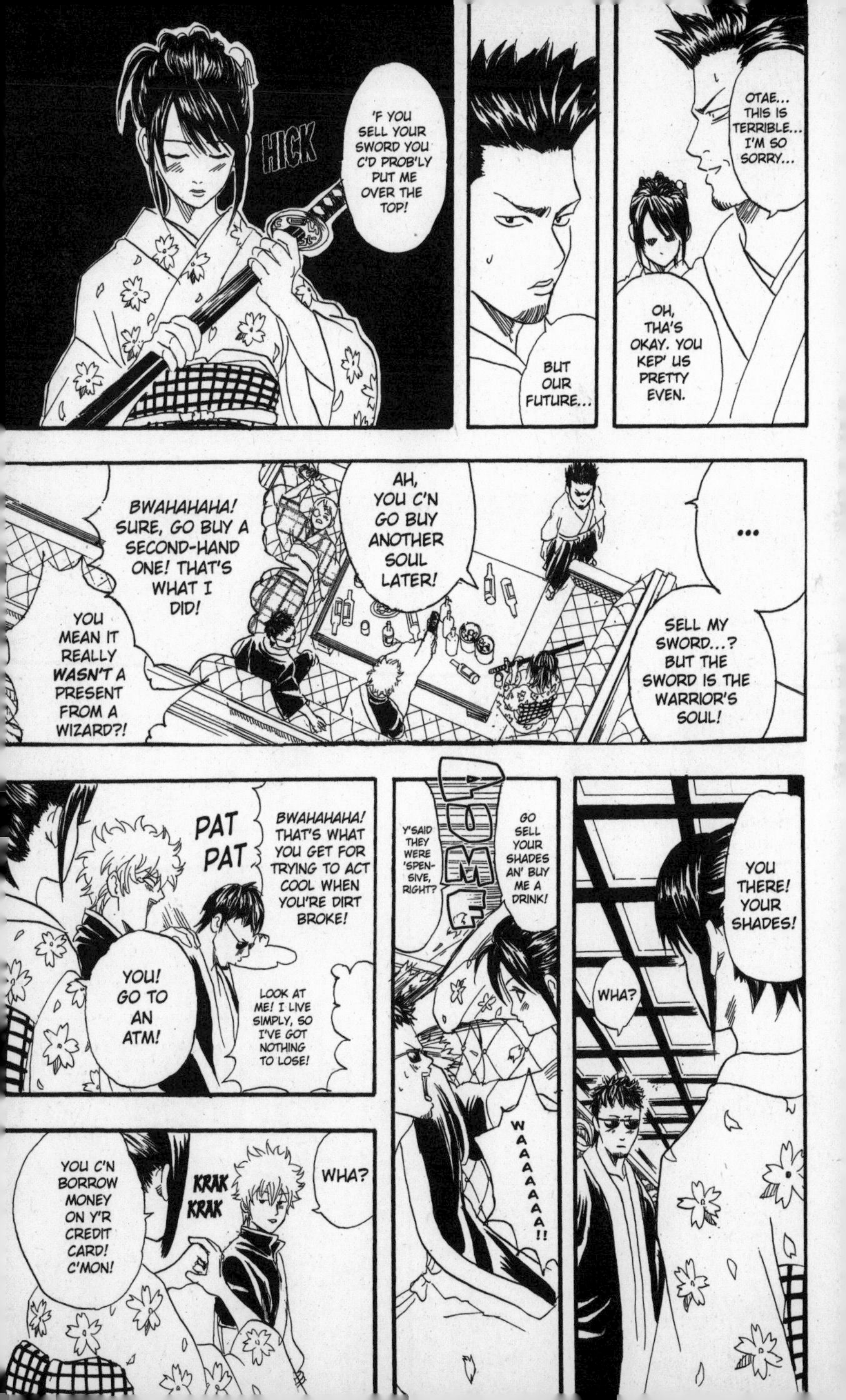
OTAE... THIS IS TERRIBLE... I'M SO SORRY...
OH, THA'S OKAY. YOU KEP' US PRETTY EVEN.
BUT OUR FUTURE...
HICK
'F YOU SELL YOUR SWORD YOU C'D PROB'LY PUT ME OVER THE TOP!
...
SELL MY SWORD...? BUT THE SWORD IS THE WARRIOR'S SOUL!
AH, YOU C'N GO BUY ANOTHER SOUL LATER!
BWAHAHAHA! SURE, GO BUY A SECOND-HAND ONE! THAT'S WHAT I DID!
YOU MEAN IT REALLY WASN'T A PRESENT FROM A WIZARD?!
YOU THERE! YOUR SHADES!
WHA?
GO SELL YOUR SHADES AN' BUY ME A DRINK!
POMF
Y'SAID THEY WERE 'SPEN-SIVE, RIGHT?
WAAAAAAA!!
BWAHAHAHA! THAT'S WHAT YOU GET FOR TRYING TO ACT COOL WHEN YOU'RE DIRT BROKE!
PAT PAT
YOU! GO TO AN ATM!
LOOK AT ME! I LIVE SIMPLY, SO I'VE GOT NOTHING TO LOSE!
WHA?
KRAK KRAK
YOU C'N BORROW MONEY ON Y'R CREDIT CARD! C'MON!

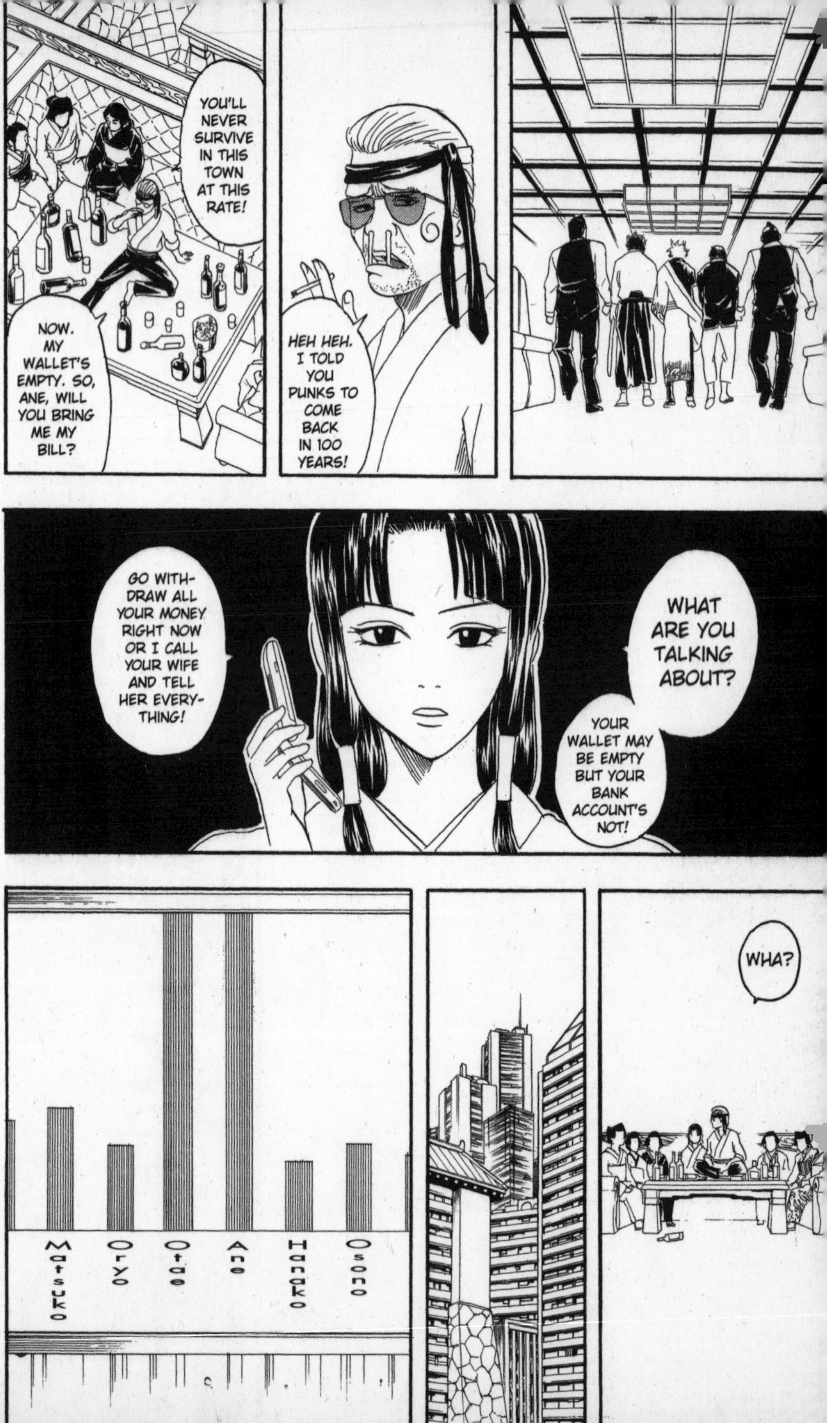
HEH HEH. I TOLD YOU PUNKS TO COME BACK IN 100 YEARS!
YOU'LL NEVER SURVIVE IN THIS TOWN AT THIS RATE!
NOW. MY WALLET'S EMPTY. SO, ANE, WILL YOU BRING ME MY BILL?
WHAT ARE YOU TALKING ABOUT?
YOUR WALLET MAY BE EMPTY BUT YOUR BANK ACCOUNT'S NOT!
GO WITH-DRAW ALL YOUR MONEY RIGHT NOW OR I CALL YOUR WIFE AND TELL HER EVERY-THING!
WHA?
Matsuko
Oryo
Otae
Ane
Hanako
Osono

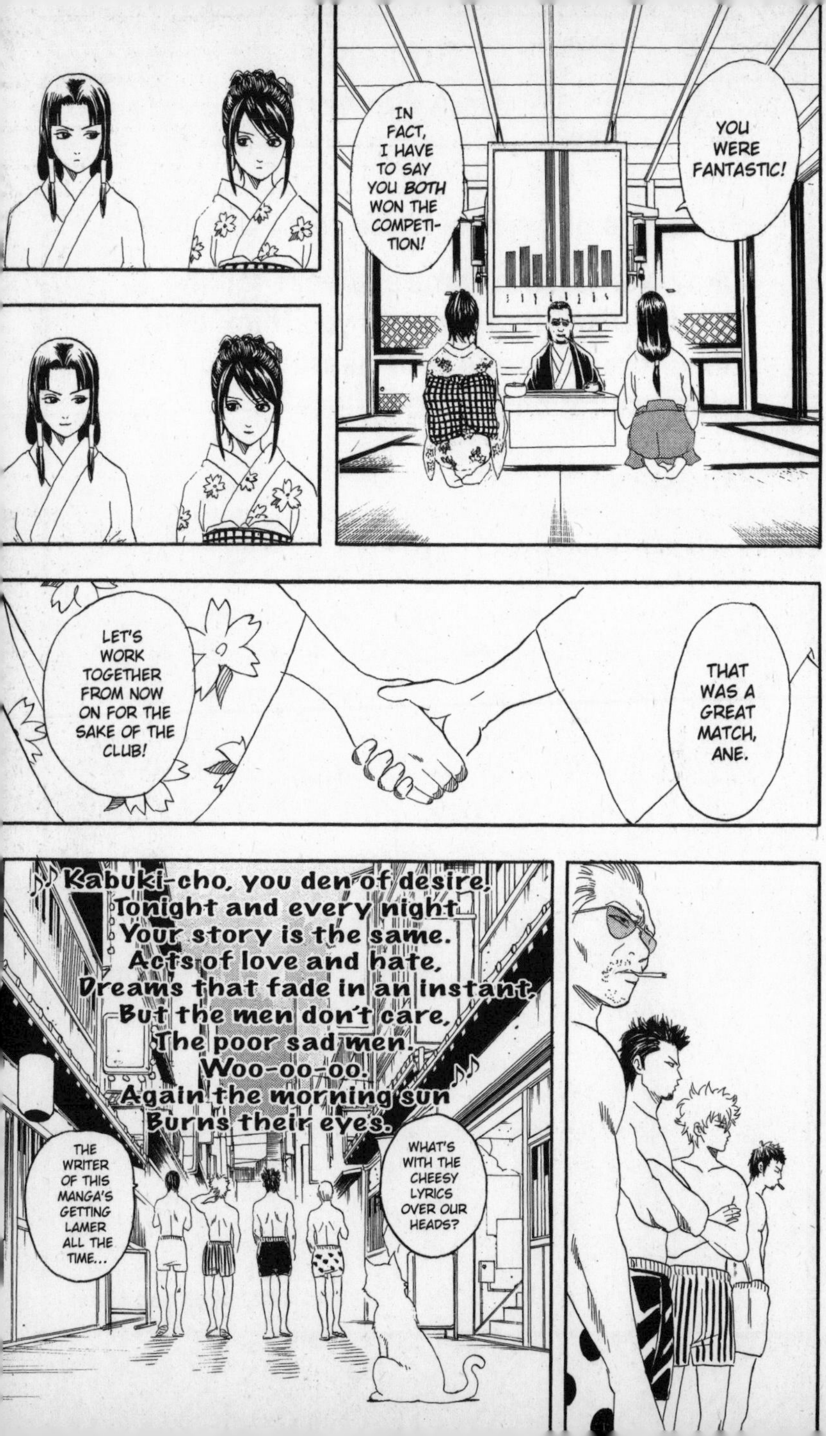

YOU WERE FANTASTIC!
IN FACT, I HAVE TO SAY YOU BOTH WON THE COMPETITION!
THAT WAS A GREAT MATCH, ANE.
LET'S WORK TOGETHER FROM NOW ON FOR THE SAKE OF THE CLUB!
♪♪ Kabuki-cho, you den of desire. Tonight and every night Your story is the same. Acts of love and hate, Dreams that fade in an instant, But the men don't care, The poor sad men. Woo-oo-oo. ♪♪ Again the morning sun Burns their eyes.
WHAT'S WITH THE CHEESY LYRICS OVER OUR HEADS?
THE WRITER OF THIS MANGA'S GETTING LAMER ALL THE TIME...

Sorachi's Q&A Corner #21

<From Amamiya-san of Wakayama Prefecture>

Okay, sensei. Gin Tama's always talking about *JUMP*...but what do you think of it? Does it really make your heart pound with inspiration and adventure?

<Answer>

Sadly, I didn't read *JUMP* when I was a kid. I read some things like *Dragon Ball* and *Knights of the Zodiac* in book form, but mostly I was into watching TV. The only comics magazine I used to collect was *WANPAKKU*. I'm always looking for people who were into it, 'cause when the conversation comes around to manga we read as kids I get all fired up about *WANPAKKU* and everybody else just gives me a blank stare. I collected it until it got cancelled, but then my mom threw away all my issues. I was so mad! Didn't anybody else read the thing?! Isn't there anybody else out there who could stay up all night talking about *WANPAKKU*?!

(Q&A #22 is on page 166)

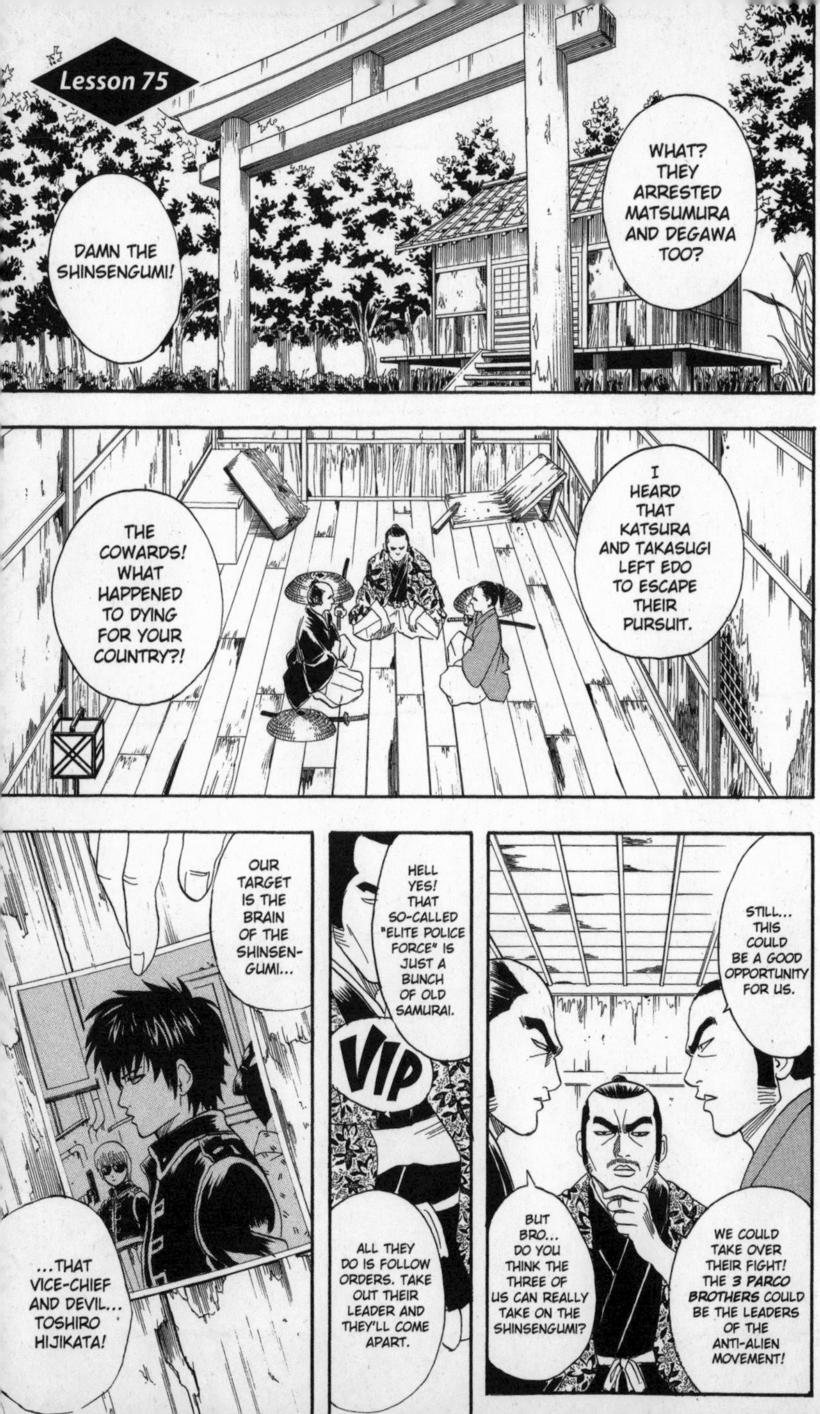
Lesson 75
WHAT? THEY ARRESTED MATSUMURA AND DEGAWA TOO?
DAMN THE SHINSENGUMI!
I HEARD THAT KATSURA AND TAKASUGI LEFT EDO TO ESCAPE THEIR PURSUIT.
THE COWARDS! WHAT HAPPENED TO DYING FOR YOUR COUNTRY?!
STILL... THIS COULD BE A GOOD OPPORTUNITY FOR US.
WE COULD TAKE OVER THEIR FIGHT! THE 3 *PARCO BROTHERS* COULD BE THE LEADERS OF THE ANTI-ALIEN MOVEMENT!
BUT BRO... DO YOU THINK THE THREE OF US CAN REALLY TAKE ON THE SHINSENGUMI?
HELL YES! THAT SO-CALLED "ELITE POLICE FORCE" IS JUST A BUNCH OF OLD SAMURAI.
VIP
ALL THEY DO IS FOLLOW ORDERS. TAKE OUT THEIR LEADER AND THEY'LL COME APART.
OUR TARGET IS THE BRAIN OF THE SHINSEN-GUMI...
...THAT VICE-CHIEF AND DEVIL... TOSHIRO HIJIKATA!

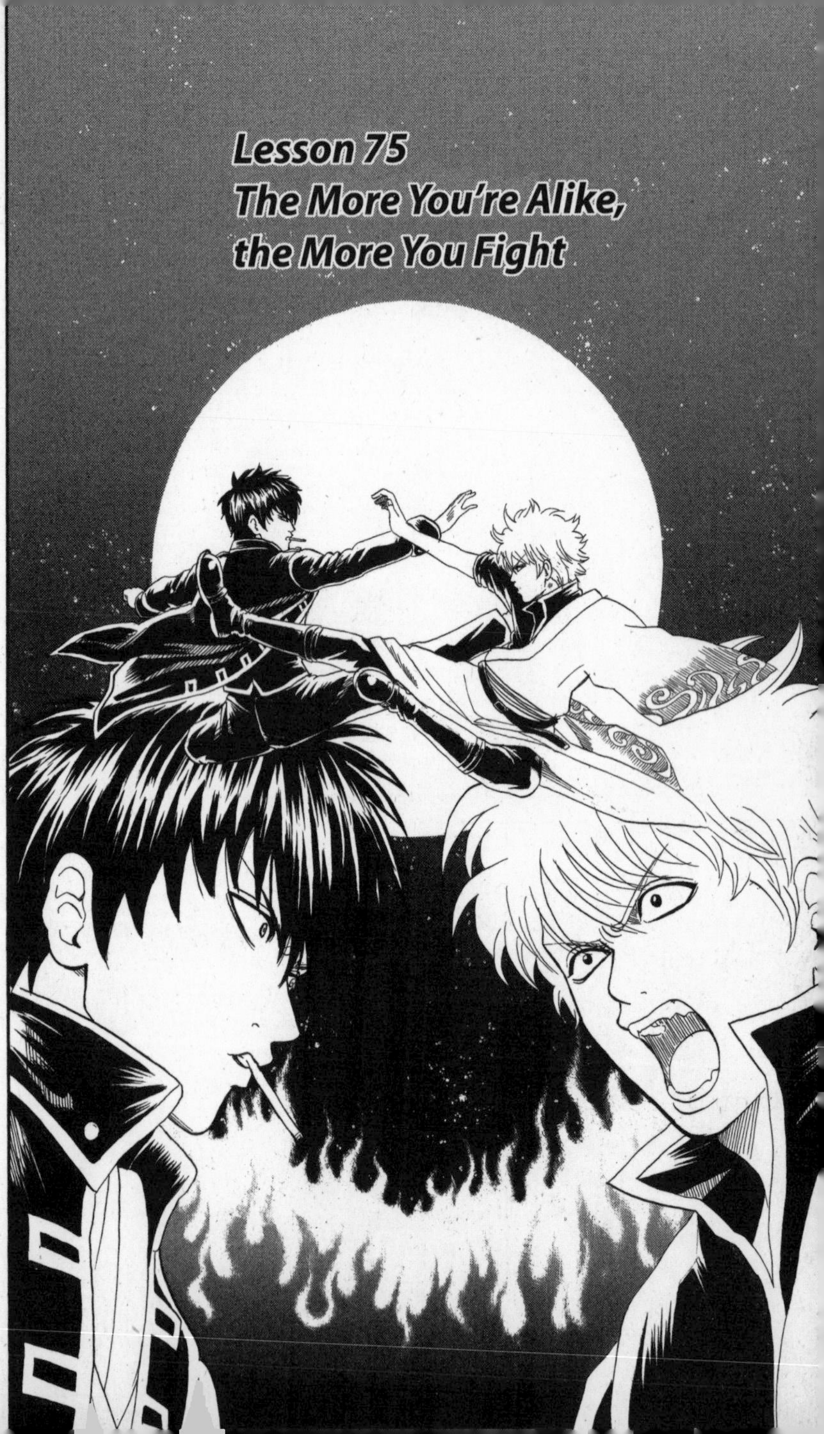
Lesson 75
The More You're Alike, the More You Fight

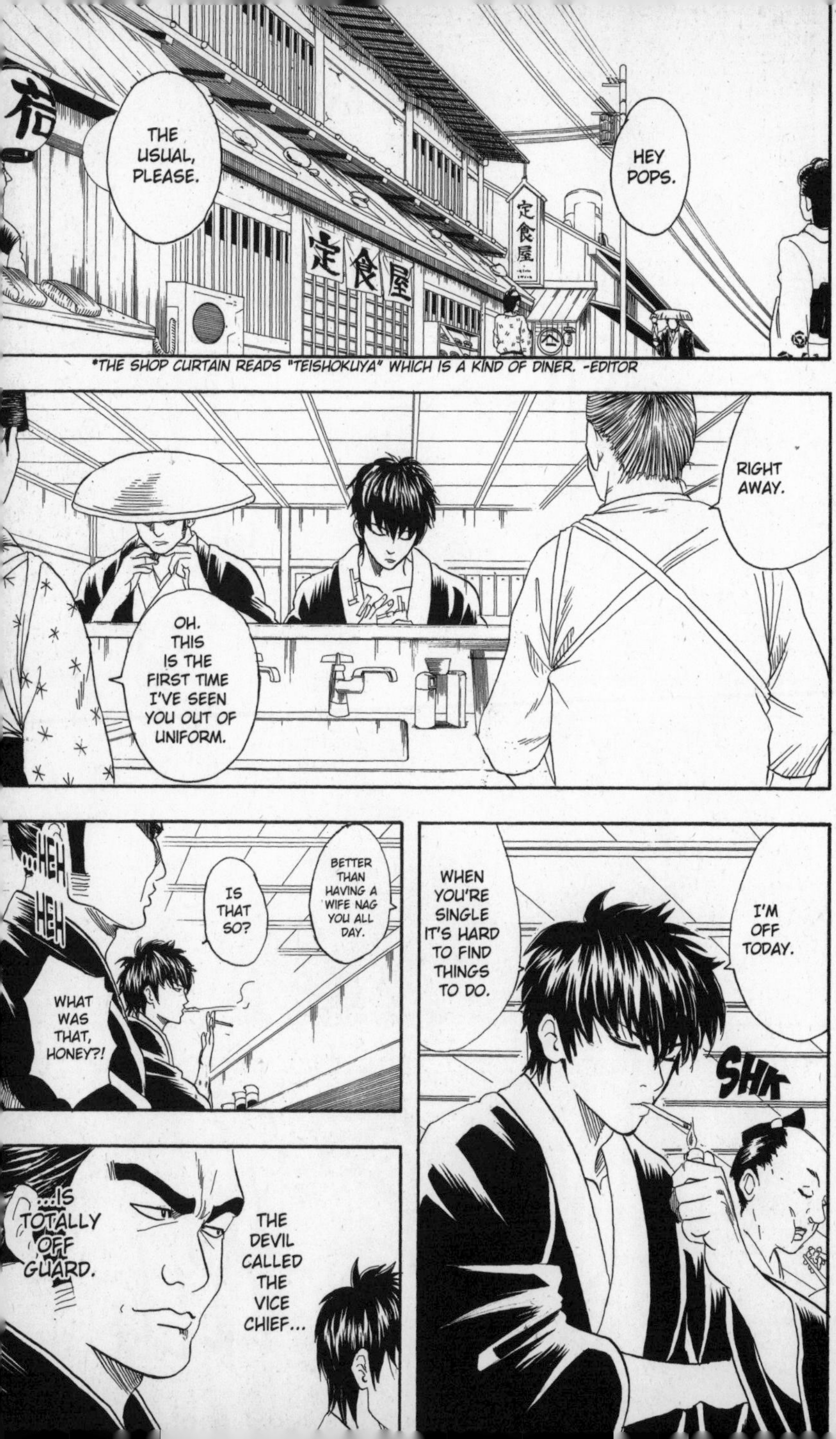
HEY POPS.
THE USUAL, PLEASE.
RIGHT AWAY.
OH. THIS IS THE FIRST TIME I'VE SEEN YOU OUT OF UNIFORM.
I'M OFF TODAY.
WHEN YOU'RE SINGLE IT'S HARD TO FIND THINGS TO DO.
SHK
BETTER THAN HAVING A WIFE NAG YOU ALL DAY.
IS THAT SO?
...HEH HEH
WHAT WAS THAT, HONEY?!
THE DEVIL CALLED THE VICE CHIEF...
...IS TOTALLY OFF GUARD.
*THE SHOP CURTAIN READS "TEISHOKUYA" WHICH IS A KIND OF DINER. -EDITOR

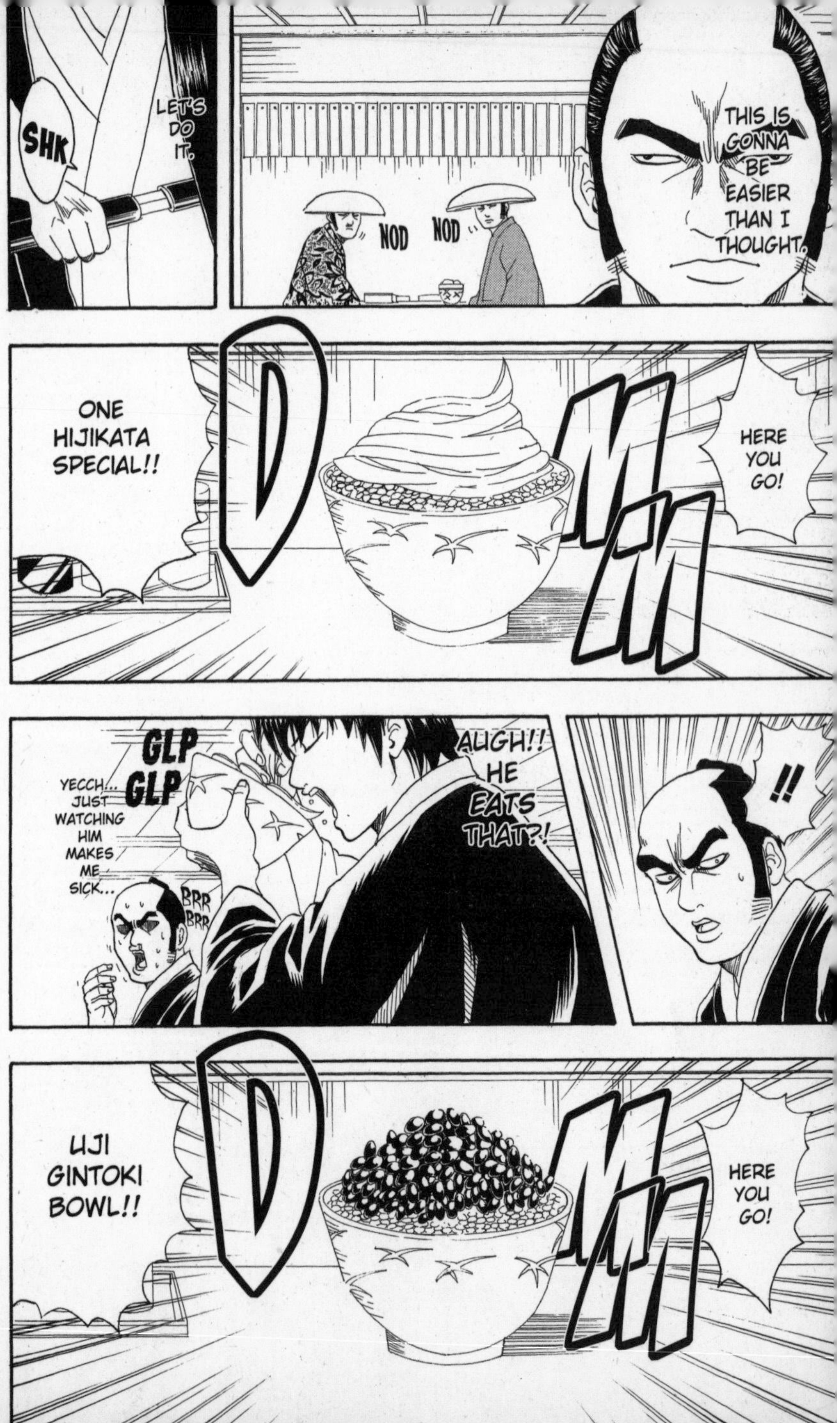
THIS IS GONNA BE EASIER THAN I THOUGHT.
NOD
NOD
LET'S DO IT.
SHK
HERE YOU GO!
DMM
ONE HIJIKATA SPECIAL!!
!!
AUGH!! HE EATS THAT?!
GLP GLP
YECCH... JUST WATCHING HIM MAKES ME SICK...
BRR BRR
HERE YOU GO!
DMM
UJI GINTOKI BOWL!!

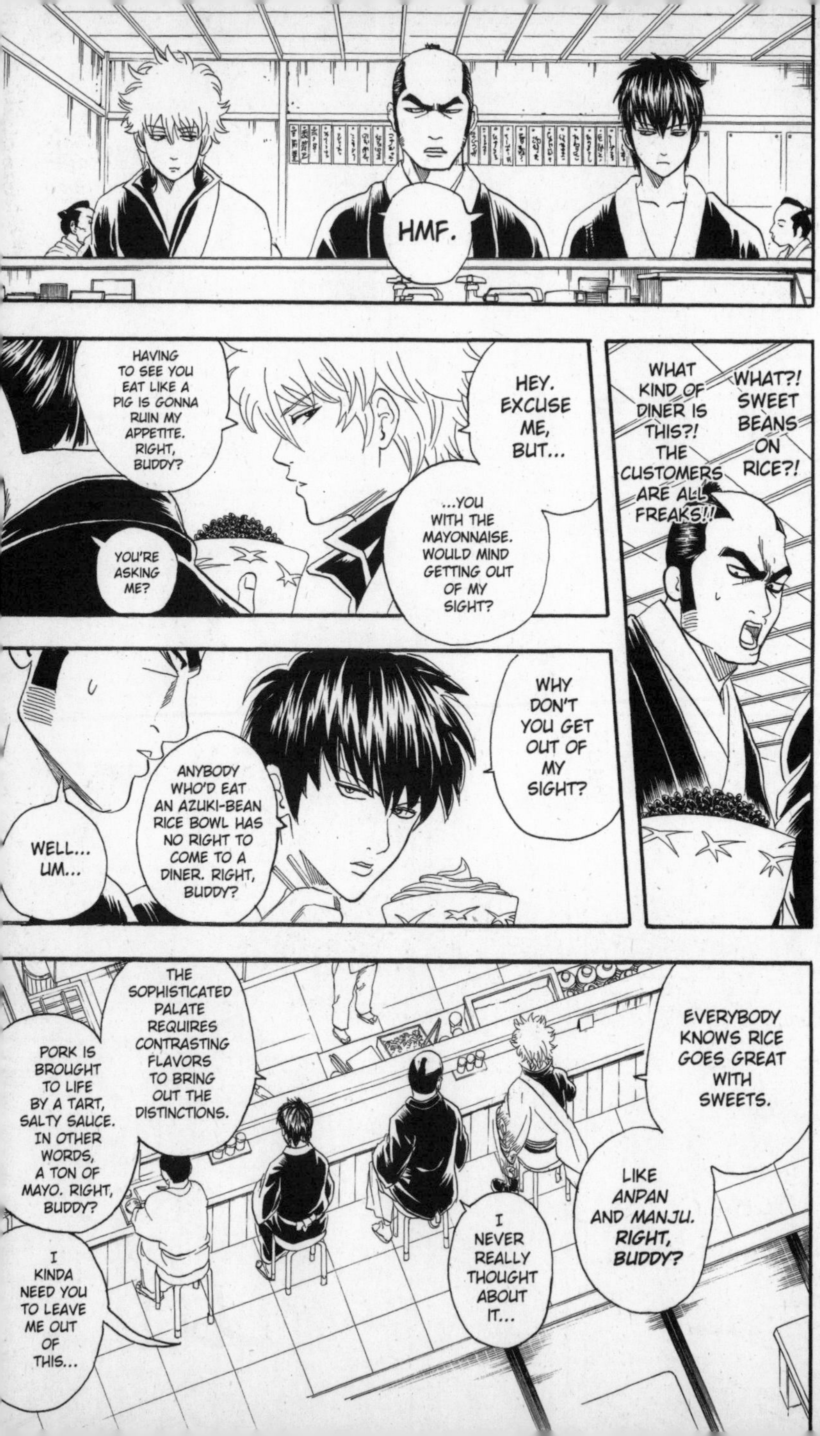
HMF.
WHAT?! SWEET BEANS ON RICE?!
WHAT KIND OF DINER IS THIS?! THE CUSTOMERS ARE ALL FREAKS!!
HEY. EXCUSE ME, BUT...
...YOU WITH THE MAYONNAISE. WOULD MIND GETTING OUT OF MY SIGHT?
HAVING TO SEE YOU EAT LIKE A PIG IS GONNA RUIN MY APPETITE. RIGHT, BUDDY?
YOU'RE ASKING ME?
WHY DON'T YOU GET OUT OF MY SIGHT?
ANYBODY WHO'D EAT AN AZUKI-BEAN RICE BOWL HAS NO RIGHT TO COME TO A DINER. RIGHT, BUDDY?
WELL... UM...
EVERYBODY KNOWS RICE GOES GREAT WITH SWEETS.
LIKE ANPAN AND MANJU. RIGHT, BUDDY?
I NEVER REALLY THOUGHT ABOUT IT...
THE SOPHISTICATED PALATE REQUIRES CONTRASTING FLAVORS TO BRING OUT THE DISTINCTIONS.
PORK IS BROUGHT TO LIFE BY A TART, SALTY SAUCE. IN OTHER WORDS, A TON OF MAYO. RIGHT, BUDDY?
I KINDA NEED YOU TO LEAVE ME OUT OF THIS...

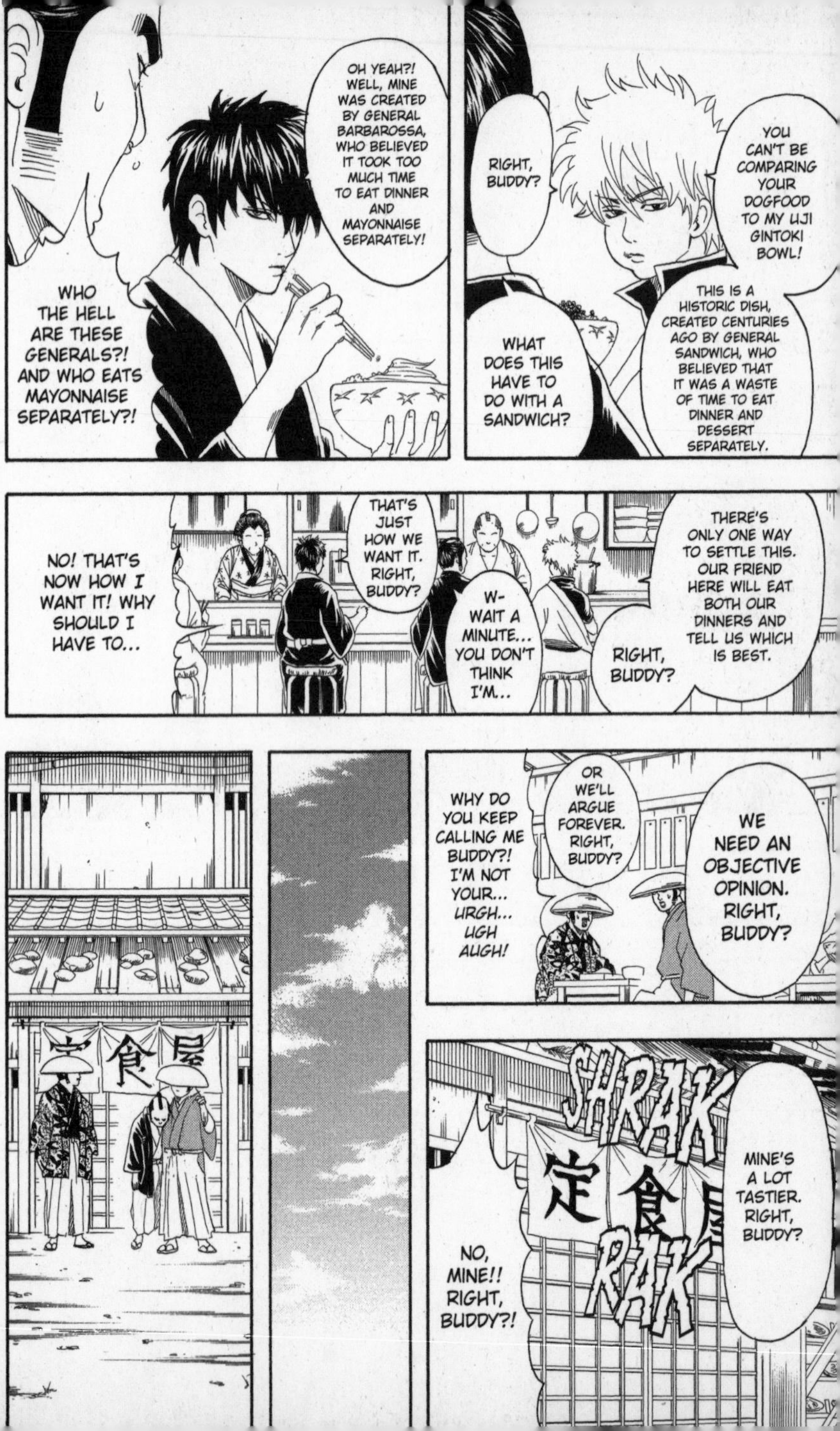
YOU CAN'T BE COMPARING YOUR DOGFOOD TO MY UJI GINTOKI BOWL!
THIS IS A HISTORIC DISH, CREATED CENTURIES AGO BY GENERAL SANDWICH, WHO BELIEVED THAT IT WAS A WASTE OF TIME TO EAT DINNER AND DESSERT SEPARATELY.
RIGHT, BUDDY?
WHAT DOES THIS HAVE TO DO WITH A SANDWICH?
OH YEAH?! WELL, MINE WAS CREATED BY GENERAL BARBAROSSA, WHO BELIEVED IT TOOK TOO MUCH TIME TO EAT DINNER AND MAYONNAISE SEPARATELY!
WHO THE HELL ARE THESE GENERALS?! AND WHO EATS MAYONNAISE SEPARATELY?!
THERE'S ONLY ONE WAY TO SETTLE THIS. OUR FRIEND HERE WILL EAT BOTH OUR DINNERS AND TELL US WHICH IS BEST.
RIGHT, BUDDY?
W-WAIT A MINUTE... YOU DON'T THINK I'M...
THAT'S JUST HOW WE WANT IT. RIGHT, BUDDY?
NO! THAT'S NOW HOW I WANT IT! WHY SHOULD I HAVE TO...
WE NEED AN OBJECTIVE OPINION. RIGHT, BUDDY?
OR WE'LL ARGUE FOREVER. RIGHT, BUDDY?
WHY DO YOU KEEP CALLING ME BUDDY?! I'M NOT YOUR... URGH... UGH AUGH!
SHRAK
定食屋
RAK
MINE'S A LOT TASTIER. RIGHT, BUDDY?
NO, MINE!! RIGHT, BUDDY?!
定食屋

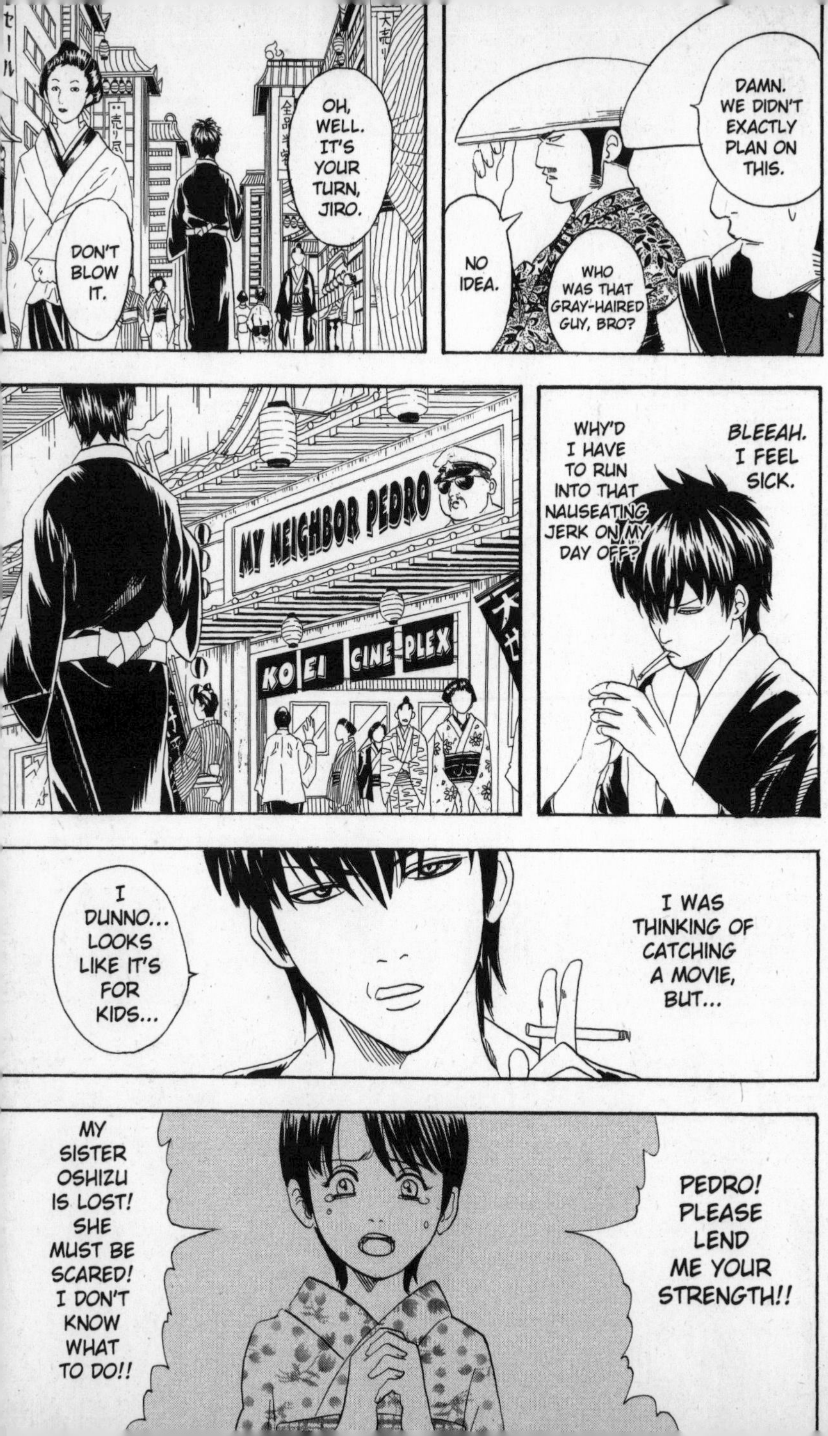
DAMN. WE DIDN'T EXACTLY PLAN ON THIS.
WHO WAS THAT GRAY-HAIRED GUY, BRO?
NO IDEA.
OH, WELL. IT'S YOUR TURN, JIRO.
DON'T BLOW IT.
BLEEAH. I FEEL SICK.
WHY'D I HAVE TO RUN INTO THAT NAUSEATING JERK ON MY DAY OFF?
MY NEIGHBOR PEDRO
KO EI CINE PLEX
I WAS THINKING OF CATCHING A MOVIE, BUT...
I DUNNO... LOOKS LIKE IT'S FOR KIDS...
PEDRO! PLEASE LEND ME YOUR STRENGTH!!
MY SISTER OSHIZU IS LOST! SHE MUST BE SCARED! I DON'T KNOW WHAT TO DO!!

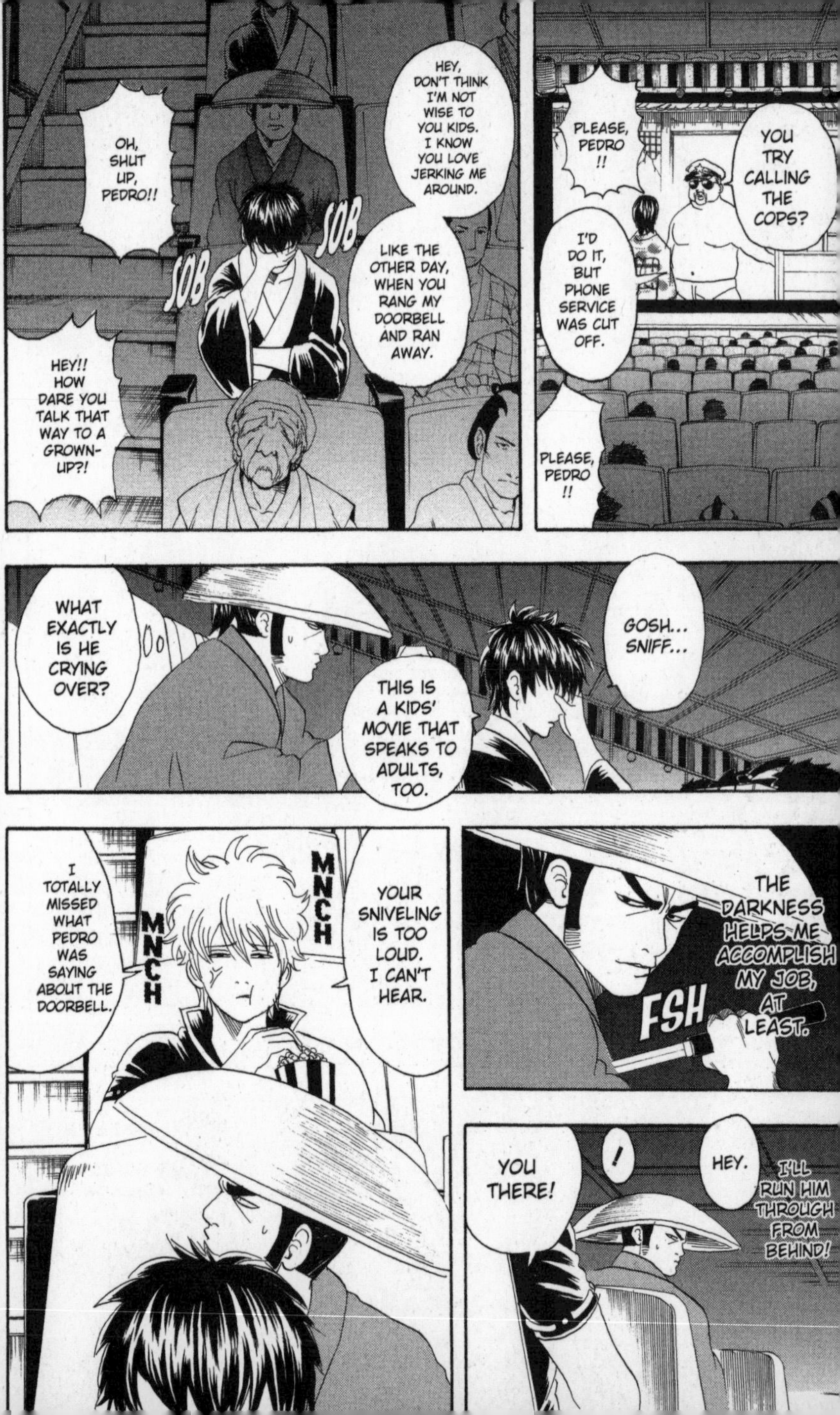
YOU TRY CALLING THE COPS?
PLEASE, PEDRO!!
I'D DO IT, BUT PHONE SERVICE WAS CUT OFF.
PLEASE, PEDRO!!
HEY, DON'T THINK I'M NOT WISE TO YOU KIDS. I KNOW YOU LOVE JERKING ME AROUND.
LIKE THE OTHER DAY, WHEN YOU RANG MY DOORBELL AND RAN AWAY.
SOB
SOB
OH, SHUT UP, PEDRO!!
HEY!! HOW DARE YOU TALK THAT WAY TO A GROWN-UP?!
GOSH... SNIFF...
THIS IS A KIDS' MOVIE THAT SPEAKS TO ADULTS, TOO.
WHAT EXACTLY IS HE CRYING OVER?
THE DARKNESS HELPS ME ACCOMPLISH MY JOB, AT LEAST.
FSH
I'LL RUN HIM THROUGH FROM BEHIND!
HEY.
!
YOU THERE!
MNCH
YOUR SNIVELING IS TOO LOUD. I CAN'T HEAR.
MNCH
I TOTALLY MISSED WHAT PEDRO WAS SAYING ABOUT THE DOORBELL.

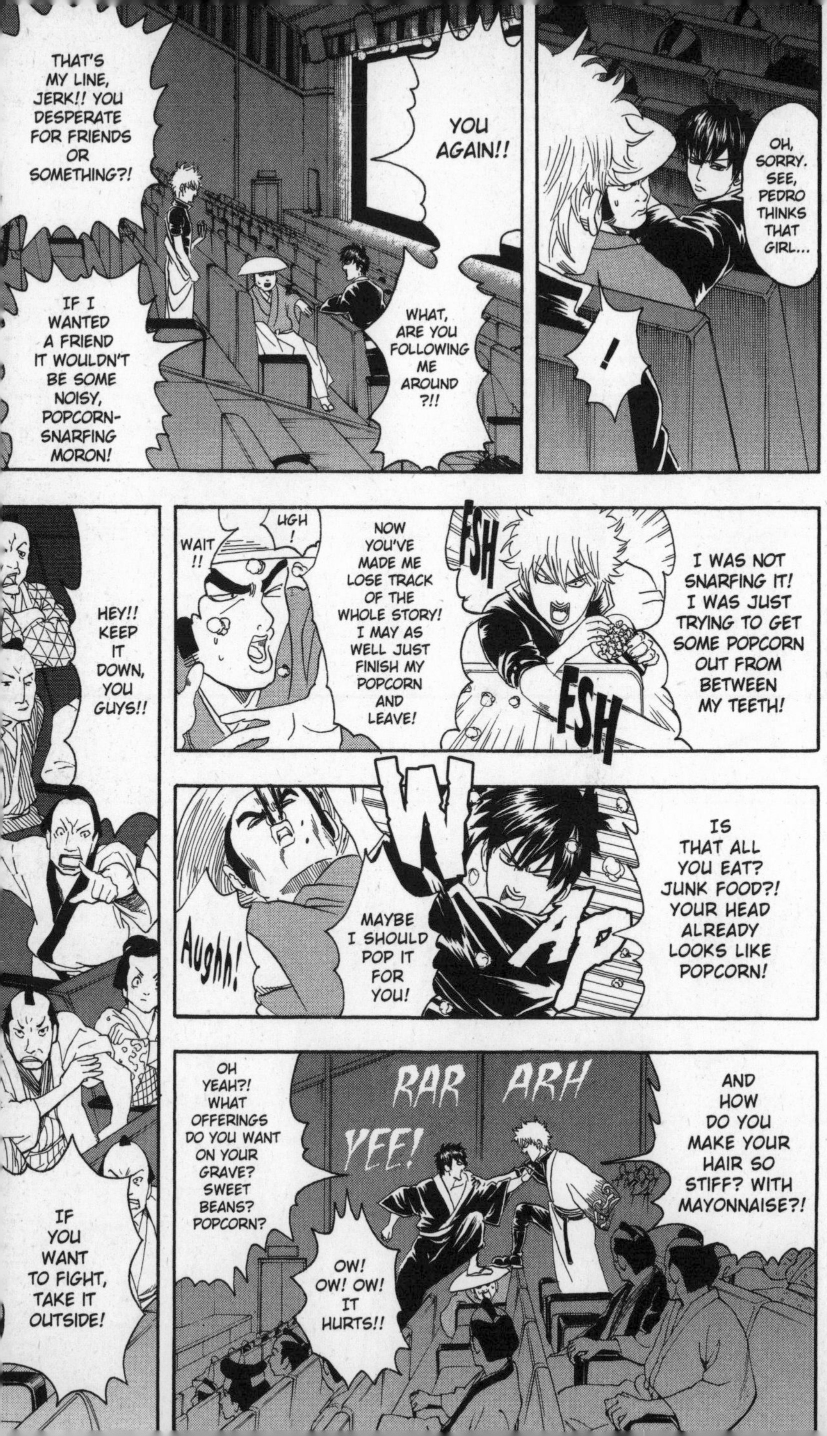
OH, SORRY. SEE, PEDRO THINKS THAT GIRL...
!
YOU AGAIN!!
THAT'S MY LINE, JERK!! YOU DESPERATE FOR FRIENDS OR SOMETHING?!
WHAT, ARE YOU FOLLOWING ME AROUND ?!!
IF I WANTED A FRIEND IT WOULDN'T BE SOME NOISY, POPCORN-SNARFING MORON!
I WAS NOT SNARFING IT! I WAS JUST TRYING TO GET SOME POPCORN OUT FROM BETWEEN MY TEETH!
FSH
FSH
NOW YOU'VE MADE ME LOSE TRACK OF THE WHOLE STORY! I MAY AS WELL JUST FINISH MY POPCORN AND LEAVE!
UGH!
WAIT!!
IS THAT ALL YOU EAT? JUNK FOOD?! YOUR HEAD ALREADY LOOKS LIKE POPCORN!
W
AP
MAYBE I SHOULD POP IT FOR YOU!
Aughh!
AND HOW DO YOU MAKE YOUR HAIR SO STIFF? WITH MAYONNAISE?!
RAR ARH
OH YEAH?! WHAT OFFERINGS DO YOU WANT ON YOUR GRAVE? SWEET BEANS? POPCORN?
YEE!
OW! OW! OW! IT HURTS!!
HEY!! KEEP IT DOWN, YOU GUYS!!
IF YOU WANT TO FIGHT, TAKE IT OUTSIDE!

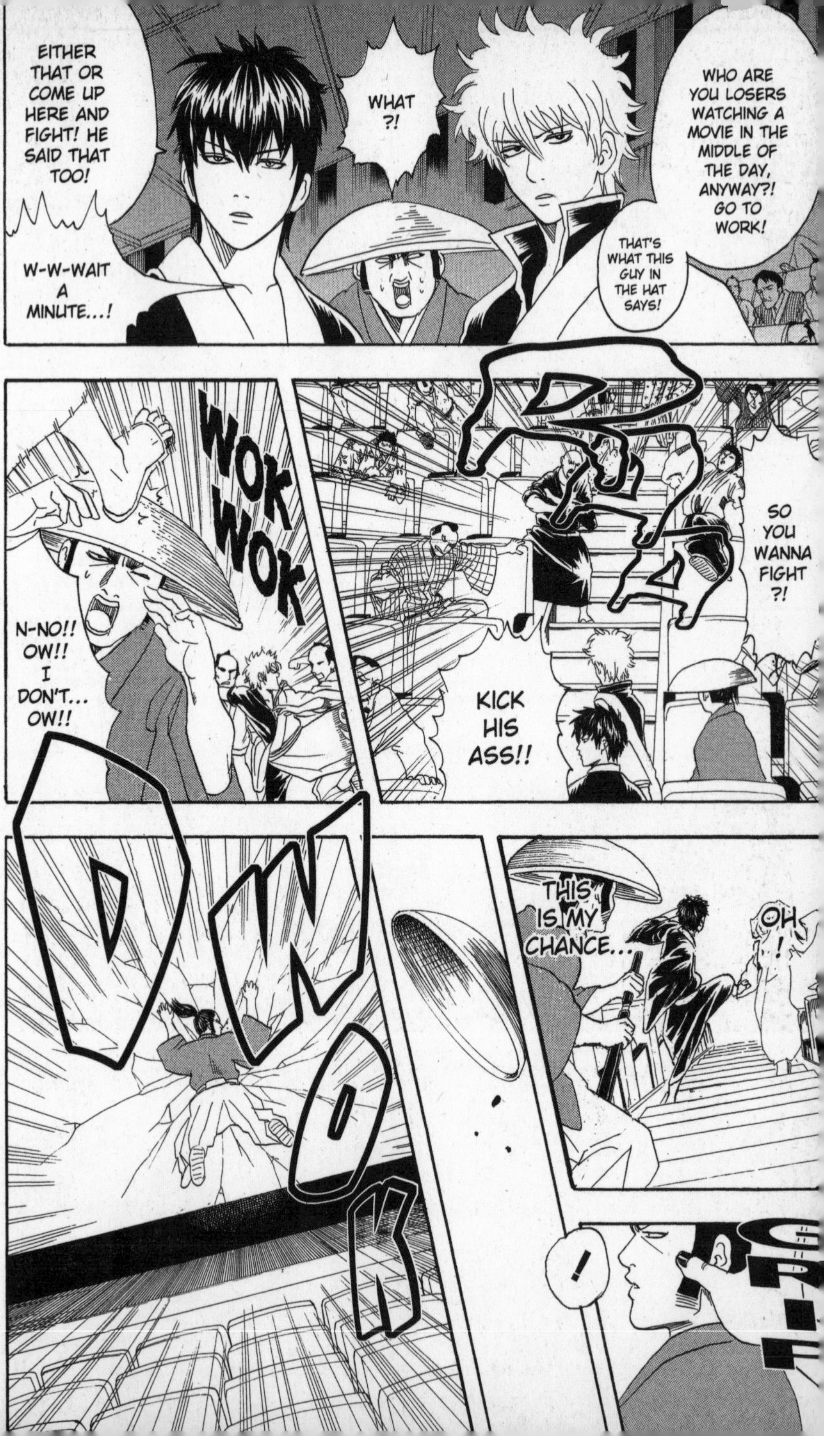
WHO ARE YOU LOSERS WATCHING A MOVIE IN THE MIDDLE OF THE DAY, ANYWAY?! GO TO WORK!
THAT'S WHAT THIS GUY IN THE HAT SAYS!
WHAT ?!
EITHER THAT OR COME UP HERE AND FIGHT! HE SAID THAT TOO!
W-W-WAIT A MINUTE...!
SO YOU WANNA FIGHT ?!
KICK HIS ASS!!
WOK WOK
N-NO!! OW!! I DON'T... OW!!
THIS IS MY CHANCE...
OH !
!

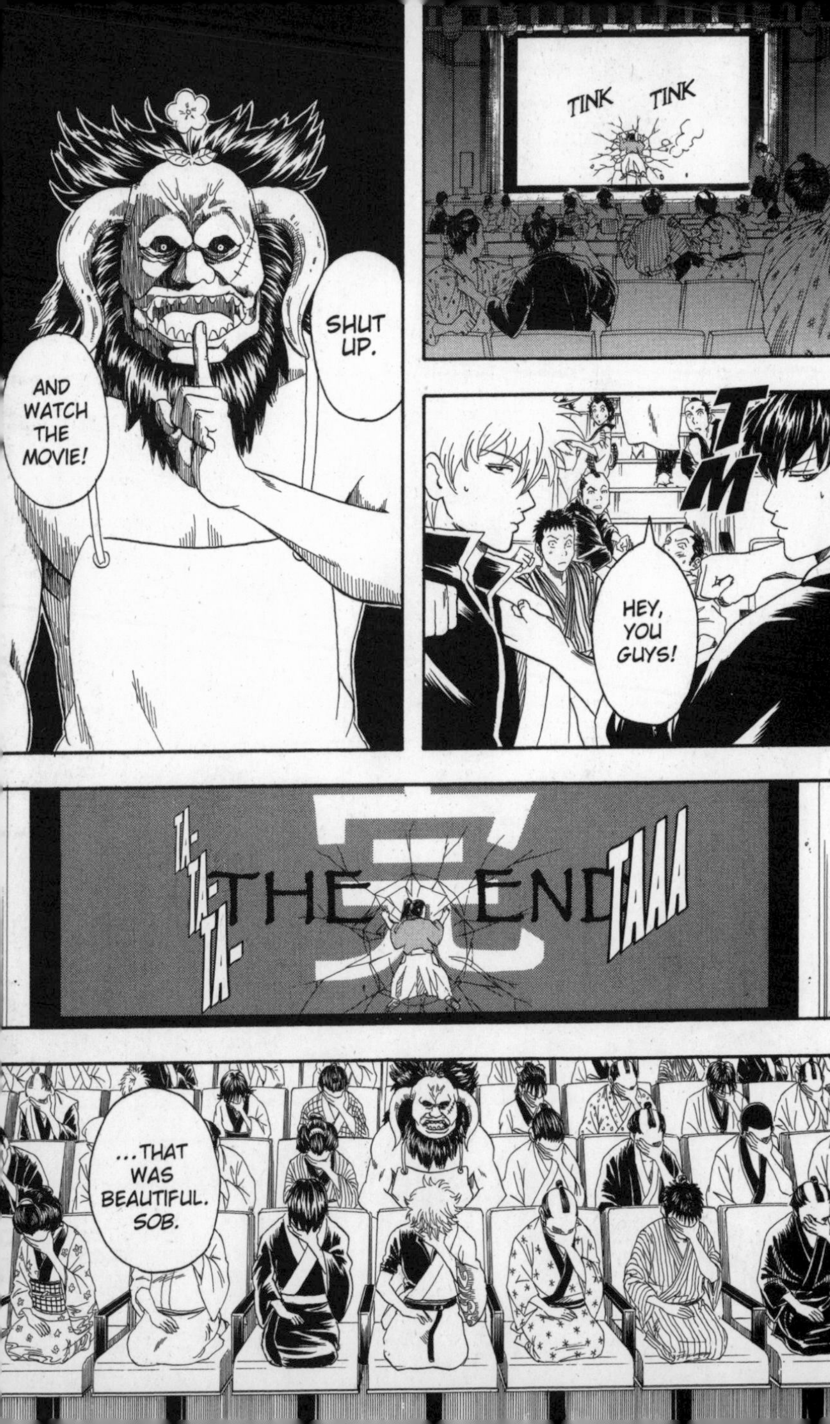

TINK TINK
TM
HEY, YOU GUYS!
SHUT UP.
AND WATCH THE MOVIE!
TA-TA-TA-
THE END
TAAA
...THAT WAS BEAUTIFUL. SOB.

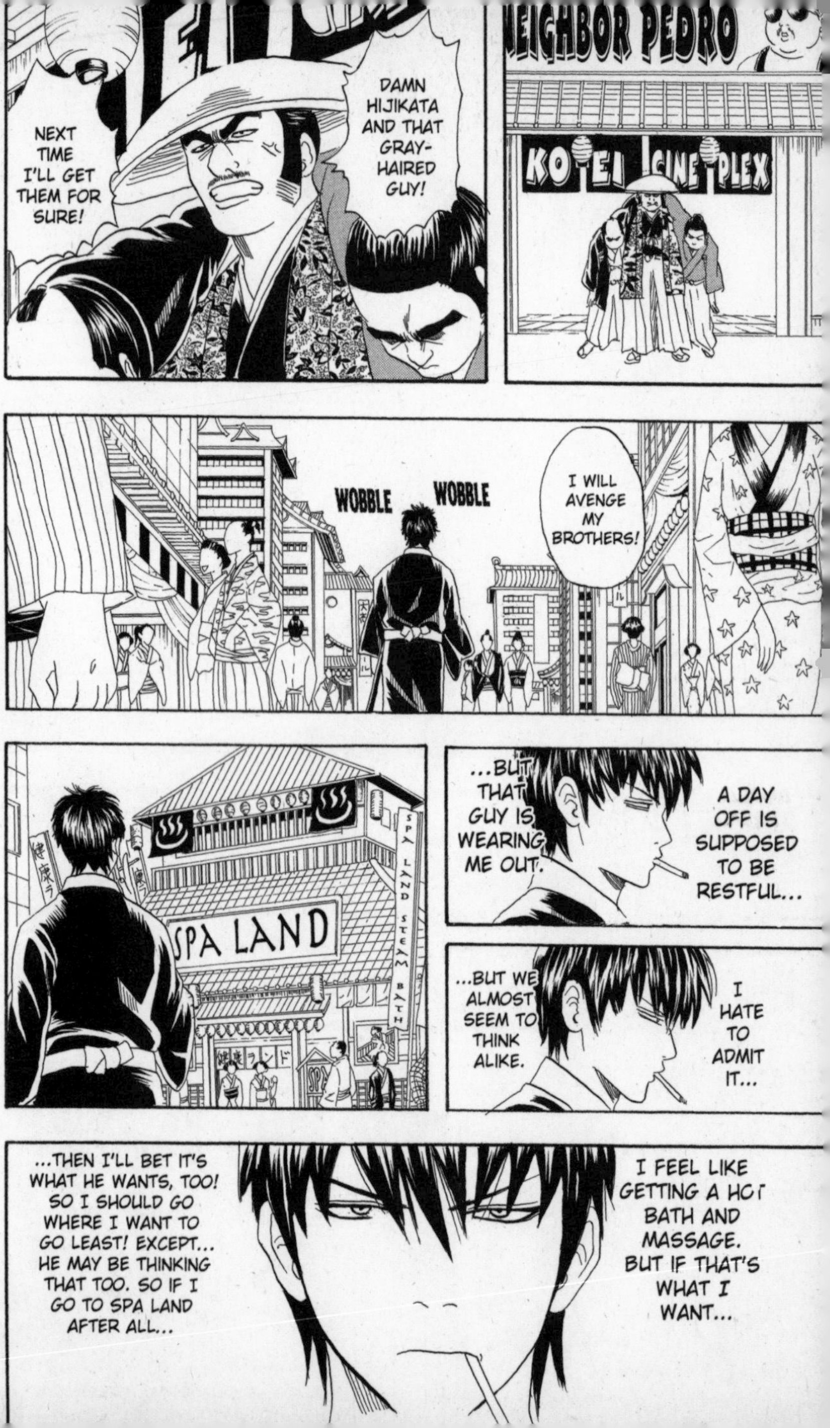
NEIGHBOR PEDRO
KOEI CINEPLEX
DAMN HIJIKATA AND THAT GRAY-HAIRED GUY!
NEXT TIME I'LL GET THEM FOR SURE!
I WILL AVENGE MY BROTHERS!
WOBBLE
WOBBLE
A DAY OFF IS SUPPOSED TO BE RESTFUL...
...BUT THAT GUY IS WEARING ME OUT.
I HATE TO ADMIT IT...
...BUT WE ALMOST SEEM TO THINK ALIKE.
SPA LAND STEAM BATH
SPA LAND
I FEEL LIKE GETTING A HOT BATH AND MASSAGE. BUT IF THAT'S WHAT I WANT...
...THEN I'LL BET IT'S WHAT HE WANTS, TOO! SO I SHOULD GO WHERE I WANT TO GO LEAST! EXCEPT... HE MAY BE THINKING THAT TOO. SO IF I GO TO SPA LAND AFTER ALL...

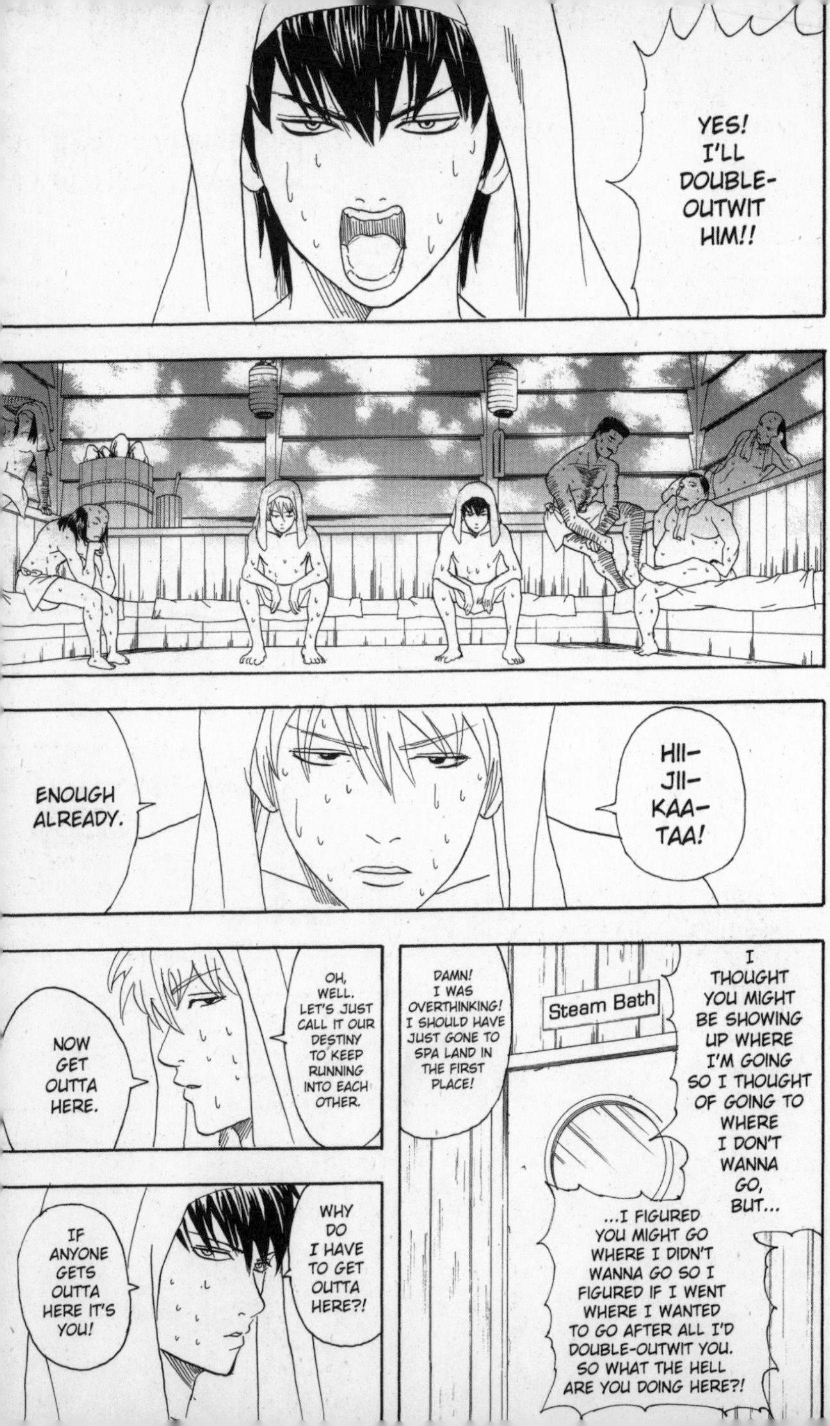
YES! I'LL DOUBLE-OUTWIT HIM!!
HII-JII-KAA-TAA!
ENOUGH ALREADY.
I THOUGHT YOU MIGHT BE SHOWING UP WHERE I'M GOING SO I THOUGHT OF GOING TO WHERE I DON'T WANNA GO, BUT...
...I FIGURED YOU MIGHT GO WHERE I DIDN'T WANNA GO SO I FIGURED IF I WENT WHERE I WANTED TO GO AFTER ALL I'D DOUBLE-OUTWIT YOU. SO WHAT THE HELL ARE YOU DOING HERE?!
Steam Bath
DAMN! I WAS OVERTHINKING! I SHOULD HAVE JUST GONE TO SPA LAND IN THE FIRST PLACE!
OH, WELL. LET'S JUST CALL IT OUR DESTINY TO KEEP RUNNING INTO EACH OTHER.
NOW GET OUTTA HERE.
WHY DO I HAVE TO GET OUTTA HERE?!
IF ANYONE GETS OUTTA HERE IT'S YOU!

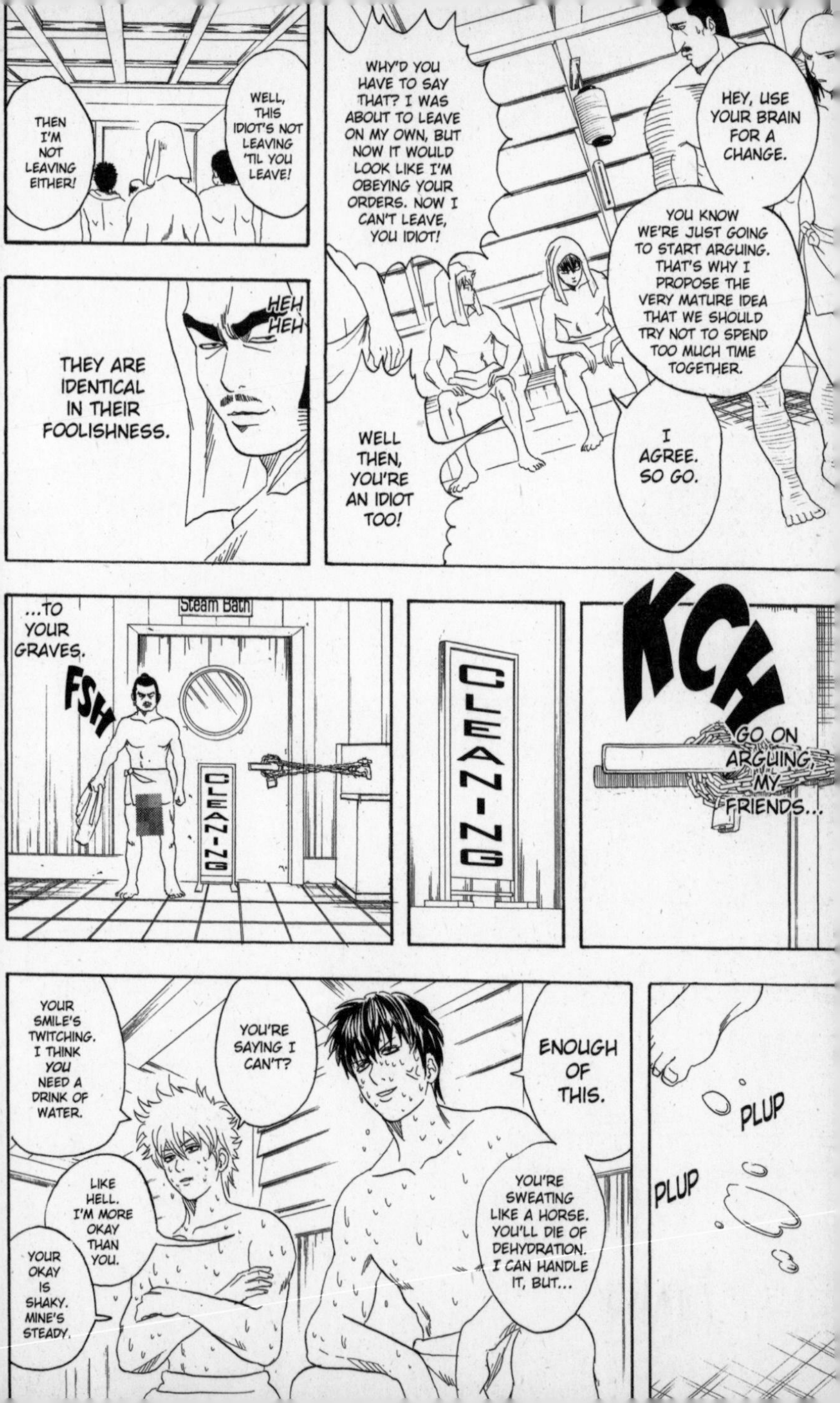
HEY, USE YOUR BRAIN FOR A CHANGE.
YOU KNOW WE'RE JUST GOING TO START ARGUING. THAT'S WHY I PROPOSE THE VERY MATURE IDEA THAT WE SHOULD TRY NOT TO SPEND TOO MUCH TIME TOGETHER.
I AGREE. SO GO.
WHY'D YOU HAVE TO SAY THAT? I WAS ABOUT TO LEAVE ON MY OWN, BUT NOW IT WOULD LOOK LIKE I'M OBEYING YOUR ORDERS. NOW I CAN'T LEAVE, YOU IDIOT!
WELL THEN, YOU'RE AN IDIOT TOO!
WELL, THIS IDIOT'S NOT LEAVING 'TIL YOU LEAVE!
THEN I'M NOT LEAVING EITHER!
HEH HEH
THEY ARE IDENTICAL IN THEIR FOOLISHNESS.
KCH
GO ON ARGUING, MY FRIENDS...
CLEANING
Steam Bath
...TO YOUR GRAVES.
FSH
CLEANING
PLUP
PLUP
ENOUGH OF THIS.
YOU'RE SWEATING LIKE A HORSE. YOU'LL DIE OF DEHYDRATION. I CAN HANDLE IT, BUT...
YOU'RE SAYING I CAN'T?
YOUR SMILE'S TWITCHING. I THINK *YOU* NEED A DRINK OF WATER.
LIKE HELL. I'M MORE OKAY THAN YOU.
YOUR OKAY IS SHAKY. MINE'S STEADY.

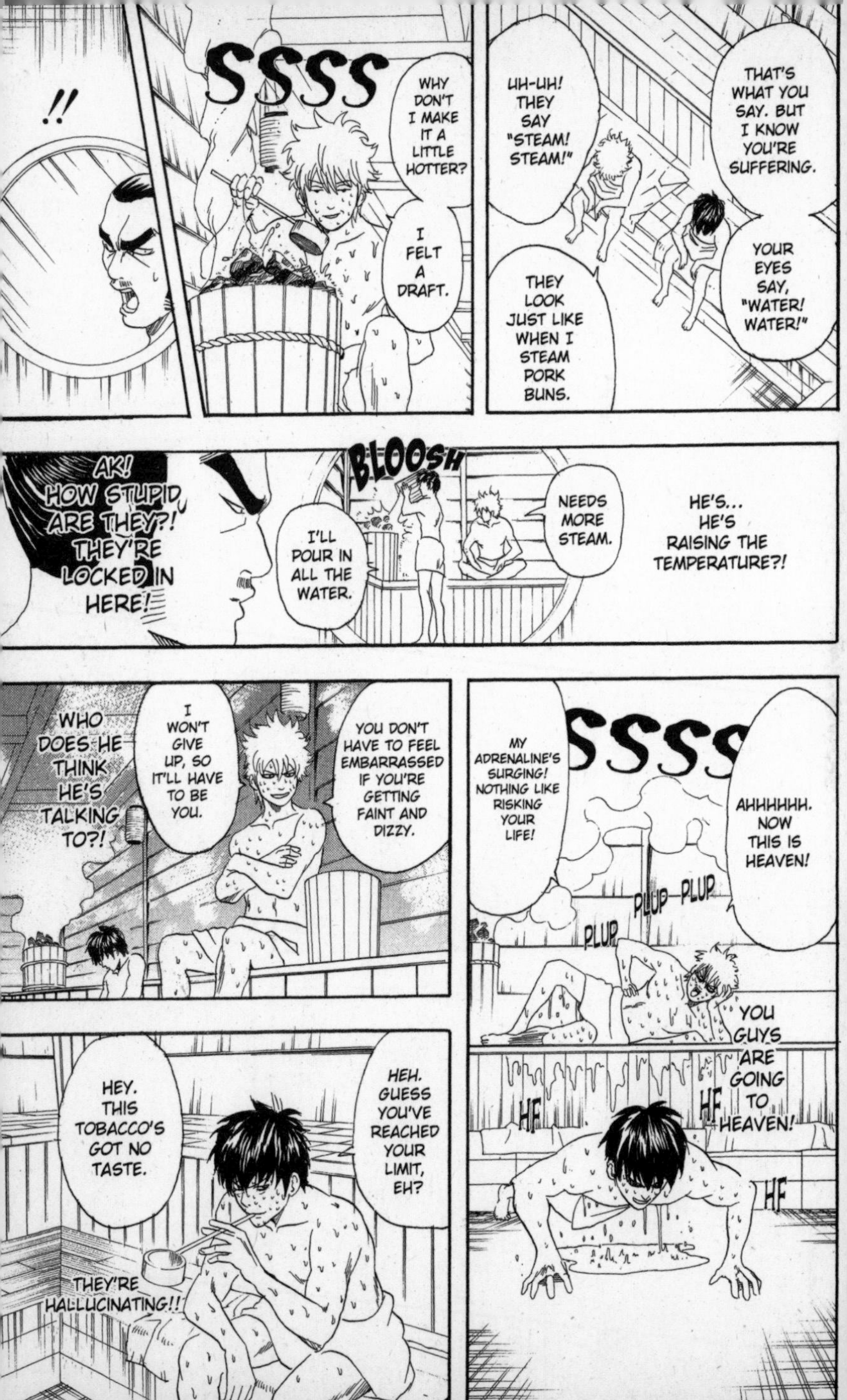
THAT'S WHAT YOU SAY. BUT I KNOW YOU'RE SUFFERING.
YOUR EYES SAY, "WATER! WATER!"
UH-UH! THEY SAY "STEAM! STEAM!"
THEY LOOK JUST LIKE WHEN I STEAM PORK BUNS.
SSSS
WHY DON'T I MAKE IT A LITTLE HOTTER?
I FELT A DRAFT.
!!
HE'S... HE'S RAISING THE TEMPERATURE?!
NEEDS MORE STEAM.
BLOOSH
I'LL POUR IN ALL THE WATER.
AK! HOW STUPID ARE THEY?! THEY'RE LOCKED IN HERE!
SSSS
AHHHHHH. NOW THIS IS HEAVEN!
MY ADRENALINE'S SURGING! NOTHING LIKE RISKING YOUR LIFE!
PLUP PLUP
PLUP
YOU GUYS ARE GOING TO HEAVEN!
HF
HF
HF
YOU DON'T HAVE TO FEEL EMBARRASSED IF YOU'RE GETTING FAINT AND DIZZY.
I WON'T GIVE UP, SO IT'LL HAVE TO BE YOU.
WHO DOES HE THINK HE'S TALKING TO?!
HEH. GUESS YOU'VE REACHED YOUR LIMIT, EH?
HEY. THIS TOBACCO'S GOT NO TASTE.
THEY'RE HALLUCINATING!!

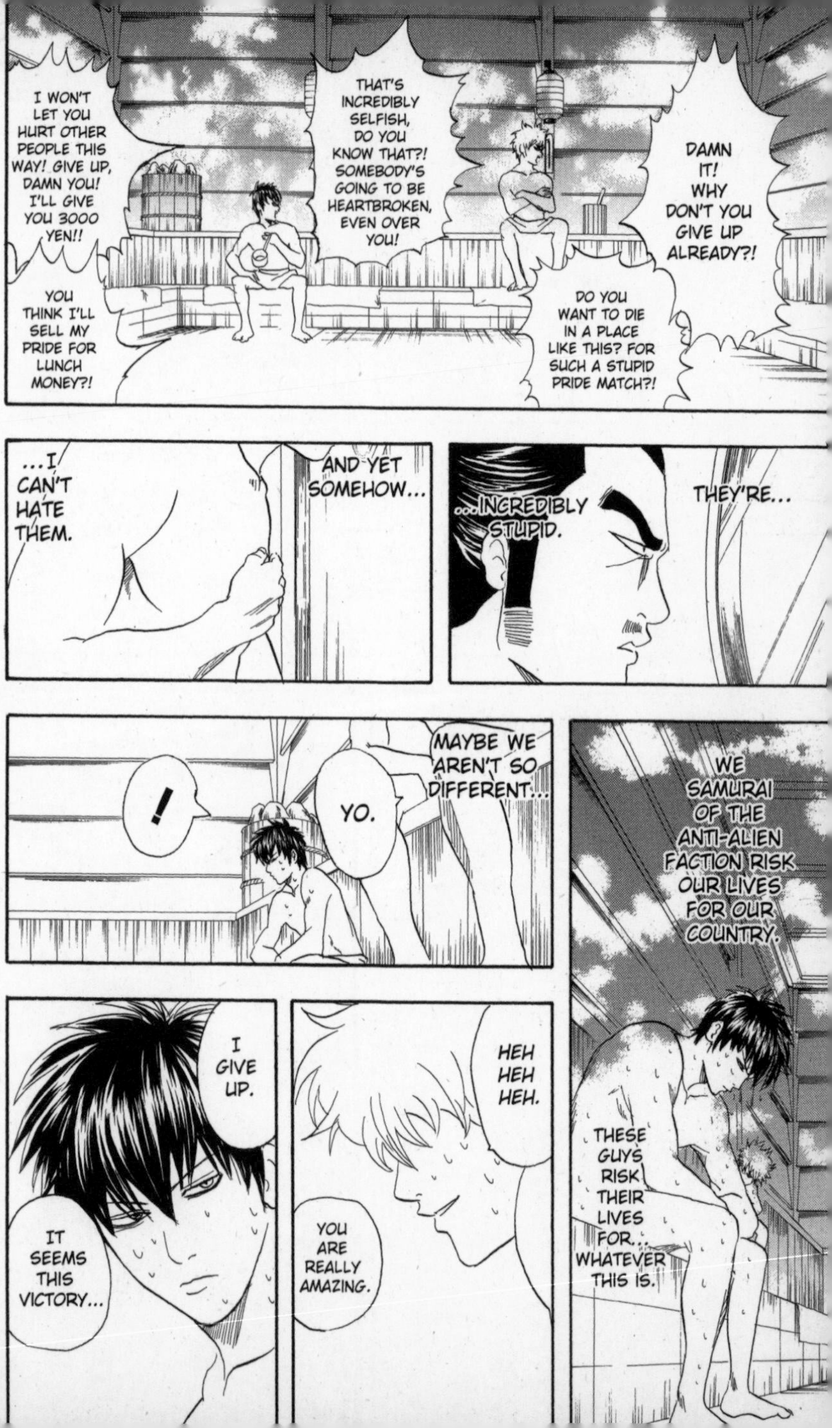
DAMN IT! WHY DON'T YOU GIVE UP ALREADY?!
DO YOU WANT TO DIE IN A PLACE LIKE THIS? FOR SUCH A STUPID PRIDE MATCH?!
THAT'S INCREDIBLY SELFISH, DO YOU KNOW THAT?! SOMEBODY'S GOING TO BE HEARTBROKEN, EVEN OVER YOU!
I WON'T LET YOU HURT OTHER PEOPLE THIS WAY! GIVE UP, DAMN YOU! I'LL GIVE YOU 3000 YEN!!
YOU THINK I'LL SELL MY PRIDE FOR LUNCH MONEY?!
THEY'RE...
...INCREDIBLY STUPID.
AND YET SOMEHOW...
...I CAN'T HATE THEM.
WE SAMURAI OF THE ANTI-ALIEN FACTION RISK OUR LIVES FOR OUR COUNTRY.
THESE GUYS RISK THEIR LIVES FOR... WHATEVER THIS IS.
MAYBE WE AREN'T SO DIFFERENT...
YO.
!
HEH HEH HEH.
YOU ARE REALLY AMAZING.
I GIVE UP.
IT SEEMS THIS VICTORY...

FUP

HEY!

I'M SORRY... TO BOTHER YOU... BUT...

WILL YOU TAKE A MESSAGE... TO THE YOROZUYA?

FLOP

...IS YOURS.

ZZZG

TELL THEM... GOOD-BYE...

I CAN'T.

...CAN'T KILL THEM.

MEN THIS COURAGEOUS... I JUST...

YOU COWARD...

SAY IT YOUR-SELF!

LIKE HELL.

!

ZZZG ZZZG

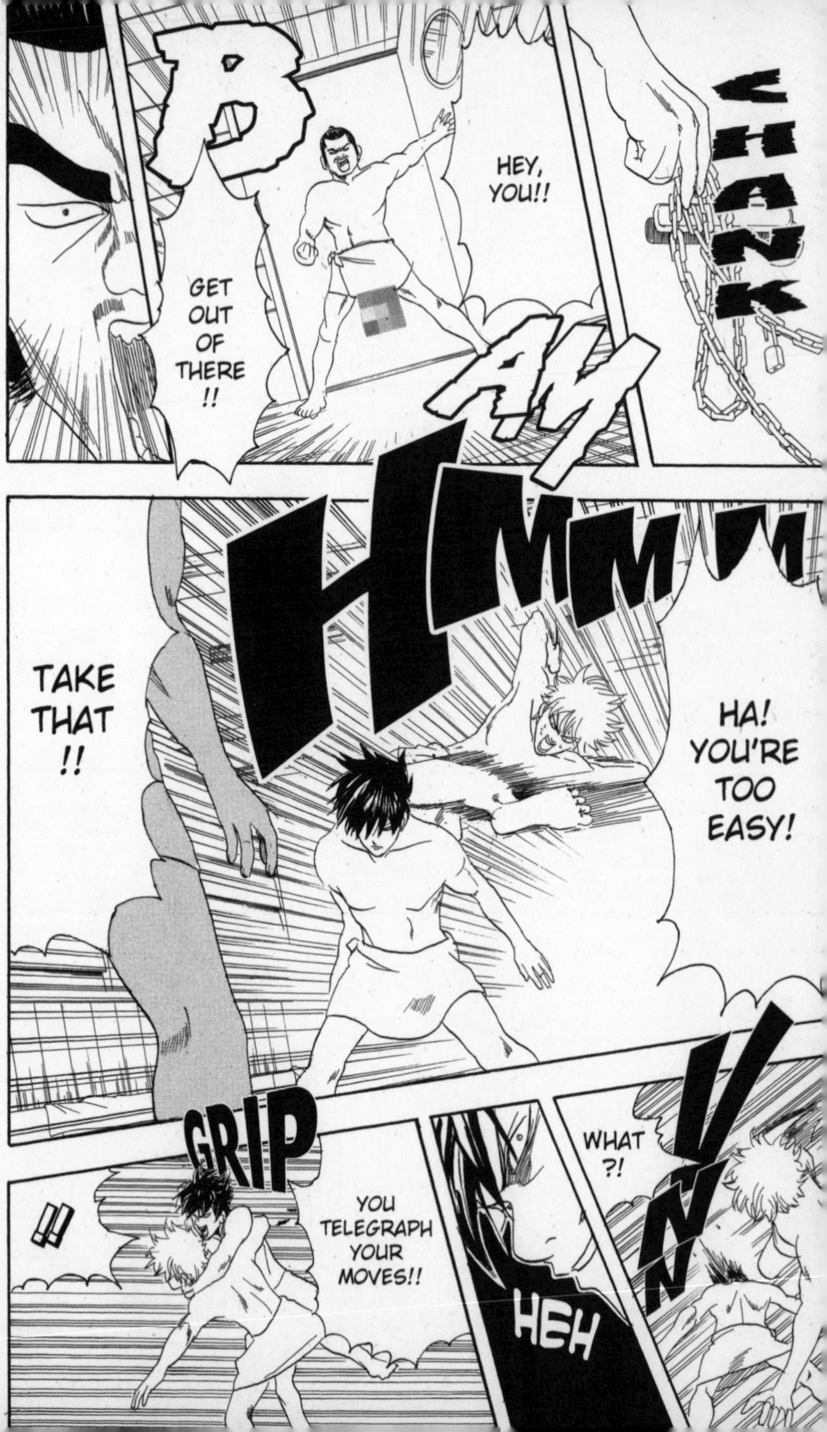
YANK
HEY, YOU!!
BAM
GET OUT OF THERE!!
HMM
HA! YOU'RE TOO EASY!
TAKE THAT!!
WHAT?!
HEH
GRIP
YOU TELEGRAPH YOUR MOVES!!
!!

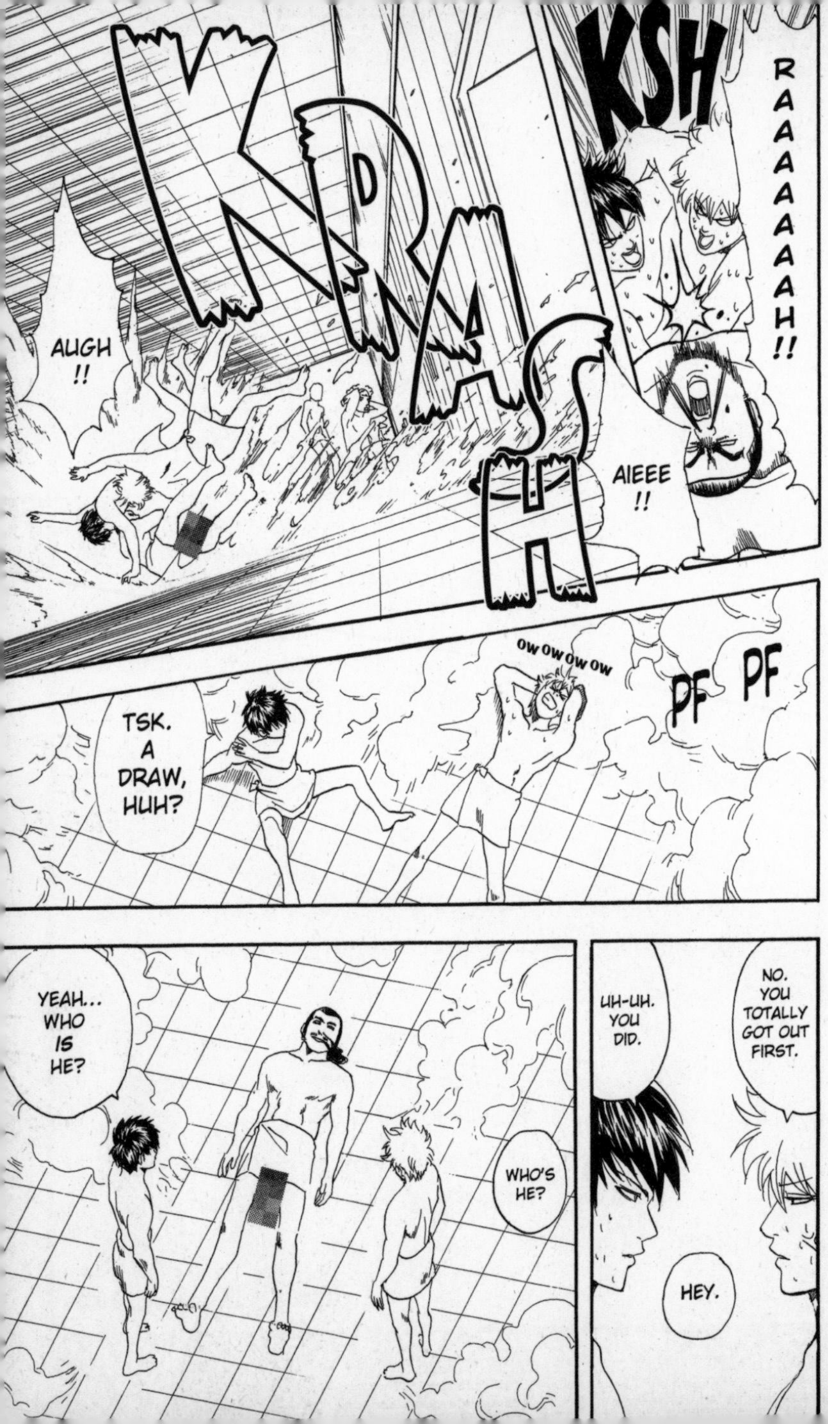
RAAAAAAAAH!!
KSH
KRASH
AIEEE!!
AUGH!!
PF PF
OW OW OW OW
TSK. A DRAW, HUH?
NO. YOU TOTALLY GOT OUT FIRST.
UH-UH. YOU DID.
HEY.
WHO'S HE?
YEAH... WHO IS HE?

Sorachi's Q&A Corner #22

<From Jennifer S. of the U.S.A.>

Original letter in Japanese

そらち先生へ
おげんきですか。私はげんきです。私は日本ごの
学生です。「ぎんたま」をよみました。「ぎんたま」は
かりゆきだね。まんがでならった ことば

「うそつき」... と
「かいぞく」... と

「あくうんのつよいやろうだ」です。
いちばん すきな ことばは

「ようするにうちゅうのキャプテンです」。
おしえてくださって ありがとございました

そして、せんしゅう 私は「ぎんたま」六 をよみました。
ゴキブリは きもい-ならきらいです。先生にしつもん
です。だれが エリザベスですか。プリーズ テルミー。

サンドバル ジェニファー より

P.S. サイン ください。
ともだちの ゆうこにも あげてください。ゆうこも
そらち先生の大 ファン。

Dear Sorachi-sensei,
  How are you? I am fine.
I am a student studying Japanese.
I read *Gin Tama*. I like *Gin Tama*
very much. Words that I learned
reading your manga are "liar,"
"pirates," and "you have the luck
of the devil." My favorite phrase is
"I'm a captain in space."
Thank you for teaching me.
Last week I read *Gin Tama* volume 6.
I hate cockroaches because they
are gross. I have a question.
Who is Elizabeth? Please tell me.
  From Jennifer S.
  P.S. Please give me your autograph.
Please give it to my friend Yuko, too.
Yuko is also a big Sorachi-sensei fan.

<Answer>

Jennifer-san sent this all the way from America. Thank you very much! You're quite fluent in Japanese. Unfortunately, the Japanese phrases I unintentionally taught you are basically worthless. You shouldn't say, "you have the luck of the devil." You might get beaten up. Be careful! I also give you my autograph. It's nothing to do with you being American or whatever...Yuko should explain these things to you 'cause she should know about it already.

(Q&A #21 is on page 186)

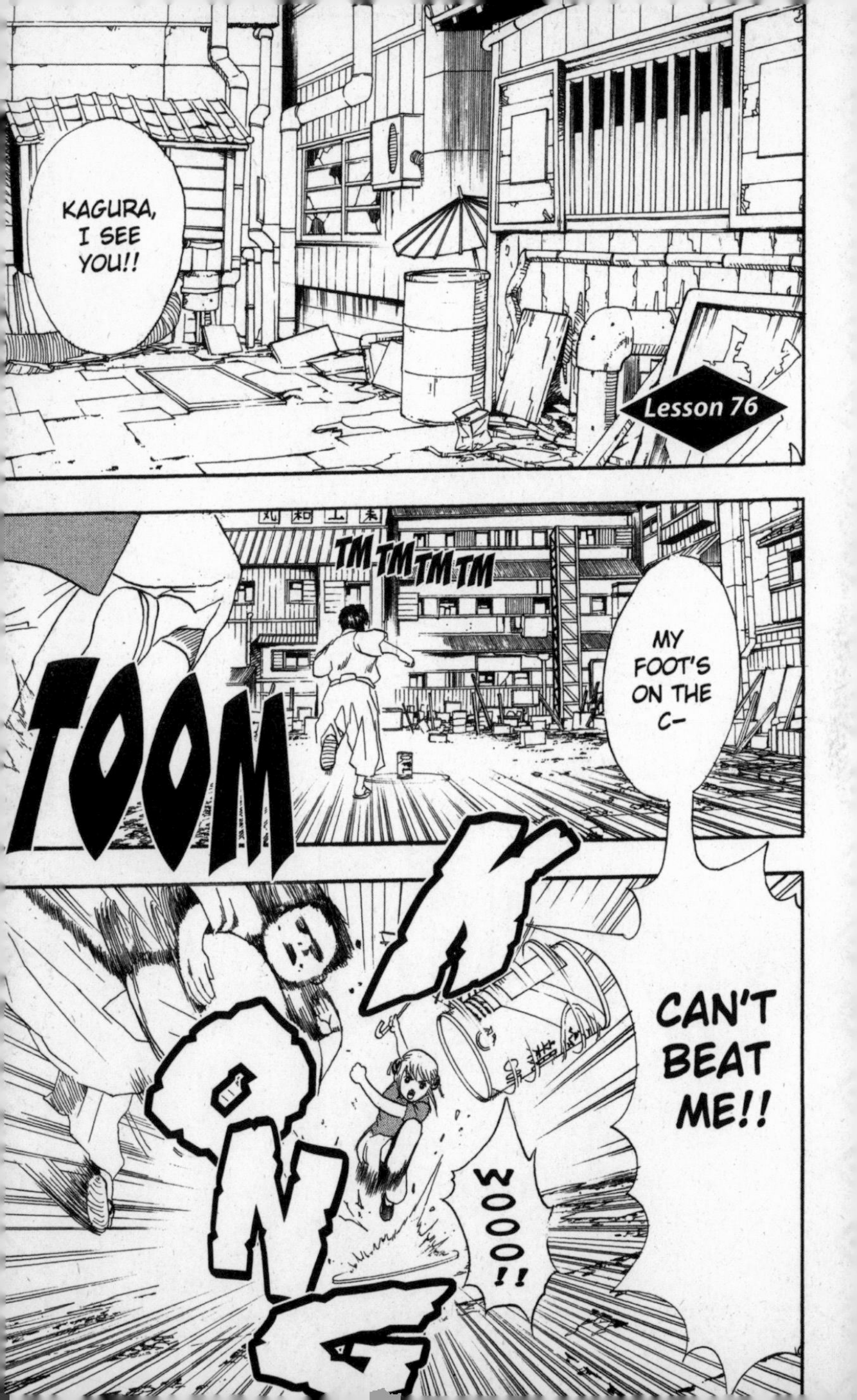
KAGURA, I SEE YOU!!
Lesson 76
MY FOOT'S ON THE C-
TM TM TM TM
TOOM
CAN'T BEAT ME!!
KANG
WOOO!!

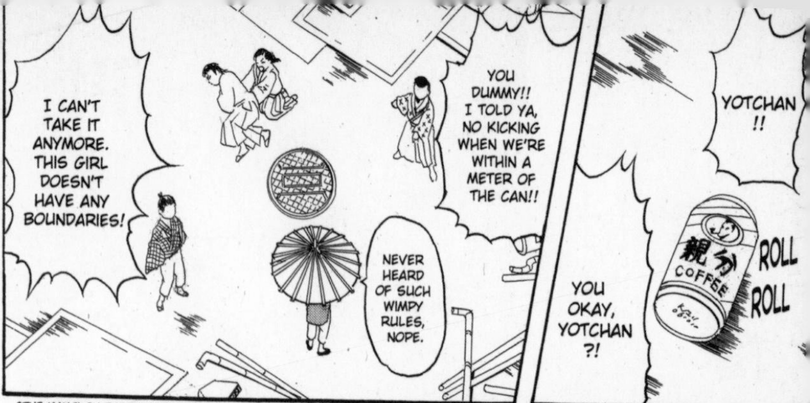
YOTCHAN !!
ROLL
ROLL
YOU OKAY, YOTCHAN ?!
YOU DUMMY!! I TOLD YA, NO KICKING WHEN WE'RE WITHIN A METER OF THE CAN!!
I CAN'T TAKE IT ANYMORE. THIS GIRL DOESN'T HAVE ANY BOUNDARIES!
NEVER HEARD OF SUCH WIMPY RULES, NOPE.

*THE KANJI ON THE CAN READS "OYABUN", WHICH MEANS "BOSS". FANS OF JAPANESE CANNED COFFEE SHOULD GET THAT ONE. -EDITOR

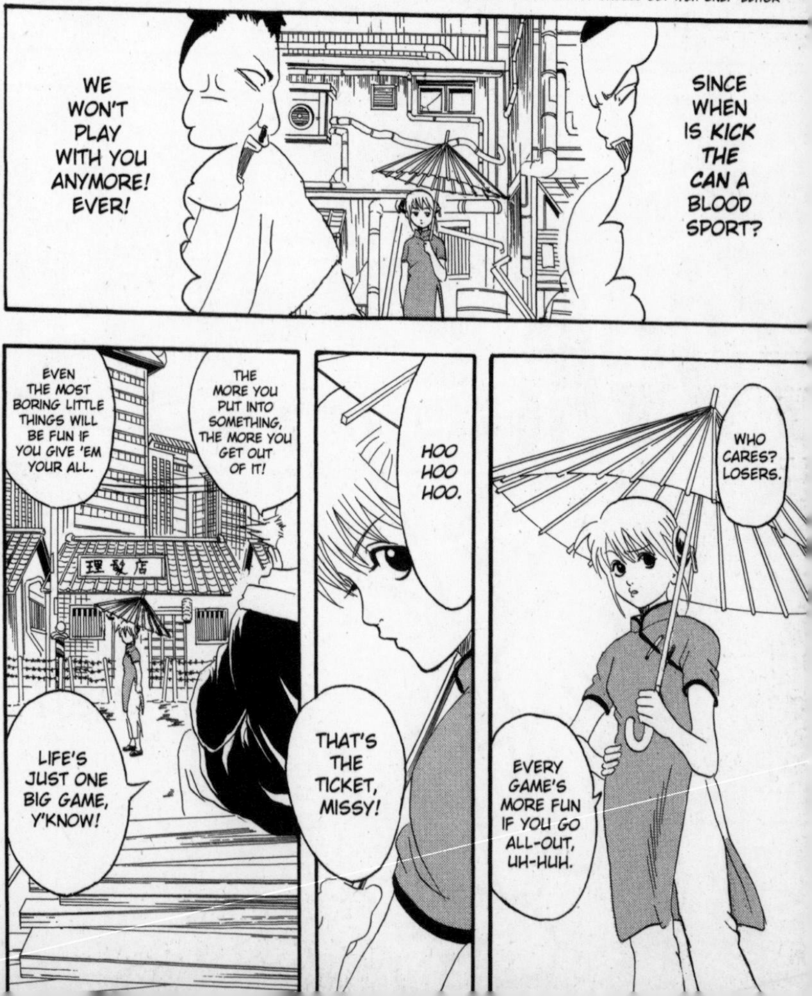
SINCE WHEN IS KICK THE CAN A BLOOD SPORT?
WE WON'T PLAY WITH YOU ANYMORE! EVER!
WHO CARES? LOSERS.
EVERY GAME'S MORE FUN IF YOU GO ALL-OUT, UH-HUH.
HOO HOO HOO.
THAT'S THE TICKET, MISSY!
THE MORE YOU PUT INTO SOMETHING, THE MORE YOU GET OUT OF IT!
EVEN THE MOST BORING LITTLE THINGS WILL BE FUN IF YOU GIVE 'EM YOUR ALL.
LIFE'S JUST ONE BIG GAME, Y'KNOW!

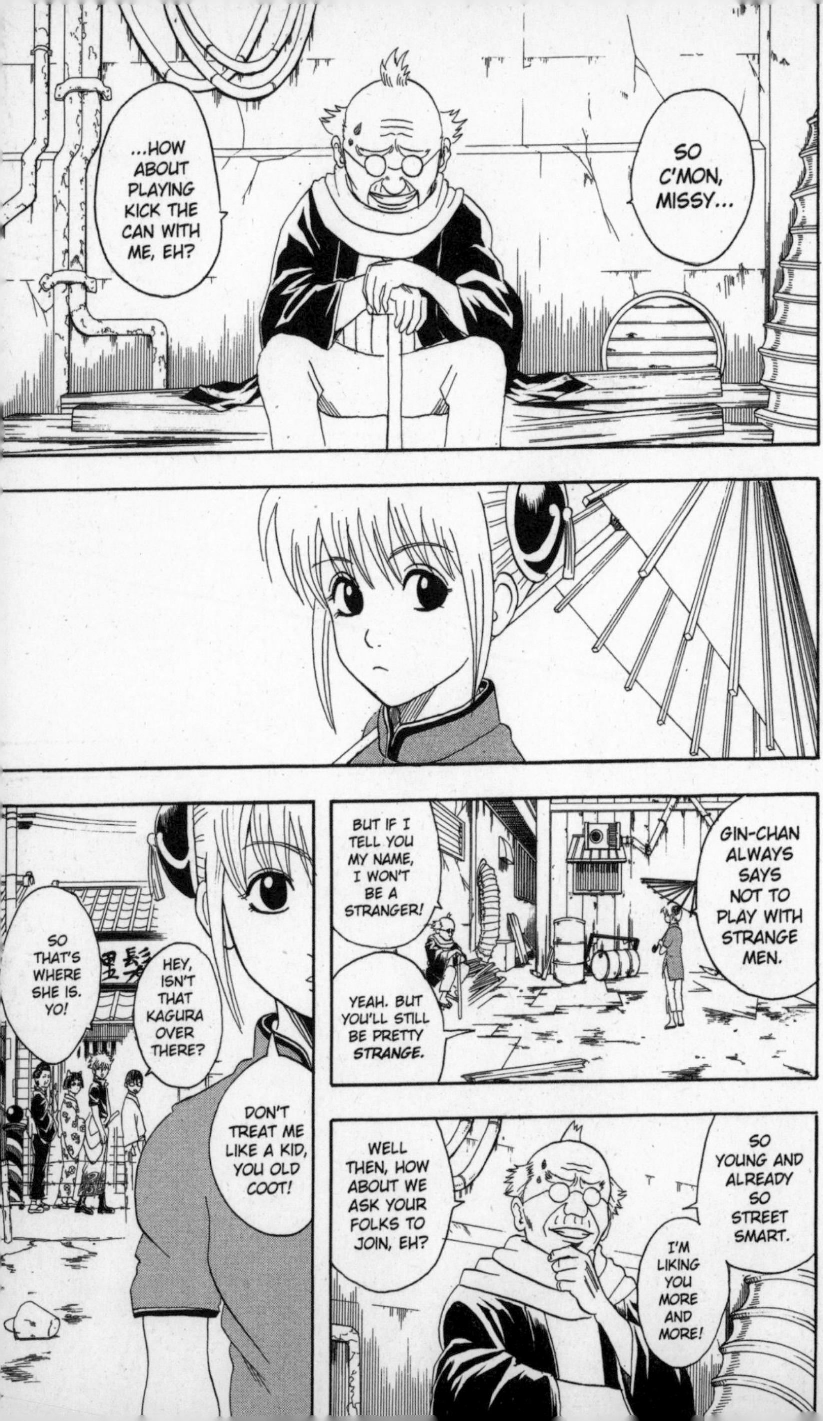
SO C'MON, MISSY...
...HOW ABOUT PLAYING KICK THE CAN WITH ME, EH?
GIN-CHAN ALWAYS SAYS NOT TO PLAY WITH STRANGE MEN.
BUT IF I TELL YOU MY NAME, I WON'T BE A STRANGER!
YEAH. BUT YOU'LL STILL BE PRETTY STRANGE.
SO YOUNG AND ALREADY SO STREET SMART.
I'M LIKING YOU MORE AND MORE!
WELL THEN, HOW ABOUT WE ASK YOUR FOLKS TO JOIN, EH?
DON'T TREAT ME LIKE A KID, YOU OLD COOT!
HEY, ISN'T THAT KAGURA OVER THERE?
SO THAT'S WHERE SHE IS. YO!

Lesson 76
Whatever You Play, Play to Win!

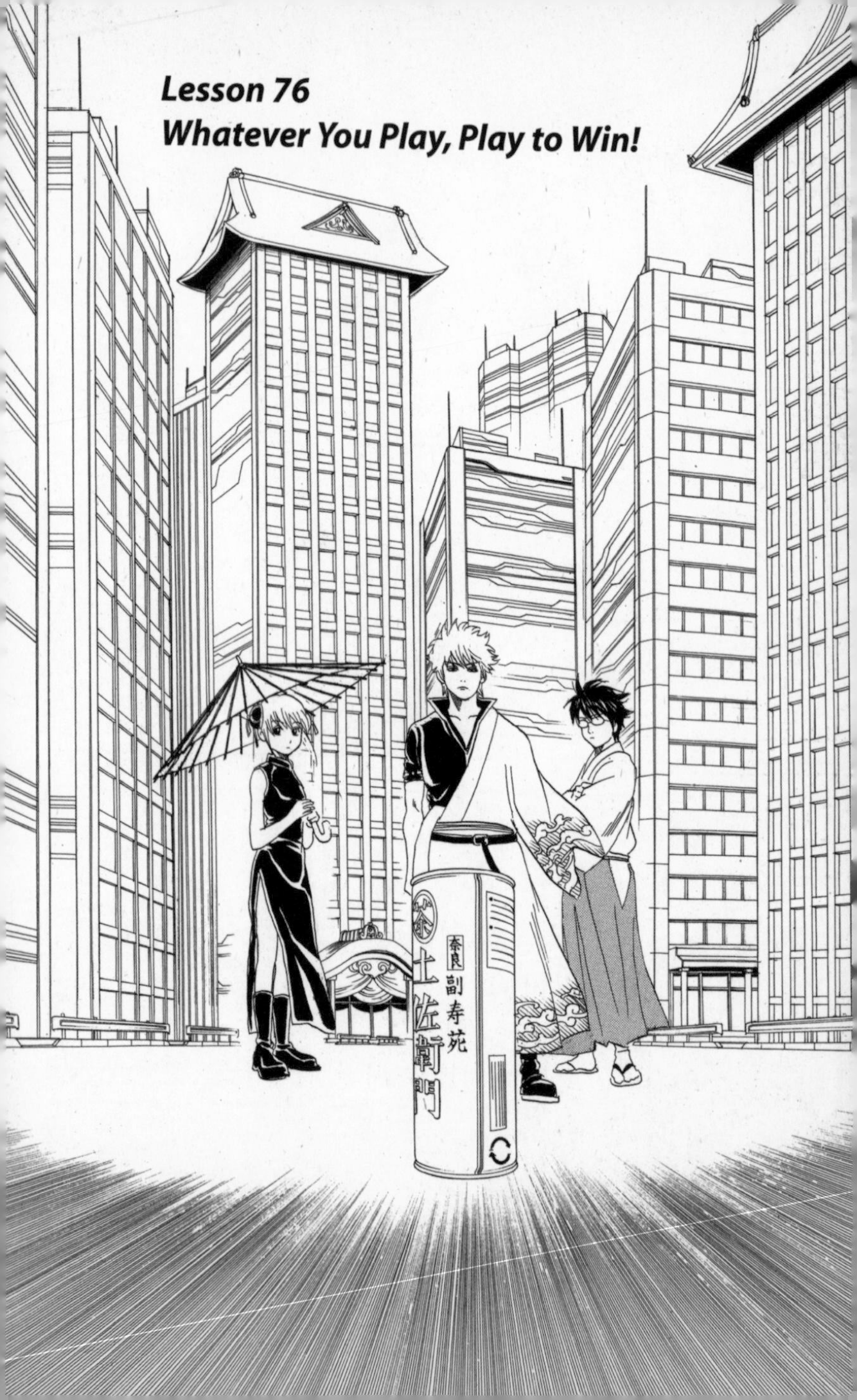

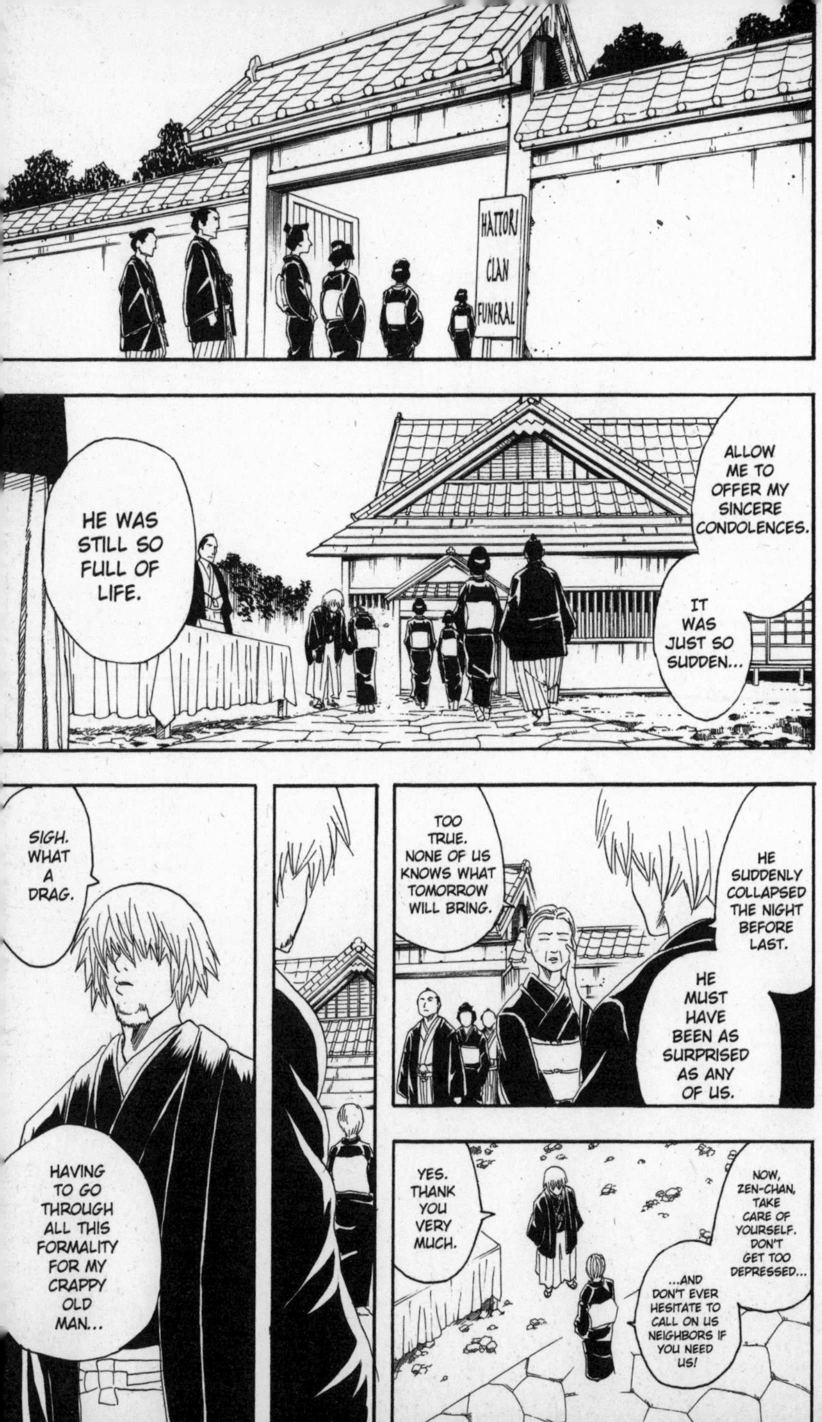
HATTORI CLAN FUNERAL
ALLOW ME TO OFFER MY SINCERE CONDOLENCES.
IT WAS JUST SO SUDDEN...
HE WAS STILL SO FULL OF LIFE.
HE SUDDENLY COLLAPSED THE NIGHT BEFORE LAST.
HE MUST HAVE BEEN AS SURPRISED AS ANY OF US.
TOO TRUE. NONE OF US KNOWS WHAT TOMORROW WILL BRING.
NOW, ZEN-CHAN, TAKE CARE OF YOURSELF. DON'T GET TOO DEPRESSED...
...AND DON'T EVER HESITATE TO CALL ON US NEIGHBORS IF YOU NEED US!
YES. THANK YOU VERY MUCH.
SIGH. WHAT A DRAG.
HAVING TO GO THROUGH ALL THIS FORMALITY FOR MY CRAPPY OLD MAN...

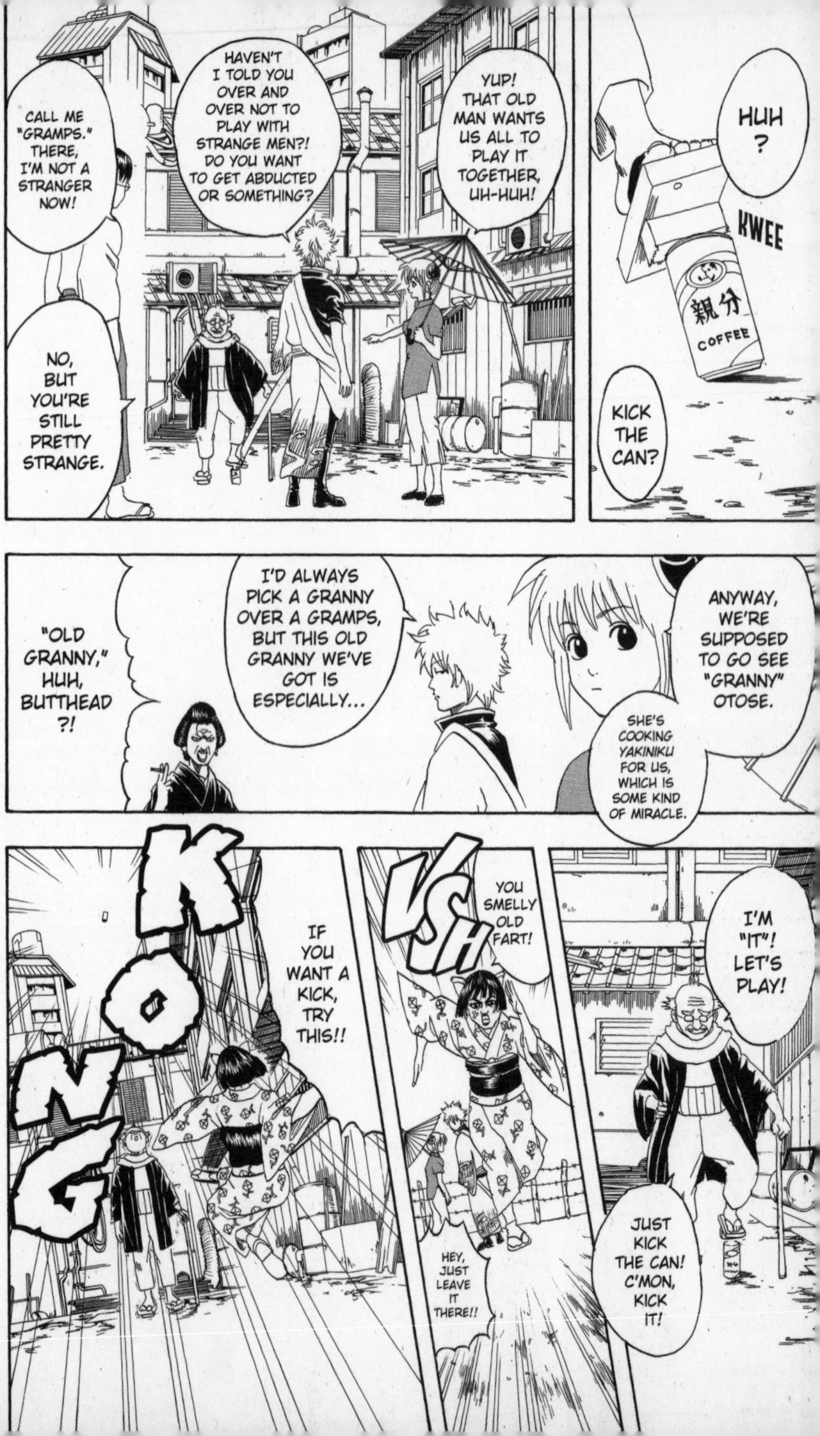
HUH ?
KWEE
親分
COFFEE
KICK THE CAN?
YUP! THAT OLD MAN WANTS US ALL TO PLAY IT TOGETHER, UH-HUH!
HAVEN'T I TOLD YOU OVER AND OVER NOT TO PLAY WITH STRANGE MEN?! DO YOU WANT TO GET ABDUCTED OR SOMETHING?
CALL ME "GRAMPS." THERE, I'M NOT A STRANGER NOW!
NO, BUT YOU'RE STILL PRETTY STRANGE.
ANYWAY, WE'RE SUPPOSED TO GO SEE "GRANNY" OTOSE.
SHE'S COOKING YAKINIKU FOR US, WHICH IS SOME KIND OF MIRACLE.
I'D ALWAYS PICK A GRANNY OVER A GRAMPS, BUT THIS OLD GRANNY WE'VE GOT IS ESPECIALLY...
"OLD GRANNY," HUH, BUTTHEAD ?!
I'M "IT"! LET'S PLAY!
JUST KICK THE CAN! C'MON, KICK IT!
VSH
YOU SMELLY OLD FART!
HEY, JUST LEAVE IT THERE!!
IF YOU WANT A KICK, TRY THIS!!
KONG

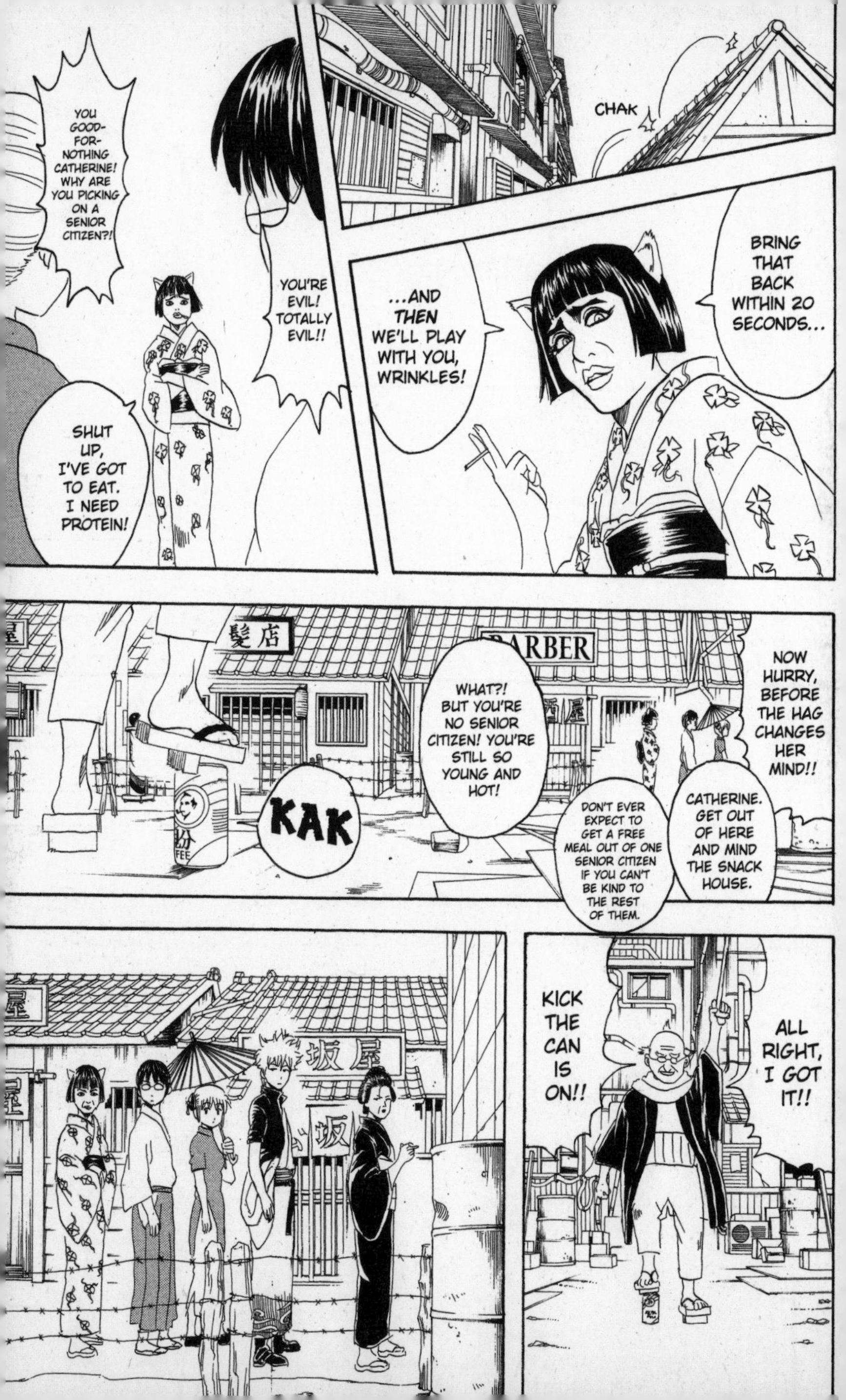
CHAK
BRING THAT BACK WITHIN 20 SECONDS...
...AND THEN WE'LL PLAY WITH YOU, WRINKLES!
YOU GOOD-FOR-NOTHING CATHERINE! WHY ARE YOU PICKING ON A SENIOR CITIZEN?!
YOU'RE EVIL! TOTALLY EVIL!!
SHUT UP, I'VE GOT TO EAT. I NEED PROTEIN!
NOW HURRY, BEFORE THE HAG CHANGES HER MIND!!
CATHERINE. GET OUT OF HERE AND MIND THE SNACK HOUSE.
DON'T EVER EXPECT TO GET A FREE MEAL OUT OF ONE SENIOR CITIZEN IF YOU CAN'T BE KIND TO THE REST OF THEM.
WHAT?! BUT YOU'RE NO SENIOR CITIZEN! YOU'RE STILL SO YOUNG AND HOT!
KAK
ALL RIGHT, I GOT IT!!
KICK THE CAN IS ON!!

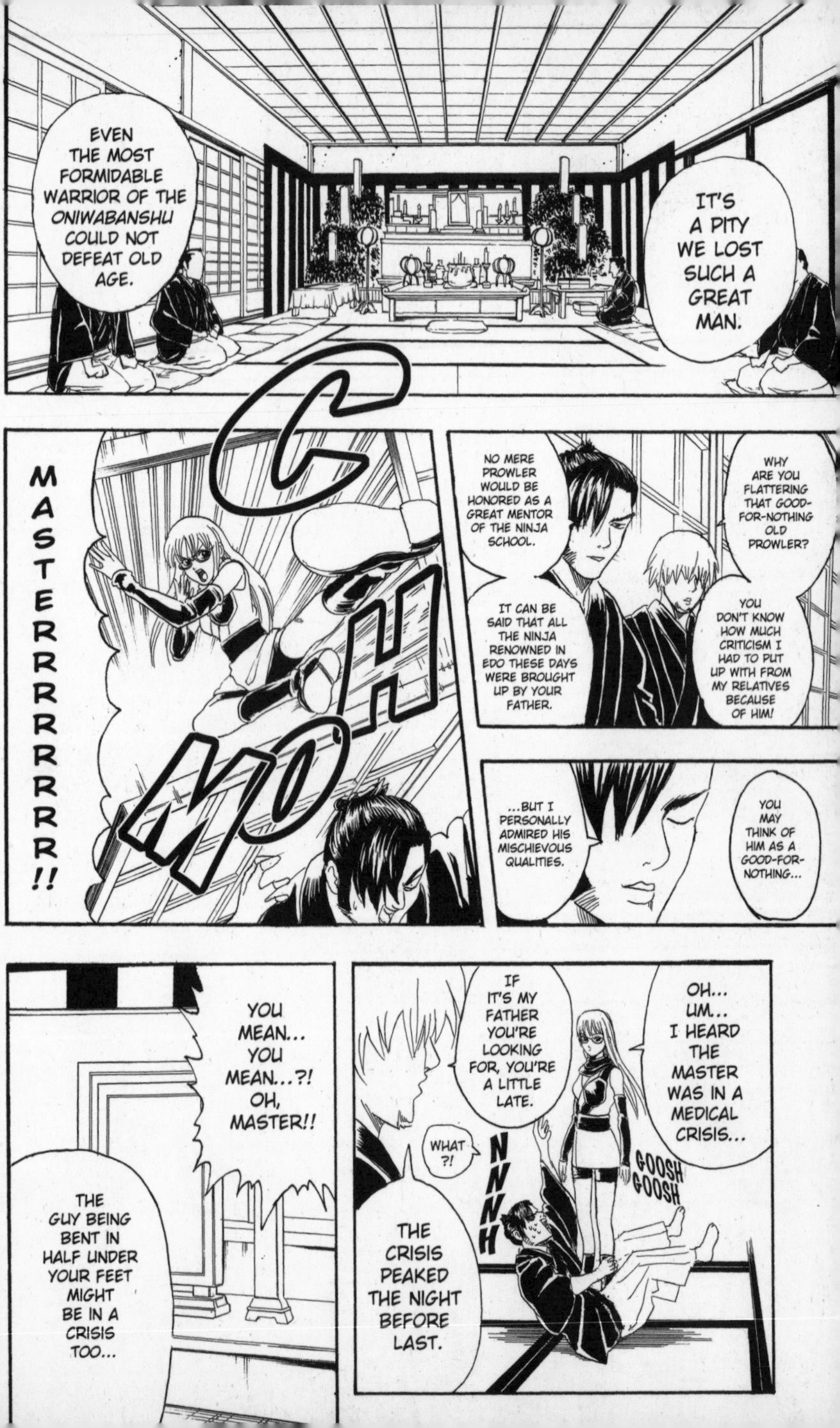
IT'S A PITY WE LOST SUCH A GREAT MAN.
EVEN THE MOST FORMIDABLE WARRIOR OF THE ONIWABANSHU COULD NOT DEFEAT OLD AGE.
WHY ARE YOU FLATTERING THAT GOOD-FOR-NOTHING OLD PROWLER?
YOU DON'T KNOW HOW MUCH CRITICISM I HAD TO PUT UP WITH FROM MY RELATIVES BECAUSE OF HIM!
NO MERE PROWLER WOULD BE HONORED AS A GREAT MENTOR OF THE NINJA SCHOOL.
IT CAN BE SAID THAT ALL THE NINJA RENOWNED IN EDO THESE DAYS WERE BROUGHT UP BY YOUR FATHER.
YOU MAY THINK OF HIM AS A GOOD-FOR-NOTHING...
...BUT I PERSONALLY ADMIRED HIS MISCHIEVOUS QUALITIES.
CHOM
MASTERRRRRRRR!!
OH... UM... I HEARD THE MASTER WAS IN A MEDICAL CRISIS...
GOOSH GOOSH
IF IT'S MY FATHER YOU'RE LOOKING FOR, YOU'RE A LITTLE LATE.
WHAT ?!
NNNH
THE CRISIS PEAKED THE NIGHT BEFORE LAST.
YOU MEAN... YOU MEAN...?! OH, MASTER!!
THE GUY BEING BENT IN HALF UNDER YOUR FEET MIGHT BE IN A CRISIS TOO...

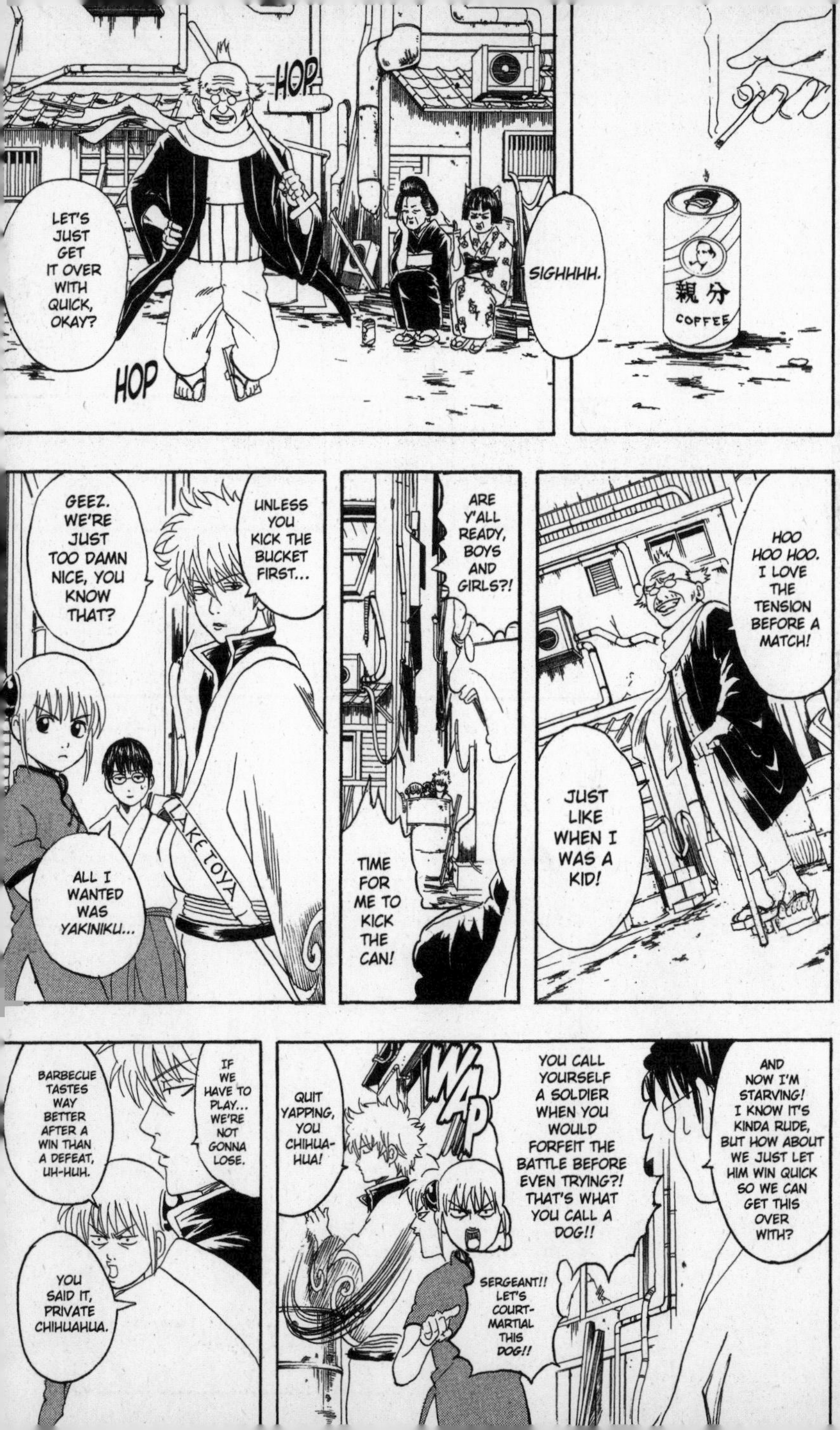

親分
COFFEE
SIGHHHH.
HOP
LET'S JUST GET IT OVER WITH QUICK, OKAY?
HOP
HOO HOO HOO. I LOVE THE TENSION BEFORE A MATCH!
JUST LIKE WHEN I WAS A KID!
ARE Y'ALL READY, BOYS AND GIRLS?!
TIME FOR ME TO KICK THE CAN!
UNLESS YOU KICK THE BUCKET FIRST...
GEEZ. WE'RE JUST TOO DAMN NICE, YOU KNOW THAT?
LAKE TOYA
ALL I WANTED WAS YAKINIKU...
AND NOW I'M STARVING! I KNOW IT'S KINDA RUDE, BUT HOW ABOUT WE JUST LET HIM WIN QUICK SO WE CAN GET THIS OVER WITH?
YOU CALL YOURSELF A SOLDIER WHEN YOU WOULD FORFEIT THE BATTLE BEFORE EVEN TRYING?! THAT'S WHAT YOU CALL A DOG!!
WAP
QUIT YAPPING, YOU CHIHUAHUA!
SERGEANT!! LET'S COURT-MARTIAL THIS DOG!!
IF WE HAVE TO PLAY... WE'RE NOT GONNA LOSE.
BARBECUE TASTES WAY BETTER AFTER A WIN THAN A DEFEAT, UH-HUH.
YOU SAID IT, PRIVATE CHIHUAHUA.

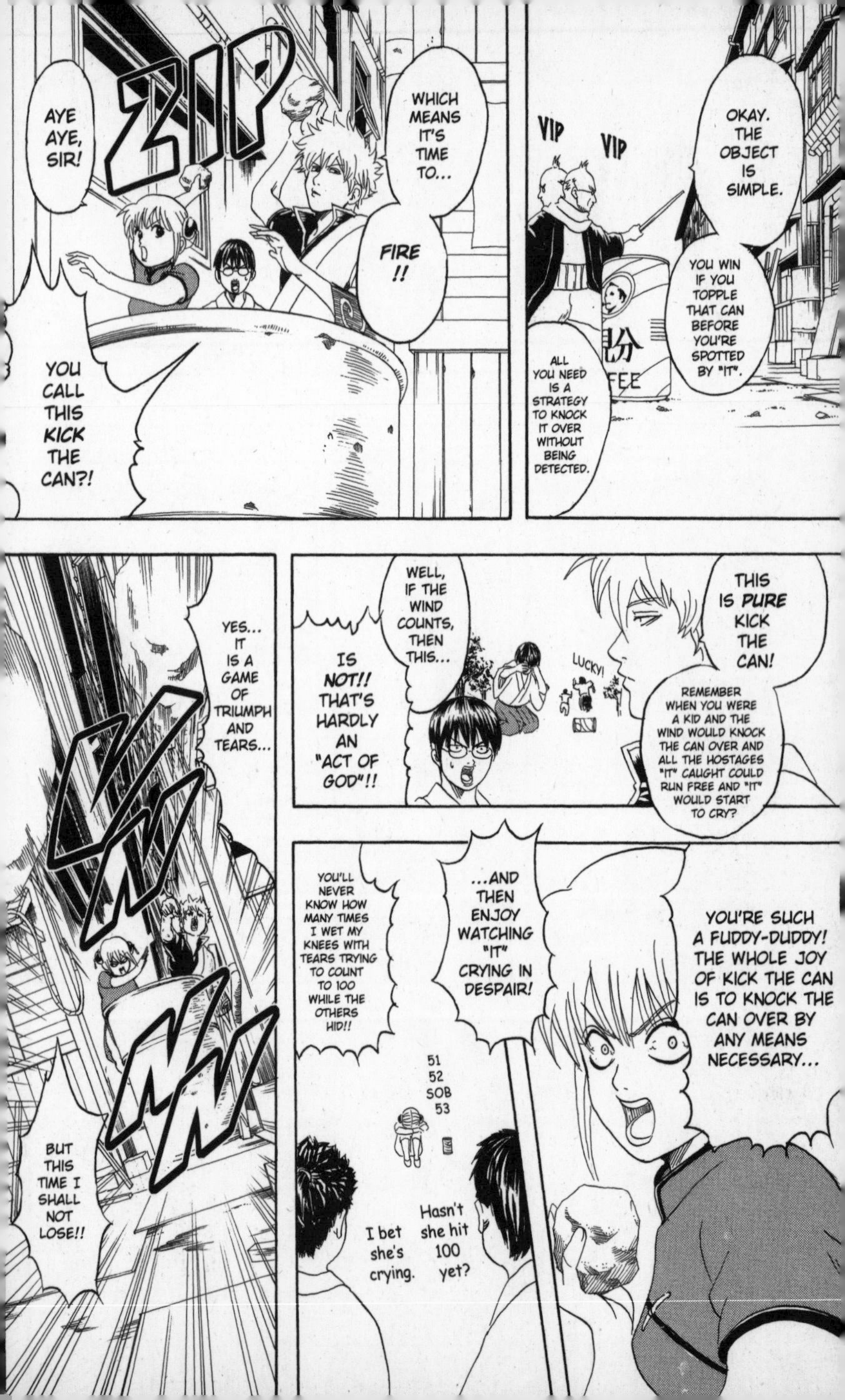
VIP
VIP
OKAY. THE OBJECT IS SIMPLE.
YOU WIN IF YOU TOPPLE THAT CAN BEFORE YOU'RE SPOTTED BY "IT".
ALL YOU NEED IS A STRATEGY TO KNOCK IT OVER WITHOUT BEING DETECTED.
WHICH MEANS IT'S TIME TO...
FIRE!!
ZIP
AYE AYE, SIR!
YOU CALL THIS KICK THE CAN?!
THIS IS PURE KICK THE CAN!
REMEMBER WHEN YOU WERE A KID AND THE WIND WOULD KNOCK THE CAN OVER AND ALL THE HOSTAGES "IT" CAUGHT COULD RUN FREE AND "IT" WOULD START TO CRY?
LUCKY!
WELL, IF THE WIND COUNTS, THEN THIS...
IS NOT!! THAT'S HARDLY AN "ACT OF GOD"!!
YOU'RE SUCH A FUDDY-DUDDY! THE WHOLE JOY OF KICK THE CAN IS TO KNOCK THE CAN OVER BY ANY MEANS NECESSARY...
...AND THEN ENJOY WATCHING "IT" CRYING IN DESPAIR!
YOU'LL NEVER KNOW HOW MANY TIMES I WET MY KNEES WITH TEARS TRYING TO COUNT TO 100 WHILE THE OTHERS HID!!
51 52 SOB 53
Hasn't she hit 100 yet?
I bet she's crying.
YES... IT IS A GAME OF TRIUMPH AND TEARS...
BUT THIS TIME I SHALL NOT LOSE!!

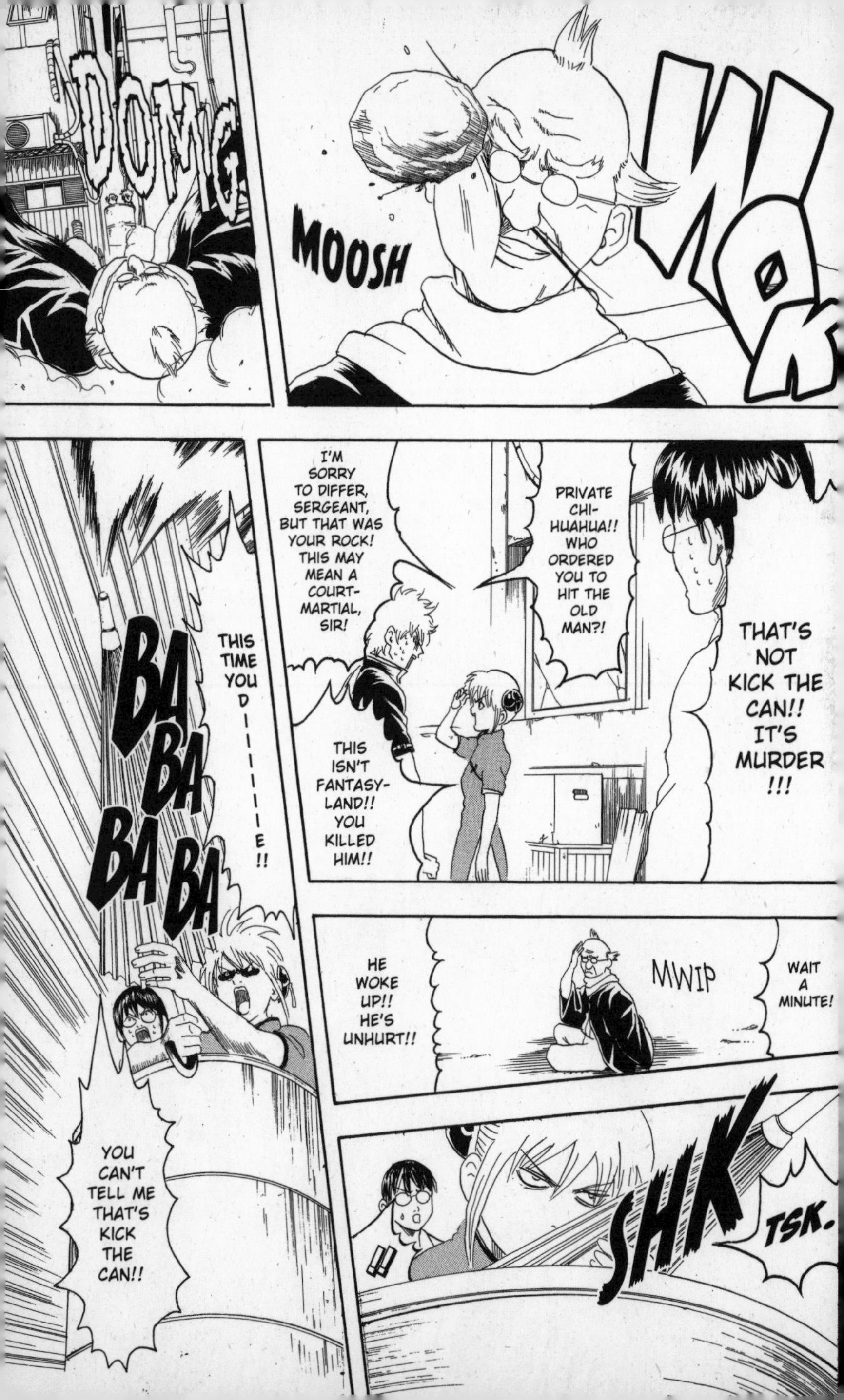
WOK
MOOSH
DOMG
THAT'S NOT KICK THE CAN!! IT'S MURDER!!!
PRIVATE CHI-HUAHUA!! WHO ORDERED YOU TO HIT THE OLD MAN?!
I'M SORRY TO DIFFER, SERGEANT, BUT THAT WAS YOUR ROCK! THIS MAY MEAN A COURT-MARTIAL, SIR!
THIS ISN'T FANTASY-LAND!! YOU KILLED HIM!!
WAIT A MINUTE!
MWIP
HE WOKE UP!! HE'S UNHURT!!
TSK.
SHK
!!
BA BA BA BA BA BA
THIS TIME YOU D------E!!
YOU CAN'T TELL ME THAT'S KICK THE CAN!!

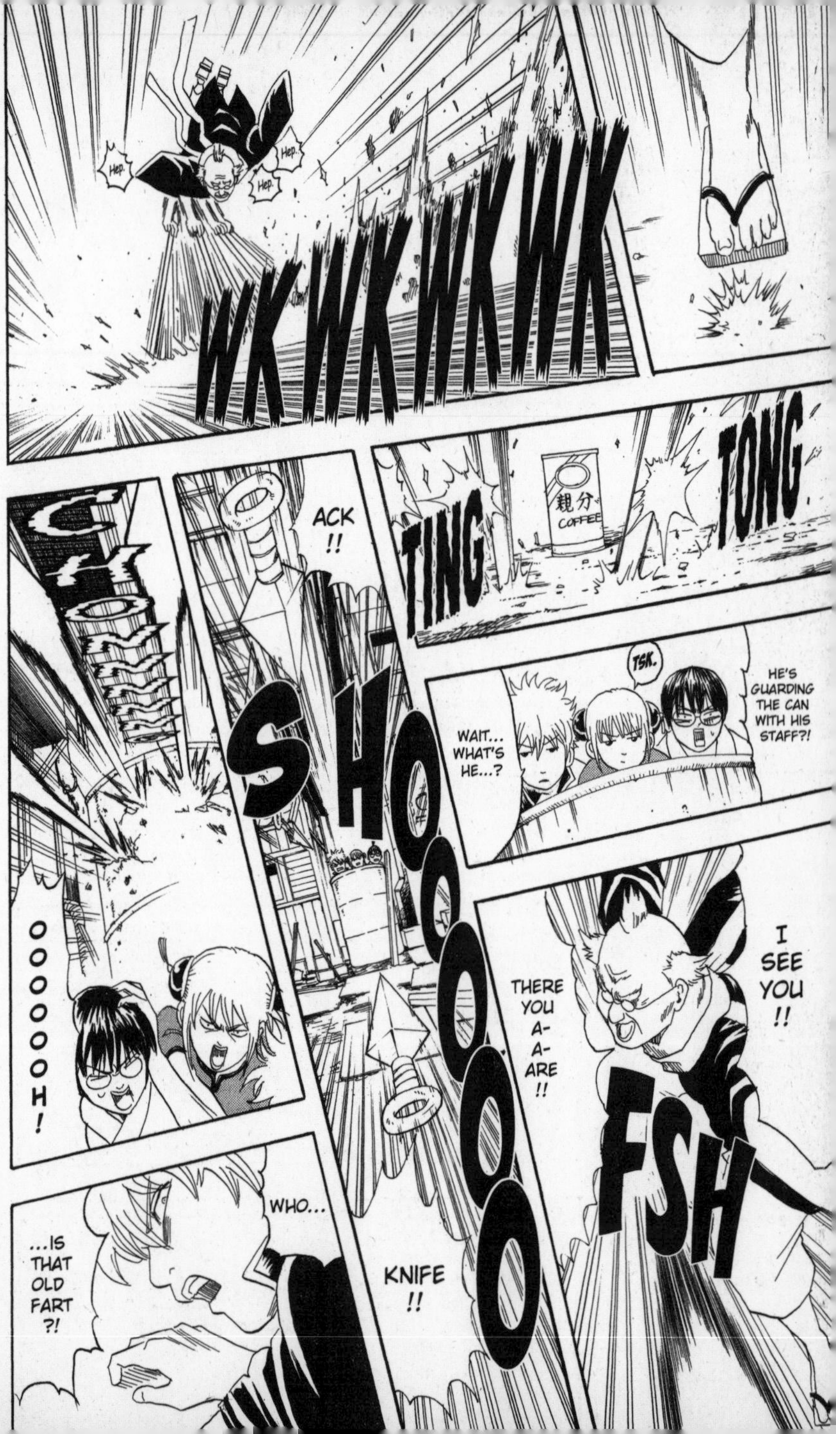
Hep.
Hep.
Hep.
WKWKWKWKWK
TING
TONG
TSK.
HE'S GUARDING THE CAN WITH HIS STAFF?!
WAIT... WHAT'S HE...?
I SEE YOU!!
THERE YOU A-A-ARE!!
FSH
ACK!!
SHOOOOOOOOOO
KNIFE!!
CHO
OOOOOOOH!
WHO...
...IS THAT OLD FART?!

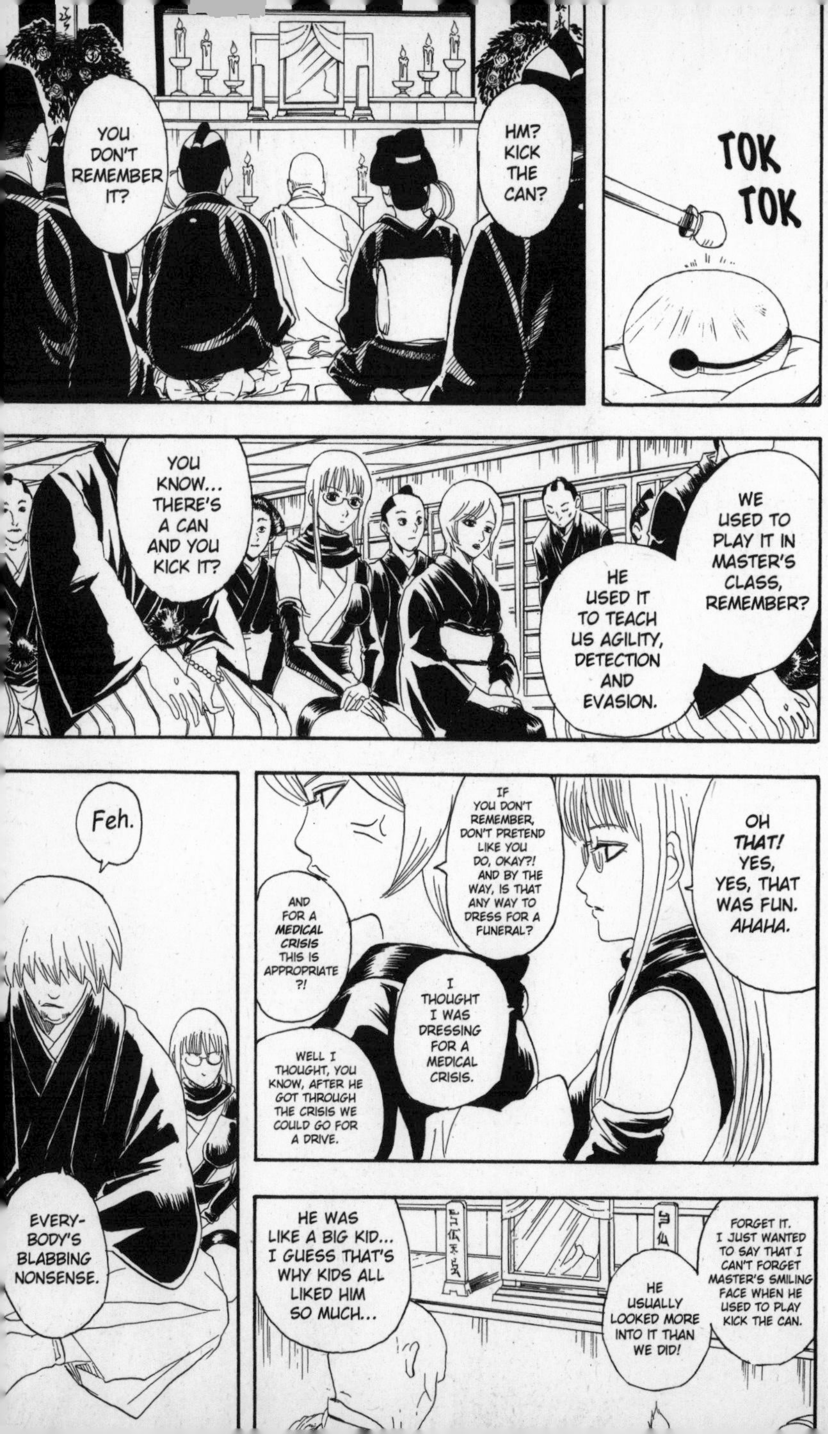
TOK TOK
HM? KICK THE CAN?
YOU DON'T REMEMBER IT?
WE USED TO PLAY IT IN MASTER'S CLASS, REMEMBER?
HE USED IT TO TEACH US AGILITY, DETECTION AND EVASION.
YOU KNOW... THERE'S A CAN AND YOU KICK IT?
OH THAT! YES, YES, THAT WAS FUN. AHAHA.
IF YOU DON'T REMEMBER, DON'T PRETEND LIKE YOU DO, OKAY?! AND BY THE WAY, IS THAT ANY WAY TO DRESS FOR A FUNERAL?
AND FOR A MEDICAL CRISIS THIS IS APPROPRIATE?!
I THOUGHT I WAS DRESSING FOR A MEDICAL CRISIS.
WELL I THOUGHT, YOU KNOW, AFTER HE GOT THROUGH THE CRISIS WE COULD GO FOR A DRIVE.
FORGET IT. I JUST WANTED TO SAY THAT I CAN'T FORGET MASTER'S SMILING FACE WHEN HE USED TO PLAY KICK THE CAN.
HE USUALLY LOOKED MORE INTO IT THAN WE DID!
HE WAS LIKE A BIG KID... I GUESS THAT'S WHY KIDS ALL LIKED HIM SO MUCH...
Feh.
EVERY-BODY'S BLABBING NONSENSE.

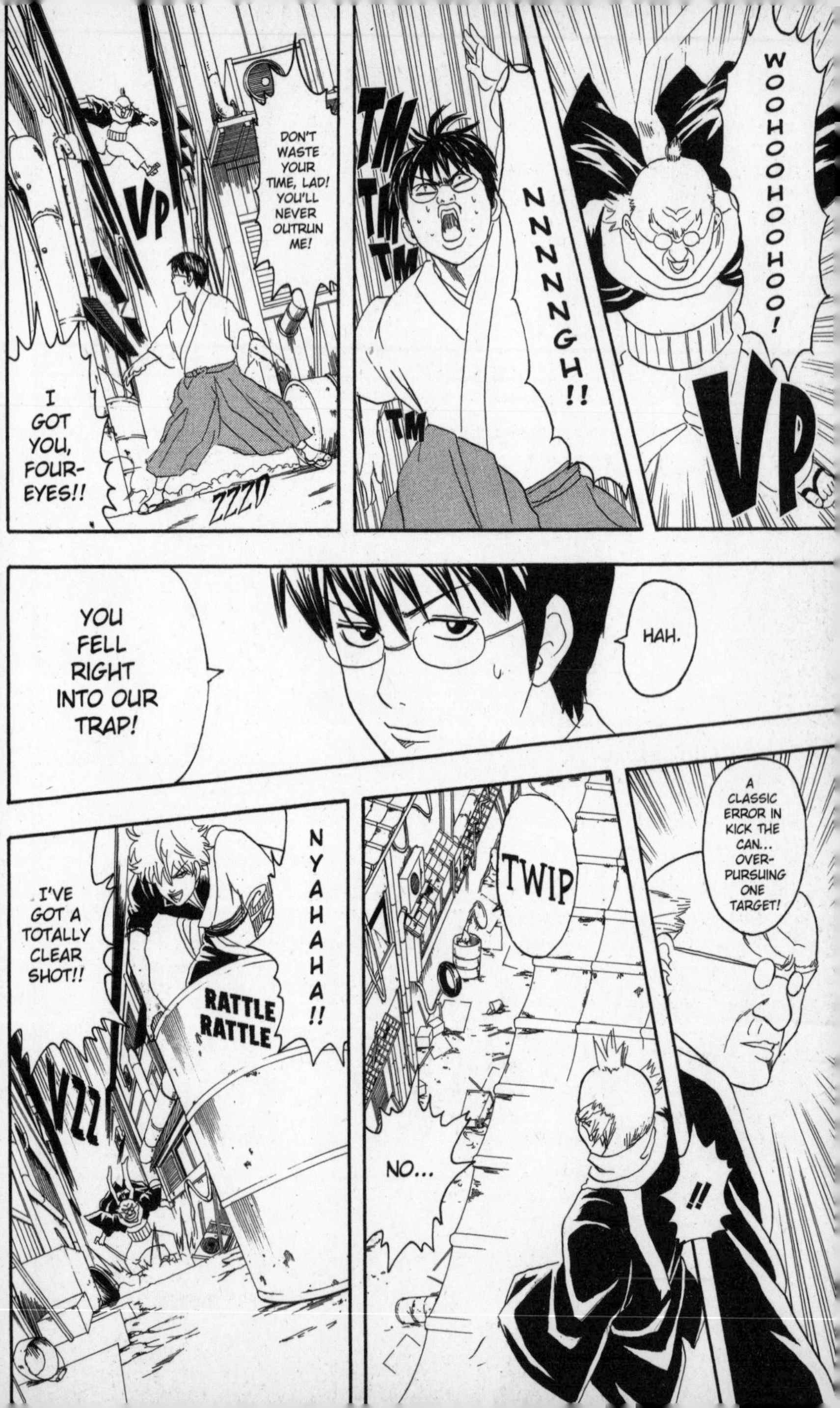
WOOHOOHOOHOOHOO!
VP
TM TM TM TM
NNNNNGH!!
TM
DON'T WASTE YOUR TIME, LAD! YOU'LL NEVER OUTRUN ME!
VP
I GOT YOU, FOUR-EYES!!
ZZZD
HAH.
YOU FELL RIGHT INTO OUR TRAP!
A CLASSIC ERROR IN KICK THE CAN... OVER-PURSUING ONE TARGET!
!!
TWIP
NO...
NYAHAHAHA!!
I'VE GOT A TOTALLY CLEAR SHOT!!
RATTLE RATTLE
VZZ

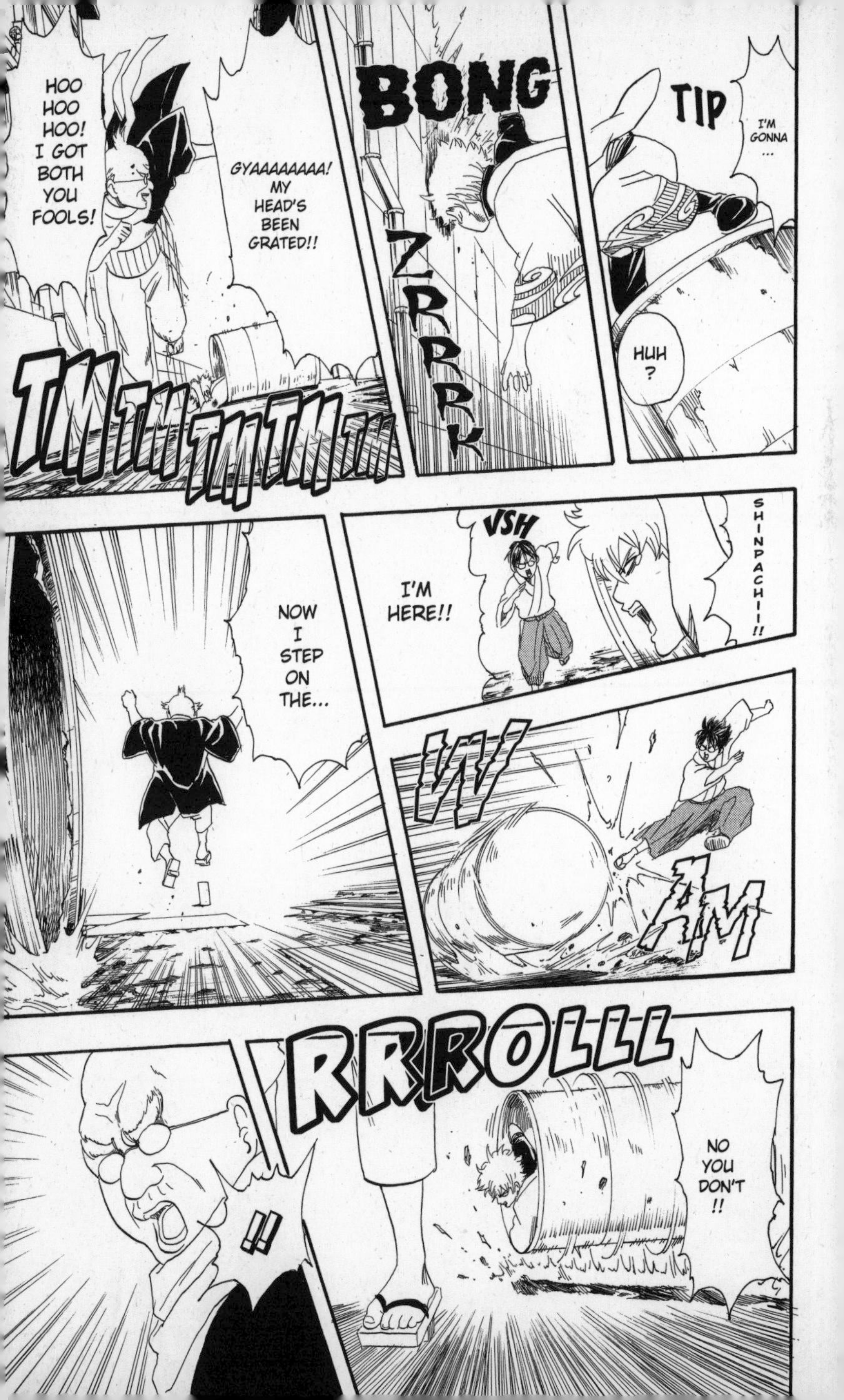
TIP
I'M GONNA ...
HUH ?
BONG
ZRRRK
GYAAAAAAAA! MY HEAD'S BEEN GRATED!!
HOO HOO HOO! I GOT BOTH YOU FOOLS!
TM TM TM TM TM
SHINPACHI!!
VSH
I'M HERE!!
W
AM
NOW I STEP ON THE...
NO YOU DON'T !!
RRROLLL
!!

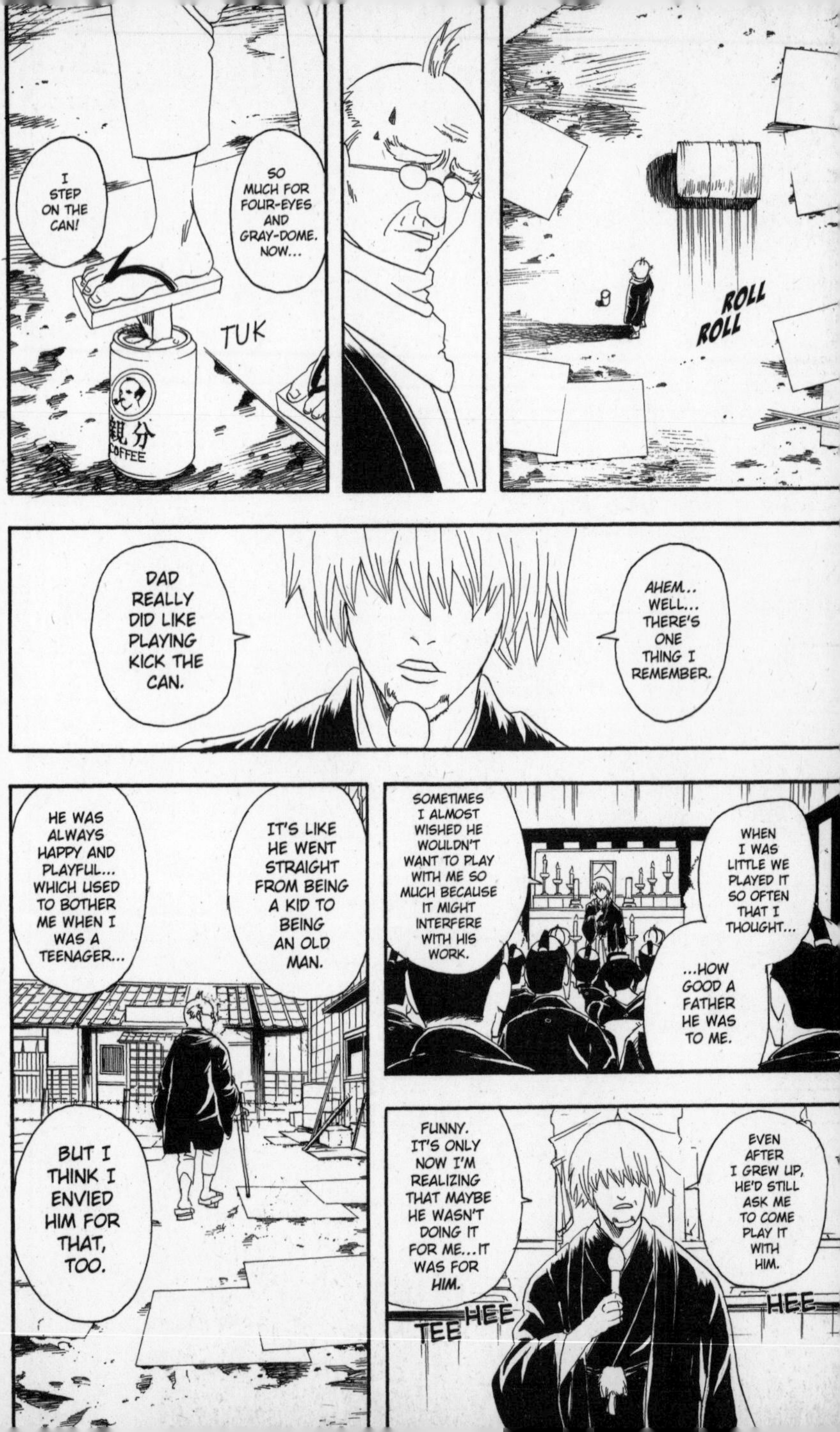
ROLL
ROLL
SO MUCH FOR FOUR-EYES AND GRAY-DOME. NOW...
I STEP ON THE CAN!
TUK
親分
COFFEE
AHEM.. WELL... THERE'S ONE THING I REMEMBER.
DAD REALLY DID LIKE PLAYING KICK THE CAN.
WHEN I WAS LITTLE WE PLAYED IT SO OFTEN THAT I THOUGHT...
...HOW GOOD A FATHER HE WAS TO ME.
SOMETIMES I ALMOST WISHED HE WOULDN'T WANT TO PLAY WITH ME SO MUCH BECAUSE IT MIGHT INTERFERE WITH HIS WORK.
EVEN AFTER I GREW UP, HE'D STILL ASK ME TO COME PLAY IT WITH HIM.
HEE
FUNNY. IT'S ONLY NOW I'M REALIZING THAT MAYBE HE WASN'T DOING IT FOR ME...IT WAS FOR HIM.
TEE HEE
IT'S LIKE HE WENT STRAIGHT FROM BEING A KID TO BEING AN OLD MAN.
HE WAS ALWAYS HAPPY AND PLAYFUL... WHICH USED TO BOTHER ME WHEN I WAS A TEENAGER...
BUT I THINK I ENVIED HIM FOR THAT, TOO.

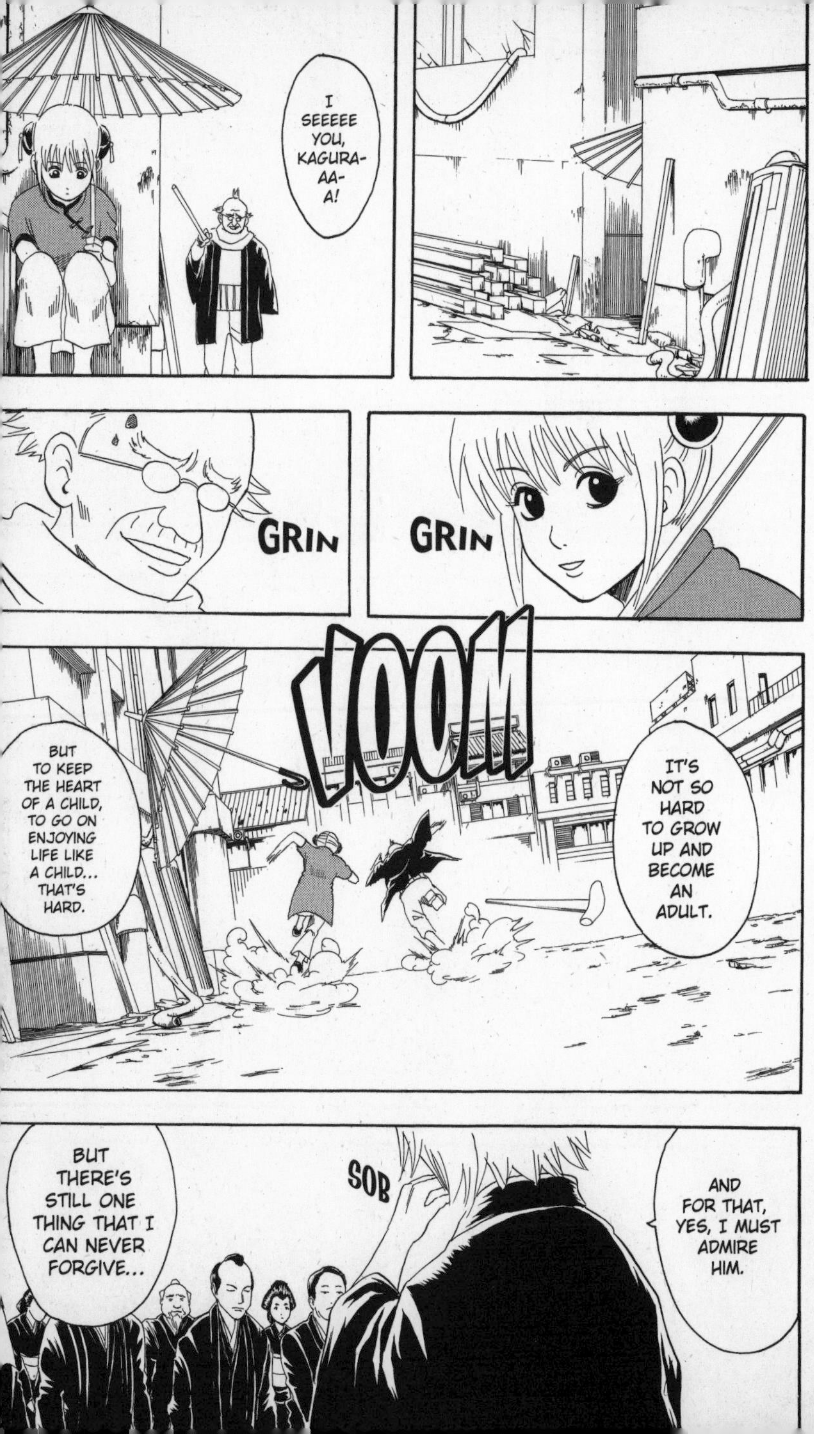
I SEEEEE YOU, KAGURA-AA-A!
GRIN
GRIN
VOOM
IT'S NOT SO HARD TO GROW UP AND BECOME AN ADULT.
BUT TO KEEP THE HEART OF A CHILD, TO GO ON ENJOYING LIFE LIKE A CHILD... THAT'S HARD.
AND FOR THAT, YES, I MUST ADMIRE HIM.
SOB
BUT THERE'S STILL ONE THING THAT I CAN NEVER FORGIVE...

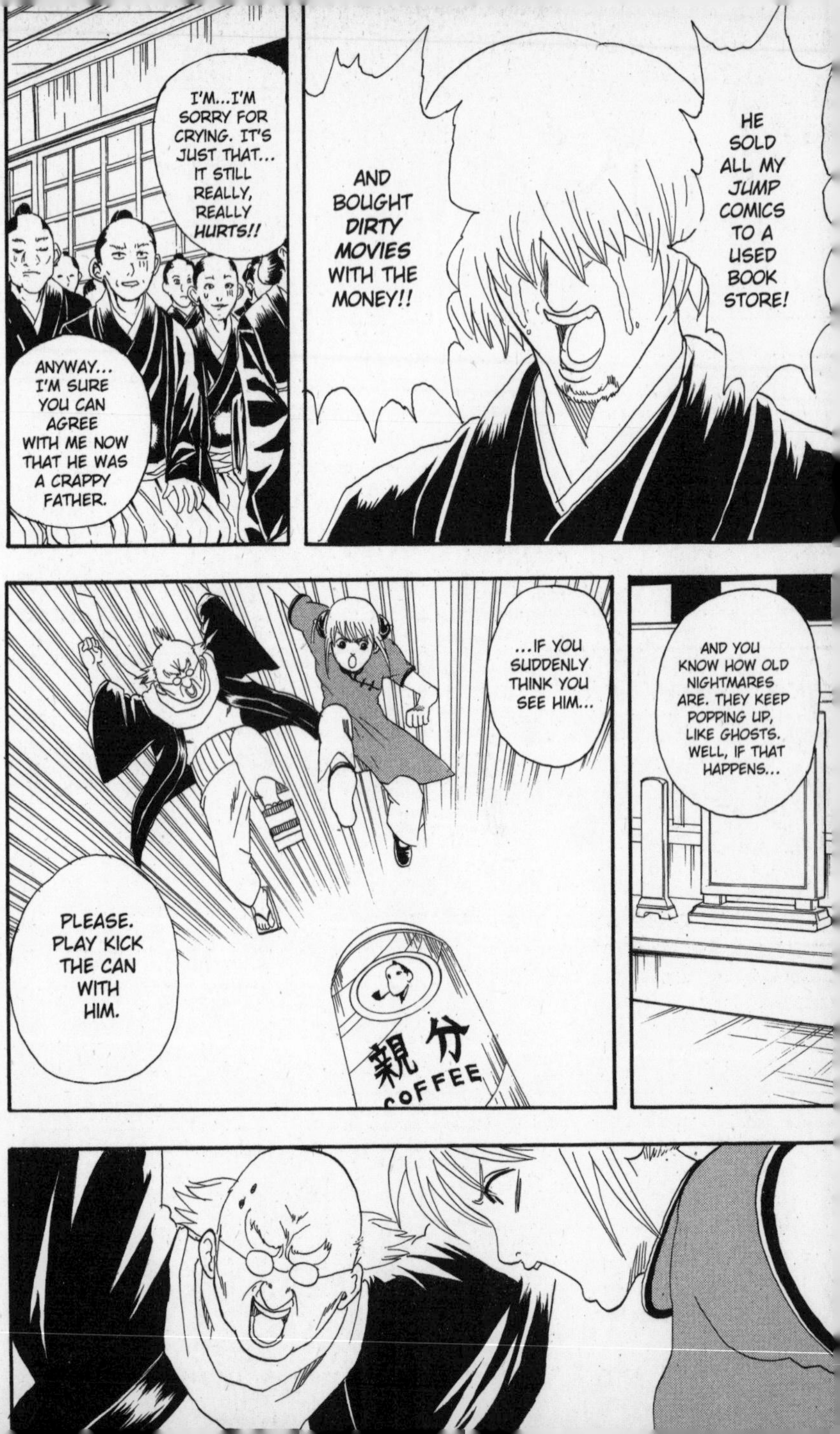
HE SOLD ALL MY JUMP COMICS TO A USED BOOK STORE!
AND BOUGHT DIRTY MOVIES WITH THE MONEY!!
I'M...I'M SORRY FOR CRYING. IT'S JUST THAT... IT STILL REALLY, REALLY HURTS!!
ANYWAY... I'M SURE YOU CAN AGREE WITH ME NOW THAT HE WAS A CRAPPY FATHER.
AND YOU KNOW HOW OLD NIGHTMARES ARE. THEY KEEP POPPING UP, LIKE GHOSTS. WELL, IF THAT HAPPENS...
...IF YOU SUDDENLY THINK YOU SEE HIM...
PLEASE. PLAY KICK THE CAN WITH HIM.
親分
COFFEE

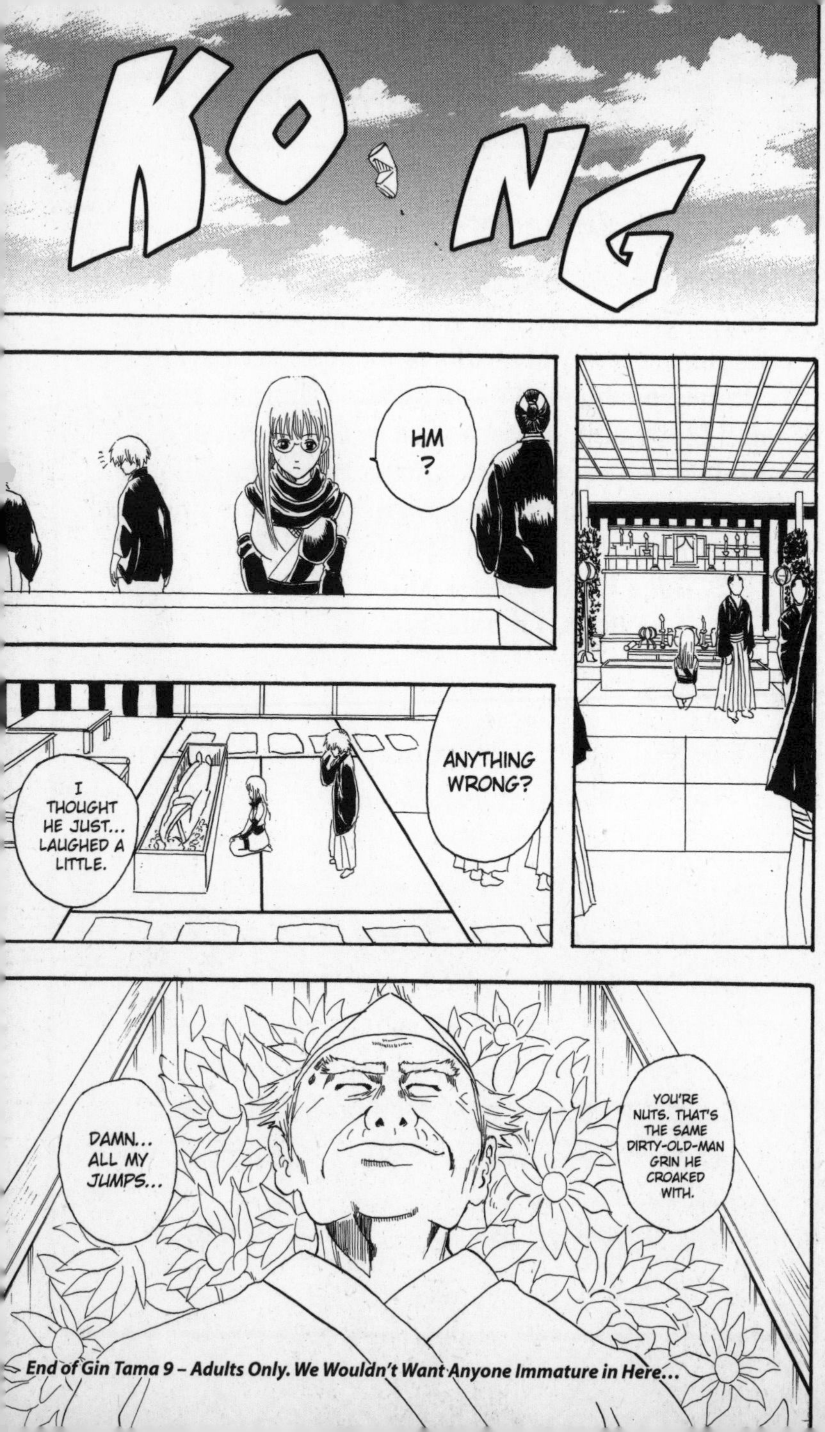
KO-NG
HM?
ANYTHING WRONG?
I THOUGHT HE JUST... LAUGHED A LITTLE.
YOU'RE NUTS. THAT'S THE SAME DIRTY-OLD-MAN GRIN HE CROAKED WITH.
DAMN... ALL MY JUMPS...
—End of Gin Tama 9 – Adults Only. We Wouldn't Want Anyone Immature in Here...

Sorachi's Q&A Corner #23

<From Kim Eri-san of Korea>

Hi, I'm Kim E. (a Korean girl) and a huge fan of yours Mr. Sorachi. Hope you understand my poor English. I really love *Gin Tama*. It's too hilarious! I think you've got a great sense of humor. Yes you do!! I love all the characters in *Gin Tama*, esp. Kintoki & Kagura & Ms. Otose. How funny they are! I really hope you're in good health all the time and great ideas never stop flowing from your heart!!
   P.S. Does Kintoki loves Killer Sacchang?
     If he does, I'll hate her. ‿

<Answer>

Kim-san wrote to us all the way from Korea! Thank you! And thanks for writing it in English, knowing we can't understand Korean...but still, why did you keep saying "Kintoki" for "Gintoki"?! Are you Sakamoto or something?! And how come you don't ask for an autograph, huh? Yuko should explain these things to you 'cause she should know about it already.
   Huh? What do you mean, "Who's Yuko?"

Well, here we are at the end of volume 9 with its special message: The world united! Both Sandoval-san and Kim-san are far away from us, but in the love of **Gin Tama,** we are always one. Still, I suggest you don't go around saying "Gin Tama Gin Tama" in public when you're in Japan. It could be dangerous by all means. You know, Yuko, you should really be explaining this.

Um...so we are still open for submissions to the Amanto drawing contest and the Q&A corner.* If you have something you want published, please send it to the address below. Okay then! See you in volume 10!

Sayo—naaara—!

* Editor's note: Sorachi-sensei is talking about a contest that ran in the Japanese *Shonen JUMP* in 2005. But you can still send us your GIN TAMA fan art and if it's really good (like good enough to impress Granny Otose— I never said this would be easy!), you just might see it in the pages of the VIZ Media version!

Gin Tama Fan Art
attn: Mike Montesa, Editor
VIZ Media, LLC
295 Bay Street
San Francisco, CA, 94133

Elizabeth

Drawing by Anonymous-san

In order for us to be able to use your fan art, you MUST include a signed release form which you can download at http://www.shonenjump.com/fanart/Fan_Art_Release.pdf

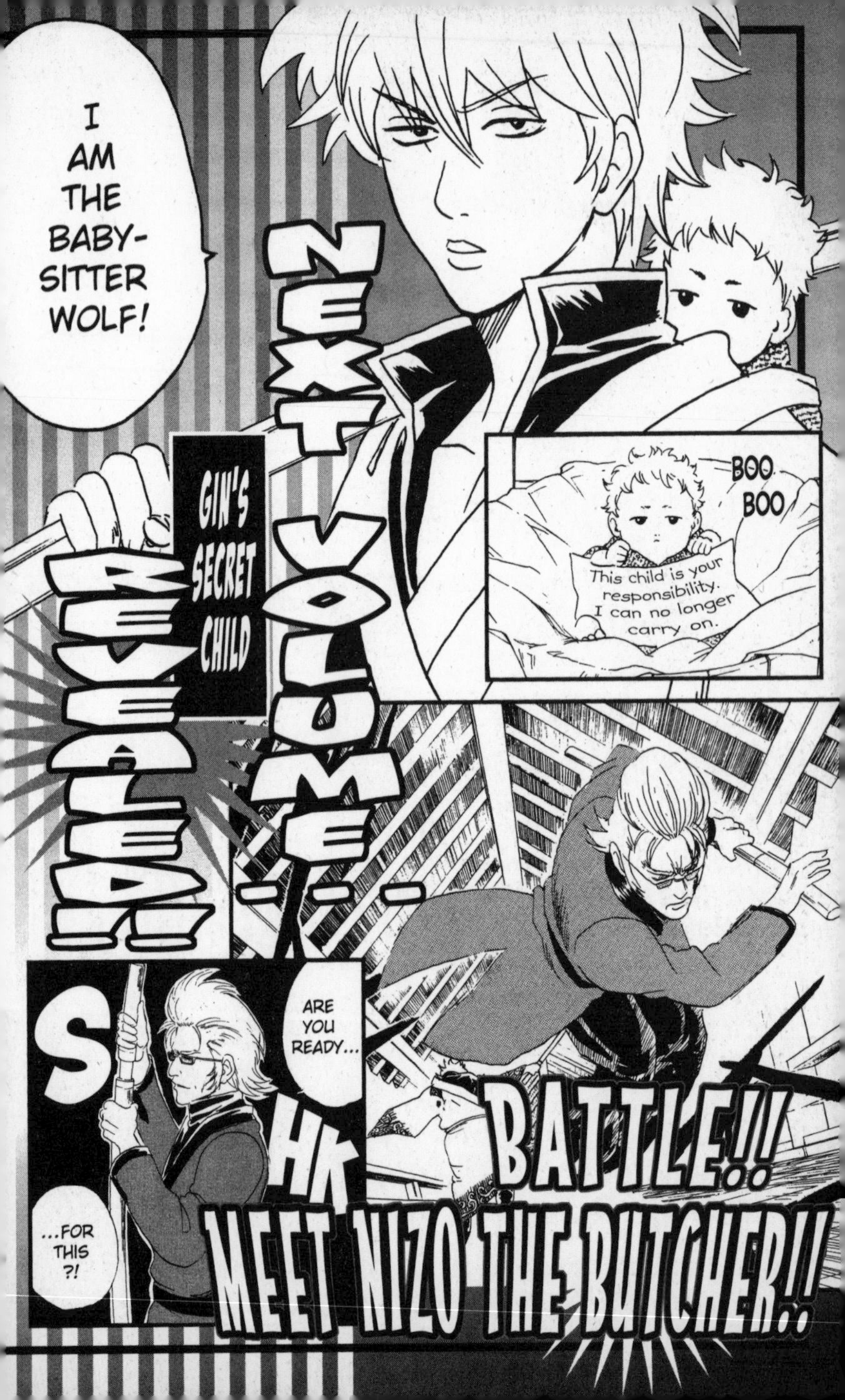
NEXT VOLUME...
GIN'S SECRET CHILD
REVEALED?!
I AM THE BABY-SITTER WOLF!
BOO BOO
This child is your responsibility. I can no longer carry on.
BATTLE!!
MEET NIZO THE BUTCHER!!
ARE YOU READY...
SHK
...FOR THIS?!

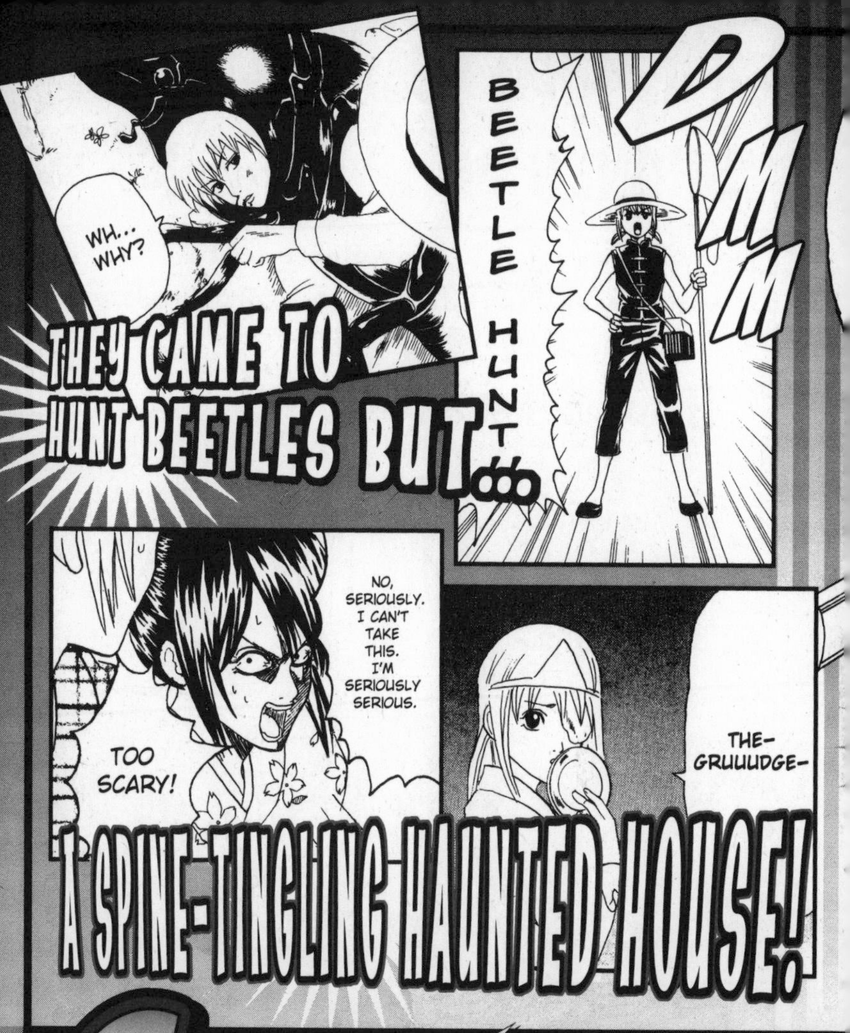
DMMM
BEETLE HUNT...
WH... WHY?
THEY CAME TO HUNT BEETLES BUT...
THE-GRUUUDGE-
NO, SERIOUSLY. I CAN'T TAKE THIS. I'M SERIOUSLY SERIOUS.
TOO SCARY!
A SPINE-TINGLING HAUNTED HOUSE!

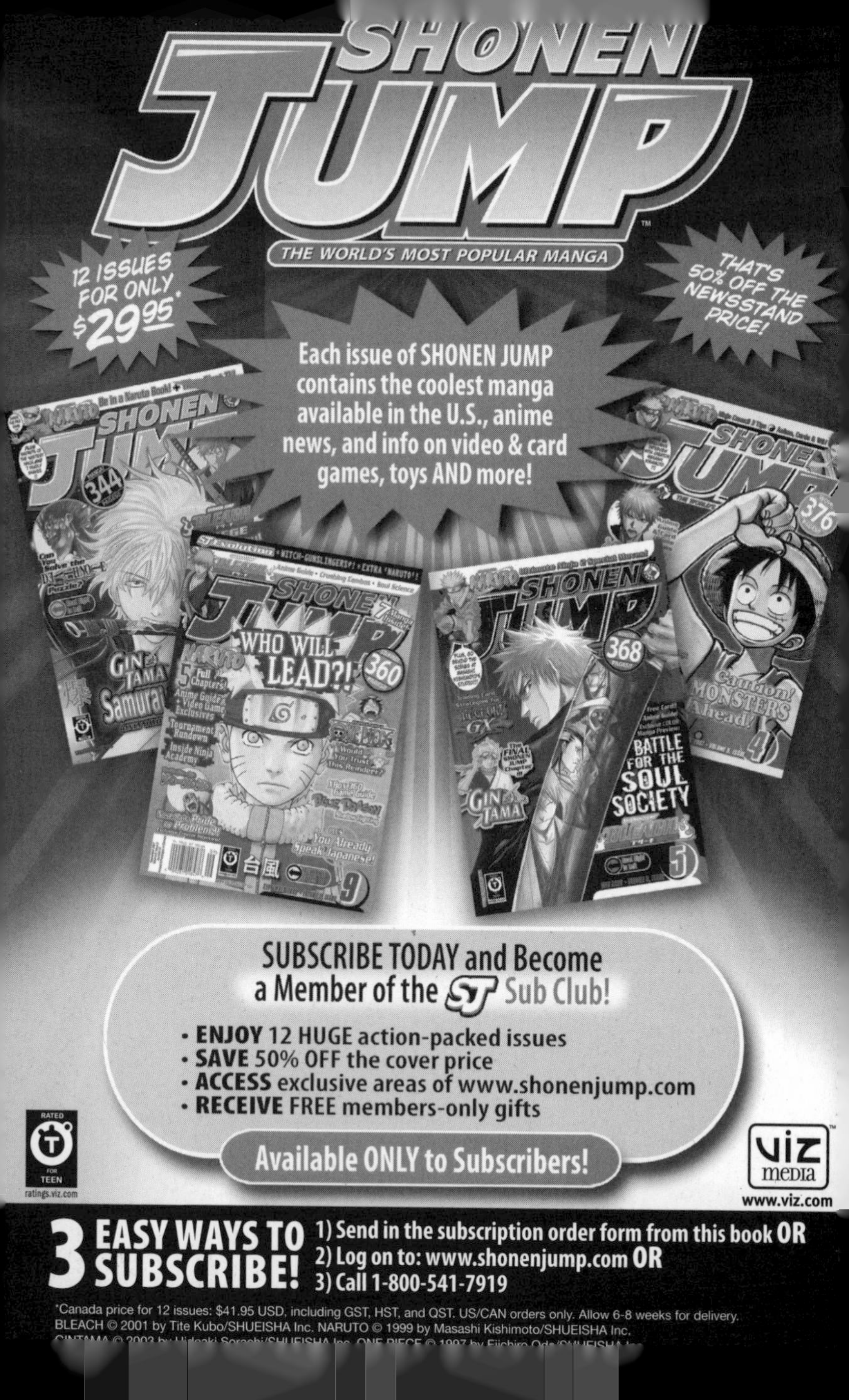
SHONEN JUMP
THE WORLD'S MOST POPULAR MANGA
12 ISSUES FOR ONLY $29.95*
THAT'S 50% OFF THE NEWSSTAND PRICE!
Each issue of SHONEN JUMP contains the coolest manga available in the U.S., anime news, and info on video & card games, toys AND more!
WHO WILL LEAD?!
Caution! MONSTERS Ahead!
BATTLE FOR THE SOUL SOCIETY
SUBSCRIBE TODAY and Become a Member of the SJ Sub Club!
• ENJOY 12 HUGE action-packed issues
• SAVE 50% OFF the cover price
• ACCESS exclusive areas of www.shonenjump.com
• RECEIVE FREE members-only gifts
Available ONLY to Subscribers!
RATED T FOR TEEN
ratings.viz.com
viz media
www.viz.com
3 EASY WAYS TO SUBSCRIBE!
1) Send in the subscription order form from this book OR
2) Log on to: www.shonenjump.com OR
3) Call 1-800-541-7919
*Canada price for 12 issues: $41.95 USD, including GST, HST, and QST. US/CAN orders only. Allow 6-8 weeks for delivery.
BLEACH © 2001 by Tite Kubo/SHUEISHA Inc. NARUTO © 1999 by Masashi Kishimoto/SHUEISHA Inc.
GINTAMA © 2003 by Hideaki Sorachi/SHUEISHA Inc. ONE PIECE © 1997 by Eiichiro Oda/SHUEISHA Inc.

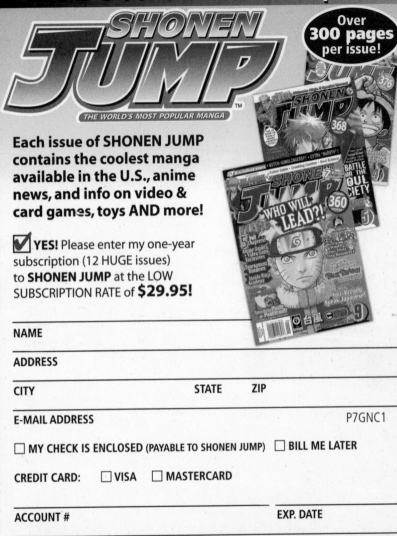